A WRITER'S LIFE

A
WRITER'S
LIFE

GAY TALESE

 RANDOM HOUSE TRADE PAPERBACKS NEW YORK

2007 Random House Trade Paperback Edition

Published in the United States by Random House Trade Paperbacks,
an imprint of The Random House Publishing Group,
a division of Random House, Inc., New York.

RANDOM HOUSE TRADE PAPERBACKS and colophon are trademarks of
Random House, Inc.

Originally published in hardcover in the United States by
Alfred A. Knopf, a division of Random House, Inc., in 2006.

The material about Gino's restaurant in Chapter 28 originally appeared
in *The New Yorker* in 1995. The material about the author's mother in
Chapter 5, and references to the author's undergraduate days at the
University of Alabama in Chapter 11, originally appeared in *The
Literature of Reality,* coauthored with Barbara Lounsberry and published
by HarperCollins, New York, in 1996.

ISBN 978-0-8129-7728-8

Library of Congress Cataloging-in-Publication Data

Talese, Gay.
A writer's life / Gay Talese.
p.   cm.
ISBN 978-0-8129-7728-8
1. Talese, Gay. 2. Journalists—United States—Biography. I. Title.

PN4874.T216A3 2006
808.0092—dc22
[B]   2005044751

Printed in the United States of America

www.atrandom.com

2 4 6 8 9 7 5 3 1

To the women in my life—Nan,
Pamela, and Catherine

A WRITER'S LIFE

1

I AM NOT NOW, NOR HAVE I EVER BEEN, FOND OF THE GAME OF SOCCER. Part of the reason is probably attributable to my age and the fact that when I was growing up along the southern shore of New Jersey a half century ago, the sport was virtually unknown to Americans, except to those of foreign birth. And even though my father was foreign-born—he was a dandified but dour custom tailor from a Calabrian village in southern Italy who became a United States citizen in the mid-1920s—his references to me about soccer were associated with his boyhood conflicts over the game, and his desire to play it in the afternoons with his school friends in an Italian courtyard instead of merely watching it being played as he sat sewing at the rear window of the nearby shop to which he was apprenticed; yet, as he often reminded me, he *knew* even then that these young male performers (including his less dutiful brothers and cousins) were wasting their time and their future lives as they kicked the ball back and forth when they *should* have been learning a worthy craft and anticipating the high cost of a ticket to immigrant prosperity in America! But no, he continued in his tireless way of warning me, they idled away their afternoons playing soccer in the courtyard as they would later play it behind the barbed wire of the Allied prisoner of war camp in North Africa to which they were sent (they who were not killed or crippled in combat) following their surrender in 1942 as infantrymen in Mussolini's losing army. Occasionally they sent letters to my father describing their confinement; and one day near the end of World War II he put aside the mail and told me in a tone of voice that I prefer to believe was more sad than sarcastic, "They're still playing soccer!"

The World Cup soccer finale between the women of China and the United States, held on July 10, 1999, in Pasadena, California, before 90,185 spectators in the Rose Bowl (the largest turnout for any women's sporting contest in history), was scheduled to be televised to nearly

200 million people around the world. The live telecast that would begin on this Saturday afternoon in California at 12:30 would be seen in New York at 3:30 p.m. and in China at 4:30 a.m. on Sunday. I had not planned to watch the match. On this particular Saturday in New York I had already made arrangements for midday doubles in Central Park with a few old pals who shared my faulty recollections on how well we once played tennis.

Before leaving for Central Park I thought I'd tune in to the baseball game that started at 1:15, featuring the New York Mets and my cherished Yankees. Irrespective of the weary, though at times wavering, counsel of my leisure-deprived and now deceased father, the Yankees had captured my heart and enslaved me forever as a fan back in February 1944 when, prompted by wartime gas rationing and its limiting effect on travel, the team shifted its traditional spring training site from Saint Petersburg, Florida, to a less warm but more centralized, if rickety, rust-railed ballpark near the Atlantic City airport, within truancy range of my school. From then on, through war and peace and extending through the careers of Joe DiMaggio and Mickey Mantle to the turn-of-the-century stardom of such newcomers as the shortstop Derek Jeter and the relief pitcher Mariano Rivera, I have reveled in the New York Yankees' triumphs and lamented their losses, and on this July Saturday in 1999, I was counting on them to divert me from several weeks of weak hitting at my typewriter.

I needed to relax, to put aside my book for a while, I decided; and I readily accepted my wife's suggestion, expressed days earlier, that we spend this weekend quietly in New York. Our two daughters and their boyfriends would be driving down to the Jersey shore to make use of our summer home, which we had bought near my parents' place thirty years ago, following the birth of our second daughter; on Saturday evening my vigorous ninety-two-year-old widowed mother was looking forward to taking her granddaughters and their boyfriends to dine with her at the Taj Mahal casino on the Atlantic City boardwalk, where she liked to have coffee and dessert in the lounge while feeding the slot machines.

During the previous month my lovely wife and I had celebrated our fortieth wedding anniversary, and I hope I will not be perceived as unromantic if I suggest that this lengthy relationship has succeeded in part because we have regularly lived and worked apart—I as a researching writer of nonfiction who is often on the road, and she as an editor and publisher who through the years has carefully avoided affiliating herself with firms to which I am contractually connected. But when we are together under the same roof, sharing what I shall take the liberty of calling a harmonious and happy coexistence that began in the mid-1950s with a courtship kindled in a cold-water flat in Greenwich Village and then moved uptown and expanded with children in a brownstone still owned and occupied by the two of us (two spry senior citizens determined not to die on a cruise ship), I must admit that I have frequently taken advantage of my wife's domestic presence as a literary professional, seeking her opinion not only on what I am thinking of writing but also on what I have written; and while her responses occasionally differ from those expressed later by my acknowledged editor, I consider myself more blessed than burdened when I have varying views to choose from, finding this far preferable to the lack of editorial access that many of my writer friends often complain about. But to writers who bemoan their lives of neglect and loneliness, let me say this: When one's own work is not going well, having a wife who is an editor can be even *more* demoralizing, particularly during those at-home weekends and nights when she is avidly reading other people's words while reclining on our marital bed under a crinkling spread of manuscript pages that lie atop our designer duvet or between the sheets, which in due time she will shake out in order to reclaim the pages and stack them neatly on her bedside table before turning out the lights and possibly dreaming of when the pages will be transformed into a beautifully bound, critically acclaimed book.

In any event, on this weekend when we decided (she decided) to remain in New York, and while she was upstairs editing the chapters of a manuscript we had slept with on Friday night, I was downstairs watching the Yankee-Mets game (the Yankees took a quick 2-0 lead on Paul O'Neill's first-inning homer, following Bernie Williams's single). Between innings I was thinking ahead to my tennis match and reminding myself that I must toss the ball higher when serving and seize every opportunity to get to the net.

I had been introduced to tennis by my gym teacher during my junior year in high school, and even though our school did not then field a tennis team, I played the game as often as I could during lunchtime recess because I could play it better than the ungainly classmates whom I selected as opponents and who also served under me as staff members on the student newspaper. That I never achieved distinction while competing on a varsity level in a major sport (football, basketball, baseball, or track) did not upset me because our school's teams were mediocre in these sports. Besides which, as the players' chronicler and potential critic (in addition to working on the school paper I wrote about sports as well as classroom activities in my extracurricular role as scholastic correspondent for my hometown weekly and the Atlantic City daily), I was suddenly experiencing the dubious eminence of being a journalist, of having my callow character and identity boosted, if not enhanced, by my bylined articles and the stamp-size photo of myself that appeared above my school-page column in the town weekly, to say nothing of the many privileges that were now mine to select, such as to travel to out-of-town games on the team bus in a reserved seat behind the coach, or to catch a ride later in a chrome-embellished Buick coupe driven by the athletic director's pretty wife.

As ineffectual as the players usually were, fumbling the football constantly, striking out habitually, and missing most of their foul shots, I never humiliated them in print. I invariably found ways to describe delicately each team defeat, each individual inadequacy. I seemed to possess in my writing a precocious flare for rhetoric and circumlocution long before I could accurately spell either word. My approach to journalism was strongly influenced throughout my high school years by a florid novelist named Frank Yerby, a Georgia-born black man who later settled in Spain and wrote prolifically about bejeweled and crinoline-skirted women of such erotic excess that, were it not for Yerby's illusory prose style, which somehow obfuscated what to me was breathtakingly obscene, his books would have been censored throughout the United States, and I would have been denied the opportunity to request each and every one of them sheepishly from the proprietress of our town library, and furthermore would not then have tried to emulate Yerby's palliative way with words in my attempts to cloak and cover up the misdeeds and deficiencies of our school's athletes in my newspaper articles.

While my evasive and roundabout reportage might be ascribed to my desire to maintain friendly relations with the athletes and encourage their continuing participation in interviews, I believe that practical matters had far less to do with it than did my own youthful identity with disappointment and the fact that, except for my skill in writing pieces that softened the harsh reality of the truth, I could do nothing exceptionally well. The grades I received from teachers in elementary as well as high school consistently placed me in the lower half of my class. Next to chemistry and math, English was my worst subject. In 1949, I was rejected by the two dozen colleges that I applied to in my native state of New Jersey and neighboring Pennsylvania and New York. That I was accepted into the freshman class at the University of Alabama was entirely the result of my father's appeals to a magnanimous Birmingham-born physician who practiced in our town and wore suits superbly designed and tailored by my father, and by this physician's own subsequent petitions on my behalf to his onetime classmate and everlasting friend then serving as Alabama's dean of admissions.

My main achievements during my four years on the Alabama campus were being appointed sports editor of the college weekly and the popularity I gained through my authorship of a column called "Sports Gay-zing," which, often blending humor with solicitousness and a veiled viewpoint, made the best of perhaps some of the worst displays of athleticism in the school's proud history. Even the Alabama football team, long accustomed to justifying its national reputation as a perennial top-ten powerhouse, suffered when I was a student through many days sadder than any since the Civil War. While gridiron glory would be restored after 1958 with the arrival of the now legendary coach Paul "Bear" Bryant, the football schedule during my time was more often than not the cause of a statewide weekend wake; and the coach of the team, a New Englander named Harold "Red" Drew, was routinely burned in effigy on Saturday nights in the center of the campus by raucous crowds of fraternity men and their girlfriends from sororities in which the pledges had spent the afternoon sewing together sackcloth body-size figures with bug eyes and fat rouge-smeared faces that were supposed to replicate the features of Red Drew.

Although Drew never complained about any of this to me or my staff, I began to feel very sorry for him, and in our sports section I always tried to put a positive spin on his downward-spiraling career. In one of my columns I emphasized the valor he had shown while serving his country as a naval officer in World War I, highlighting an occasion on which he had jumped two thousand feet from a blimp into the Gulf of Mexico. This leap in 1917, when Drew was an ensign, established him as the first parachute jumper in naval history, or so I wrote after getting the information from a yellowed newspaper clipping that was pasted in an old scrapbook lent to me by the coach's wife. I also illustrated what I wrote with a World War I–vintage photograph showing a lean and broad-shouldered Ensign Drew standing in front of a double-winged navy fighter plane at a base in the Panama Canal, wearing jodhpurs and knee-high boots and an officer's cap decorated with an insignia and bearing a peak that shaded his eyes from the sun without concealing an understated smile that I hoped my readers would see as the mark of a modest and fearless warrior— thinking, naïvely, that this would arouse their patriotism and extinguish a few of the nighttime torches that they raised in vilifying Coach Drew and also at times his venerable assistant, Henry "Hank" Crisp, who specialized in directing Alabama's porous front line of defense.

In yet another futile attempt on my part to divert the fans from such disastrous performances as were customarily presented throughout such seasons as 1951, for example, when the team lost six out of eleven games, I dramatized the tragedy partly with words lifted from Shakespeare:

> To be, or not to be: that is the question:
> Whether 'tis Drew or Crisp who must suffer the
> slings and arrows of outrageous blocking, or to take
> arms against football writers, and by opposing end
> them?
> To win: to lose: to get wrecked, routed, o'erwhelmed
> and consumed by prissy Villanova. . . .
> Ah, to sleep, for in that sleep of death one dreams
> of our opponents who plunged and fled with leather football
> under arm, around, under, and over Bama walls. . . .

I left Red Drew to his own fate following my graduation in the spring of 1953. A year later I read that he had resigned in the wake of his team's 4-5-2 record, which might have been considered outstanding if compared with the accomplishments of his successor, J. B. "Ears" Whitworth, who in 1955 lost ten games without winning even one. During these two years I did not return to the campus to witness any of these engagements, being assigned for my military service to an armored unit in Kentucky much of the time, and then stationed with that unit in Germany for part of the time, until my discharge in June of 1956 enabled me to accept a reportorial job in the sports department of the *New York Times*. I had actually worked briefly for the *Times* as a news assistant in the summer and fall of 1953 prior to entering the army, having been recommended to the paper by an Alabama classmate and friend whose uncle from Mississippi, the journalist and editor Turner Catledge, had become managing editor of the *Times* in 1951. Mr. Catledge had arranged for my initial hiring after seeing me in his office and fingering through some of my clippings; and during the time I was away in the military, as you might well imagine, I was not remiss in remaining in touch with him.

It was he who later proposed that I work in the sports department, which he made no secret of criticizing for what he saw as its tendency to cover games in the same serious and stodgy manner that the *Times* then covered everything else; but for some reason he singled out the sports section for reform, hinting that the writing there might be more diverting, original, and (since the *Times* did not publish comics) more entertaining. And while he said nothing clearly disapproving of the sports editor, a rotund and rosy-cheeked elderly man known in the office for his long lunches at Longchamps, I somehow got the impression that the career prospects of the sports editor were no more auspicious than those of Red Drew.

As an ambitious young sports journalist, I nevertheless continued to read and be influenced primarily by writers of fiction, although my tastes were no longer exemplified by the lingerie literature that had heated up my hormones in high school. At Alabama I had read novels and short stories by William Faulkner, Thomas Wolfe, and other southern-born writers who had been urged upon me by Turner Catledge's nephew, who himself possessed such poetic sensibilities that he swore to me in advance that he would never do what I would later do so eagerly—capitalize on his uncle's connections in journalism.

Each day in the *Times* building I made note of the authors whose names I saw on the covers of the books held under the arms of my elders in the elevators, and sometimes I overheard discussions about these books while lunching in the cafeteria. Since I was now reading literary supplements and subscribing to *The New Yorker* for the first time, I was becoming aware that even some renowned fiction writers occasionally dealt with sporting events and athletes in their novels and short stories. When reading examples of these, I kept reminding myself that what I was reading had been *imagined;* these efforts were, after all, labeled "fiction." And yet after finishing a short story by John O'Hara, for example, one in which the esoteric game of court tennis was precisely and gracefully described as it presented itself within the oddly angled interior walls of the New York Racquet & Tennis Club—a locale that I had visited and was familiar with—it did not seem to matter in this case whether or not O'Hara was writing "fiction"; insofar as he had woven into his story the facts and details about the club and the game, he had met the demanding standards of accuracy as upheld daily by the desk editors in the *Times* sports department.

I had moreover been impressed by O'Hara's ability to make me feel as if I was *there* within the Racquet & Tennis Club, watching the game from a bench overlooking the court; and I was also *there,* on a football field, rooting for a swivel-hipped halfback who elbows his way toward a touchdown in Irwin Shaw's story "The Eighty-Yard Run"; and *there* on a snow-covered golf course, shivering next to a lovelorn caddy in F. Scott Fitzgerald's "Winter Dreams"; and *there* in the dining room of a racetrack, sitting next to a horse trainer, who, looking up from his meal, notices that he is about to be joined by a jockey friend—an aging, ill-tempered rider presently experiencing much difficulty in controlling his weight—and the trainer is overheard saying in a voice that the jockey does not hear (but is quoted in the excerpt of Carson McCullers's "The Ballad of the

Sad Café" that I had read in *The New Yorker*): "If he eats a lamb chop, you can see the shape of it in his stomach an hour afterward."

I wanted quotes like these in my sports pieces, but I also knew I could not make them up. I was a reporter, not a fiction writer. And yet if I could get close enough to some of these athletes I was now meeting in New York and could convince them to trust me and confide in me as had many of the players I had known back in high school and college—when I used to commiserate with them and encourage them after each defeat; I was the Miss Lonelyhearts of locker rooms—I might be able to write factually accurate but very revealing personal stories about big-time athletes while using their *real* names, and then get these stories published in the strait-laced *New York Times*, which Mr. Catledge was trying to loosen up in the area where I worked. Again, without faking the facts, my reportorial approach would be fictional, with lots of intimate detail, scene-setting, dialogue, and a close identity with my chosen characters and their conflicts.

And so while I sat in the back of the sports department one afternoon interviewing a glamorous visitor named Frank Gifford, the star halfback of the New York Giants, I was thinking about "The Eighty-Yard Run"; and when I was at Yankee Stadium trying to communicate with the unglamorous Roger Maris, a home-run king on a team led by the beloved Mickey Mantle, I was as empathetic as I usually am with those who are designated second-best; and after I had befriended an up-and-coming pugilist named José Torres, I shortened my sentences, like Hemingway, and wrote:

> At 22, the prize fighter has sad, dark eyes. He has jagged, small facial scars and a flattened nose that has been hit by obscure amateurs he has already forgotten.
>
> He has had six professional fights as a middleweight. Nobody has beaten him. In the closet of his $11-a-week furnished room at 340 Union Street, Brooklyn, he has eight suits, a dozen silk shirts and fourteen pair of shoes. He also has a girl named Ramona. Both were born in Puerto Rico.
>
> Each week Ramona, who is also 22, and her mother come to clean the fighter's room. The mother complains that it is always dirty, that he never picks up his socks, that he has too many shoes. Soon, he says, he will marry Ramona and will move to Manhattan, close to Stillman's Gymnasium, far from the mother.

Although baseball as played by the Yankees would continue to command my emotions as a fan, it was the realm of professional prizefighting—as personified by boxers who were inevitably disappointed, who were often ignored in defeat, and who just as often contemplated comebacks—that I tried hardest to ennoble in the sports pages of the *Times*, being joined in this quest by a nearby novelist or two who were regulars at ringside. It was fortunate for me that during the late 1950s into the 1960s the heavyweight ranks included a remarkably candid and articulate champion named Floyd Patterson, whom I got to know so well that I often thought of him as my literary property. I wrote more than thirty articles about Patterson during my nine years as a *Times* reporter (from 1956 through 1965); and although I left sports in 1958 in order to have access to the more varied subject matter available in general news, I nonetheless continued to volunteer constantly for sports assignments—particularly if it was a World Series game involving the Yankees, or a heavyweight fight in which Patterson was a contestant.

On the late afternoons of fight nights I would sometimes spend an hour or more talking to him near his bed in a hotel suite, surrounded by his trainers and sparring partners, who were either playing cards on the dining room table or snoozing on one of the sofas. Later, as fight time approached, and I squeezed into the limousine that would transport him and his invited guests to the arena, I could feel my sweat rising as I anticipated what might be inflicted upon the body and face of this amiable, well-mannered man who sat silently in the back, glancing out at the sidewalk with seeming nonchalance, indistinguishable in his conservatively tailored suit and subdued silk tie from an average black executive who might be employed by IBM. Soon he will be standing nearly naked in the ring, I kept thinking, along with other thoughts that might seem simplistic and melodramatically banal except at times like this, when I feared that he was a few hours away from becoming seriously hurt, battered and knocked senseless because he was not really vicious and talented enough, and because he was also very light for a heavyweight, perhaps twenty pounds lighter and with a much shorter reach than his primary contenders—the menacing Sonny Liston and the arrogantly confident Muhammad Ali, both of whom would eventually annihilate him.

But even after they did, leaving him puffy-eyed behind dark glasses and with his ribs so sore that he winced with each breath, Patterson allowed me to go to his home for a postfight interview, in which he replied to questions that I might not have asked had other reporters been in the room. In 1964, after a first-round knockout by Liston, and after an assignment editor at the *Times* told me that the paper was at this point satiated with my stories about Patterson, I spent a weekend with him in order to do an article for *Esquire*, in which, among other things, he described what it is like being knocked out.

"It is not a *bad* feeling when you're knocked out," he told me. "It's a *good* feeling, actually. It's not painful, just a sharp grogginess. You don't see angels or stars; you're on a pleasant cloud. After Liston hit me in Nevada, I felt, for about four or five seconds, that everybody in the arena was actually in the ring with me, circled around me like a family, and you feel warmth toward all the people in the arena after you're knocked out. You feel lovable to all the people. And you want to reach out and kiss everybody—men and women—and after the Liston fight somebody told me I actually blew a kiss to the crowd from the ring. I don't remember that. But I guess it's true because that's the way you feel during the four or five seconds after a knockout. . . .

"But then," he continued, pacing the room, "this good feeling leaves you. You realize where you are, and what you're doing there, and what has just happened to you. And what follows is a hurt, a confused hurt—not a physical hurt—it's a hurt combined with anger; it's a what-will-people-think hurt; it's an ashamed-of-my-own-ability hurt . . . and all you want then is a hatch door in the middle of the ring—a hatch door that will open and let you fall through and land in your dressing room instead of having to get out of the ring and face those people. The worst thing about losing is having to walk out of the ring and face those people. . . ."

Although he had never complained that he had perhaps been too open with me in the long and revealing piece that appeared in *Esquire*—indeed, I later coauthored a shorter piece with him in the same magazine, and we continued to see each other socially until we approached our senior years and his memory began to fade, and he could not always remember my name—my own lingering regret about that piece was that the editors had entitled it "The Loser."

While it is true that Patterson was never a match for Liston or Ali, and that he had probably been knocked down more times than any highly ranked heavyweight in history—he went down *seven* times in a *single* fight in 1959 while losing his title to Sweden's Ingemar Johansson—it is just as true that Patterson was the all-time heavyweight leader in getting up off the floor. He was climbing to his feet after Johansson had decked him for the final time in 1959, but the referee stopped the fight. In a return match a year later, Patterson knocked out Johansson, becoming the first man ever to regain the heavyweight title; and he subsequently stopped Johansson in their third and final fight. And so instead of thinking of Floyd Patterson as a "loser," I consider him an exemplar of perseverance, a man who never quit and always tried to get up, even during moments of staggering disappointment and defeat.

Not long after Patterson had retired from the ring, the Yankees also became known as losers, having fallen from first place in the American League in 1964 to sixth in 1965, tenth in 1966, and ninth in 1967. The Yankees were owned by CBS, which had become the controlling partner in 1964, but I never knew what, if anything, the network's ownership had to do with the team's uncharacteristically poor record. I myself was now out of New York regularly, and I rarely went to see games in Yankee Stadium. After leaving the *Times* in 1965 to freelance for magazines and write books, I spent much of my time between the mid-1960s into the 1970s residing in hotels and apartments in various parts of California—in Beverly Hills to do a profile of Frank Sinatra during his autumn years; in San Francisco to write about the fifty-one-year-old Joe DiMaggio still mourning Marilyn Monroe, and also wondering what was wrong with the present-day Yankees; in San Jose, where I completed research on a book about the exiled Bonanno crime family, which had been driven out of New York by rival mafiosi in the late 1960s after losing the "Banana War"; and in Topanga Canyon, near Malibu in Los Angeles County, where I frequently hung out, from 1971 through 1973, in order to interview dozens of nudist freethinkers and free-love couples in a commune called Sandstone, which was one of the locales I used while researching and writing a book that outlined the historical and social trends that I believe made America in the 1970s so much more permissive and less prudish than the postwar, pre-*Playboy* days of my youth, when my confessed admiration for Frank Yerby's novels prompted my parish priest to predict, perhaps rightly, that I was predestined for degeneracy and an afterlife of purgatorial punishment.

One evening, while I was residing in Topanga Canyon, I drove down to Beverly Hills to dine with a writer friend I knew from New York who was now making a fortune in Hollywood working on scripts that, as far as I know, were never made into movies. He was a Yankee fan, and as we were finishing dinner, he introduced me to one of the restaurant's managers, who was a devotee of the Red Sox—a charming and gregarious Irish-American in his early thirties who stood more than six-four and wore a trimly tailored double-breasted suit and a bow tie and was named Patrick Shields. After joining our table for a while and treating us to an after-dinner drink, Shields took the opportunity to toast the continuing decline of the Yankees.

I saw him in the restaurant a few times after that; and before I had returned to New York during the spring of 1974, we had exchanged phone numbers and had made tentative plans to meet during one of his East Coast visits, which he said he would try to arrange while the Red Sox were playing the Yankees at the Stadium. I next heard from Shields a year later, when he phoned to inform me that he had moved to New York and wanted me to be his guest at a private dining establishment and disco that he was managing on the Upper East Side of Manhattan.

His place was called Le Club, and, as I would learn from frequent visits, its membership included many of New York's business tycoons who were not only sports fans but sometimes investors in one or more of the local teams—they might own a piece of the Yankees, the Mets, the Jets, the Giants, the Knicks, the Nets, the Rangers, or morsels of several of them. In any case, they traveled by limo to sporting events and usually sat in commodious, glass-walled mid-level boxes that, while offering an expansive overview of the playing area, muted much of the noise and spirit emanating from the crowds in the nearby seats and the spectators and athletes below. And yet—because most of these enclosed boxes had air-conditioning, heating systems, upholstered furniture, bartenders, waiters, and buffet tables offering a variety of seafoods, meats, and salads—the tycoons and their friends, both male and female, were able to attend games without being deprived of their accustomed comforts and amenities, to say nothing of their option to do here (as many of them did) what they might have done had they stayed home—watch the game on television, since there were usually two or more screens affixed to the walls of the boxes.

After the game was over—and often long before, if it was not a very interesting contest—the men and their friends would perhaps be driven back to Le Club for a late supper or nightcap. I enjoyed watching Patrick Shields moving and mingling among them at their tables near the dance floor; what most impressed me was the ease with which he comported himself while in the presence of these affluent and at times abrasive and fickle individuals who, having hired him, could also have banded together at any time to fire him. But to me he never seemed to be concerned or deferential in the manner often exhibited by maître d's even in New York's more exclusive restaurants. It was as if he *had* something on these people, something more than the usual extramarital dalliances that most restaurateurs discreetly accept as part of the decor of a New York dining room. Or maybe what Patrick Shields had going for him was merely the fact that he could seat these people wherever he wished, which in itself would make him a force, at least during the evening hours, when I believe most people's sensibilities and stability undergo an altering process that makes them more dependent upon the flattering light and ego-feeding rooms that good restaurants and clubs can provide, along with the choice tables that such hirelings as Patrick Shields could reserve by way of confirming the status that most of these people take for granted during the day.

I have long believed that in such vast and vacillating cities as New York even some very significant citizens can often feel insignificant at night, in part because their offices are closed and they are remote from their support systems and the attentions of their underlings, and they are sometimes even forgotten by their limo drivers, who await them in front of restaurants but have fallen asleep behind the wheel, and will wake up only after a few sharp knuckle raps on the side window or windshield. And so the nocturnal necessity of restaurants as extensions of important people's daytime prominence are essential ingredients that have nurtured the successful careers of all the great culinary figures—the legendary Henri Soulé of Pavillon, Sirio Maccioni of Le Cirque, Elaine Kaufman of Elaine's, and dozens of younger restaurant owners and men like Patrick Shields, who, though not an owner, was akin to them as an enterpreneur of the evening.

He was also an excellent conversationalist, and, as he passed out menus to his guests while towering over their tables, he forthrightly expressed his opinions on those subjects that were most often under discussion—the national economy, local politics, and professional sports.

Each morning, Patrick read five newspapers—the *Wall Street Journal*, the *Times*, and three local tabloids, including *Women's Wear Daily*, whose editor was a member of Le Club. During the latter part of the afternoons, while the waiters were preparing the tables for dinner, he was on the phone with his broker discussing some of the stock tips he had picked up the night before while cruising the tables. His bachelor apartment was in a high rise in the neighborhood, and what hung from the wooden hangers in his closet were bicoastal rows of tailored jackets and suits purchased from the finer shops of Rodeo Drive and Madison Avenue; and parked below in the garage was his leased Lincoln Town Car, which was spacious enough to accommodate his long limbs. Among the attractive women whom he escorted around Manhattan when he took a night off from work—and was not playing backgammon or bridge in the tearoom of a Park Avenue hotel with a few trophy wives he had met at Le Club—was his friend the actress Jennifer O'Neill, as well as some other performers he had known in Los Angeles or had met since moving to the East Coast. He himself might have qualified for camera work. His lean and handsomely haggard facial features and blue eyes reminded me at times of the film star Peter O'Toole. But Patrick Shields's height—he was nearly six-five, as I said, and his proudly erect posture and lean frame made him seem even taller—might not have served his potential acting career as much as I think it helped to define his role as an uncommon character at Le Club, as a man who, as perhaps I have emphasized too much already, could not be cast as a glorified servant.

I have actually never known very tall people to be obsequious. Such individuals may be shy, or, as I saw Patrick Shields on occasion, reserved. But because of their stature they are rarely challenged, I think, because shorter people—even those who might be known as Napoleonic bullies in their offices—tend to modify their behavior, to become less assertive when facing men who hover over them, as Patrick Shields did every night at Le Club, casually conversing with CEOs, real estate moguls, corporate lawyers, and other people who might own a percentage of a basketball team but whose view of tall men was usually limited to what they saw from luxury boxes or courtside seats in Madison Square Garden. And yet this *was* close enough for them to note that there surely were advantages to size and reach, and they could observe as well how aggressive tall men can be in action—as, for example, the Knicks player Latrell Sprewell, whose acceptance years later by the local fans all but smothered the notoriety he had earned after choking the coach of the West Coast team on which he had previously played.

I am certainly *not* hinting here that there was anything threatening or ill-tempered about the demeanor of Patrick Shields. I am merely suggesting that his being very tall was perhaps a factor in his capacity to be both beholden to and independent from the men who paid his salary at Le Club. Whether his height, along with his general efficiency and geniality, was entirely responsible for his apparent sense of security at Le Club, I do not really know, but my impression nonetheless was that he was very comfortable with the membership, and it is certain that they sometimes invited him as a single man to dinner parties in their homes, and also provided him with tickets to sporting events and even passes allowing him access to their boxes. One individual who did this, somewhat to my surprise, was the owner of the New York Yankees, George Steinbrenner.

Patrick Shields never concealed his ongoing affection for the Red Sox after he had moved to New York, and among the board members of Le Club who were aware of this was the Yankees owner, who was known in the media for his indifference to people with opinions other than his own. As a tabloid cartoon subject, Steinbrenner was sometimes portrayed as an antedated, barrel-chested Prussian military officer with a square-jawed scowling face partly hidden under a large spiked helmet. But since acquiring the Yankees from CBS in November 1973 (after the team had finished fourth for three straight seasons), he immediately put his considerable wealth and win-at-any-cost attitude into the organization and saw it improve within the next eight years to five first-place finishes, three trips to the World Series, and two world titles.

Among those who regularly watched these winning seasons from Steinbrenner's box was Patrick Shields, who often showed his gratitude for Steinbrenner's largesse by walking into Yankee Stadium wearing one of his Armani suits and a Red Sox baseball cap. I know this is true because I often accompanied him, having also gotten my name on Steinbrenner's list after Shields had introduced us and had expounded upon my lifetime devotion to the Yankee franchise. Much as I appreciated Shields's efforts in laying the foundation for what would become my enduring and amiable acquaintanceship with the boss of the Yankees, I must also say that I quietly worried about Shields's choice in headgear each time we entered the owner's luxurious box. While at first everyone appeared to be amused by it, including Steinbrenner, and while it was eventually ignored—or accepted as one might accept a touch of eccentricity or dishabille from an otherwise elegant and reputable individual—I always believed that unless Patrick Shields (no matter how tall he was) soon began wearing a more appropriate chapeau to Yankee Stadium, the two of us would unavoidably end up in the bleachers.

The six-foot-one-inch Steinbrenner was in essence taller than anybody in our midst. And as he had already demonstrated in the way he ran his team—by haggling over tiny matters in big contracts, by impulsively rotating his managers (he would hire and fire Billy Martin no fewer than four times within a dozen years), and by insisting that his players trim their beards and have close-cropped hair and *definitely* eschew such Afro-bouffant styles as a few black outfielders had tried to contain within their Yankee caps—he cared deeply about many things that were not always rational, reasonable, or predictable. But saying this is saying nothing that will explain why the reputedly tyrannical boss of the Yankees would continue for years to welcome a Red Sox idolizer into his private box in the Stadium; in fact, the relationship between them would rapidly develop into a warm and openly expressed bond of fraternalism. My guess is that Steinbrenner privately respected Shields's stubborn and stalwart allegiance to the Boston team that in Patrick's mind represented (no less than the Celtics or the Kennedy family that he also adored) the hub and soul of the immigrant Irish work ethic and Catholic suffering. Absolute loyalty in good and bad times had been one of the mandates of Steinbrenner's military school upbringing; and even when he himself deviated from such principles, for example, in his dealings with ex-Yankee players who became his managers—Yogi Berra refused to speak to him for fourteen years because, after being told that his managerial job was secure, he was inexplicably fired by Steinbrenner and learned of it through secondary sources—the Yankees' owner was nonetheless capable of being enamored with and affected by manifestations of loyalty when he saw them demonstrated by such adherents as Patrick Shields. It is perhaps true as well that in condoning Shields's fidelity to the Red Sox, the Yankees owner was able to refute the media's image of him as an intolerant martinet. On the other hand, Steinbrenner's affiliation with Shields might also be comparable to that of a missionary man seeking to reform an infidel, for he presented Shields with gifts that might have been proffered in the hope of Shields's conversion, such as a Yankee uniform that was tailored to fit, and also pregame passes that allowed Shields into the Yankee clubhouse and dugout, and along the fringes of the field and behind the batting cage, where he was free to converse with the players. As a result, Shields became friendly with many of them, so much so that he admitted he favored them over all other players except those on the Red Sox team. At the same time, he pressed Steinbrenner to allow him to demonstrate his presumed talent as an Irish tenor by selecting him to sing "The Star-Spangled Banner" one night before a game in the Stadium.

Steinbrenner responded with what he thought was an even better idea: He would (and did) rent Town Hall for a single evening in order to sponsor Patrick Shields's debut as a concert soloist. All the tickets were issued gratis to Shields's friends from Le Club and elsewhere in the city; and one of Steinbrenner's corporate colleagues, whose sister was a nun, enlarged the size of the audience by having busloads of parochial school students transported to the hall in midtown Manhattan. Before the program and during it, Patrick Shields received generous rounds of applause, which testified less to Shields's skills as a singer, which were barely evident, than to the persuasive Citizen Kane–like response of George Steinbrenner and the rest of the claque in the front rows. Later that night at Elaine's restaurant uptown, a few of the diners who had gone to the concert were ridiculing it in voices loud enough to be heard across the room by the restaurant's ample-figured proprietress, Elaine Kaufman, who had also been to Town Hall.

"That show tonight was a goddamned disaster," said one of the men at the table.

"Shields can't sing a lick," another man agreed, adding, " Steinbrenner was a damned fool to get himself mixed up in this thing. . . ."

"Will you guys knock it off?" Elaine Kaufman shouted from her bar stool. "Patrick at least had the balls to get up there and give it a shot. That's a lot more than any of you guys would have done."

A framed photograph of Patrick Shields, wearing his Yankee uniform, hung on the wall near the front of her restaurant, and she and he were close friends at this time, often going to the games and sitting together in Steinbrenner's box—except on those occasions when the Red Sox were in town and Shields preferred watching alone (as Steinbrenner had arranged) in a single seat behind the Boston dugout. Shields sometimes flew up to Boston to see the Red Sox in Fenway Park when his work schedule permitted, but he was too ill with the flu to watch the September 1978 play-off game in which the visiting Yankees triumphed over the Red Sox primarily because a New York shortstop named Bucky Dent (a .243 hitter who in 1978 had only five home runs) managed to hit one of these during the late innings of this important game, a "fluky little denty poke," as Shields would describe it while watching it on television at Le Club, that nevertheless rose loftily along the left-field foul line and landed beyond the playing area to ultimately decide the contest in the Yankees' favor and terminate the season for Boston.

"Oh, George," said Shields to Steinbrenner after the latter had returned from Boston, "how could you have done this to me? You have all those sluggers, all that high-priced talent! And you break my heart with *Bucky Dent!*"

These Yankees of 1978 would move on to play in the World Series and defeat the Los Angeles Dodgers, as they had the year before. But when the two teams next met in the World Series of 1981 (the Yankees failed to qualify in 1979 and 1980), the Dodgers would retaliate, winning four of six games. After that, the Yankees would flounder through many years of ineptitude and vanishing managers and Steinbrenner's ranting and raving, which would not cease until the Yankee team of 1996, managed by Joe Torre, finally produced another world champion.

During these many years, I continued to go to the Stadium with Elaine Kaufman but often without Patrick Shields, who during the latter 1980s began to complain of his diminished energy and enthusiasm for the game. But what he did not tell us was that he was slowly dying. He was dying of what we did not know about his private life, *his* nighttime life as he had lived it after he had closed Le Club at 4:00 a.m. and welcomed into his apartment the young men with whom he shared his cocaine and affections.

A woman who was Patrick Shields's longtime secretary and confidante, and who knew for more than two years that he was suffering from AIDS, said that he seemed to be very pleased by the fact that he had so long and convincingly presented himself as "straight" to all the people he associated with in Steinbrenner's box and Le Club and to the women whom he escorted back to their homes at night before his dawn life began. In his final will and testament, Patrick Shields left all of his possessions, including his Red Sox cap, to the last of his lovers, a young fashion model who had been born in Puerto Rico and was known in the New York garment industry and the discos as "Romeo."

2

THE YANKEES THAT I HAD BEEN WATCHING PLAY THE METS ON television on this July afternoon in 1999 were not playing like the world champions they had been the year before, when the team had won 114 games and swept the San Diego Padres in the World Series. On this particular Saturday, with the Yanks leading the Mets 6-4 going into the bottom of the seventh inning, a Yankee relief pitcher named Ramiro Mendoza gave up a double to the Mets' Rickey Henderson and then, following a walk to John Olerud, Mets catcher Mike Piazza whacked a 2-1 pitch over Shea Stadium's left-field wall and suddenly the Yankees were behind, 7-6. While I shook my head, the television set resounded with the cheering of Mets fans and there on the screen was the picture of the burly Piazza rounding the bases with his fists clenched.

My telephone was also ringing. Hoping that my wife, who was upstairs, would interrupt her reading to answer it, I let it ring. Finally I picked it up. It was my tennis partner, who was supposed to be coming by in a taxi that would take us to our doubles game in Central Park, but now he was saying that it had been canceled. He had injured his right ankle earlier in the afternoon in a fall on Lexington Avenue while on an errand with his wife, he said, adding that he had called two or three times to tell me this but my phone had constantly been busy. (I later learned that my wife had been communicating enthusiastically and at length on the bedroom extension with a literary agent in Connecticut who represented the author whose manuscript the two of us had slept with the night before.)

I was unhappy about not playing tennis, for I had been looking forward to getting a workout and practicing my service toss at a higher elevation. The slow-moving slugfest between the Yankees and Mets had already dragged on for nearly four hours, with no relief in sight from either team's bullpen. All three of the Mets relievers who had worked in the eighth and ninth innings had put men on base, while the Yankees had added two runs to retake the lead, 8-7—which remained the score as the Mets came to bat in the bottom of the ninth. One of the announcers said that the Yankees' fourth pitcher of the afternoon would be Mariano Rivera. He was perhaps the best reliever in baseball, and I was confident that he would soon be blinding the Mets' batters with his speed and would surely secure the victory.

As Rivera made his way to the mound to begin his warm-up pitches, and as the television channel began to inundate its audience with commercials, I impatiently switched to another channel to see what the Chinese and American soccer women were up to in the Rose Bowl, and how the United States' comely star, Mia Hamm, was doing in her quest to live up to the current media hype, which virtually equated her athleticism with that of Michael Jordan. While up to now, as I already suggested, I had no more passion for women's soccer than tiddlywinks, I had recently read a few sports page articles about Hamm and her teammates; on television, in an often-repeated Gatorade commercial, she was shown getting the better of Michael Jordan in various indoor and outdoor sports activities, all of them accompanied by the musical refrain "Anything you can do, I can do better."

In addition, this China-USA World Cup finale was being staged subliminally not only as the international Super Bowl of women's soccer but as a face-off between the daughters of two contentious nations presently at odds over a number of governmental grievances. It is often the case that athletes become unwittingly conscripted to the military and political interests of their nations, being called upon to transform a sports arena atmospherically into a battlefield and to help propagandize a cause by winning a game—and this was particularly so this summer with regard to the young women of the Chinese national soccer team.

In early May an American war plane had bombed the Chinese embassy in Belgrade while participating in the NATO anti-Serbian offensive in Yugoslavia, causing heavy casualties, three deaths, and a cost in damage and property losses of $28 million. Although the United States government claimed that the raid was accidental, an unintended target selected from an outdated map, the disbelieving Chinese immediately reacted by attacking the American embassy in Beijing with rocks and Molotov cocktails, causing a fire and more than $2 million in damages. Preceding this, and continuing concurrently, were charges and countercharges between the two nations concerning such matters as spying, human rights violations, copyright infringement, imperialism, intransigence, ignorance of the truth as each government saw it, and an animus tinged on both sides with what each believed was hypocrisy: an accusing finger from the West pointing to the plight of the Falun Gong spiritualists and the Dalai Lama, and Communist threats to the security of the Taiwanese; while an accusing finger from Beijing cited the U.S. government's destruction of the Branch Davidians, the nation's long history of prejudice and oppression against minorities, beginning with the Native Americans, and its prolonged boycott that had brought suffering to ordinary people in Cuba.

What all this portended for China's soccer women was either more pressure on them to defeat the Americans during their scheduled visit to the United States or maybe the nullification of their opportunity to compete in the United States if China's Party rulers decided to cancel their trip as a political gesture of ill will. Surely this was not wanted by the American sponsors of the 1999 Women's World Cup. This event took place every four years in different countries—it was like the Olympics, but never held during the same year—and in 1999 the host country was the United States. It had invited teams representing sixteen nations out of a total of more than sixty soccer-playing nations with well-organized programs, all sixteen invitees having previously demonstrated their superiority by advancing through qualifying rounds in their areas of the world. In the United States they would be involved for three weeks in a thirty-two-match tournament held in various American stadiums on the East Coast, in the Midwest, and in the far West—for example, at Giants Stadium in the New Jersey Meadowlands; at Soldier Field in Chicago; at Spartan Stadium in San Jose—and from these contests would emerge two teams with the best records and the right to face each other for the title in Pasadena's Rose Bowl.

Even before the games had begun, it was generally agreed by most sportswriters and the aficionados of women's soccer that the two best teams in the competition were from China and the United States; and while the promoters of the tournament privately welcomed the political tension between these countries as a potential boon to the World Cup's television ratings and the ticket sales in the eight stadiums chosen as game sites, the absence of the Chinese was nervously anticipated. This presaged not only reduced profits and media interest but also a missed opportunity to showcase the superior talent of Asian women who were eager to compete and who at the same time shared the promoters' aspirations to lift women's soccer to a higher level of global marketability, wanting to attract through intense rivalries more financial support from governments, industries, and businesses (especially businesses that manufactured products for women), and also to appeal to greater numbers of emotionally involved fans (including more soccer moms and schoolgirls) who would identify with and support this game as a celebration of female agility, endurance, power, and aggressiveness.

After some days of uncertainty, the Chinese women in early June were given permission by their leaders in Beijing to proceed with their flight plans to the United States. And true to form—while appearing before large crowds in Portland, Oregon, and San Jose, in the New Jersey Meadowlands, and in Foxboro, Massachusetts—they recorded victories over all the teams they had been matched with, successively defeating the women of Sweden, Ghana, Australia, Russia, and Norway. Meanwhile, the American women were also undefeated after taking on Denmark, Nigeria, North Korea, Germany, and Brazil.

And so the promoters ultimately had what they wanted, which was the closest thing that the World Cup could approximate to a Cold War confrontation with a bit of sex appeal, a battle between bevies of phyically fit young athletes with their hair cut in the style of pageboys, or bobbed or ponytailed, all of the women wearing shorts and numbered shirts and having fine legs. The United States' uniforms were white with red trimming and on the players' feet were Nike-swooshed black leather sneakers, which, as I would soon see on the television screen whenever an American was upended while tussling for the ball, were studded with red cleats. The Chinese women wore red uniforms with white trimming, and, like the Americans, displayed on the left side of their shirts a national symbol and on the right side the logo of their uniform's manufacturer, which in the case of the Chinese was Adidas.

Brand-name merchandise from the West had been distributed and also made in China for many years, encouraged by the trade policies of Deng Xiaoping, who became the Party ruler in 1978 (two years after Mao's death) and proclaimed, "To get rich is glorious." But now in 1999, as this nation of 1.3 billion people was about to mark a half century of Communist rule that had been inaugurated by Mao's triumphant entrance into Tiananmen Square in October of 1949, China was hardly rich; I had read in a newsmagazine that China in 1999 was still poorer than any non-Communist East Asian nation, and that to drive one hour outside a Chinese town was to enter a rural tableau that was "medieval." Still, it was reported in the Western press that China's leading cities were rapidly becoming towering temples of modernism, with pagoda-topped skyscrapers and five-star hotels, with shopping malls featuring world-famous designer boutiques, cappuccino machines, the latest in computer software and CD releases, and the biggest of the fast-food franchises.

In Beijing alone there were now six Pizza Huts, thirty-three Kentucky Fried Chickens (in the capital's streets there were more pictures of Colonel Sanders than of Chairman Mao), and fifty-seven McDonald's. It was now possible in China to ascend the Great Wall in a ski lift and descend in a toboggan; to tour Beijing's Imperial Palace while being guided by the audiotaped voice of Roger Moore; to be acoustically accompanied in parks by the single-string sounds of erhu players and by boom boxes blaring with the music of the Back Street Boys; and to travel through congested city streets swarming with beehives of bicyclists, diplomat-licensed limos with flag-flapping fenders, pedal-pumping rickshaw drivers, and any of the half dozen extraordinarily expensive sporty Italian vehicles sold in the past year at Beijing's newly opened Ferrari dealership.

"Without contradictions, nothing would exist," wrote Mao. But what I believed I was seeing as I stayed tuned to the televised soccer finale from the Rose Bowl—watching the Chinese players running up and down the field, pushing and bumping against the Americans, and being pushed and bumped in turn—was not in the category of a Maoist contradiction, but a contrasting and updated view of the kind of Chinese women whom Mao once imagined were holding up half the sky. These modern globe-trotting, cleat-sneakered Chinese finalists in the 1999 World Cup were in some cases the granddaughters or great-granddaughters of women who once hobbled around their homeland on bound and therefore deformed feet. These soccer players were in a historical sense part of an ongoing long march, a great leap forward into the twenty-first century, where, as future mothers in a technically advanced and burgeoning superpower, their competitive genes might epitomize the energy and resolve by which newer generations of Chinese might vie with the Americans to blow each other off the map.

But in the Rose Bowl, so far the score was 0-0, and while the rules and strategies of this game confounded me, there was something compelling enough to delay my channel-surfing back to the Yankees. My curiosity was engaged. As I sat in front of the television screen watching the players in motion without fully appreciating the intricacy of their movements, I kept wondering what it was that I was *not* seeing that was prompting the crowd's constant roars of approval and sighs of regret. What I could see, or thought I could see, rising along the grassy turf of the sun-bathed stadium was the sweat seeping through the red and white uniforms of these women who vigorously pursued and swarmed around the ball, often interlocking one another's limbs and entangling at times even their ponytails. With their soft-leather-covered feet they massaged and moved the white round ball in one direction, then another, sometimes losing it to an opponent, who often lost it just as quickly—in basketball these are "turnovers," and whenever a player on the home team commits one, he can expect boos or jeers from the onlookers. But here in the Rose Bowl, where apparently the expectations of dexterity were not applied to athletes advancing a ball with shod feet, there were no sounds of condemnation from the spectators.

President Clinton appeared on my television screen, smiling and waving from the shadows of his enclosed box. There were many Asians in the crowd, perhaps most of them residents of Southern California. In the press section were hundreds of American and foreign journalists with their laptops and cameras, focusing on the field-level forays and retreats and the fancy footwork of this Saturday-afternoon spectacle that 100 million people in China were now watching before sunrise on Sunday.

I continued to wait for someone to score, wishing it would be soon. I was disappointed that Mia Hamm, the only player whose name and face I was familiar with, was not showing any of her Jordanesque dazzle when she had the ball. In no way did she distinguish herself from the rest of the players. Whatever they were doing, she was not doing better.

I decided to take a quick peek at the Yankee game, thinking it might already be over and that Mariano Rivera had probably blanked the Mets in the bottom of the ninth to preserve the 8-7 lead and seal yet another Yankee victory.

But the scene that greeted me from Shea Stadium was a picture of frustration on the face of Mariano Rivera. He had been unable to control his pitches, having walked the Mets' Rickey Henderson; and then the Mets' Edgardo Alfonzo had smashed one of Rivera's ninety-five-mile-an-hour fastballs deep into center field for a double, sending Henderson to third. As I stood up and watched, doing as most of the fifty thousand fans in the ballpark were now doing, although they were also clapping and shouting for the Mets' rally to continue, Rivera deliberately walked Mike Piazza. This loaded the bases. There were already two outs, and issuing an intentional walk to a slugger like Piazza was a predictably intelligent managerial move. The last time Piazza had come to bat, two innings before, facing the Yankees' middle-relief pitcher Ramiro Mendoza, he had hit a three-run homer. All that Rivera had to do now was induce the next hitter to make an out, and this long game would be over.

The Mets sent up a pinch hitter named Matt Franco. I had never heard of him, but I normally do not watch Mets games. Whoever Franco was, I reasoned, he was surely not as threatening as Piazza. Franco strolled up to the plate and, with the bat on his shoulder, took his position, ready to swing. Rivera glared at him from the mound. Rivera then took a deep breath, went into his pitching motion, and hurled one of his signature fastballs that was supposed to look like an aspirin as it streaked past the hitter for a called strike. But Franco saw it clearly and hit it perfectly, whacking it out to right field beyond the Yankee outfielder's reach, and suddenly Henderson and Alfonzo had raced home to score two runs, and now the Mets were the winners, 9-8. As the Mets' fans leaped and screamed in celebration, and as Franco was embraced by his teammates, Mariano Rivera walked slowly with his head lowered toward the Yankee dugout.

I sought my relief by walking into the kitchen for a can of beer. For me this afternoon so far had been a total loss—no tennis, no Yankee pitching, nothing to do until dinner (if my wife ever came down from her reading room) except to click back to the soccer women. I did not know how many minutes had been played, but there was still no score, and *still* the banner-waving and noisy fans continued to give the impression that they were excited by what they were seeing on the field. This game that my foreign-born father used to refer to as "a waste of time" seemed to be wasting what was left of my afternoon, and yet I continued to watch and wait for something to happen that I would find satisfying or conclusive. That this women's contest had attracted so many spectators, and was featured on American network television, was definitely a point of interest. Soccer might well be the world's most popular sport, played in the past by such renowned millionaires as Pelé and Maradona, and at times personified by rabbles of passionate fans who started riots in the stands and ran berserk through the towns in which their beloved teams were matched against loathed rivals; but the many millions of foreigners who had come to the United States and assimilated during the nineteenth and twentieth centuries had not seen this sport assimilate with them into the American mainstream. They had left the game behind in the Old Country, as my father had, leaving it to male relatives whom he somehow suggested to me were village laggards and POW candidates.

And yet here in the Rose Bowl, this manly foreign game was being profitably promoted to Americans through network television by young women—foreigners in the sense that Chinese players were involved, and foreign in the sense that the American women were, in style and manner, foreign to many men of my generation and certainly to the immigrants of my father's time.

Since I am about to sound somewhat knowing about these women and this sport about which I have heretofore proclaimed so little knowledge or interest, I must explain that, in addition to the newspaper and newsmagazine articles I had been reading recently about the World Cup competition, I had also been receiving abundant information about soccer via E-mail and the postal service from a soccer mom in her late thirties who the previous spring had attended a writing seminar that I had been invited to conduct on a campus not far from my home. This woman was aspiring to complete a book entitled *Confessions of a Soccer Mom,* and, while her literary skills at this point in her life were not much developed beyond the singing talents of the late Patrick Shields, she was consumed with confidence and recommended that I give her work in progress to my wife.

Among the drawbacks that I associate with my participation in seminars and with the part-time teaching that I sometimes do at universities within their graduate and undergraduate writing programs is meeting students and other people who have book ideas and manuscripts for my wife and who regard me as part of a courier service that will transport their efforts expeditiously and personally into her office. I have actually done this, carried away from a classroom a thick envelope or package addressed to my wife; but since the results have too rarely been satisfactory to anyone, I now strive to remain uninvolved, although it is often not that simple with people possessing the stamina and single-mindedness of this soccer mom from the suburbs of northern New Jersey. Even though my wife or one of her colleagues did finally read and politely turn down what the woman herself had delivered to the office receptionist, and despite my own courteous avoidance of the opportunity she extended to me as her chosen ghostwriter or even the coauthor of her book, she nonethless continued to send me massive amounts of material about women's soccer that she herself had collected while attending games and picking the brains of the cognoscenti along the sidelines or while she was at home communicating on the Internet with fans of women's soccer around the world, including many soccer moms in China.

A typical Chinese woman lacked the resources to buy a sport-utility vehicle, she informed me, acknowledging that she herself had two SUVs, one left behind by her former husband (it had a broken axle), and so in China the young girls who were escorted to practice by their mothers did so on the backs of bicycles. If any of these girls indicated signs of exceptional ability on a practice field, she continued, they were practically snatched from the backs of their mothers' bicycles by one of the regime's talent scouts, who would then enroll the girls as full-time students for years in a special academy, where they would receive an inadequate education in everything except the development of those physical skills that might qualify them finally as Olympic contestants in soccer, or gymnastics, or volleyball, or swimming, or whatever sport they were capable of performing on a world stage so well that their male coaches and the Party bureaucrats would have no fear of losing face.

While five of the twenty-two Chinese women players on the 1999 national squad were married, none could have children if they wished to remain affiliated with the team. With their average incomes being about five thousand dollars a year, and with financing in China unavailable to help cover the high cost of such items as, for example, an automobile, only four members of the squad owned and operated cars (three of the women had working husbands who shared expenses; the other was the unmarried daughter of a successful family from Shanghai). The majority of their teammates did not even have a driver's license and saw no point in taking lessons to obtain one. None of the women on the national team had a college education. The only one with classroom experience on a campus was the team captain, Sun Wen, who dropped out early in her first year. Drinking, smoking, and dancing in discos late at night—a not-unfamiliar routine with some male soccer players following practice sessions and games—would have caused a woman player's dismissal had such behavior come to the attention of the national team's ascetic male coach, Ma Yuanan, who considered himself permissive when he allowed one of his wedded sequestered soccer-playing sprites to accept a husbandly visit in her dormitory bedroom late on a Saturday night.

The women of the United States team, on the other hand, were free to partake in nighttime interludes with husbands and/or admirers of either sex. Two of the five married players on the American squad had children (one had two), and when these women were on the road with the team, the organizational budget covered the travel costs and living expenses of the accompanying nannies. All the American players had college degrees or were in the process of getting them. All drove cars, and, with their team salaries and bonuses and their forthcoming game fees as participants in the newly formed National Soccer League, the women would soon join the lucrative six-figure ranks of professional athletes. With the exception of the goalkeeper, who was black, all the American starters were white women, who as a group were fair-haired and photogenic enough to be courted by the makers of commercials in the mainstream market and to be poster-perfect for schoolgirls in the suburbs. The American players also tended to be larger, taller, and yet just as fast as the Chinese—I could see this myself from watching the Rose Bowl game on television—and it also appeared to me that the Americans' bodies were more curvesome and fully feminine than the Chinese. The latter were inclined to be quite narrow-hipped and boyish in figure, and, with one or two exceptions, to have smaller breasts than the Americans. Actually, I had not noticed large-breasted women on either team. Perhaps there were some seated among the substitutes, but, since the television cameras were not catering to the sensual concentrations that might enliven my afternoon, any women so endowed existed beyond my purview.

Still, from what I had read about the American team, they were not especially prudish. One of the starting players was apparently proud enough of her body to pose in a bikini for *Sports Illustrated*'s swimsuit issue. Another starter was photographed in a squatting position in *Gear* magazine, wearing no clothes at all while holding a soccer ball in front of her breasts. I could not imagine the Chinese coach allowing his players these liberties even if they were so disposed, but this was conjecture on my part, the musings of an elderly man who, for lack of anything better to do at this particular time, was watching fleet-footed and sweating female athletes chasing one another around the playing field while momentarily imagining them gamboling in G-strings in a rain forest on the Playboy Channel.

This game was now nearly over and the score was still 0-0. The regulation time of a soccer match is ninety minutes—two forty-five-minute halves—and so far every shot aimed at the net had either been misguided or blocked by the opposing goalkeeper. The Americans got off more kicks than the Chinese, and they seemed to boot the ball harder and farther and to cover more ground as they roved widely around the field before settling into their offensive or defensive formations. But the Chinese impressed me as having the edge in teamwork and in anticipating where the ball was going to be before it got there. They were prescient about what footwork and ball movement would lead to, and, like the onetime rebounding basketball star Dennis Rodman—a veritable geometric genius in the way he foresaw and acted upon the projections of errant shots caroming off backboards and rims—the Chinese women arrived just ahead of time at the spot where a pass from a teammate was due or where they might intercept an intended exchange between their opponents. The Chinese minimized their own turnovers by advancing with short passes, and they also maintained possession of the ball through feigning— keeping the ball between their feet while *pretending* they were about to kick it. Instead of kicking it, they sidestepped it, danced around it, did the jig, the rumba, then wiggled their hips and their heads just enough to keep the opposition off balance and allow sufficient space through which they could get off a quick kick downfield toward a teammate dashing in the direction of the rival goalkeeper.

At one point in the closing minutes, the Chinese had an opportunity to break the deadlock. After the Americans had allowed the ball to roll out of bounds on the sidelines deep in their own territory, the Chinese corner kicker booted the ball back into play at an angle that spun inward through the air and then tailed down within reach of two Chinese players who stood ready to kick or head it in for a score. But before they could get to it, the American goalie leaped forward with a clenched fist to punch it away, clobbering not only the ball but also the head of a teammate with such force that the American girl was knocked sprawling to the ground. Unconscious for a few moments, and unable to maintain her balance after being helped to her feet, the groggy American was carried away and was never able to reenter the contest. Her substitute filled in well enough, however, and the game continued without further scoring opportunities from either side until the clock expired.

After a brief respite, during which the two eleven-player teams huddled separately along the sidelines, drinking water and talking to their coaches, the referees waved them back onto the field for fifteen minutes of overtime—which from then on would both extend and heighten the spectators' expectations and their noise level as they sat forward in their seats, observing the ongoing foot-to-foot combat that went back and forth on this grassy turf that measured 116 by 72 yards and was rimmed by big-business billboards—Coca-Cola, MasterCard, Fuji film, Bud Light— and that earlier in the day had been buzzed from above by four streaking U.S. F-18 fighter planes that were perhaps trying to communicate to any of the Chinese spies in the crowd, or their bosses back in Beijing, that such jets were part of Uncle Sam's answer to China's potential military aggression along the coastal areas of Taiwan.

The people of Taiwan were now, in fact, completing a half century of isolation from mainland China, having first become a self-governing entity under Generalissimo Chiang Kai-shek following the latter's military defeat by Mao's forces and his escape to the island in 1949. Arriving with what was left of his downtrodden Kuomintang army and nearly a million mainland refugees and all of China's gold reserves, the Generalissimo subsequently established Taiwan as a small but stalwart abutment against communism while he continued to see himself as the legitimate leader of the mainland, from which he had been so rudely removed. When he died in 1975, he left behind a people made more secure through United States support and with a standard of living higher than that of their counterparts on the mainland, but neither he nor his political successors could restore his notions of grandeur, and the Taiwanese women who played on the island's soccer team in 1999 were a level below the Chinese now playing in the Rose Bowl. Not only the Taiwanese but *all* the teams of Asia—the Japanese, the North and South Koreans, the Thais, and the rest—were inferior to the soccer women of China, and had been so for nearly a decade.

However, the Chinese were now being tested on the other side of the world by this more physical force from the United States while being surrounded by a partisan crowd consisting of spectators cloaked in the Stars and Stripes, and by confetti-tossing teenagers with their faces painted red, white, and blue, and by an energy-sapping sun and the 105-degree heat under a stadium sky jet-streamed with jingoism. Still, the Chinese women kept pace with the United States through the overtime period, and they nearly won the game in the tenth minute when one of their players headed a ball over the American goalkeeper, and were it not for a spectacular save near the back line by a leaping American defender, the ball would have penetrated the net.

With neither team staging another serious attack during the remaining five minutes, nor during the *second* fifteen-minute overtime period that followed—fatigue was slowing down many of the women, especially those who had performed without substitutes during this grueling and sweltering ordeal that had so far lasted two hours—the referees ordered that the outcome be resolved by penalty kicks, a situation in which five women from each side would be selected by their coaches to take turns trying to kick a ball spotted twelve yards in front of the net into the goal that was guarded by the rival team's goalkeeper.

The odds were always with the kickers, since it is very difficult for a defender standing alone to react quickly enough to block a hard-hit shot booted at such close range toward a net that is eight feet high and eight yards wide, practically the size of a two-car garage. Still, scoring was not automatic—errant shots sometimes *did* occur due to a combination of factors that might include the nervousness or carelessness of the kicker, or the defensive acrobatics and/or good guesswork of the goalkeeper.

The World Cup winner would now be decided while the majority of the players stood watching along the sidelines as their five appointed teammates, alternating with five opponents, would singularly appear on the western end of the field and place the ball on a white spot in the grass in front of the net, and then, after stepping back several paces, and after the referee had blown the whistle, each player in turn would run toward the ball and kick it in a way she hoped would elude the outstretched hands and moving body of the goalkeeper and land somewhere within the net. If each of the teams' five kickers were successful, resulting in a 5-5 tie, the coaches would then summon a sixth member to go one-on-one against a rival; and if these two also scored, they would be succeeded by another pair of competitors, and then another and *another* if necessary, until one of the two had faltered as a result of missing the net or having the ball blocked. This title match could not end in a draw. The kicks would continue indefinitely until there was a winner and a loser. It would be demoralizing and heartbreaking for the individual who would ultimately fail to get her penalty kick into the net, knowing that she alone would be responsible for the defeat of her entire team, but this would inevitably be the fate of one of these women on this day in the Rose Bowl.

Since the Chinese won the coin toss, they were the first to send a kicker onto the field. She was a round-faced, ponytailed brunette who wore the number 5 and seemed to be a bit taller and sturdier than her characteristically petite teammates. She was not, however, as imposing in appearance as the burly 150-pound black American goalkeeper who stood in front of her, staring at her, although the Chinese girl paid little attention as she slowly lowered the ball with both hands and positioned it on the white grass spot that marked the twelve-yard target site. She was said to be China's most reliable penalty kicker, which was why the coach had assigned her ahead of the others, expecting her to get his team off to a good start. She was also functioning with full energy, since she had not played long in today's heat, having entered the game as a substitute late in the second overtime. After hearing the referee's whistle, she charged the ball and kicked it so swiftly and surely that the American goalie could only watch it sail high over her own right shoulder into the left corner of the net. As the kicker's teammates and the coaches clapped along the sidelines, China took a 1-0 lead.

The first American kicker was the team captain, wearing number 4, a lanky chestnut-haired woman with delicately refined facial features and the reputation for being an indelicate and indefatigable defender. But she would also prove to be a surefooted kicker on this occasion, unhesitatingly attacking the ball and driving it low and hard past China's goalie into the opposite side of the net that the first Chinese kicker had hit. Jubilantly, after watching her ball slam into the cords, the American pumped her fist in the air and then jogged back to the sidelines while most of the stadium's crowd stood cheering and her teammates came forward to embrace her. The score was now 1-1.

The second Chinese kicker was a slender brunette who wore number 15. She had seen action earlier in the game as a substitute and was not a key player on the team except in times like this. She was an excellent penalty kicker. Some of her teammates considered her the equal of their premier penalty converter, the surefire number 5. I had read that there were some fine players among the Chinese—and among the Americans and other teams, as well—who had stage fright when confronting penalty-kick situations. They were more comfortable running and kicking while surrounded by crowds of scrambling opponents than they were when standing alone behind an unmoving ball spotted on the grass and having to boot it twelve yards toward a spacious net that was guarded by a solitary defender in a one-on-one matchup being scrutinized by every fan in the stadium and perhaps millions of watchers on television. There were players who practically begged their coaches not to select them for the penalty spotlight, which could subject them to such vast humiliation should their booted ball be blocked or, worse, should they fail to hit the net.

But the second kicker for China, the reputably unflappable number 15, was known within the team as being a rather narcissistic young woman who welcomed as much attention as she could get and was a very focused performer when all eyes were upon her; and so after she had taken her running start and had struck the ball cleanly to her left, she paused to watch with apparent satisfaction as it glided beyond the goalie's fingertips and went crashing into the cords, bringing smiles from her coach and her teammates, if not from the overwhelmingly pro-American assemblage in the stands. Then she turned around and trotted back to the sidelines in an unhurried stride that suggested to me both self-assurance and a lingering interest in being watched. And so China had regained the lead, 2-1.

The second kicker for the United States was also known for exhibiting poise under pressure, and, while not renowned for being self-absorbed, she acquitted herself well when in center-stage situations. She was a thirty-one-year-old Californian who wore number 14 and had been a U.S. team leader for nearly a decade, having taken leave from the sport only intermittently to bear two children and to recover from a broken right leg suffered while competing in 1995. Although her forte was defense—it was she who singularly stopped the Chinese from scoring during this game's first overtime by leaping into the net to deflect a shot that had sailed over the head of the U.S. goalkeeper—she was also formidable on the attack, having scored the third goal in her team's 3-2 triumph over Germany during the quarter-final round of this World Cup. Now, as a penalty kicker, she approached the ball slowly but with practiced deliberation and deception, freezing the Chinese goalkeeper in a fixed position near the middle of the box while the ball soared into the net yards beyond the goalie's upraised left hand. And so the score was again tied, 2-2.

The third kicker for China was a twenty-five-year-old native of Beijing who had close-cropped black hair and a straight-lined figure, and she wore the number 13. She had been a member of the national squad for six years, and a starting player for the past two, developing into a scoring threat as well as a steadfast defender. Her versatility and diligence meant that, except when she was injured, she was not replaced by a substitute if the score was close, and on this afternoon in the Rose Bowl, she had been active during each and every minute of this long and debilitating test of wills and tenacity.

As she prepared for her penalty kick—the announcer introduced her as Liu Ying, it being one of the few Chinese names I could pronounce—she was being watched by the stout and sturdy American goalkeeper, Briana Scurry, who stood waiting twelve yards in front of her in a crouched and challenging stance. Briana Scurry had been a youth-league football player in her hometown of Minneapolis, and later a high school trackster and basketball player as well as an outstanding performer in this sport of soccer, for which she would win a scholarship to the University of Massachusetts. Beginning in 1994, she would achieve whatever distinction went with being the one black woman on the otherwise all-white starting lineup of the U.S. national team. She once described herself to a reporter as "the fly in the milk." In a *New York Times* article that was published a few weeks *after* this game, she recalled that when the third Chinese kicker, the aforementioned Liu Ying, had positioned herself behind the ball, "Her body language didn't look very positive. It didn't look like she wanted to take it. I looked up at her and said, 'This one is mine.'"

The *Times* article also reported that during this crucial moment, Briana Scurry had decided to try to limit Liu Ying's effectiveness by defending against her improperly, moving forward a couple of steps in front of the net even *before* Liu Ying's foot had touched the ball, reducing the angle of the kick. This was a goalkeeper's ploy that Briana Scurry and other teams' goalies occasionally resorted to, hoping it would offset some of the disadvantage of being on the receiving end of what goalkeepers often compare to Russian roulette. Sometimes the referee's whistle signaled a goalkeeper's unauthorized movement, allowing the shooter a second chance if the ball had not gone into the net. At other times the referees failed to see, or were too uncertain to confidently call, an infraction; it was frequently very difficult to determine if a goalkeeper *had* stepped forward a split second before the kicker's toe had touched the ball. With regard to Briana Scurry in the Rose Bowl, it appeared to some reporters and other onlookers that she had moved forward ahead of time against the *first* Chinese penalty kicker, number 5, but there had been no whistle—and number 5 had made her shot anyway.

But China's third kicker, Liu Ying, was less fortunate. Her shot was not well hit. Her footwork seemed to be tentative during her approach. Perhaps she was distracted by Scurry's movement, if the latter *had* moved too early. There had not been a whistle. Still, Scurry instinctively sensed or rightly guessed that the ball would be coming to her left side, and as it sailed off Liu Ying's right foot, Scurry was already leaping toward it, her outstretched body surging through the air parallel to the ground with both of her arms fully extended and the fingers of her gloved hands elongated and rigid until being bent back by the force of the ball, which was nevertheless deflected and sent bouncing inconsequentially toward the sidelines.

As Scurry fell heavily to the turf—she said later that as she lay in pain she feared she'd chipped a hipbone and mangled a stomach muscle—she was immediately revived by the applause that surrounded her and the sight of far-flung confetti and the enthusiasm of her teammates jumping and hugging one another near the bench. Scurry leaped to her feet and pumped her arms several times while the captain of the U.S. team raised her own index finger above her high-browed forehead, signaling perhaps that the Americans were now alone at the top.

If this was the captain's intention, it was a premature gesture. The game was not over. It was true, however, that if all the remaining shooters (the three Americans and the two Chinese) were successful, the final tally would favor the Americans, 5-4, and the World Cup trophy would become the property of the United States.

Ultimately, this is what happened. China's last two kickers—number 7 and number 9—both aimed accurately beyond Scurry's reach, the first player shooting to the right, the second to the left. But the trio of Americans—which included Mia Hamm, who shot fourth—were also flawless. The American who made the fifth and decisive kick was number 6, Brandi Chastain, a ponytailed blond Californian with a suntanned and gracefully delineated muscular figure that *Gear* magazine had photographed in the nude ("Hey, I ran my ass off for this body" was her response to the media; "I'm proud of it"). After she had blasted her winning shot to the left side of the lunging Chinese goalkeeper, Chastain pulled off her shirt and fell to her knees in front of the net, wearing a black sports bra as she clenched her fists in a triumphant pose that would make the cover of the next issue of *Newsweek* under the headline GIRLS RULE!

I stood in front of my television set without elation as the victorious U.S. team continued to celebrate on the field, and I kept watching as the roving eye of the camera zoomed in on the stadium's multitudes of American revelers with their smiling and patriotically painted faces and their party hats and horns, embracing and kissing—it was a midsummer prelude to New Year's Eve, and overlooking the scene was a big balloon, the Goodyear blimp. But my own thoughts were now concentrated on an individual who had disappeared from the screen, the young woman from China, Liu Ying, who had missed her kick.

I imagined her at this moment sitting tearfully in the locker room. Nothing in the life of this young woman of twenty-five could have pre- pared her for what she must have been feeling, for never in the history of China had a single person so suddenly been embarrassed in front of *so many* people—including 100 million from her home country. Was she surrounded now in the locker room by sympathetic teammates? Was she sitting in isolation after being rebuked by her coach? Was the coach at fault for selecting her as a kicker when he might have known that she was too physically exhausted and mentally distracted to meet the test? Would the bureaucrats who ruled over the Party's sports apparatus soon replace the coach? If he retained his job, and if Liu Ying were not demoted from the national team, would the coach choose her in the future to take a penalty kick in an important game?

I was asking questions as if I were a born-again sportswriter with access to the locker room, and if I were, *she* would have been my story, she who would probably not sleep tonight and might forever be haunted by the remembrance of her woeful moment in the sun while much of the world was watching. Or was I overdramatizing, overstating the sensibilities of this young athlete? Among the supposed strengths of a successful athlete is the capacity to overcome one's shortcomings and mistakes by not dwelling upon them, by not obsessing over them, by *forgetting* them, and—quoting the tiresome term of the 1990s—moving on. And yet it seemed to me that Liu Ying's failed penalty kick was momentous and heartrending in ways well beyond the blown save by Mariano Rivera of the Yankees, and even the pounding humiliation that I can recall watch- ing decades ago as it was being inflicted by Muhammad Ali upon Floyd Patterson.

Losing the 1999 World Cup soccer title to the Americans when China was simmering with political tension, rivalry, and resentment toward the United States lent significance to this World Cup match that it would not have otherwise warranted, and it brought forth wishful expectations and nationalistic passions within the Chinese population that would not be gratified by the conclusion of this game. I could not imagine a longer and more uncomfortable airplane ride than the one scheduled to trans- port this player and her teammates from Los Angeles back to Beijing. In China, where it is acknowledged that most parents lack enthusiasm for the birth of females, what amount of enthusiasm would greet this particu- lar female when she returned to her homeland? What would her family say to her? What would I say were she my daughter? What would be the response from the people who lived in her neighborhood, and from the men who headed the regime's sports commission?

The television cameras focused on the Americans receiving their medals. It was now nearly 6:45 p.m. I had been watching television for about five and a half hours. I was restive. My wife was still upstairs reading. Her door was closed. She had called down earlier, requesting that I lower the sound coming from the television. She also suggested that we dine out in a restaurant that night, but not before 8:30. I was about to turn off the program, but hesitated. Usually after a major sporting event—a World Series game, a championship prizefight, tennis from Wimbledon, the Super Bowl—the losing competitors were invited to the microphones to offer their views and explanations concerning the outcome. I was hoping to hear something from the Chinese, especially from Liu Ying. But the network terminated its World Cup broadcast shortly after 6:45 without a word from her and without any information about how she was bearing up.

Why did I care? Why did I quietly think about her throughout dinner while I listened listlessly to my wife and a few of our friends who had joined our table at Elaine's? Why was I so disappointed and displeased the following morning after I had perused several newspaper articles about the game and learned nothing that I wanted to know about Liu Ying? Later in the week when the newsmagazine cover stories that featured the World Cup also failed to include even a brief interview with her, or any information that would satisfy my curiosity about her, I telephoned an important editor I knew named Norman Pearlstine, who oversaw the publication of Time Warner's many periodicals—among them *Sports Illustrated*, *Time*, and *People*—and I asked if he might consider ordering a story in one of his magazines that would describe how the Chinese people had responded to Liu Ying's return, and how she herself had reacted and was reacting to her Rose Bowl experience, and, finally, what if anything this had to say about contempory attitudes and expectations with regard to young women in a changing China.

If I was sounding a bit lofty on the phone as I impersonated being an editor to one of the most savvy and successful editors in New York, it did not greatly concern me. I was sixty-seven. He was maybe fifty. At my advanced age, I have become accustomed to being indulged by younger people, many of them no doubt encouraged by the fact that they will not have to indulge me much longer. And so I let Norman Pearlstine indulge me. I elaborated and digressed without any interruption on his part, and while at no point did he commit himself or even pass judgment on my idea, he also voiced no objection when I volunteered to send him a memo expressing my thoughts in writing.

I faxed him at once.

Dear Norman:

As I was saying on the phone, I believe that last week's single blocked kick of the Chinese World Cup soccer player, Liu Ying, might provide us with a story angle by which we may measure China and the United States in ways well beyond the realm of sports competition.

There's a photo in today's *New York Times* showing President Clinton greeting the triumphant American women in the White House. How did China's officials greet the Chinese women after their return to their homeland? Who was at the airport? . . . the story should be told through this one woman, Liu Ying, a step-by-step account of how her life has gone since her foot failed her in the Rose Bowl.

Back in the 1950s I began my *Times* career as a sportswriter, and I've always found losers' locker rooms as learning experiences; and I think that the losing effort by the Chinese women last week in California might tell us a lot about our comparative societies.

I'd be happy to assist if you and your other colleagues think I can. I could assist your China-based correspondents with an interview, or sidebar writing, or whatever.

I'd surely be interested in visiting the mainland if you think I'll be a help . . . so after you have had time to think it through, let me know. . . .

After I had faxed the memo, I wished that I had deleted the last two paragraphs. My phone call had been entirely prompted (or so I told myself) by my desire to have my idea accepted by Pearlstine, with the assumption that he would later turn it over to be developed and written by members of his organization. In a sense, I had been doing him a favor. I had come up with an uncommon approach to a story that the rest of the press had apparently overlooked, and I was giving it to him gratis.

But at the end of my fax I had gracelessly insinuated myself into the assignment, promoting the notion that Pearlstine might like to send me halfway around the world (at his expense) so that I might "assist" his China-based correspondents with my story idea. How utterly *stupid* of me to propose that! If his China-based correspondents needed my assistance, they were unqualified for their jobs and should be fired. I was also appalled by the tone of false modesty in my final paragraph and the obviousness of my opportunism in seeking to take professional advantage of my personal relationship with the magazine czar at Time Warner. It is one thing to make a suggestion and quite another to belatedly try to horn in on an assignment or reappropriate a story idea after I had relinquished my proprietary claim to it with my call soliciting Pearlstine's help in publicizing what was of interest to me.

Maybe I was making too much of this, I reasoned, and for all I knew Pearlstine had liked my memo, and had already forwarded it with his approval down to one of his magazines, and soon I would be consulted by the corporation's travel department, asking me how soon I could leave for China.

A few days later I received a call from a high-ranking Time Warner executive who explained that Norman Pearlstine was traveling but that the editors had found my idea very interesting and were grateful that I had contacted them about it. Even though they would not be using it, he assured me that they were sincere in wanting me to continue sending them ideas in the future. I promised that I would.

As I hung up, I was quite disappointed, but also relieved. China was very far away. I had my overdue book to deal with. The World Cup was yesterday's news. Liu Ying had invaded my thoughts for more than a week, and now I could thank the Time Warner people for bringing me to my senses. Who wanted to read anything centered on a little Chinese soccer maiden who could not kick straight? The twenty-first century was upon us, and I had new things to think about.

If this was the case, why did I soon find myself on a jet airplane flying toward China (at my own expense, without an assignment, and without knowing where in that vast country I might find Liu Ying), anticipating my rendezvous with her?

3

IN TRUTH, AFTER I HAD LOST ALL HOPE THAT THE MONETARY COST OF my potential wild-goose chase in China would be underwritten by the largesse of Time Warner, I procrastinated for nearly three months before dipping into my own pocket to pay for the trip—which, until the day of my departure (Tuesday, October 12, 1999), I decided I would discuss with no one, including my wife.

It was not that I was shying away from whatever might be her reaction. I doubted that my wife would find anything about me to be shockingly out of character after forty years of marital familiarity with my various impulses and errant ambitions. It was rather that I myself had misgivings about my motives. Did I seriously believe that this was a valid story worthy of my involvement? Or was I merely reaching out to Liu Ying as a kind of muse, an alluring figure in a mirage that would inspire my meanderings across the mainland of China while I avoided my main professional obligation at home, at my writer's desk, where I was struggling with my book? When there is a creative lapse in a writer's work, I reminded myself, a writer can be very creative in finding ways to escape it.

And so I decided in late July, after the polite declination from Time Warner, to try to forget about Liu Ying and adhere to the daily schedule that I have always sought to follow when attempting to write books at home in New York or at my home on the New Jersey shore, a rambling Victorian beach house that is winterized and that I commuted to regularly, with or without my wife, while visiting my mother, who lived nearby and who, at an advanced age, no longer wanted to drive her own car at night when going out to restaurants and casinos; but she *still* wanted to go out. So I was her chauffeur and escort.

When I am writing, each morning at around eight o'clock I am at my desk with a tray of muffins and a thermos filled with hot coffee at my side, and I sit working for about four hours and then leave for a quick lunch at a coffee shop, followed perhaps by a set or two of tennis. By 4:00 p.m. I am back at my desk revising, discarding, or adding to what I had written earlier. At 8:00 p.m. I am contemplating the numbing predinner delight of a dry gin martini.

Whether I am at home in New Jersey or New York, I work in a single room behind a desk that is U-shaped, formed by three tables at right angles, and I sit on a firm-backed cushioned swivel chair that has armrests and rollers—and, as I shift about, the roller sounds (whether in New Jersey or New York) emit precisely the same squeaks. In both locations the workroom walls—or, rather, the walls that face and flank my desk—are covered with white panels of Styrofoam insulation material, each panel ten feet long, two feet wide, and an inch thick; in my opinion, these Styrofoam panels are more desirable as bulletin boards than are the wood-framed cork examples customarily sold in stationery stores. Each panel, selling for three or four dollars, is much less expensive than a corkboard of similar size, which costs twenty or thirty dollars or more, and in addition to being light enough to be affixed to walls with heavy tape reinforced maybe by a couple of thumbtacks, the Styrofoam panels are softer than cork and easier to penetrate with the dressmaker pins that I use when hanging up instructional notes or reminders to myself, or, on those rare occasions when my work is flowing, the many manuscript pages filled with finished prose that dangle overhead like a line of drying white laundry, fluttering slightly from the effects of a distant fan.

Most of the desk utensils and machines that I work with in New Jersey and New York are duplicates; whenever I see things that I like and need, and also foresee the day when these things might be outmoded or out of stock, I invariably buy two of them—one for each house; and so now I have twins in computers, printers, typewriters, photocopiers, wastebaskets, pencil sharpeners, fountain pens, and such other regularly used items as electric shavers, tennis rackets, bathrobes, shirts, and pairs of shoes. Being by nature impetuous, one who often deviates from prearranged travel plans and whose tendency to overpack is offset by a lack of zeal for hauling luggage, I seek comfort in knowing that, at least when commuting between New Jersey and New York, I may carry little more than house keys. But since I rarely throw anything away, except pages of my own writing, I am surrounded within these homes by things no longer manufactured and marketed and that in some instances are inoperative—for example, a desk lamp in New Jersey with a corroded switch.

Although my portable Olivetti manual typewriters purchased during the 1950s are dented and wobbly after my having hammered out more than a million words through miles of moving ribbons (I have also secured several loose letters to their arms with threads of dental floss), I nonetheless continue to use these machines at times because of the aesthetic appeal of their typefaces, their classical configuration imposed upon each and every word. But the Olivetti keyboards are characterized by a springed resistance that I find fatiguing after more than an hour of typing. So in the late 1970s, motivated by a mild case of digital arthritis, I purchased a pair of IBM electrics that offered more speed with a softer touch; they also came equipped with a number of interchangeable print wheels that provided me with the time-wasting opportunity to dally over my phrases and sentences as I rewrote them in diversified fonts that I believe often reflected my changing moods, ranging from the serenity of "Script" to the assertiveness of "Boldface."

In 1988, influenced by writer friends who claimed that it is easier to write when using a word processor, I acquired two Macintosh 512Ks at a discount price through my publisher and subscribed to introductory courses in the new technology offered by various young college-educated people who made house calls and seemed to have no career ambitions of their own.

Within a few months, however, my eyesight seemed to be fading (I could no longer read the baseball batting averages printed in agate type on sports pages), and while I initially attributed this condition to my advancing years, I also began to blame it on the hours during which I had sat facing the flickering glare of the Macintosh 512K computer screens. These screens were also quite small, having a viewable area of six by seven and a half inches, not much larger than a postcard. When, after acclimating myself to my first pair of prescription glasses, I *still* had difficulty reading my words on the screen, I decided to trade in my 512Ks for the big-screen Macs that were then being heavily advertised in newspapers. But the computer-store managers I approached refused to give me any trade credit for my 512Ks. These machines had zero retail value, I was told by one man, who added that consumers had begun to see them as obsolete about two years ago, and he doubted that there were people around still using them.

Angry at myself for having been so unaware and so unwise as to launch myself into the computer age with antiquated merchandise that only months before I had considered myself lucky to buy wholesale from my publisher's no doubt shady distributor, I now stubbornly refused to invest in new equipment unless I received some financial compensation for my supposedly worthless pair of 512Ks. And thus they remained untouched on my desks in New Jersey and New York for most of the next three years, collecting dust.

But my resistance to upgrading myself also concerned me. Often I saw myself as a Luddite, an old-fashioned, stagnating reactionary—and I particularly felt this way when I was in the company of fellow writers who raved aloud about their newly acquired "state-of-the-art" computers that were practically *writing* their books for them; even my wife, with whom I presumably shared a time-honored belief in the enduring value of slowly evolving, painstaking literary labor, was now smitten with the speed and facile efficiency of the cutting-edge technology available in her office and that she herself embraced with the devotedness and blithe sense of discovery often associated with late-in-life religious converts.

The corporation also provided her with extra computers and printers for her home use at night and on weekends, requiring that we install an additional telephone line in each house. Whenever she was traveling around the country or overseas—to sales conferences in Florida or Arizona in wintertime, or to European book fairs in autumn—she toted within her carry-on luggage a slim and stylishly elongated laptop that, when I first saw it, I realized had a screen considerably larger than that of my Macintosh 512K. But her journeying laptop and the corporate equipage that cluttered her reading rooms in New York and New Jersey were much too complicated and sophisticated for me to borrow, not being manufactured by Macintosh and, in any case, beyond my patience and the limited technical skills I retained as a result of reading and rereading my deskside instructional book, *Macs for Dummies*.

In 1992, however, about four years after I had bought the 512Ks— which, incidentally, I had recently recrated in their original boxes and stored under my desks—I finally did invest in a pair of au courant computers, the Macintosh IIci. Motivating this purchase to some degree was the substantial royalty check I had received that week from Tokyo, sent by a Japanese publisher who in the early 1980s had arranged for the translation of a book of mine about American sexual practices, which he predicted would become a perennial best-seller in his country because it would make the Japanese people feel morally superior. I first saw the Macintosh IIci while shopping for tennis balls in a New Jersey shopping mall. It was displayed in the front window of a computer shop, with a poster bearing the endorsement of a Pulitzer Prize–winning writer of my acquaintance. The store manager allowed me to sit down and type for a while on a demonstrator model, and what I liked about the Macintosh IIci was, of course, its sizable screen (double that of the 512K) and also the fact that it offered a variety in fonts as bountiful as the ice-cream flavors at Baskin-Robbins.

And so I arranged for the delivery of a Macintosh IIci to each of my residences, not realizing until they were put in place that they dominated my desks with their density and their space-commanding sprawl, requiring that I rearrange everything else that had previously surrounded me (my Olivetti, IBM, Canon photocopier, stacks of Racerase paper, rows of plastic cups containing paper clips, rubber bands, staples, and dressmaker pins) in order to accommodate the new computers' many component parts: the hard drive encased in a flat-topped heavy gray metal box that resembled an aircraft carrier; the slant-backed printer and its spiral-corded keyboard, both plugged into the hard drive; the long-tailed mouse that was linked to the keyboard; the wrist-lifting green felt slats that fronted the keyboard, and the slick rubber mouse pad at angles intended to protect the user from various carpal ailments. The computers' most prominent part, which I placed in the middle of my U-shaped arrangement, was their hunchbacked beige box, which was metallic and featured in front a rectangular-shaped glass screen that I preferred to think reflected my adjustment to what was contemporary and technically advanced in America.

But in actual fact, after the novelty of owning this new computer had diminished, as it did within a month, I probably made less use of it than did my daughters and their companions, who occasionally came to dinner in New York and spent weekends at the Jersey shore. I am not claiming that I ever completely abandoned this model, as I had the 512K, for I regularly did turn to it (along with my IBM and Olivetti) as a *typing* instrument, if not a *writing* instrument. I continued to enjoy fiddling with the many Macintosh fonts as I composed, in varying type sizes and shapes, my personal correspondence, fax messages, shopping lists, folder labels, instructional notes to deliverymen, and the outlines for scenes and situations that might appear in a future chapter of my book. Owning a Macintosh also allowed me to store much of my research material on one or two gingersnap-thin plastic discs that I carried easily in the breast pocket of my jacket while driving between New York and New Jersey.

Nevertheless in 1998, after one of my daughters' friends who knew a lot about computers told me that my Macintosh model IIci was now a valueless antique, adding that Macintosh had just introduced the wondrous *iMac*—which was superior in all ways to everything currently on the market—my reaction to this young man's information was one of unmitigated indifference. I had bought my last computer. The new technology got old so fast that it was constantly close to becoming a misnomer, I thought, but I reminded myself that this no longer mattered to me. I was now reconciled to accepting what I had experienced throughout my working life: Whatever serious writing I was capable of doing would be done most likely in my own handwriting, on a yellow-lined pad, with a pencil.

4

TAKING PENCIL IN HAND EACH MORNING DURING THE LATE SUM-
mer of 1999 while resisting for the time being the temptation of
taking off for China, I began to write—or, rather, to *print*—one
word after another on a yellow pad until I finished what I hoped would be
a readable sentence and a tiny linear leap forward toward the completion
of my book. I had been involved with this book for about four years. Even
when taking into account the systematically slow and exacting process by
which I have always produced prose, a virtual Stone Age method that I
regrettably discovered to be my most natural mode, I could not be contented with the paltry number of pages that I had turned out between
1995 and 1999. During this period, to be precise, I had accumulated fifty-
four and a half typed pages. All the words had initially been hand-
printed, as I explained, and several of them had been erased and replaced
many times with other words until I thought I had finished a sentence or
that a sentence had finished me. I always linger over a sentence until I
conclude that I lack the will or skill to improve upon it, whereupon I
move on to the next sentence, and then to the next. Ultimately—it
could take days, an entire week—I have hand-printed enough sentences
to form a paragraph, and enough paragraphs to fill three or four pages of
the yellow pad. This is when I usually put down my pencil and move to
the keyboard of my Olivetti, or the IBM, or the Macintosh IIci, and begin
transcribing what I have composed by hand.

If I double-space the sentences and narrow the margins as much as possible, I can fit about five hundred words onto each white sheet of Racerase
paper measuring eleven by eight and a half inches. I then remove the
page from the typewriter or the computer's printer and read it carefully.
Should I find typing errors or a phrase or word that I want to alter, I redo
the page; while doing so, new ideas often come to mind that I think
should be expressed on this particular page. And that is why, but not

entirely why, it had taken me so long to compile fifty-four and a half neatly typed pages.

There is also the matter of research. At least half of the time I have devoted to this current book, as well as to my earlier ones, has been spent collecting and assembling information that I obtained from libraries, archives, government buildings where public records are kept, and from various individuals whom I have sought out and interviewed. I believe that face-to-face contact is necessary because I want not only a dialogue but a visual sense of the interviewee's personal features and mannerisms, as well as the opportunity to describe atmospherically the setting in which the meeting took place. Whatever valuable insights and facts are derived in this manner, however, often cost me considerable sums of money in transportation and hotel expenses, and the dining and wining of sources—and frequently what is said and seen during these interviews contributes nothing at all to the progress of the book. Were I paid at an hourly rate for my research efforts, I would be remunerated in pennies, not dollars. This is not meant as a complaint, for if earning a high hourly income was paramount, I would have long ago aspired to becoming a divorce lawyer in Beverly Hills or a Freudian analyst with an office on upper Fifth Avenue. Yet it is pertinent to acknowledge that during my forty-year career as a researching writer, I have invested heavily in the wasting of time.

I have spent weeks negotiating interviews with reluctant individuals who, when they finally did speak to me, revealed nothing informative. I have traveled hundreds and thousands of miles in pursuit of leads that in the end led me nowhere. Eighty percent of the information I have collected from people ends up in the wastebasket. Nonetheless, I could not have discovered the useful 20 percent without picking my way through the other 80 percent, which in the final analysis is refuse. However, as I was getting older—and this constantly concerned me during the summer of 1999—I feared that I had become so selective, so deliberate and fastidious in my way of working, that I would not live long enough to see the end of this book.

My fifty-four and a half pages comprised not even a tenth of the length of any of the four manuscripts that I had completed since I had begun writing books full-time in the mid-1960s. My most recent manuscript totaled more than seven hundred pages and took more than ten years to research and write, much of the research being done in Italy. It was edited and made into a book—entitled *Unto the Sons*—in 1992, and it told the story of the mid-ninteenth-century decline of the ancient Neapolitan kingdom of southern Italy and the subsequent departure of such people as my father, who at seventeen left his home and his soccer-playing townsmen to find work as a tailor in America.

In 1980 I finished a manuscript of about 650 pages that dealt with the contemporary definition of sexual morality in America and how and why this definition was so radically different from the mid-twentieth-century standards that were advocated during my youth. It took me nine years to research and write that book, and it owed its inspiration to my altar boy days on the New Jersey shore and my parish priest's Sunday sermons urging the censorship of novels and films that he believed threatened the stability of family life in our parish. One of the novels we were told on many occasions not to read was Kathleen Winsor's *Forever Amber*. After reading it, I thought it generated a lot less heat than did the smoldering fiction of my favorite author, Frank Yerby, whose name went unmentioned in the sermons. Our priest had probably not heard of the author until I senselessly mentioned my familiarity with his works during confession, which is how Mr. Yerby's novels later came to be advertised in our parish's list of forbidden books and no doubt brought him new readers.

In 1971, after six years of sporadic research and writing that was often interrupted for many months due to reasons beyond my control (my sources were being shot at), I delivered a 575-page manuscript about the Bonanno crime family, which had been driven out of New York during the latter 1960s by rival Mafia factions and forced to resettle on the West Coast and in Arizona. Prior to this dispersion I had befriended the Bonanno clan leader's eldest son, Bill Bonanno, and it was through him that I gradually gained access to his father and other inhabitants of this insular and at times terrifying way of life. Bill Bonanno was an American-born college-educated contemporary of mine, with an ethnic background and family traditions similar to my own. What separated us was his father's career and Bill Bonanno's willingness to become part of it. He would spend much of the latter half of his life in prison. It was his convent-bred wife who suggested to me the ironic title I selected for my book: *Honor Thy Father*.

The discontinuity that had characterized my working relationship with Bill Bonanno and his henchmen while they were preoccupied in the underworld, their whereabouts unknown to me until one of them made the headlines after being killed in an ambush, meant that I had lots of free time during the 1960s to consider writing about other topics. The one that most engaged me was the century-long saga of the *New York Times* and the interpersonal relationships of the people who had significantly contributed to its history. I have no doubt that my interest in this subject, and even much of the research that infused my 698-page manuscript, which was published in 1969 as *The Kingdom and the Power,* had been enterprisingly prioritized in my brain for at least five years before I had first entered the *Times* building as an intern in the summer of 1953, following my graduation from the University of Alabama.

During the postwar 1940s, my father made suits for a white-haired author and onetime editor of the editorial page of the *Times* named Garet Garrett, who, though he kept an apartment in New York, was then writing books full-time at his more remote residence along the Tuckahoe River in southern New Jersey, a few miles inland from our island resort of Ocean City. I believe that Mr. Garrett first became my father's customer during the winter of 1948. I was then sixteen and, in addition to helping out in the store after school, I was active on the student newspaper and I usually delivered early each Thursday evening one or two articles on sports and other scholastic activities to the editor of our town weekly. I would have liked it if my father had mentioned this to Mr. Garrett; but since he did not, and since I was not supposed to talk to customers, my relationship with the former *Times* man was limited to observing him from the office balcony that overlooked the front of the shop. Sometimes, when I was able to create a chore for myself downstairs behind one of the counters, I was able to eavesdrop.

Garet Garrett was a short, slender, and loquacious man with a strong voice, and although he was probably then nearing his seventies, he gave no indication of physical frailty. His stride was vigorous, and so was his handshake when greeting my father, who always stopped whatever he was doing to welcome Garrett at the door. I saw many stylish men in my father's shop, but none possessed the jauntiness of Mr. Garrett, who reminded me of one of those continental boulevardiers often photographed in *Esquire,* a magazine sent to us as a gift from the Philadelphia fabrics manufacturer that sold material to my father. Garrett usually arrived at the shop with his fedora rakishly tilted forward over his right eyebrow and sometimes with an ebony walking stick swinging at his side, held lightly in his left hand, which was encircled by a leather loop attached to the stick's silver knob. After he had removed his jacket to try on something that my father was making for him, I could see cuff links gleaming at the ends of his shirtsleeves, and the embroidered leather galluses that extended over his narrow shoulders, and the fact that his trousers had three pleats on each side of the fly front. As he stood on a footstool while my father held a tape measure down to Garrett's trouser cuffs and across his midsection, and as I tried to seem busy while leaning forward from behind a counter, I would listen as he spoke in a worldly manner about things that I knew little about; nonetheless, he personified for me the metropolitan splendor to which I someday hoped to escape.

Garrett had joined the *Times* editorial board during World War I and enjoyed a close working relationship with Adolph Ochs, the *Times*'s owner and patriarch of the family that to this day maintains proprietary control over the paper. Garrett seemed to enjoy reminiscing about his days on the *Times* and the daily editorial meetings he used to attend in the presence of Adolph Ochs, and there was not a tailor in America who was more interested in hearing about Ochs and his newspaper than my father. As a newly arrived immigrant in the 1920s, he would peruse the *Times* every day and, with the aid of a nearby dictionary, would enlarge upon his vocabulary while learning what mattered most to Americans. When the Allied armies invaded southern Italy in the summer of 1943, my father relied upon the military coverage of the *Times* to give him a sense of his widowed mother's security as she dwelled in a tent city with her relatives and friends along the open fields below their hillside village—which was as far as they could get from the cross fire of the combative soldiers in the highlands. The Germans, and what was left of Mussolini's loosely disciplined army, were still trying to defend the region. But as my father could tell from studying the *Times*'s battlefield maps with their directional arrows, the Allies were always advancing. They were overwhelming their adversaries not only on the ground but in the air and from the ships that hugged the shorelines and bombarded the German-occupied seaports and hill sites. As the arrows on the *Times*'s maps each day moved closer and closer to the area that included my father's birthplace, he became increasingly hesitant as he reached for the paper in the morning. Not until the arrows had bypassed his town of Maida and headed north toward Naples—leaving behind no reports of civilian casualties in his town—did he seem to regain his composure.

But there were tears in his eyes months later when the *Times* printed on its front page a photograph of a burning, bomb-shattered hilltop monastery northwest of Naples called the Abbey of Monte Cassino. This building had been a scholarly center for Benedictine monks since the sixth century. My father had visited it as a fourteen-year-old when he himself had contemplated becoming a monk, although his spiritual mentor in those days, and throughout his entire life, was a monk unaffiliated with the Benedictines. My father's guardian was a Franciscan—a bearded, brown-robed fifteenth-century mystic later canonized as Saint Francis of Paola. This monk had spent time in and around my father's village, meditating and levitating, curing the crippled and sometimes reviving the dead, or so it was reported by eyewitnesses. Across the road from my father's birthplace, Saint Francis built a sanctuary that has endured into the twenty-first century as symbolic of Catholic belief in the omnipresent possibility of miracles.

My father prayed daily in front of a wall portrait of Saint Francis while kneeling on a prie-dieu in our living room. In the niche at the bottom of our staircase was a four-foot-high statue of Saint Francis holding a crosier and exuding a facial expression that seemed to vary between agony and ecstasy, depending, it seemed to me, on how briskly the sea breezes seeped through the cracks of our door frame and whipped against the wicks of the vigil lights, which sent alternating reflections from the statue's base upward past the saint's sandaled feet and tattered robe to the vacant stare of his upturned eyes under the hood shading his scraggly-bearded face. In all my days as a churchgoer, I had never seen a statue or portrait of a saint more gruesome than Saint Francis.

What my father must have seen was a beatific beauty that eluded me. My father's belief in the meaningfulness of monastic life must have also influenced his emotions and brought tears to his eyes on the day the *Times* depicted the ruination of the Abbey of Monte Cassino. The Americans justified the air raid because there had been intelligence reports claiming that German troops were using the abbey as a fortress. These reports turned out to be false. Meanwhile, six hundred tons of bombs were dropped on the abbey and its grounds by U.S. planes. It was the first time the Allies had deliberately targeted a religious site.

Although the *Times* was owned by Jews, my father believed that it was the only major newspaper in America worthy of being read by committed members of the Catholic Church. The *Times* covered the Vatican comprehensively and respectfully as an autonomous state. When the Pope issued an ecclesiastical message, the newspaper printed every word of it.

Except for my father, the only other *Times* subscriber in our parish was our Irish-born pastor. While I had seen signs of the latter's imperiousness toward some Italian parishioners, especially those who sent him jugs of homemade wine in lieu of cash in response to his fund drives, he and my father were extremely cordial and like-minded on the main political and social issues of the day, including the need to protect church members from the sinful behavior that might be aroused as a result of the distribution of indecent films and such books as those that I was then keeping under my bed.

During one of his sermons, our pastor complimented the *Times* for printing articles and editorials calling attention to the nationwide antipornography campaign led by the Catholic Legion of Decency. My father's words of praise to the priest after Mass affirmed for me the bond

that existed between them as subscribers to the *Times*, as adherents of
this seemingly God-fearing and certainly high-minded periodical that
eschewed comic strips and, reflecting what I later knew to be the bourgeois sensibilities and sexual prudery of the *Times*'s guiding spirit, Adolph
Ochs himself, published each day hundreds of thousands of words and
many images from which lewdness and profanity were extracted, and taw-
driness was tempered, and the genitalia of racehorses and show dogs was
airbrushed from photographs designated for the sports section.

The references to Mr. Ochs in Garet Garrett's conversations with my
father gave me the idea of writing a term paper about the owner of the
Times, who died in 1935. I would have liked to have interviewed Garrett
about his former boss, but my father advised against it, fearing perhaps
that my intrusiveness might cost him a customer. But I had kept some
notes on what I had overheard, and later I found information about Ochs
in our town library, which during those days was located within a wing of
my school building, Ocean City High School—on the front of which,
high above the entrance in ornate stone lettering, appeared the name:
OCHS.

Although I had been attending classes in that building for two and a
half years, I had never paused to look up at the lettering until I began
working on my term paper, and indeed I had never heard of Adolph Ochs
until he had been ushered into my consciousness within my father's store
by Garrett. But now my school building suddenly seemed to be elevated
in my mind in ways both majestic and magical, and as I sat in the library
gathering information about Mr. Ochs from biographies and encyclope-
dias, I believed that I had been preordained to write about this man whom
in my five-page term paper I would call "The Titan of The Times." Twenty
years later, in 1969, I would think of this high school effort as the genesis
of my 698-page manuscript on Ochs and his dynasty. It was edited and
published by a company that specialized in printing and distributing
Bibles. The editors there were pleased that I was calling my book *The Kingdom and the Power* because, in addition to whatever appeal the book might
have with a general audience, the editors believed that it might sell many
extra copies to spiritually minded readers who would mistakenly believe
the book carried a religious message. The book became a number-one
best-seller in the United States in 1970. When I first wrote about Ochs
and his *Times* in my term paper, my English teacher gave me a B-minus.

I know why I did poorly as a student in such subjects as chemistry and
mathematics, both of which I found boring and confusing, but to receive
mediocre grades in English upset me very much because I *did* pay attention in class and I *was* interested in the subject—and, to make matters

worse, my failure to excel in English gave impetus to my father's argument that my true talents might someday be realized in my capacities as a tailor.

I was his only son. I was his main hope as the inheritor of his business, as a follower in this craft that had been pridefully practiced by some elders in his family since the era of Napoleonic rule in southern Italy. And so as my schoolboy journalism continued to absorb most of my free time, and as my academic standing in my junior year fell below the level required by our principal to earn his recommendation for college-entrance consideration, my father became more insistent that I sit for a few hours a week in his workroom practicing certain rudiments under his guidance, such as how to cut and secure a pair of trouser cuffs, and how to make button-holes, and how to baste the inner lining of a jacket. At the very least, he explained, tailoring was "something I could fall back on." He also tried to reason with me while repeating an offer that, in my darkest moments of self-doubt, I must admit held a modicum of appeal.

"Wouldn't you like to live in Paris after you're out of high school?" he would ask. All that was required of me, I knew, was to occupy a guest room in the Paris apartment of an older Italian cousin of my father's who had left their village for Paris as a tailor in 1911, and who now owned a thriving shop on the rue de la Paix where I could work as an apprentice. I had also been told that this cousin's clientele included General Charles de Gaulle, several French film directors and performers, and other prominent people who my father hoped would convince me that there was a glamorous side to the tailoring profession. But I knew from watching my father at work that tailoring was tedious, time-consuming, and physically demanding, and that it often brought considerable pain to his back muscles and fingers. He made each suit stitch by stitch, avoiding the use of a sewing machine because he wanted to *feel* the needle in his fingers as he penetrated a piece of silk or wool and moved at a worm's pace along the seam of a shoulder or a sleeve. If whatever he did deviated from his definition of perfection, he would pull it apart and do it again. He hoped to create the illusion of seamlessness, to attain artistic expression with a needle and thread. Much as I admired his aspirations, I was never tempted to become a tailor, and yet I listened respectfully whenever my father alluded to my possible apprenticeship in Paris—which he did more than once after my diligence and weeks of work on my term paper had earned me only a B-minus.

I tried to defend myself as my father shared my disappointment with the grade. My teacher's standards in English were not necessarily relevant to my future in journalism, I insisted. My research indicated that the great Adolph Ochs had begun his career without encouragement from his English teachers—he, too, had been an average student, one whose intelligence and talents became apparent later in his life. He had started out in journalism as a floor sweeper on a small newspaper in Knoxville, Tennessee. I was also convinced, although my reasoning was based on emotion, without a shred of evidence, that my English teacher's assessment of my classroom work was influenced by personal factors, such as the fact that she privately loathed me, or at least disapproved of me, and thus graded me harshly. The B-minus was not the lowest mark I had received in her class. I got mostly C's, sometimes D's, and once—after I had misspelled Shakespeare's name twice in an essay on *Hamlet*—an F. She wrote notes of explanation across the front page of each student's composition. On mine, she criticized me constantly for writing sentences that were "too wordy" and "indirect," and sometimes she underlined sentences in red ink and wrote in the margin a single word: *syntax*. This word might appear two or three times on the same page with exclamation points: *syntax! syntax! syntax!* Although I looked up the meaning of the word in different dictionaries, I was never entirely sure how it related to what was wrong with my grammar, and yet I was reluctant to approach her. I felt intimidated by her in ways that I did not when in the presence of other teachers. I had transferred to this public high school after eight years in parochial school, and my immediate reaction to the new building was liberating. Here the faculty members were predominantly Protestant, and they were definitely less strict and oppressively virtuous than the nuns I had known. In this particular English composition class, however, I felt even more indecisive and detached than I had years before in parochial school, where my main concern had been in keeping my distance from the big Irish boys in the schoolyard who often ganged up on Italian-Americans during recess. In those days we constituted a small minority within the larger minority of Irish Catholics on this Protestant-governed island of Ocean City, founded in 1879 by Methodist ministers. But my teacher in this English composition class had all but reduced me to thinking that I was foreign-born, that English was my second language. My position on the student newspaper and my bylined articles in the town weekly and sometimes in the Atlantic City daily, articles that then represented my sole claim to whatever capabilities I possessed, never drew a word of encouragement from my teacher, nor did she even mention them to me in private before or after class. I could not believe that she never saw them in print, or that she remained silent about them because they were not pertinent to my work in her classroom. No matter how low her opinion of journalism might have been, nor how little regard she might have had for those editors who considered my articles publishable, her omission in this situation surely was connected to some personal dislike of me, I repeatedly told myself, although beyond this I did not know what to think. Or rather what I *did* think only added to my frustration and bewilderment. I think that in a strange way—strange to everyone except the kind of teenage boy I was in that time and place, a pimply-faced sixteen-year-old in the apex of ignorance and wonderment about women—I was in love with her.

Each afternoon I sat waiting eagerly for her to enter the classroom. She was a slender, blue-eyed blonde with a long-legged stride who held her head high and who often wore tight-fitting tweed suits that accentuated her figure. She was then in her early twenties, perhaps teaching teenagers for the first time, which might have explained why she seemed to be so high-strung, and at times timorous, and always quick in trying to assert her control over her students, who were probably only five or six years younger than she was. She had come to us as a substitute teacher, filling in for an elderly and ailing veteran of the faculty, whose longtime popularity with his students had been sustained by his generous nature in grading them—but, much to my regret, this gentleman with coronary problems was never able to regain his health and his presence in English composition class. He resigned shortly before the start of my junior year; and due to scheduling problems and other matters, the more experienced teachers who might have stepped in for him were not as free and flexible as was this lovely female newcomer to the faculty, who would soon become the source of my romantic fantasies and my grief.

My difficulties began on the very first day of her arrival. Our class was scheduled to meet immediately following lunch. While most of us were chatting at our desks awaiting the arrival of our new teacher, my other schoolmates were leaning out of the open windows, calling to their friends entering the building from the street. It was a warm September day, and the breezes blowing across the nearby dunes carried the salty smell of the sea into our classroom, giving us a lingering sense of summer.

As the bell rang and everyone hastened to their seats, our teacher entered, smiling. She said nothing as she surveyed the room. She wore a yellow short-sleeved linen dress; her blond hair was held back by a blue velvet ribbon; her face and arms were suntanned and, compared to the dowdy female faculty members whom we were accustomed to seeing, she glowed with the incandescence of a starlet in an MGM musical—and two boys seated on either side of me in the rear row began to whistle.

She stiffened. Her smile disappeared. She quickly turned toward the back of the room, standing on her toes for a better look, and angrily asked, "Who whistled?"

She seemed to be staring directly at me. I slid down in my seat, my head bent as I examined my shoes, a pair of penny loafers that I had polished the night before. I suddenly saw myself as the prime suspect, and if I did not quickly clear myself, and if word of this indescretion got back to my parents, it would be very embarrassing to them, especially to my father, my Catholic Legion of Decency–devoted father, the only Italian in our town who wore a suit and tie and was looked up to even by the Protestants. And yet I knew that I could *not* squeal on the two friends I sat between. One was the starting quarterback on our football team. The other was his favorite receiver. I always sat among the varsity players in the back rows of classrooms, it being among my perks as their chronicler and occasional spinmeister.

"Who *whistled?*" she repeated.

I continued to look down and did not glance sideways, which might have implicated my friends. The rest of the class in front of us also remained silent. As the seconds passed, I could hear the teacher's feet tapping impatiently, and a few flies buzzing overhead, and the floor-creaking sounds of a desk shifting under the weight of a fidgety student. But the two culprits next to me remained perfectly still and soundless, not a muscle moving, it seemed to me, nor could I even hear them breathing. I was surprised that they did not finally stand up, tell the truth, and accept the consequences. What could she have done to *them?* The coach would have protected them. The season was just beginning, and they were essential to the team's aerial attack. But they just sat in the classroom like the rest of us, blending in with the crowd, apparently fainthearted in the presence of this thin-skinned female teacher. This did not augur well for our forthcoming football season.

"All right, let us proceed," she then said with a sigh, although she seemed to continue to look at me. "It's a sad but obvious fact that we have someone among us today who is unwilling to assume responsibility. But let this be a word of warning to all of you. If I *ever* catch anyone whistling, it will lead to your instant expulsion. Am I making myself clear?"

There were nods and murmurings of agreement from myself and the rest of the students, including the football players.

"This is a *classroom,*" she continued, "and here we *will* maintain proper standards of behavior. . . ."

After more nods from the students, she stepped toward the desk at the front of the room, introduced herself after she had taken her seat, and then proceeded to outline what subjects we would cover in this English composition class that in the ensuing months would bring me so little joy.

5

THROUGHOUT MY HIGH SCHOOL YEARS AND DURING MOST OF MY boyhood, my parents made our home in an apartment above their store. The conversations my mother and father had upstairs usually involved things going on downstairs, and the ringing of the telephone and the doorbell was simultaneously heard above and below. The extra mirrors from the store that my father installed in our living quarters multiplied everything we saw, deflecting rather than reflecting any sense of intimacy and domesticity.

While the apartment did have an adequate kitchen and dining area, I do not recall ever sitting down and enjoying a relaxing and satisfying home-cooked meal. This was due not only to the interrupting phone calls from customers but to the fact that my preoccupied parents rarely made the effort to shop properly for food even when they had the time to do so on weekends. My mother was one of the few Italian-American women of her generation who disliked being in the kitchen.

She was a businesswoman, an entrepreneurial individual whose best customers were her best friends, and she entertained them in her boutique (dispatching me to get them sodas, tea, or ice cream from the corner drugstore) as if they were guests in her true and only home. Here she held private conversations with them, earned their confidence and trust in a way that sooner or later inclined them toward buying most of the dresses she recommended. The merchandise my mother featured catered to decorous women of ample figures and means. These were the ministers' wives, the bankers' wives, the bridge players, the tale bearers. They were the white-gloved ladies who in summer avoided the beach and the boardwalk to spend considerable amounts of time and money along the main avenue in places like my parents' shop, where, amid the low humming of the fans and the attentive care of my mother in the dressing rooms, they would try on clothes while discussing their private lives and the happenings and misadventures of their friends and neighbors.

The shop was a kind of talk show that flowed around the engaging manner and well-timed questions of my mother; and even when I was hardly taller than the counters behind which I used to pause and listen, I began to learn much that would be useful to me years later when I began interviewing people for articles and books. I learned never to interrupt when people were having difficulty in explaining themselves, for during such halting and imprecise moments (as the listening skills of my patient mother taught me) people often are very revealing. What they hesitated to talk about told much about them. Their pauses, their evasions, their sudden shifts in subject matter were likely indicators of what embarrassed them, or irritated them, or what they regarded as too private or imprudent to be disclosed. However, I later overheard many people discussing candidly with my mother what they had earlier avoided—a reaction that, I think, had less to do with her inquiring nature or sensitively posed questions than with their gradual acceptance of her as an individual in whom they could fully confide. My mother's best customers were women less in need of new dresses than the need to communicate.

Most of them were born of privileged Philadelphia families of Anglo-Saxon or Germanic stock, and they were generally tall and large-sized in a way typified by Eleanor Roosevelt. Their suntanned, leathery, handsome faces were browned primarily as a result of their devotion to gardening, which they described to my mother as their favorite summertime hobby. When one of these women came into the store, my mother was unavailable for phone calls, relying on my father or one of the employees to take messages, and while there were one or two women who abused her forbearance as a listener, droning on for hours, I was interested in most of what I heard and witnessed there. In fact, in the decades since I have left home, during which time I have retained a clear memory of my eavesdropping youth and the women's voices that gave it expression, it seems to me that many of the social and political questions that have been debated in America since then—the role of religion in the bedroom, racial equality, women's rights, the adulteries of public officials, the advisability of films and publications featuring sex and violence—I overheard in my mother's shop during my elementary and high school years of the 1940s.

My mother, born Catherine Di Paola on Mulberry Street in Manhattan's Little Italy to parents originally from my father's native village in Calabria, moved as a young girl into Brooklyn with her large family after her father had found steady work as the chauffeur and general factotum of a real estate developer in that borough. When my mother was twenty-one and employed as an assistant buyer in the dress department of Abraham & Straus, a store that had hired her after her graduation from high school, she met my father at a Brooklyn wedding in the mid-1920s that united one of her sisters to one of his cousins. Within a few years she and my father were married and residing in Ocean City, beginning a relationship of more than sixty years that combined their love and compatibility with their shared interest in wearing and selling fine clothes and their capacity to cover up their lives in ways that I might prefer to call mysteriously romantic but that as a youth I found troubling and confusing.

There is such a thing as having parents who are too much in love, whose essential needs are so completely met by each other that no one else is essential to their well-being, including their own children. As a Catholic couple, they produced only two children, my younger sister and myself, and we grew up thinking we were in the way of our parents' relationship, that our main function was merely to complete the picture of their completeness, to accompany them to Sunday Mass and then stand beside them on the sidewalk, smiling while being introduced to their fellow parishioners, and later in the day to stroll with them on the boardwalk in nearby Atlantic City among the casually dressed crowds and roving photographers who usually mistook us (with our fine clothes and familial formality) for a family of visiting dignitaries from abroad, which is, I think, precisely the impression my parents wished to convey. After my mother had left Brooklyn and my father had severed his ties to Italy, they reconstructed their lives together in a place where the social atmosphere differed greatly from anything they had previously known (an island mandated by prohibitionist Protestants who disallowed the sale of even a glass of wine), and yet here my parents were at liberty to associate with mainstream Americans without being surrounded by masses of immigrants who might confirm the worst early-twentieth-century stereotype of their countrymen as clannish, garlic-smelling laborers with dark-garbed wives and lots of aggressive children who were delinquent in school and destined to prosper only in the realm of organized crime.

This island was my parents' point of departure from all traces of Ellis Island, a midway point before melding in, and here they carefully walked hand in hand on weekends and were inseparable during the week in their store and after hours in our home, which was more or less an annex of the store. They had earlier bought a white cottage by the sea on the northern end of the island, but after my birth in 1932—in the fourth year of their marriage—my mother did not want to be so far away from the store during those hours she was caring for me, and so she encouraged my father to move the business into a building that had an upper floor. This he did almost immediately, renting a two-story commercial property on the main street for a few years until he was able to purchase a large brick building two doors away that had been the site of the town's second weekly newspaper, an enterprise that had recently gone bankrupt and that my father acquired on excellent terms during the years of the Great Depression.

Mirrors are what I most remember about living in that spacious apartment, large—ten-by-twelve-foot—mirrors that covered the portable partitions that concealed the bedrooms in the rear area, which had once been occupied by linotype machines, and smaller mirrors that had been mismeasured or otherwise found inappropriate for the store below and were affixed to the walls upstairs in various places, reflecting every feature and piece of furniture existing in that wide and high-ceilinged hundred-foot-long room that we called home but could have been better utilized as a dance studio. In fact, my parents occasionally used it as that, and perhaps my earliest consciousness of the harmony and interiority of their relationship occurred one evening when, as they heard waltz music coming from their favorite classical radio station in Philadelphia, they suddenly interrupted a discussion they had been having with me to stand up and embrace each other, and then to begin dancing around the room for ten or fifteen minutes without ever once turning to look in my direction, to wave or wink or otherwise acknowledge that I was in the room, next to the coffee table, where they had left me, sitting on one of the red leather chairs that matched the ones used by my mother in her shop. I was then eleven or twelve, and while I do not wish at this late date to try to revive and interpret my emotions of more than a half century ago—other than to concede that I would never in my life feel comfortable on a dance floor, nor would I ever accept an invitation to a dinner dance—I do recall feeling miserable at the time and being misty-eyed when my parents paused to turn off the radio and the room lights, and, before heading toward the rear of the apartment together, to call out and remind me that it was well past my bedtime, that my sister had been asleep for hours, and that tomorrow was a school day.

One might assume if one were unlike myself that I would have used the remoteness I felt from my parents to my own advantage, that I would have gone off and done as I pleased, would have cultivated my own separateness, would have disappeared for hours and maybe even run away from home—would they even have noticed?—or that at the very least I would have a boyhood history that would venture well beyond parental reflections in the mirrored room by which I measured myself. But I was captivated by the two of them, was in awe of them; they were the romantic leads in my ongoing interior movie. My slender and stylishly brunette mother was a stand-in for my favorite actress, Gene Tierney, and my custom-suited, rather exotic father was a second Valentino. I also felt captured with my parents in the confining complexity that prevailed in our household during the World War II years, when my father's homeland was allied with the Nazis and his brothers were armed to confront the Allied invasion.

In public my mother and father always behaved patriotically in the politically conservative community in which we lived. Like the other merchants on the block, my father each morning carried an American flag on a twelve-foot pole out to the sidewalk in front of the shop and inserted it in a hole near the curb. My father also joined a local citizens group that surveyed our coastline around the clock for signs of enemy submarines, performing this task at a time when great numbers of Italians in America were declared enemy aliens and when many were interned at a camp in Montana. Other Italians living within coastal communities were sometimes forced to move inland and surrender to the Coast Guard any fishing boats they had. One who relinquished his boat and temporarily vacated his home along the northern California coastline was the Sicilian-born father of the baseball star Joe DiMaggio.

While my father's commitment to America was never openly questioned in our town as far as I knew, he nonetheless always spoke in public with the same care as he dressed and comported himself, and this remained equally true after the war. My father never discussed the war with me directly, and in this case I welcomed his aloofness. I had learned enough about the war from the Saturday-afternoon newsreels and from two of my tough Irish classmates in parochial school. After one of their uncles had died in action as an American infantryman while attacking the Anzio coastal area, the boys began referring to me in the school yard as "Mussolini" and "dago bastard," insulting me in voices just quiet enough to be unheard by the nuns; one day they followed me home and beat me up behind a vacant summertime hotel, slashing my left wrist with a long nail, which left a scar I can see today.

I remember running frantically through my parents' shop, dripping blood on the rug, alarming my mother and her customers, and not stopping until I had reached my father back in the alteration room, where, after examining my wrist and hearing my account of the incident, he comforted me while washing my wound and then wrapping it with strips of basting cloth. My mother was soon there as well, leaving her customers to be attended to by the salesgirl she had originally hired as a baby-sitter. Although the doctor's office was only two blocks away, my mother and father took me there in their car, and during my week of recovery and my absence from school, my parents bestowed upon me the attention they usually reserved for each other. At the same time, however, my father did not want to hear me complaining any more about my wrist or the boys who had attacked me, nor did he file charges against them with the school.

"Just forget about it," he said; "you've only got a scratch." And more than once he emphasized, "Don't be a sissy."

My father's solution to making me feel better was comparing our boyhoods in ways that portrayed his as far worse. He reminded me that back in 1914, when he was my age, his own father had suddenly died of an uncommon and untreated respiratory ailment, leaving his mother responsible for the rearing of her four children. There was a constant lack of food and coal throughout the postwar years in southern Italy, my father recalled, adding that on one particularly frosty night, while snow covered the nearby mountain peaks, a pack of prowling wolves descended into the village to terrify the people and devour dozens of chickens and pigs, until they themselves were annihilated by the shotgun fire of the angry and anxious men standing on balconies and rooftops. In the village of Maida, as my father described it, there was no escape from the ferocity of wild nature and misfortune. Here the hill people dwelled perilously under the mountain heights, from which rocks fell during earthquakes, and below them was the coastal area salvaged and thus made malarial by the Romans, but perhaps also avoided by the superstitious villagers because of its mythic association with the region's sailor-swallowing sea monster Charybdis, as well as its being the entry point for the ships that had historically brought pirates and conquerors into southern Italy.

During my father's time in Italy, none of the villagers walked along the coast or learned how to swim, he told me, not having to acknowledge what I already knew: He *himself* did not swim, and during the seventeen years I lived in Ocean City prior to going away to Alabama, I believe that we as a family visited the beach on fewer than six occasions. We would situate ourselves closer to the dunes than the water, and after renting an umbrella and a pair of wood-framed folding canvas chairs stenciled with the name of the concessionaire, my parents in their dry bathing suits and white terry-cloth robes would spend the time in conversation, while my sister and I would kneel nearby with our tin buckets and shovels, building castles and trying to dig deeply enough to reach the muddy water and feel the soft pricklings of the sand crabs scampering through our fingers. But should we venture out into the water and stand where the waves splashed around our knees, my father would quickly rise from his chair and come running out toward us and summon us back to the beach.

And thus did I grow up along the Atlantic Ocean, instilled with my father's boyhood fear of the Mediterranean Sea.

6

I N DEFERENCE TO MY MOTHER'S DEFICIENCIES IN THE KITCHEN, MY father would often drive us at night to a small hotel dining room in our community, or to a seaside inn across the bay, or to one of his favorite Italian restaurants in Atlantic City, where we would usually be greeted, served, and fed in a manner that brought a pleasant conclusion to the day.

My mother, attired in one of the expensive suits or dresses she had been unable to sell the season before, enjoyed being seen in restaurants, regarding them as an extension of her showroom and a modeling opportunity for herself. The appeal of restaurants to my younger sister and myself was augmented by the fact that after dinner we were not expected, as we were at home, to clear the table and help with the dishes. And in my father's case, quite apart from my mother's cooking, I think that going to restaurants catered to a need in his nature that could never have been adequately satisfied at home.

In restaurants he became a changed person, was less remote, less tense, more kindly and communicative than he ever was in our apartment or while working behind my mother's boutique in the alteration room, where he spent the day lengthening or shortening dresses, or making a suit for one of the ever-decreasing number of men who valued his skills and would pay the high costs of a custom tailor. My father sometimes sewed silently for hours, listening to classical music on the radio or the record player, seemingly detached from all else around him; but when we dined out in Atlantic City, or in a larger Italian restaurant on certain weekends in Philadelphia, my father immediately and buoyantly burst into Italian while greeting and embracing the owners and waiters, who in some cases were natives of his area of Italy. And even though their language was entirely foreign to me, and remains so to this day, I immediately perceived its liberalizing effect upon my father, adding color to his countenance, a brightness to his expression, and as we settled down to dinner—our table was usually near the bar, where the owner sat on a stool, sipping wine and toasting each of our courses—my father continued to speak out animatedly and even exchanged jokes in his native tongue with his compatriots, doing this while gesturing freely with his hands and arms in a manner I had never seen at home.

I had two fathers in this period of my life: a residential father and a restaurant father. Only with the latter was I happy as a son. And during my high school years, especially during moments when I was feeling most inadequate as a student, I saw myself as entering the restaurant business someday, owning an Italian restaurant that would appeal to men like my father and bring laughter into their lives, and in which I would stand out as a debonaire figure in a festive crowd, wearing a white dinner jacket like Humphrey Bogart in the film *Casablanca,* and having my own piano player, and buying drinks for my friends, and enjoying flirtation privileges with the pretty waitresses.

From what I read in the newspaper columns by Walter Winchell and Leonard Lyons, the ownership of a successful restaurant was an easy and felicitous route to recognition and prosperity, an opportunity to become a celebrity's celebrity in the way that Toots Shor had with America's sports heroes, and Vincent Sardi had with the leading Broadway stars, and as the management at the "21" Club had with the nation's business tycoons and their trophy wives.

Long after my fantasies of restaurant ownership had faded and I settled instead for the life of a writer who uses restaurants as an escape from the solitude that my father had undoubtedly shared when he was sewing, I became a nightly patron not only of neighborhood places but also of such renowned establishments as the "21" Club, where I soon became accustomed to the handshakes and arm pats from the proprietors each time I entered into what surely is one of the great glad-hand centers of New York City. Here the faithful customer is welcomed not only by a primary greeter but by a virtual receiving line of bowing gentlemen courtiers who in an earlier age could have served the Sun King at Versailles. While I initially thought that the corridor of the "21" Club was overcrowded with greeters and strokers, it soon occurred to me that this restaurant had not prospered for more than sixty years by underestimating the insecurities of its leading customers. Indeed, it probably knew very well that most of its big expense-account clientele sensed that they were but a golden parachute away from having to bail out as the corporate boss, and when this happened, they would lose their prestigious table against the west wall in the dining room; but *until* it happened, they and their greeters at the door would reinforce one another with their handshakes and embraces, which linked the management of the restaurant with the management of the nation's power and wealth.

So at the "21" Club I saw on a grand scale what I had already glimpsed as a boy in New Jersey: restaurants as rooms of recognition, salutation, and reassurance. And I indulged in what they had to offer, which for me was not what was featured on the menu but, rather, the surrounding sights and sounds that drew me out of myself, a magical sprinkling of a certain spice in the gestalt that elevated me to levels of response and appreciation that I often experienced when attending the theater.

The lighting in the better restaurants is, in fact, often arranged by Broadway stage technicians who view dining rooms as sets and manipulate the mood of the evening meal with a luminescence that will display most enhancingly the character of the clientele that is most fundamental to the restaurant's image and financial stability. If the restaurant is what one technician described to me as a "high-energy" place, a trendy spot for young couples and what he called "the beautiful people," then the lighting should be bright and intense "because everybody wants to see who's there." In the more sedate and elegant restaurants intended for an older affluent crowd, the light bouncing off the table linen onto the diners' faces should be quite soft and intimate, he said, but not physically revealing. "Everyone must look younger," he explained, adding that a pinkish light is often used to achieve this effect, as it is by morticians upon caskets in viewing rooms in order to put the best face on the dead. In restaurants and clubs aimed primarily at a homosexual following, he went on, the lighting is customarily very dark and indirect, "taking into account that a number of people in the place prefer a bit of privacy. They want to survey the room, and maybe even cruise a little, without it appearing to be too obvious."

Whether it is the influence of the lighting, or the accompanying liquor that one consumes, or the supplementary sense of release and stimulation that captivates people like me after I leave my desk and join a lively and amiable gathering composed primarily of strangers closely quartered within rooms that are ideal for making eye contact and assumptions that have little to do with reality, I have come to regard restaurants as extensions of the proscenium, as centers for grand entrances and exits, as showcases for drawing room scenes and improvisational sketches, as location sites for mysterious plots and shady transactions, as venues for romantic encounters and illicit trysts and potential gangland bloodbaths and burlesque sideshows of the sort I saw in a Manhattan restaurant one night when a middle-aged man from the bar approached the table of the movie star Anthony Quinn and proceeded to masterfully impersonate the actor's dance steps and movements from *Zorba the Greek*—an imitation that brought applause from around the room, but only scowls from Quinn, prompting the maître d' to toss the star's dancing rival out into the street.

"Dinner lubricates business," wrote James Boswell, but I believe he was referring primarily to lunch, for during the daylight the dramaturgy in restaurants is more methodical and less whimsical than it is at night; lunchtime is more sober, more programmed, more conducive to shoptalk and sales figures than the figures seen at night wearing dresses and skirts, not all of them worn by women. At night restaurants reflect more fully the variety of roles that they are playing in people's lives at this time when millions of Americans in major cities are dining out, on average, four nights a week, according to the Zagat survey, and when more and more women, like my pioneering mother, serve the needs of their jobs during the day and at night expect dinner to be served by someone else.

Restaurants are echo chambers for veteran eavesdroppers like myself. Even when partaking in the conversations at my own table, I am often tuned in to the talk of people seated nearby, silently sharing in their debates and arguments, their confessions and restitutions, their jokes and rumormongering, their attempts at seduction and their efforts to extricate themselves from deeper romantic involvements. A tearful young woman at a table next to mine at Cafe Luxembourg in the West Seventies in Manhattan is telling her gray-haired companion that she wants to leave her husband, but her companion, shaking his head and touching her arm, responds, "Darling, you promised we weren't going to talk this way. . . ." Nights later, from behind me at Coco Pazzo on East Seventy-fourth Street, someone is saying, "I hear Perelman's looking to unload Revlon," and his dinner partner says, "Bullshit." During the following week, at Elio's on Second Avenue, I sit near a large table where the talk is all about book publishing and real estate prices in the Hamptons. And on a subsequent evening, I am farther uptown at Elaine's, where I go so often that I rarely hear or observe anything new.

I have known the proprietress, Elaine Kaufman, for more than thirty-five years, having met her in the early 1960s, soon after she took over a failing Austro-Hungarian tavern on Second Avenue near Eighty-eighth Street called Gambrino; after renaming it in her honor, she gradually converted it into a late-night gathering place for writers and other creative people whom she went out of her way to cultivate. She had been an avid reader of literary works since her girlhood in Queens, and in later years, during her off-hours as a waitress in Greenwich Village, she attended poetry readings, art shows, and the avant-garde theater. When she moved uptown to start Elaine's in 1963, she might well have been the only restaurateur in New York who had ever finished reading a book.

Although most of the writers of her acquaintance who frequented her place were not yet known to the general reading public, she seated them at her front-row tables, and sometimes picked up their checks if she knew they were experiencing financial difficulties, and she decorated her restaurant walls with framed photographs of their faces and the covers of their books. The presence of literary writers lent an intellectual aura to Elaine's that in time attracted some recognized intellectuals, along with leading book reviewers and publishers, playwrights and directors, painters and art patrons, politicians and business tycoons, socialites, gossip columnists, Hollywood actors, and press agents. But no matter how prominent or affluent some of these newcomers happened to be, neither Kaufman nor her waiters—though they were never unnecessarily rude to anyone— permitted pampered movie stars, or renowned louts from the sports world, or mighty moguls from Wall Street, to behave in an imperious or contentious manner while in the restaurant.

One evening Elaine Kaufman's headwaiter, a Genoese Italian named Nicola Spagnolo, whom she had worked with at Portofino restaurant in Greenwich Village, was being pestered by a prominent stockbroker who, standing among his seated guests at a round table in the rear of the room—his guests included two high-fashion models and an anchorman from one of the local television channels—kept demanding that Nicola bring over the wine list, or the *carte du vin*, as he insisted on referring to it.

"I already told you, we don't have a *carte du vin* around here," Nicola called to him from across the room, having earlier explained that Elaine's wine selection was too limited to warrant such a list.

"Oh, I'm *sure* there's a *carte du vin* near the bar," the man said. "Go over and get it."

Nicola turned and walked toward the front of the room. Moments later he returned holding a fifteen-hundred-page copy of the Manhattan telephone directory, and after thumping it down on the table in front of the stockbroker, he announced, "Here's your *carte du vin*." Everyone at the table laughed except the stockbroker. "This is my first and last time in *this* place," he said.

"That's okay with me," Nicola replied, anticipating, correctly, that when the broker later paid the bill, there would be no gratuity.

A few weeks after this, which was during Elaine's second year in business, a leading art dealer brought in some friends, and as he sat down he asked Nicola for a glass of rosé wine. Without admitting that Elaine Kaufman had not gotten around to stocking her bar with rosé, since no customer had previously requested it, Nicola strolled to the side bar and filled a stemmed goblet almost entirely with white wine, added a little red, stirred it vigorously with a spoon, and then carried it to the art dealer's table. The latter held up the glass and smelled it. As his companions watched, he slowly began to sip it, closing his eyes momentarily. Nicola stood quietly behind him, not knowing what to expect.

"Ah, very good, *very* good," the man said finally. "What is it?"

"Balaggola," Nicola replied, using the first word that had popped into his head. It was a word he had grown up with in Genoa, and it referred to matters of little importance or quality.

"Ah yes, *Balaggola*," the man repeated, with seeming appreciation and recognition, as he took another sip.

At various times during my lengthy patronage of Elaine's I have contemplated writing a book about Nicola Spagnolo and Elaine Kaufman and the groups of literary figures and other personalities that interacted with one another there every evening; I believed—during rare moments when I was intoxicated with optimism—that I might be capable of producing a New York version of Ernest Hemingway's Paris-based *A Moveable Feast*, or George Orwell's *Down and Out in Paris and London*. Orwell's book recounted his travels and travails as a young Englishman who, in addition to other demeaning but enlightening undertakings, earned his livelihood as a worker in a fetid, sweltering kitchen in a Paris hotel, where his colleagues included "fat pink cooks," "greasy dishwashers," and such food-smuggling dining room waiters as Boris from Russia and Valenti from Italy. Orwell wrote of Valenti:

Like most waiters, he carried himself well and knew how to wear his clothes. With his black tail-coat and white tie, fresh face and sleek brown hair, he looked just like an Eton boy; yet he had earned his living since he was twelve, and worked his way up literally from the gutter. Crossing the Italian frontier without a passport, and selling chestnuts from a barrow on the northern boulevards, and being given fifty days' imprisonment in London for working without a permit, and being made love to by a rich old woman in a hotel, who gave him a diamond ring and afterwards accused him of stealing it, were among his experiences. I used to enjoy talking to him, at slack times when we sat smoking. . . .

Orwell described the kitchen in which he worked as "a stifling, low-ceilinged inferno of a cellar, red-lit from the fires, and deafening with oaths and the clanging of pots and pans"; and beyond the double door of the kitchen, Orwell saw the dining room: "There sat the customers in all their splendour—spotless table-cloths, bowls of flowers, mirrors, and gilt cornices and painted cherubim"; and when a waiter walked out of the kitchen into the dining room, Orwell observed:

> a sudden change comes over him. The set of his shoulders alters; all the dirt and hurry and irritation have dropped off in an instant. He glides over the carpet, with a solemn priest-like air. I remember our assistant maître d'hotel . . . pausing at the dining-room door to address an apprentice who had broken a bottle of wine. Shaking his fist above his head he yelled . . . "You're not fit to scrub floors in the brothel your mother came from" . . . then he entered the dining-room and sailed across it dish in hand, graceful as a swan. Ten seconds later he was bowing reverently to a customer. And you could not help thinking, as you saw him bow and smile, with that benign smile of the trained waiter, that the customer was put to shame by having such an aristocrat to serve him. . . .

Until I had read Orwell's book in the early 1970s—it was first published in the early 1930s—I had never contemplated writing about the restaurant world, but as I gave some thought to it, I convinced myself that I was ideally suited to the task. I had been reared as a restaurantgoer. Menus had been my childhood literature. I could measure out my life with coffee spoons. As a young bachelor in New York, and during my forty-plus years as a married man, I have dined out, on average, four or five times a week. I am alone all day, producing prose with the ease of a patient passing kidney stones, and so at night I prefer to dine out, seeking diversion and usually finding it in any of the half dozen restaurants that I patronize—places where I am able to walk in without a reservation even on heavily booked evenings and receive a smile of recognition and the next available table from the maître d' (to whom there is no greater aide-mémoire than a twenty-dollar bill).

Sometimes my wife accompanies me, but just as often she chooses to remain at home. She has manuscripts to read and welcomes the quiet hours alone after her busy days in the office. While she enjoys cooking and will happily put aside her reading whenever the two of us are eating in—compared to the culinary talents of my mother, my wife is a four-star chef—I still respond inharmoniously to home cooking, associating it no doubt with the isolating and dutiful dinners I was forced to endure in my parents' kitchen above the store, where I was expected to pay attention to what was being said (that is, the shoptalk of my parents) and where the telephone rang incessantly with customers' calls, and where the meal would conclude with me helping to clear the table and then participating in the washing and drying of the dishes.

While none of this applies to my marriage, the echo of the shop probably pervades my dinners at home, and occasionally we *are* interrupted by calls from one of my wife's authors or business colleagues, and I must admit that whenever my wife seems to be especially cheerful, I am prone to attribute it to good news she received in her office—perhaps that a new book by one of her authors will be reviewed favorably on the front page of next Sunday's *New York Times Book Review*.

While it is true that my own demeanor is no less influenced by my work, and that my nightly moods are invariably linked to whatever I did or did not do at my desk that day, it is also true that in restaurants I seem to gain some distance from my domestic sense of obligation. I have the option of tuning out, half-listening, drifting about mentally while glancing around at the crowded and noisy dining room, watching almost simultaneously a sporting event being shown on television above the bar, an attractive blonde sitting sideways on a stool, and a fat man sitting at a nearby table with his mouth open, about to devour a piece of fish, a slender slice of flounder; and suddenly I imagine the fish coming to life, jumping off the fork, wiggling along the floor, and being retrieved by a waiter, who carries it in a napkin back to the kitchen, where I have visions of the fish swimming backward in time, a flashback fish floating freely ten days before in the Labrador Sea of northeastern Canada, a fish that is flat-bodied and pancake-size and has two eyes on the same side of its head, a Picasso fish, cruising easily along the muddy bottom of the sea in search of a shrimp until, five minutes before sunrise, it glides into a net, is trapped, is confused, is frightened, but is not alone—hundreds of other Picasso-eyed flounder are ensnared there, swirling around, bumping into one another, angling to flip over to their seeing-eye side, hoping to figure out what's going on—but then they are squeezed together as the big net soars drippingly out of the sea and scrapes along the side of a ship that is piloted by a bearded, brandy-breathed, scrawny, wife-abusing French-Canadian fisherman, who had been illegally trawling in that area all week, and who now, after grabbing fistfuls of wiggling fish out of the net with his gloved hands, hurls them into an ice-filled hold in the stern of his ship, and then starts up his engine for the six-hour journey to the dockside depot of a seafood distributorship in Newfoundland, from which the fish will be flown a day later in refrigerated aluminum containers to JFK airport in New York, where Mafia-affiliated teamsters will receive them and drive them to the Fulton Street market, then deliver them into the hands of wholesale dealers whose vans on the following morning will be double-parked in front of myriad Manhattan restaurants, including Elaine's, where the fish will be counted and examined by Elaine's Neapolitan chef, and will be cleaned by her Spanish-speaking scullions, and will be prepared and offered that night as a fresh fish special—flounder meunière almondine, twenty-nine dollars—and this is what was ordered by, and brought to, the fat man I saw sitting in front of me with his mouth agape.

So many hands, so many people from all over the world, so many middlemen, merchandisers, restaurant managers, chefs, and their helpers are involved in the acquisition, the processing, and the presentation of every piece of fish, every chunk of beef, every lima bean, every carrot and potato that makes its way onto a menu; and the primary concern of a kitchen staff is not only with the cuisine but with the synchronized dispatching of several dozen different appetizers, entrées, and desserts to various tables at the moment when the customers should receive them. "It is not the cooking that is so difficult," Orwell wrote, but rather "doing everything to time"; and he added, "It is for their punctuality, and not for any superiority in technique, that men cooks are preferred to women."

Although he was referring to the 1930s, it seemed to me that little had changed in subsequent decades; a vast majority of the most respected and best-known chefs I was aware of in New York and elsewhere were male. But in addition to the cooking and timing, contemporary chefs are interested in the *look* of the food, the *design* of the food, the architecturally interesting way in which food might be placed on a plate—a technique that in the parlance of the practitioners of American nouvelle cuisine is called "plating."

Initially inspired by the chefs of Japan and elaborated upon by those in France—which is where many graduates of America's best cooking schools have traditionally gone to intern in the baptismal dish waters of the Michelin-approved kitchens of Paris and Provence—plating is a means by which chefs can make visual statements, can sculpt and *stage* their food in ways that can transform plates into miniature theaters in the round, edible art that is intended to appeal at once to the aesthetics and appetites of customers while at the same time (I suspect) indulging the fanciful natures of those chefs whose childhoods were marked by their mothers' admonitions about playing with their food at the family dinner table.

Indeed, plating is *all* about playing with food, toying with it, reshaping it, reimagining it, metamorphosing it, stacking it like building blocks—balancing beef tips and black olives on a brioche that rests atop a circular silver mold filled with sautéed spinach; cantilevering the rib bones of lamb chops across a bird's nest of couscous and a rice field lined with coolie laborers wearing shiitake mushroom caps; choreographing a water ballet of baby clams within a leek-ribboned watercress soup that resembles a lily pond; presenting a shrimp cocktail in the form of a Spanish galleon, with bows of protruding prongs, masts of bread sticks, and billowing sails shaped by potato chips. And plating is also about advertising the creative chefs' elevated status in the better restaurants and their power to prevent the captains in the dining room from tampering with their inventiveness as was once routinely done in the days when food left the kitchen in lidded platters to be placed at tableside next to a stack of empty plates on wheeled wagons that were really the captains' vehicles for displaying their dexterity and surgical skills as spooners and carvers and occasionally as pyrotechnical wizards with steak flambé and crêpes suzette.

Yes, I love the modern restaurant world, and I respect all restaurants—the good and the not so good—as fundamentally sincere and intrinsically democratic establishments whose kitchens are Ellis Islands of opportunity for thousands of hardworking immigrants who, initially speaking limited English, can nonetheless hone their skills and rise through the ranks to become the next Henri Soulé of Pavillon fame, or the next Sirio Maccioni of Le Cirque, or any of the young proprietors whose names now appear on restaurant marquees, or in the newspaper columns next to the names of those celebrities and socialites whose presence can establish a restaurant as the place to be—until they tire of it, and *it* tires of their inflated egos and unpaid bar bills. The essence of every restaurant's ingredients is based on hope, trust, and optimism. There is the hope that people will enjoy what is served. There is the trust that they will later pay for it. And there is the optimism that an investment in restaurants will be rewarding and rewarded, bringing satisfaction not only to the owners, the managers, the chefs, and their clientele but also to all the others involved—the servers and bartenders, the suppliers of food, linen, candles, and music, as well as the sweepers of the after-dinner table crumbs, who may briefly brush against the shoulders of the seated moguls and movie stars and other achievers while hoping that some of the luck and success will rub off.

7

WHILE I VIEWED GEORGE ORWELL AS A QUASI-DANTE portraying a purgatory of pots and pans in his book *Down and Out in Paris and London*, I saw myself as producing a *Decameron of Dining Rooms*, feasting on the tales of the customers, the restaurateurs, and their personnel, and somehow blending this material into a cohesive narrative. At first I did not approach Elaine Kaufman or Nicola Spagnolo for interviews, preferring to wait until I had a better idea of what I was doing, but I did begin keeping a restaurant journal in the 1970s, one in which I noted what I had observed and overheard during my nightly visits to Elaine's and other restaurants, and I continued this practice on and off for the next thirty years. Indeed, it was the restaurant world that I was writing about during the summer of 1999 when I saw the China-USA women's World Cup soccer match on television. The fifty-four and a half typed pages that I had then completed—and that were stacked on my desk as I took a respite from my work to spend a Saturday afternoon channel-surfing, during which time I happened upon Liu Ying's sad moment in the Rose Bowl—were pages that I had rewritten many times in the past and were distilled from two hundred other pages that I had written and thrown away.

Often I involve myself with two or three unrelated subjects at the same time, and I shift from one to another when I become bogged down and believe it wiser to put aside what I am doing and reappraise it at some point in the future. In 1974 I had begun to describe many restaurant scenes and situations that I had witnessed, but they seemed to be too fragmented and diffused. So I moved on to another subject that I had under consideration, and finally in 1979 I saw this one through to the end. It was *Thy Neighbor's Wife*—one of four books that I had begun and completed between 1965 and 1999; but during this period I had also started several other books and had finished none of them. My curiosity drives me in different directions, but until I have invested lots of my time—

months, years—I have no idea whether a chosen subject will sustain my interest. Sometimes I toss into the trash various drafts of what I have written, while at other times I put them aside, file them away, reread them a year or two later, rewrite and refile them perhaps, or decide that they are not worth saving after all, and so I tear them up and rid myself of them forever.

Writing is often like driving a truck at night without headlights, losing your way along the road, and spending a decade in a ditch. It had been much simpler when I worked as a journalist. In those youthful days I was ordered by an editor to write a certain story, was permitted a limited time in which to complete it, and, whether or not I was entirely pleased with the results, I was forced to surrender it before the deadline to the editor, who passed it on to the copyreader, after which it went to the printers, and that was the end of it until it appeared in the next edition of the *Times*. On the following day, the process was repeated.

The book I was under contract to finish by the 1990s, but had so far failed to deliver to my patient, anxious publisher, was to be the sequel to *Unto the Sons*. This last book had centered on my parents and my Italian ancestry; the sequel was supposed to be *my* story, an autobiographical account of my semiassimilated life as I experienced it in America during the second half of the twentieth century. I began this book in 1992, wrote and rewrote the opening section dozens of times, but never got very far with it. What blocked me, I think, was the imprecision of my persona and the fact that I did not know where to establish my story. I had no idea what my story was. I had never given much thought to who *I* was. I had always defined myself through my work, which was always about other people. So when I confronted the sequel, and sought a location in which to situate myself, I was hesitant. This had not been a problem in my earlier works. The main locale for *Unto the Sons* had been my parents' shop. The principal location for *Thy Neighbor's Wife* had been a hillside manor in Los Angeles owned by a nudist couple, John and Barbara Williamson, and shared by their extended family of eroticists. The backdrop for *Honor Thy Father* had been the suburban home outside San Francisco occupied by Bill Bonanno, together with his wife, his children, and his bodyguards. The fourteen-story *Times* building had provided the focal point for *The Kingdom and the Power*. The steel columns and span of New York's Verrazano-Narrows Bridge, still unconnected when I began my research there in 1962, provided the foundation for my story about the agile, hardhatted steelworkers portrayed in *The Bridge*. My first book, *New York—A Serendipiter's Journey*, published in 1961, concentrated on neighborhoods of obscure people dwelling in the shadows of a skyscraper city.

Since my days as a schoolboy reporter, and continuing through my ten-year career on the *Times* writing staff, I had been told that we in journalism were not part of the story. Where we were, who we were, and what we thought was not relevant to what we wrote. In Orwell's chronicle, *he* was the main character, the first-person narrator who held everything together with his commanding voice, his I-was-there account of what it was like to be Orwell working in a French kitchen with duplicitous waiters who were bow-tied serfs and rogues; with perspiring chefs whose sweat trickled off their white toques into pots filled with gravy and soup; with itinerant tribes of dishwashers and brass polishers, mysterious men with aliases and borrowed working papers, who were sought for questioning by the authorities in their native villages and towns of Africa, Asia, or Arabia.

Unlike Orwell, I could not write as an "insider" in the culinary world unless I pursued my onetime fantasy of becoming an owner or partner in a restaurant. A former colleague of mine at the *Times*, Sidney Zion, who, I think, enjoyed hanging out in restaurants as much as I did, took over as the proprietor of Broadway Joe's restaurant in the Manhattan Theater District for a couple of years, but I think it turned out to be an uninspiring experience, and to my knowledge, he never wrote about it. Whenever I dined at Broadway Joe's, he greeted me courteously at the door, escorted me to a fine table, and introduced me to his show business clientele, which sometimes included Frank Sinatra. But I believe that after a few years Sidney was bored with running a restaurant. He was restricted almost every night to the same place. He had to pay attention to his business, to keep an eye on the kitchen help and their pilfering tendencies, and on the bartenders, who might otherwise be offering too many free drinks to their friends. If I owned a restaurant, I assume my fate would be similar to Zion's. I would be unable to rove around at night, would not have the option of dining each week in a variety of restaurants. I'd be confined to a single place. I might as well stay home.

Still, I had a contract to do a book. I had signed the contract for the sequel in 1992, and I also had accepted at that time a six-figure advance from my publisher, a sum of money that was supposed to cover my operating expenses during the three-year period deemed sufficient for me to research, write, and finally deliver a manuscript to my editor that was worthy of publication and would, it was hoped, become a best-selling book. At the end of 1995, having delivered not a word to my editor—although regularly reassuring him through the mail and faxes that I was making progress—I was technically in default of the contract. The publisher could have sued me for the return of the advance, but I heard nothing from them, not even as my tardiness continued throughout 1996 and then into 1997. What saved me from being sued, I think, was my publisher's knowledge that I had been four or five years late in delivering *Unto the Sons* and *Thy Neighbor's Wife,* both of which became best-sellers. In any event, I was not asked to return the advance, for which I was grateful, because by the end of 1997 I had spent every dollar of it. While I was hardly destitute at the time, being able to draw upon savings from my earlier works, I knew that I could not continue indefinitely with my method of shifting from subject to subject. I *must* make up my mind, I told myself, hearing again the authoritative voice of my late father. I must devote myself to *one* topic and then *finish* it, be *done* with it—or else I'd spend the rest of my life spinning my wheels in a ditch.

Thus motivated, I decided (albeit tentatively) that my sequel would be set in a restaurant. So I reached into my metal filing cabinet and pulled up a thick and long-ignored folder that was labeled "Restaurants—a work in progress." This folder contained more than ninety single-spaced typed pages of notes that I had begun accumulating in the 1970s and had added to sporadically throughout the 1980s and into the 1990s. My notes described much of what I had seen and overheard during my nocturnal peregrinations in restaurants; my account of the interviews I had conducted with several restaurant owners and their employees; and the many false starts and unfinished paragraphs that represented the opening chapter of my loosely defined "work in progress" about the restaurant industry. Also tucked into my folder were photocopied pages of other people's writings about restaurants—copies of many pages from Orwell's book were included here, and from another book I admired, Joseph Wechsberg's *Dining at the Pavillon,* a biography published in 1962 about Henry Soulé, the French owner of perhaps New York's most renowned dining establishment, located on the ground floor of the Ritz Tower on Park Avenue and Fifty-seventh Street. With my yellow fluorescent marker pen, I had highlighted some of Wechsberg's remarks:

> . . . the maître d'hotel must be a subtle compromiser, capable of soothing not only the resentment of waiters toward overbearing guests but the far more deep-seated resentment of cooks toward waiters—a resentment based on the cooks' feeling that they do all the work and the waiters collect all the tips . . . the great restaurateur must be a showman, a business man, and an artist. Like a great conductor he needs both a first-rate audience and a first-rate orchestra to perform. To be able to cast a spell over his audience he must have full control over his orchestra. The experienced restaurateur

builds his kitchen brigade and dining room staff just as a conductor builds various sections of his orchestra, trying to get the best experts he can afford . . .

Wechsberg not only celebrated the culinary talents and business acumen of Soulé but also his organizational ability, which allowed him to maintain his standards even while dividing his time between the Pavillon and a second restaurant that he owned and operated a few blocks away, La Côte Basque, on West Fifty-fifth Street; and, during the summer months, Soulé was frequently in Long Island, overseeing his third restaurant, the Hedges. He attracted a large and faithful following wherever he happened to be *without* ever spending a dollar in restaurant advertising, Wechsberg emphasized; it was strictly word-of-mouth campaigning that drew crowds of diners into his orbit.

"Elaine Kaufman doesn't advertise, either," I scribbled in the margin of the photocopied page of Wechsberg's book. I further noted that in Elaine's case, the word-of-mouth factor that had propelled her career was all the more remarkable because her restaurant was located in a working-class Upper East Side neighborhood that was very inconvenient to nearly all of her regular customers—most of whom had to travel at least ten or twenty blocks to get there—and, moreover, the media's restaurant reviewers had written quite negatively about the quality of her food, portraying her as New York's doyenne of dyspepsia.

What most bothered these reviewers, it seemed to me, was their powerlessness in influencing her business with their criticisms. She was critic-proof, so admired and appreciated by her nightly clique, to whom she was their Jewish mother and steadfast supporter, that it mattered not at all what others thought about her or her chef. I myself never found fault with the food at Elaine's, and while I admit that such an endorsement coming from me is of little consequence, I was confident that within the ambience of Elaine's I would find an accommodating homesite for my sequel. Even though I did not have a specific story in mind, certainly not one in which I saw myself as a central character, the restaurant offered several interesting people for me to draw upon, an eclectic nightly gathering of intellectuals and pretenders, actresses and activists; and there was the leading lady herself, Elaine Kaufman, and her personable, though at times prickly, majordomo, Nicola Spagnolo.

I saw them as an odd couple—the rotund Elaine, 240 pounds of amiability and angst, swatched in exquisite silk frocks costing one hundred dollars a yard, and the lean, dark-haired, limber-legged Nicola, moving around the dining room, balancing trays with the grace of an adagio dancer. The two of them worked well together, though they often bickered throughout the evening while striving to keep their voices below the sound level of their customers. If in writing my sequel I used the third-person narrative form, as I had in my other books, I believed that I could channel much of what I wanted to say about the restaurant world—and my place within it as its devotee and self-appointed writer-in-residence—through my characterization of these two individuals, both of whom I could identify with and knew well enough to be able to write about interiorly, casting them as *my* narrators, *my* stand-ins for what would be *my* story projected through them and other people whom I might add later.

In certain ways, Elaine reminded me of my mother. Elaine was all business, and yet a very patient and attentive listener to her customers. Her restaurant was her raison d'être, but without her as its magnate, it would undoubtedly be doomed. She had been raised within a conventional family in Queens, and from an early age was determined to cross the bridge into Manhattan. Being an omnivorous reader who had spent her after-school hours in libraries, and who enjoyed an acquaintanceship with distinguished authors through the books they had written, did not prepare her for any particular career or calling of her own, and so she sought contentment temporarily as an appreciator of talented people while she paid her rent to live within the vibrant vortex of Manhattan while working at subservient jobs on a short-term basis until she found something that she hoped would fulfill her.

She was employed variously as a hatcheck girl, a clerk in a used-book store, and a pitchwoman selling cosmetics at the Astor Hotel's pharmacy in the Times Square district. She worked in the stamp department of Gimbel's Department Store in Herald Square, and as a waitress in an uptown restaurant on 116th Street and one downtown on Tenth Street. While waitressing at Portofino on Thompson Street at Bleecker in the Village, she fell in love with the owner, a Genoese gentleman named Alfredo Viazzi, who years before, as a waiter on a luxury cruise ship, had cultivated a courtly manner in an effort to impress the better-looking of the widowed women who were traveling alone in first-class accommodations. Elaine and Alfredo Viazzi lived together above the restaurant on the fifth floor of a walk-up apartment building in which the tenants included a Mafia enforcer named Vincent "The Chin" Gigante and his mother, around whom Vincent was invariably dutiful and compliant. Elaine's affair with Alfredo ended bitterly when he became romantically involved with a stage actress, and this is what prompted her to move uptown in 1963 and, with financial help from a partner she would eventually buy out, acquire the run-down Austro-Hungarian tavern she would rename Elaine's.

In addition to her friends from downtown, Elaine's uptown patrons who helped to launch her restaurant included the editor and writer Nelson Aldrich and the poet Frederick Seidel, both of whom were connected editorially with the New York–based literary magazine *The Paris Review*, a quarterly founded a decade earlier on the Left Bank by George Plimpton, Peter Matthiessen, and other young American writers then living abroad. The quarterly's contributors and supporters who were also in Paris then included the novelists William Styron, Terry Southern, and John Phillips Marquand, the latter being the first lover of a comely debutante who during the early 1950s was a regular visitor to the city—Jackie Bouvier, future wife of John F. Kennedy and Aristotle Onassis. Marquand told me during the 1980s that when he and Jackie had first made love in a small Left Bank hotel, she had looked up into his eyes and inquired wonderingly, in her whispery little-girl voice, "That's *it?*"

The courtesy and respect that Elaine Kaufman showed toward poets and writers in her restaurant—to say nothing of the free after-dinner drinks and the fact that she decorated her restaurant's walls with framed photos of their faces and book jackets, correctly assuming that they would have no objection to eating and drinking in a place where they were surrounded by reminders of themselves—helped to establish Elaine's as a highbrow tavern in a low-rent district where the blasé clientele would hardly bat an eye if on any given night they saw Elaine escorting to a table the Dalai Lama accompanied by a ghostwriter and a representative from the William Morris Agency. It was often close to dawn before she locked her doors, waiting patiently while a few of her regulars finished their nightly backgammon or card game at one of the rear tables. She rarely gambled at cards herself, or bet on sporting events, but she was busily engaged in the stock market, profiting from the wisdom she received from one of the few Wall Streeters who were part of her inner circle. In 1968, five years after opening Elaine's, she had earned enough money from her business and stock investments to purchase the entire four-story apartment building that included her restaurant.

Nicola Spagnolo began working for her during her second year of operation, in the spring of 1964, and he functioned as her headwaiter for the next ten years. He attended to the front tables, where he was on a first-name basis with the regular customers, and he soon knew as well as they did what they liked to eat and drink and how they wanted their food to be seasoned and served. Since dropping out of school at fourteen in his native village, located between Genoa and the French border, Nicola had followed his male relatives into the realm of restaurant service, which would become his lifelong undertaking. Beginning as a pot washer and apprentice in a local bar and patisserie, he next found seasonal work in the kitchens of resort hotels and inns extending along the beaches from Nice to Marseilles, and in winters he often signed on as a kitchen helper on cruise ships. While employed as a cook's assistant on an Italian merchant marine vessel that was docked in Bayonne, New Jersey, in late November 1956, Nicola decided to jump ship. At the time, he was nearly thirty, a bachelor with no dependents and a carefree disposition. So he slipped away from the crew one night, hailed a taxi into Manhattan, and traveled by subway to the Bronx, where he had the name and address of an Italian compatriot whom he knew would temporarily shelter him and would eventually get him a job in one of the many New York restaurants and hotels that employed illegal aliens in their kitchens.

A year later, still undetected by the American immigration authorities who had been notified about his defection, Spagnolo was a hireling in the kitchen of the St. Regis Hotel on Fifty-fifth Street off Fifth Avenue in Manhattan. Although he had not yet mastered English, his fluency in French and Spanish as well as Italian meant that he had no difficulty in communicating with the many foreign-born people who worked at the St. Regis and in the other places where he moonlighted during his off-duty hours. As he continued each day to ride the subway back and forth to work between the Bronx and Manhattan, and as he enlarged upon his sense of the city through his after-hours strolls and his widening social contacts, he guessed that he was one of several hundred or maybe one of several *thousand* fugitives who earned their keep "off the books" in the kitchens of restaurants or hotels, as well as in the factories of the Garment District and in the construction yards of the city's five boroughs, and at numerous other job sites that were linked to the vast underground economy that flourished in New York.

Nicola was pleased that this situation existed, having no misgivings about its being criminal or mendacious or unfair to dues-paying unionists. From what he had heard from his friends in the Bronx, the margin of profit in the restaurant business was so small, and the operating costs and various risks involved were so high, that if the bosses were to adhere strictly to the law—that is, hire only licensed workers and pay them according to union standards—it would drive most restaurateurs into bankruptcy.

What would also lead them toward bankruptcy, unless they could control it better than the St. Regis's executives seemed to be doing, was the employees' habit of stealing food, liquor, and other commodities out of the kitchen and elsewhere in the hotel with such brazenness and regularity that Nicola was certain that there would soon be a crackdown and the entire workforce, including himself, would be discharged and maybe prosecuted in a court of law. Still, the workers' prodigious purloining of food supplies and numerous other portable items went on with impunity, week after week, month after month; what amazed Nicola most of all about it was how casually and openly the workers indulged in their larcenousness, how unafraid they seemed to be about being caught while looting the larder, the pantry, the freezer, and the liquor cabinet. They even spoke aloud among themselves about what they planned to take home after work, never defining it as stealing, but using instead a euphemism—"valising." They would ask one another, "What are you going to valise tonight?" They customarily referred to a coworker as a "valise": "Who's that new valise the chef just hired?"

After Nicola had been at the St. Regis for a few weeks without revealing larcenous tendencies, a fellow worker approached him one night and asked, "Hey, how come you don't valise anything around here?" Nicola explained that he did not have a refrigerator in the single-room apartment he rented in the Bronx, and since he also lived alone and nibbled on the job, he had no reason to practice valising. "You'd better find a reason," the man said, adding that otherwise Nicola might be seen as behaving disrespectfully toward his coworkers. And so Nicola became a valise, doing as the others did, coming to work often with an empty shopping bag folded inside his shirt, or a canvas carrier strung over his arm, into which he might later deposit assorted vegetables or a few filet mignons or whatever he thought would be appreciated by the wife of his landlord in the Bronx, a man who had a large family to support and who had always been lenient regarding overdue rent.

One night, Nicola was riding home on the subway, standing next to a St. Regis busboy who, unknown to Nicola, was carrying several raw eggs in the pockets of his jacket and trousers. Suddenly, as the subway lurched and screeched to a halt, one of the passengers lost his balance and fell against the boy, cracking open all the eggs and causing a gluey mess to trickle down the boy's legs, onto his shoes, and then across the floor—sending Nicola and the other passengers into quick retreat. Nicola later wondered why the boy would be stuffing his pockets with things so fragile and so relatively inexpensive as four or five eggs. It was certainly worth the trouble to walk off with a few filets, or a tin of caviar, or occasionally a bottle of cognac, as he had done—but fewer than a half dozen *eggs*? A few nights later, just before closing time in the St. Regis kitchen, Nicola watched as another worker inserted only a single onion, a piece of garlic, and some parsley into his coat pocket, and Nicola asked him on the way out, "Why bother taking that stuff?" "My wife needs it," the man said. "It isn't worth much," Nicola replied. "Yes," the man said, "but my wife would have to buy it. A penny here, a penny there, it all adds up to dollars I don't have to spend and the hotel will never miss."

The St. Regis workers who were employed outside the kitchen seemed to be far more flagrant as freebooters than were Nicola's coworkers. A few of the former once arranged for the permanent disappearance from the hotel of a number of Persian rugs that had been set aside to be cleaned and repaired; on another occasion, three pianos in need of tuning were carefully rolled down the hotel's ramp and placed within a truck that would never return with them. There were investigations by the management, but Nicola never knew of a case in which an investigation produced incriminating evidence. And he believed that the workers more or less justified their valising as compensation for their lowly wages and also as a reaction to the great wealth, privilege, and waste that they saw all around them, as personified by the hotel's guests.

Coming from a family background in which little was spent and nothing was wasted, Nicola was overwhelmed by the bountiful squandering that was evident whenever he and his coworkers began to clear the tables in the ballroom after each banquet and then returned to the kitchen carrying plates of uneaten food, and several uncorked bottles half-filled with champagne, and more flowers than would adorn a mafioso's funeral, and bundles of decorative crepe paper that was partly torn and speckled with dried wax, and dozens of frivolous and forgotten party favors, and countless chips of delicate dessert cookies that Nicola sampled and that sweetened his appetite while reducing his scruples about leaving the hotel later with a few uncooked chunks of beef wrapped in tinfoil and tucked under his hat. Furthermore, he reminded himself that what he stole was not out of his own greed, but for the benefit of the needy family of his landlord; a second reason that valising seemed harmless to Nicola was his belief that the hotel's executive chef and the other department heads were aware of what was going on within their domains and they quietly condoned it as long as it did not threaten their positions with their superiors in the main office.

To be sure, there *had* been a few incidents that had taxed the patience of the normally easygoing chef Nicola worked under, and such an occasion was the theft of one of the two baby lambs reserved for a private dinner in the Louis XV Suite that was to be hosted by the hotel's owner, Vincent Astor. Although the chef's follow-up investigation indicated that no one in the kitchen had been responsible, the experience had motivated within him an uncharacteristic surge of scrupulousness; and a few days after the baby lamb's disappearance, as the chef was saying good night to one of his cooks—a cook whom the chef had earlier observed placing a pound of butter under his hat—the chef said to the cook, "Wait a minute, don't go yet. I need to talk to you. Let's go into my office."

The chef's office was a small glass-partitioned room located next to a boiler tank. The room was very hot, since the overhead fans had been turned off and the boiler was still hissing steam. The cook, wearing a heavy overcoat and porkpie hat that was tilted forward over his round and swarthy face, sat down in front of the chef's desk and waited. The chef, after seating himself and unbuttoning his shirt collar, opened a drawer to his desk. He removed a few pages from a folder and spread the pages in front of him. As he read, he began to fiddle with the steel-rimmed glasses that rested on the nose of his raw-boned, ruddy face. He removed the glasses and wiped the foggy lenses slowly and repeatedly with a linen cocktail napkin. He paid no attention to the cook. With his glasses back on, the chef resumed reading.

The cook unbuttoned his overcoat and remained seated, waiting patiently, perspiring noticeably. The chef, after reading for about five minutes, reached across the desk for the phone and dialed a number. Someone soon responded on the other end, and for the next ten minutes the chef chatted in a friendly fashion with this person about matters unrelated to the hotel. The cook was now squirming in the seat and, with both hands on the rim of his hat, he pulled downward, trying to reduce the flow of the unctuous yellowy liquid that was trickling down from his forehead and dripping from his earlobes onto the collar of his coat.

The chef chatted on for another three or four minutes. After hanging up the phone, he looked directly at the cook, whose face was now glistening thickly with a kind of lava flow of melted butter.

"You know," the chef said, "you don't look good. I think you should hurry home and call a doctor."

The cook nodded and, after easing himself up, again pulled down on his hat and said good night.

8

NICOLA SPAGNOLO SPENT THE BETTER PART OF FIVE YEARS WORK-
ing at the St. Regis. As he gradually mastered English, having
taken lessons at a community center in the Bronx, he found
extra work as a waiter or kitchen helper in other restaurants during his
off-hours from the hotel. Most of these restaurants were undistinguished
places located along the side streets of mid-Manhattan, but sometimes,
aided by the fact that he could speak French, he was able to fill in as an
assistant waiter at the Pavillon. Nicola would never speak a word of Italian inside the Pavillon, knowing that Henri Soulé did not approve of it
any more than he did the Italian custom of cooking with oil instead of
butter. All the elite restaurants in New York were French, and Soulé was a
Francophile in the extreme. Working at the Pavillon was for Nicola a
prideful and humbling experience.

Everything about the restaurant bespoke the best and the most expensive—the glassware was Baccarat, the centerpieces vaunted with long-
stemmed roses (three thousand freshly cut roses were inserted every
week), and the restaurant's silver serving wagons, exclusively designed in
Paris with built-in burners and chafing dishes, and equipped with ball
bearings, rolled smoothly along the Pavillon's carpeting and could turn
on a dime. Mr. Soulé was constantly in motion between the dining room
and kitchen, overseeing the cooking and the serving while being assisted
by his cadre of watchful captains and his meticulous and vigilant French
chef. The underlings working at the Pavillon knew well that the condi-
tions there were not very conducive to valising.

During this time, Nicola's fourth year since jumping ship, he was having an affair with an adventuresome and impetuous young woman from
Texas who worked behind the St. Regis's reservation desk. A year later, in
1960, she encouraged him to revisit Italy. She accompanied him on the
trip, and the two of them decided suddenly to get married while visiting
his home village, thus accelerating the process by which he would later

gain his American citizenship. But except for the fact that he and his wife were both working at the St. Regis, they discovered soon enough that they had little else in common, and their period of marital cohabitation lasted only a few years and was characteristically tempestuous. Although they would not get around to finalizing their divorce until the late 1960s, Nicola had moved out of their marital apartment in Queens in 1963 and at the same time severed all connections with the St. Regis. This is when he began working with some regularity at Portofino, owned by his Genoese friend Alfredo Viazzi, and it was there that he became acquainted with Elaine Kaufman, and then subsequently joined her uptown after she had started Elaine's.

But after ten years as her headwaiter, the couple began to disagree on so many matters that Nicola decided in 1974 to quit Elaine's and open a restaurant of his own. He quietly revealed this to me late one evening when I was in the restaurant dining alone and Elaine was in the back, having an after-dinner drink with her playwright friend Jack Richardson and a few others playing backgammon.

I was very upset by Nicola's news.

"You *can't* quit," I said. "This book I'm doing takes place in Elaine's, and you're a main character. You'll both get lots of free publicity when I finish it."

"I can't take her shit anymore," he said. He was leaning over my shoulder, speaking directly into my left ear while clearing the table.

"You *can* take it," I insisted, looking up from my brandy glass, which was half-filled with the green crème de menthe that Elaine had sent over earlier. "You've been sniping at one another every night for ten years. And then you always kiss and make up."

"We'll see," he said, walking off with an armload of dishes.

At the time, I was confident that I had convinced him to remain, at least for a few months. By then, I believed, I could finish my research at Elaine's and concentrate on the writing. What I had in mind varied from week to week, but I always saw the presence of Nicola and Elaine as vital to what I thought I was doing, which was to present in book form the panorama of a place that, in addition to being a restaurant, was also a way station for writers escaping the blank pages of overdue books, and a therapy center for unemployed actors allergic to solitude, and a halfway house for husbands between wives, and a rendezvous spot for men and women who, as evening approached, were not sure with whom they wished to dine, or with whom they wished to sleep after they dined, or even if they wished to sleep. It was a restaurant for insomniacs and the indecisive, a late-night talk show without cameras and microphones or commercial interruptions. Here I saw gangsters, police commissioners, and clergymen ordering dinner at separate tables but on the same night, and here I observed elegantly dressed women walking in with theater programs tucked into their handbags and pausing at the bar while their tuxedoed escorts were being delayed outside by an aggressive pair of panhandlers. I had seen chauffeured moguls making their grand entrances into Elaine's one step ahead of a federal indictment or a skip into Chapter 11, and a porno actress wearing a Laura Ashley dress give a birthday party for her two nieces and their young friends, spending the better part of the evening correcting their table manners. Among the customers at Elaine's had been members of the Beatles, the Black Panthers, the New York Yankees, and Hell's Angels. A young muscleman named Arnold Schwarzenegger came in for dinner one night and presented Elaine with an inscribed copy of the newly published book *Pumping Iron,* in which he was featured. On another occasion, Jackie Gleason walked in, and before joining his friends at a table, he stood behind the bar and entertained the crowd with his famous "Joe the Bartender" routine from his television series. Jazz musicians would stroll in and pound the keys on Elaine's piano, which had a cappuccino machine on top. Elaine's also lured other restaurateurs— Vincent Sardi of Sardi's, Danny Lavezzo of P. J. Clarke's, and Ken Aretsky of the "21" Club—who while eating tried to conceal the fact that their eyes were roving around the room, counting the house.

All these bits and pieces of information were in my notes, along with much more of the same, and sometimes I feared that what I was collecting was too lighthearted and insubstantial for a full-length book— too replete with table-hopping scenes featuring famous people making cameo appearances; it was as if I were interested in adapting my material for a stage review or a musical comedy. I could almost imagine it on Broadway with songs by Stephen Sondheim—A *Funny Thing Happened on the Way to Elaine's,* starring a hefty actress who could sing and dance as gracefully as the lumpish Zero Mostel while surrounded by a chorus of black-tied waiters kicking up their heels and spinning trays above their heads. At other times, I was satisfied with how my research was going, reminding myself that I was progressing as I had when doing books in the past, sucking up massive amounts of trifling details as indiscriminately as a vacuum cleaner, and then later sorting it all out with care.

However, if Nicola Spagnolo left Elaine's to open his own restaurant, I did foresee procedural problems for my work in progress. I could, of course, present the story entirely from Elaine Kaufman's vantage point, doing a full-length portrait of her and her place in the manner that Joseph Wechsberg had done in his book about Henri Soulé and the Pavillon. But then my book might turn out to be more Elaine's than mine, more a biography of her as a famous woman than about me as a writer in search of a story set in the world of a restaurant, the only place where I had witnessed my father being happy.

When Nicola went ahead and quit Elaine's two nights after our talk, infuriating Elaine and making news in the tabloids, I resigned myself to putting the project away for a while, delegating it to the back of my filing cabinet. With the exit of Nicola from my location site, I had lost one of the pair of clashing, colorful characters that I had been counting upon to lend a perception of stability to what was still forming in my mind. I had likened the presence of Elaine and Nicola to two poles supporting my tent show, two ringmasters around whom my rotating cast of characters could revolve, two alter egos through whom I might reflect my views as an outsider in both the mainstream of America and the Italy of my ancestry.

Elaine was a contemporary of mine, the only smart Jewish woman I'd ever met who had an affinity for Italian men. We were both newcomers to Manhattan at the same time, and, though we did not meet until she started Elaine's, we lived a block apart during the mid-1950s in Greenwich Village, hung out in many of the same sawdust-floored bars, attended many of the same poetry readings, listened to the same music on the jukebox, and, remaining residents of the city for the rest of our lives, we similarly appreciated and responded to what E. B. White called "the vibrations of great times and tall deeds."

Nicola Spagnolo was my Italian insider in the restaurant trade, my "down-and-out" Orwellian wanderer whose fugitive lifestyle fascinated me and that as a writer I intended to emulate vicariously. Nicola and I had established a sense of familiarity and kinship shortly after we had first met at Elaine's, and I think this was reinforced by the fact that we strongly resembled each other physically. The regulars at Elaine's often mentioned this, asking if we two were related. Our features and profiles were strikingly similar, both of us having large brown eyes and Roman noses and chiseled cheekbones that gave us, in repose, the brooding, pensive expression often projected in the posed photos of matadors. Our dark hair was graying at the temples in the same place and was thinning equally at the crown as we entered our forties; and in the ten years that followed at Elaine's, neither of us had noticeably gained weight. He commented admiringly on the suits I wore into the restaurant, the tailoring done by my father or my Italian cousin in Paris, and since Nicola was my size, he often reminded me that if I should die before him, he would like to inherit my wardrobe.

Within weeks of his departure from Elaine's, I was on a plane to California to resume my work on what was to become *Thy Neighbor's Wife*. But during my regular visits to New York, I continued to see Elaine Kaufman (her new headwaiter was another Italian she had known from her Village days at Portofino, Elio Guaitolini), and I also remained in contact with Nicola Spagnolo, whose restaurant—Nicola's, at 146 East 84th Street—Elaine found irritatingly close to her own place north of Eighty-eighth, and she also alleged, through her attorney, that Nicola was trying to steal her customers.

Fortunately for him, and a main factor in his successful defense, was the lack of any evidence that he had made overtures to her patrons; he had not mailed them circulars, nor made phone calls, nor otherwise informed them that he was opening a place of his own. What he did do, however, though it was difficult to criminalize, was decorate the walls of Nicola's with framed photographs depicting several of the authors and cultural figures he had met at Elaine's, and like moths to bright light, many of these people were drawn to him, but never in such numbers on any given evening, nor with any consistency in the following months or years, that would threaten the continuing popularity and prosperity of Elaine Kaufman's business. Whatever trade she lost, she replaced with other customers to whom she offered front tables and gratuitous cordials, and, moreover, it was soon clear that the two restaurants functioned differently and were not dependent on the same type of loyal patronage.

Elaine Kaufman's restaurant remained as it had always been—a late-night informal place that reflected the personality of its magisterial mistress. She was the Night Mother, the nurturer of the psychological and dining needs of the Quality Lit set and their accompanying poseurs. Since she enjoyed puffing on cigarettes, her own and other people's, smoking was allowed at the front tables of Elaine's, including cigars; anyone who objected was sent to one of the tables closer to the back, or to an adjacent room that was usually reserved for private parties and was referred to as "Siberia."

Nicola Spagnolo's place, on the other hand, posted NO SMOKING signs and was patronized by a relatively early-to-bed group of achieving people who, more than at Elaine's, were representative of Wall Street, television networks, advertising agencies, fashion magazines, cosmetic surgery, and—until they became the targets of environmentalists and animal activists roaming the sidewalks armed with spray cans—the city's leading furriers and their runway models. Writers were treated as cordially and respectfully by Nicola as they were at Elaine's, but since neither he nor his waiters were regular readers of anything more high-toned than the *Daily Racing Form* and the local tabloids, there was a limit to his ability to enlarge upon his circle of literary customers.

Nicola's career as a proprietor was financially profitable from the start, and he was also now married for a second time and the father of a young son. He had met his second wife, a petite hazel-eyed blonde named Linda, during the early 1960s, when she and her fellow employees from an investment banking firm frequently dined at Portofino. Following his divorce from the Texan, Nicola married Linda in 1968, and after their son was born, she willingly left her job in order to have more time for their home life as well as assisting her husband with the financial management of Nicola's and the outside investments he was making with his share of the profits. The couple occupied a comfortable apartment in a modern high rise on a well-maintained street a few blocks east of the restaurant. As a result of their continuing good fortune throughout the 1970s and into the 1980s, their son grew up in circumstances similar to those of the other privileged children of the neighborhood. As a toddler, he had been doted upon by doormen. During his adolescence, he attended private schools on Manhattan's Upper East Side. After his father had purchased a home near Palm Beach, close to those occupied by some of the entrepreneurs and executives who regularly patronized Nicola's, the boy would become accustomed to winter vacations in the sun.

In 1980, as Nicola Spagnolo celebrated his fifty-third birthday and sixth year as the proprietor of Nicola's, his hair was almost entirely gray and his lean figure an inch thicker in the middle, but he retained his youthful appearance and energy and the conviction that he did not have a worry in the world. His unrelenting optimism and devil-may-care attitude worried Linda at times, although during their courtship these were the very qualities that had attracted her to him, since she believed that recklessness and Pollyannaism were a positive part of his nature. How else could he have jumped ship and landed on his feet? But what had seemed boldly romantic in the past was less appealing now that she had given up her job to devote herself exclusively to their marital life and to maintaining an expensive lifestyle entirely dependent on her husband's sizable but uncertain income. That his restaurant was doing well was a comforting thought, but it was not something that could be taken for granted. She had noticed while walking around town that a few restaurants that had been hugely successful in the past, so popular that every night crowds of people used to stand patiently for a half hour or more waiting for tables, were suddenly and inexplicably out of business. She often reminded her husband of this whenever he returned home complaining—as he regularly did during his eighth and ninth year of running Nicola's—that he was becoming bored with the nightly routine and needed a new and greater challenge. He also admitted to her with a certain reluctance that he was having disagreements with a few of the men who were his partners. The issues were relatively minor, he reassured Linda, and no one was entirely at fault. He attributed it to the middle-aged crankiness of the men involved, including himself, although he remembered that he had felt similarly as a young man when he had been at sea too long working on cruise ships. Being confined for prolonged periods had often unnerved him and everyone around him, he recalled, bringing an edginess and impatience into conversations that otherwise would have been casual and friendly exchanges of ideas. Now these irritable feelings existed in his restaurant, he said, making his relationship with his partners thorny and stressful, and he was ready to leave. The financial rewards could not compensate for the fact that he had been doing basically the same thing in the same place in front of the same crowd almost every night for nearly ten years. The solution was not in working fewer hours, or taking longer vacations, both of which Linda had suggested as a solution; what he needed now, he insisted, was a permanent change. Ten years was his limit in any one place. He had been at Elaine's for ten years. And now he was approaching his tenth year at Nicola's. And furthermore, as he confided to Linda before informing his partners at Nicola's, he had recently found a vacated place in which he thought he could revive his spirit and enthusiasm by starting a *new* restaurant, with fewer partners this time, and with the ultimate goal of succeeding at this particular location, where *two* restaurants had already failed.

This rentable space consisted of the lower two floors and the basement of an old five-story commercial brick building situated within a residential side street in the East Sixties, about twenty blocks downtown from Nicola's. Since the partnership he was abandoning would still own the name Nicola's—and would continue to run the restaurant under that name at 146 East 84th Street into the twenty-first century—Nicola Spagnolo decided that he would call his place Gnolo, inspired by the last five letters of his surname. His new restaurant would be larger than Nicola's. In addition to Gnolo's main dining room on the street level, and the spacious basement that the departed restaurant owners had used for their freezers, wine cellar, and preparatory kitchen, there was a staircase leading up to the second floor, which the two earlier restaurants—Le Premier had been a tenant from September 1977 until December 1978, and the

Bistro Pascal from February 1979 until July 1983—had reserved for private parties, corporate social functions, and as a second public dining room on those rare occasions when the floor below had been overbooked.

While Nicola did not anticipate altering this arrangement, he was confident that the two floors and the basement he was renting would be put to more profitable use than anything imagined by the restaurateurs who had been there before. He had known only success for twenty years, having contributed heavily to it at Elaine's from 1964 to 1974, and at Nicola's from 1974 to 1984; and at Gnolo he would not be shackled with four partners, as he had been at Nicola's. At Gnolo he would have only two—one being his attorney, and the other a gentleman he had first met while waiting on his table at Elaine's, the scion of Harry Winston's jewelry establishment on Fifth Avenue.

After Nicola had signed the lease and made plans to have the place repainted and redecorated in time for Gnolo's opening in the fall of 1984, he telephoned to invite me and my wife to be among his first-night guests in the middle of October. I was glad to accept and looked forward to seeing him again after a lapse of many months. From 1982 through the summer of 1984, I had been living mainly in Italy, researching what would become, seven years hence, *Unto the Sons*. During this period, my visits to New York had been frequent but brief, and I can recall dining at Nicola's place on East Eighty-fourth Street no more than three or four times, which had been sufficient for me to assume that his days there were numbered. He candidly told me that he was restless, displeased with most of his partners, and depressed. I also found him depressing to be around, as he lacked the sprightly spirit I had always associated with him. And therefore I was relieved as well as pleased to hear the ebullience back in his voice when he telephoned me to announce the launching of Gnolo.

"What's the address?" I asked.

"It's on Sixty-third between Second and Third avenues," he said. "It's closer to Third Avenue. The address is Two oh six East Sixty-third."

I was astonished.

"I've been keeping a file on *that* building for twenty-five years!" I exclaimed. "I've often thought of writing about it."

"Well, now's the time," Nicola said.

"It went up as a warehouse about eighty years ago," I went on. "It used to be filled with old bureaus, pianos, and family heirlooms, and there was a stable below for the horses that pulled the moving carts. Later there was a garage for trucks. Then the place was gutted and converted into a five-story commercial building, and the upper floors were rented out as office space to a travel agent, and a studio photographer, and, I think, a shoe importer—and there's also a Gypsy fortune-telling parlor on one of the floors there now. There used to be restaurants on the ground floor that I went to, but they're both out of business now. . . ."

I was boring him, or so I assumed from his interruption at this point.

"Look, I don't care a lot about the horses and other stuff," he said. "All I know is, I'm moving in next month, and it's going to be great."

After he hung up, I reached into my filing cabinet and retrieved what I had been collecting about the building since I had first noticed it during the late 1950s, which was when I drove a sports car around New York (a 1957 Triumph TR-3) and was garaging it directly across the street from 206 East 63rd. I was then researching and writing what would become *New York—A Serendipiter's Journey*, in which I called attention to many of New York's old buildings and obscure people whom I thought characterized survival and perseverance in an ever-changing city. I would have asked the photographer Marvin Lichtner, who was taking pictures for *Serendipiter's Journey*, to take one of the ex-warehouse at 206 East 63rd, but unfortuntely the publisher's deadline in 1961 closed in on me before I could gather enough historical data about it to include it in the book.

Still, it continued to occupy my thoughts as I saw it every day while coming and going from my garage. So in 1964, after I had finished *The Bridge*—which included photos by Bruce Davidson showing the iron-workers in action—I proposed in a memo to my publisher that we do a follow-up book entitled *The Building*, which would present in words and pictures the history of this edifice on Sixty-third Street that had captured my fancy and that (as I suggested in my sales pitch) stood as a monument to American durability and adaptability, having existed from the horse-and-buggy era into the period of motorcars and then into the high-tech time of microchips without a single brick being chipped from its fortress-like facade! There was nothing flimsy about this structure, I emphasized in my memo; it had been solidly constructed during the golden age of brick masonry in America, and the early-twentieth-century artisans who had begun laboring on it in 1906 had obviously taken great pride in their craft even while aware that what they were constructing would be occupied at night only by a dozen ungrateful dray horses. It was my appreciation of the workers' dedication to detail that had initially attracted me to this building, which was designed in the Renaissance style and was fronted with light brown iron-dotted brickwork that was corbeled and frieze-lined and had window arches crowned with keystones and other touches of entablature testifying to many extra hours of early-century effort.

On the inside of the building was a freight elevator that ran along the

interior western wall between the top floor and the ground level, the latter being where, until the late 1940s, the loading and unloading of the
customers' cargo had been done with the aid of horse-powered winches.
The upper four floors were sectioned off into cubicles, each containing
the individual customers' belongings. I was once permitted to tour the
interior after introducing myself as a prospective client, and what I saw as
I ventured from floor to floor were objects that I assumed were expendable
items of sufficient sentimental value, if not actual value, to preserve them
from the junk heap. There were many grandfather clocks, sideboards,
armoires, and sofas. There was also a suit of armor, a spinet, an oil paint-
ing of a white-haired, black-robed magistrate, and a stately large-wheeled
perambulator bearing a croquet set. There were many rolled-up rugs,
stone and marble statuary, candelabra, and a couple of finely crafted oak
wood sleds (Rosebuds?) and some steamer trunks bearing the stickers of
ocean liners no longer afloat.

It also occurred to me that the warehouse served, at least in part, as a
repository for what had been willed and was unwanted. It was where a
younger generation had stowed away the evidence of their rejection of
the inherited tastes and values of their elders. The floors here were the
final resting place for the reupholstered love seats that had once known
familiar contact, care, and affection. This place was now an orphanage for
antique dolls. It was an art gallery for the portraits of departed patriarchs
no longer deemed worthy of family wall space. It was a memory bank
filled with reminders of good and bad times, a vault packed with
redeemable inventory that was traceable to people with stories to tell—
stories that I could tell if my reluctant publisher would eventually endorse
my proposal for The Building.

In my memo I conceded that though this place lacked the imprimatur
of landmark status and was overshadowed by modern skyscrapers reflecting a soaring modern economy, it nonethless stood tall in the annals of
antediluvian stubbornness; it simply refused to erode and disintegrate, and
I was confident that within its cubicles I would find the inspirational
essence of human drama and pathos that would be worthy of public attention. I recalled a line from Arthur Miller's Death of a Salesman, in which
the wife of Willy Loman—a man whose best days are behind him and is
disrespected by his sons—excoriates these sons, reminding them that their
father is a worthy human being, one to whom "attention must be paid."
And she insisted further: "He's not to be allowed to fall into his grave like
an old dog. Attention, attention must be finally paid to such a person. . . ."

I saw this old warehouse on Sixty-third Street as the Willy Loman of
buildings in New York.

9

THE FIRST OWNER OF THE BUILDING WAS A STOUT AND AUTO-
cratic man named Frederick J. Schillinger, a German-born furniture mover who died in New York at seventy-two in 1927 and
whom I tried to revive whenever I sat thinking about him and trying to
write about him at my desk.

Sometimes I looked up to study several fading sepia photographs of
him that were pinned to my bulletin board. In the clearest and most
detailed of these, Schillinger was shown standing on the sidewalk with
apparent satisfaction in front of his then newly opened five-story warehouse at 206 East 63rd Street. The photo was taken on a wintry day in
1907, and except for the absence of the advertising signs that were
then affixed to the brick-walled exterior—signs reading SCHILLINGER'S
STORAGE: *Furniture Packed and Shipped . . . Pianos and Safes Moved and
Hoisted*—the building today is unchanged in its outward appearance.

When he posed for the picture in 1907, Frederick J. Schillinger was
fifty-two, gray-haired, square-jawed, mustachioed, and quite distinguished
in attire. A black bowler rested on his broad head, a dark tie fronted his
white shirt and was knotted triangularly under his chin, and covering his
thick chest and his muscular furniture-lifting arms and shoulders and
extending below the knees of his dark trousers was a velvet-collared gray
chesterfield overcoat. While it might be supposed that this man in the
moving business who carried a scent of horses was dressed as he was in
order to appear fashionable in the photograph, I was told by some of his
elderly grandchildren and other relatives who had given me the pictures
that he was always clothes-conscious and also somewhat vain and
pompous. He was a man who emulated the stodgy manners of the butlers
who too often kept him waiting in the vestibules of the large East Side
homes to which he and his workmen were summoned to carry away furniture that could not be accommodated in the more modest living quarters
that his no-longer-rich clientele would soon be compelled to occupy.

To Schillinger's right in the photograph, parked under the uplifted paneled doors leading into the stable, was one of his high-roofed padded vans with three of his employees sitting forward on the carriage bench, holding the reins of a pair of chestnut-colored horses paused with their hoofs flat on the sloping sidewalk. In the background stood his ornate warehouse, designed by a Bronx architect named Fred Hammond, and built at a cost of twenty thousand dollars on the south side of Sixty-third, which was then a noisy and trembling street darkened all day by the shadows of the elevated tracks that reverberated up and down Second and Third avenues. Schillinger himself resided in a quieter neighborhood six blocks uptown, in a four-story brownstone at 340 East 69th Street, occupying it with his wife, Eliza, and their four children and some of his wife's relatives. His older children and his in-laws assisted him in performing administrative or secretarial chores in his warehouse, and they accompanied him daily to and from work on foot, doing so along Second Avenue's cobblestone sidewalks and unpaved streets, which were enshrouded with the lattice-patterned shadows formed by the elevated tracks and structure of the overhead railway. Although electric traction cars had replaced steam engines a few years before, in 1902, the fabric awnings of some of the avenue's shops still displayed burn holes formed by blazing bits of coal that had come flying down from the older trains, and nearly all the buildings in the neighborhood were darkened by varying shades of soot.

When the Schillinger warehouse opened for business in 1907, it was the newest addition to a block that had long catered to the household and personal needs of those wealthier New Yorkers who dwelled westward, closer to Fifth Avenue and Central Park. Here, on this service street between Second and Third avenues on Sixty-third, Mr. Schillinger's neighbors included a beer-bottling plant, a wholesale baking factory, a lumberyard, a carriage manufacturer, the workshop and family apartment of a blacksmith (the current site of Bravo Gianni restaurant at 230 East 63rd), and a massive dark-bricked four-story public school building—P.S. 74, its enrollment primarily made up of Irish and German immigrant children who had been pressured by truant officers into regular attendance partly as a result of the rising antipathy within the city toward child labor.

Across the street from the warehouse was a vacant lot that would presently become the site of the rumpside annex of the Manhattan Eye, Ear & Throat Hospital, which fronted on Sixty-fourth Street. Frederick Schillinger's most friendly and accommodating neighbors on his side of the street, next to the school, were the proprietors of a piano factory, who accorded him exclusive delivery rights to the department stores and other retail outlets that sold their products, and also to their special customers (such as concert performers) who received pianos directly at reduced prices, or even gratis if they were very famous.

If anyone had cornered the piano-moving market in New York City in the early twentieth century, it was probably Frederick J. Schillinger. He had earlier received introductions to pianists and to shop owners and manufacturers from his wife Eliza's parents and other relatives who owned and operated a small factory that manufactured keyboard parts near Times Square, then called Longacre Square. The factory was well known to members of New York's musical community, and Eliza herself, throughout her courtship and the early years of her marriage to Frederick J. Schillinger (himself an able violinist), made certain that all of her family's clients and friends with pianos to be moved were aware of his capabilities.

Eliza and Frederick's three daughters and one son, Fred junior, were excellent piano players, although the girls became more accomplished as light classical singers on New York's radio station WEAF (one of them also sang in the Metropolitan Opera's chorus), while young Fred's musical talents were most conspiciously noticed at his father's warehouse after he had begun working there in 1920, having just graduated without honors from high school and with no ambition to go to college. He did not like working in the warehouse, either, but he did enjoy serenading his fellow employees at the keyboard while they were pushing pianos in and out of moving vans.

Since no other family member would agree to take over the warehouse following the elder Schillinger's death in 1927 of bronchopneumonia, Fred junior became his father's successor by default, and while he would gradually replace the horses with trucks, he did little else during the next twenty-five years to keep pace with his rivals in the small but very competitive furniture-moving and storage business in New York.

"He slowly ran his father's business into the ground," I was later told by Fred junior's wife and widow, Charlotte Schillinger, who added that in 1952 he was grateful to dispense with the entire five-story building for the low price of $64,200.

The man who bought the building, and continued to operate it for the next twenty years as a storage and moving business, was an Italian-American named Frank Catalano, a short, balding, and compactly built individual in his late forties who had successfully owned and managed other warehouses in New York and who wasted no time in revitalizing the trade at 206 East 63rd Street after he had removed all the advertising signs bearing the name Schillinger. The building was now the site of Dard's Express and Van Co.

The new owner named it Dard in memory of his grandfather, Dardinello Catalano, who had been born and reared in the hills of Calabria, not far from my own family's ancestral village. A son of Dardinello Catalano who was named Salvatore left Italy at twenty-three to work as a coal miner near Pittsburgh. But within ten years, Salvatore Catalano's ailing lungs made it impossible for him to continue with his job in the mines, and so he left the Pittsburgh area for New York, where he found work as a laborer with a construction company. A disabling injury a few years later forced Salvatore to quit and begin earning his living as the proprietor of a fruit and vegetable store near the East River on Forty-ninth Street. In the neighborhood, he met and would soon marry an Italian-American woman with whom, during the next decade and a half, he would have nine children. The second of these, a son born in 1914, would prove to be the most energetic and resourceful, Frank Catalano.

As a child, when Frank was not helping his father in the store, he was on the sidewalks shining shoes in front of the Grand Central Post Office. As a young teenager, Frank rose daily at dawn to drive a horse and wagon downtown to fetch the produce for his father's store before going on to class at Public School 135 on Fifty-first Street and First Avenue. During the 1930s, after persuading his father that the high cost of purchasing a truck was a prudent investment because of its time-saving value, Frank put the produce truck to use during his off-hours from the store by moonlighting as a furniture mover. Within a few years, while taking night courses to complete his high school education, Frank Catalano was buying trucks on his own, and employing his younger brothers and sisters to help with his moving and storage business, which was initially centered within a warehouse on East Forty-ninth Street. In 1952, needing more space and knowing about the mismanaged warehouse belonging to Fred Schillinger, Jr., Frank Catalano paid him a visit and found him more than eager to sell.

After I had moved into the neighborhood, I would sometimes see Frank Catalano helping his men as they loaded or unloaded trucks behind the opened paneled doors, and once I ventured in to introduce myself and tell him about my interest in his building. He was reluctant to talk to me, and I did not press him. But I continued to see him and to acknowledge him with a few friendly words or a wave while walking to my then girlfriend Nan's apartment, which was located on Sixty-third Street east of Second Avenue; and in 1959, after we had gotten married and began exploring the city together in my aggressively stylish, sleek white TR-3— an English sports car I bought secondhand but have maintained and continue to drive today—I parked it directly across the street from Frank

Catalano's warehouse in an underground garage where the monthly rates were low but where my low-slung vehicle was often nicked or dented by one of the wiry, wine-drinking attendants as they backed into my fenders and headlights while maneuvering larger cars with higher bumpers. It was impossible to accuse anyone, since I could never identify who was at fault, although I did complain constantly and futilely to the management about the abuse being rendered upon my beloved TR-3, whose every dent was like a hole in my heart.

One warm autumn afternoon in 1963, after I had arrived at the garage and had lowered and snapped my car's canvas top down, I noticed that one of the red plastic taillight covers mounted to the back fender had been smashed, and it was the third time this had happened in recent weeks. I always stored extra taillights and covers in the trunk in anticipation of their breakage, but for some reason on this occasion—though the fender itself was not damaged—I succumbed to rage. Unable to direct my frustration at the garage attendants, since none was in view, I turned toward a metal trash can that stood in front of a concrete post and kicked the can halfway across the floor of the garage, hurting my foot.

Limping into my car and turning on the ignition, I began to gun the motor and discharge noxious puffs of dark smoke from the exhaust pipe. Then I shoved the wooden knob of my stick shift into first gear and roared up the ramp with my horn honking, alerting any and all pedestrians above that I was to be reckoned with. Arriving on the sidewalk, I saw to my left a fast-approaching garbage truck that would have blown me away had I kept going, and so I slammed my ailing foot down on the brake pedal and skidded to a stop at the curb. Close behind the garbage truck were other vehicles that were soon blurring past my windshield—taxis, limos, buses, private sedans, and vans, many of them coming from the Sixty-third Street exit of the FDR Drive along the East River and all of them now churning forward almost bumper-to-bumper on this wide westbound one-way street toward Third Avenue.

I waited impatiently at the curb, gunning my motor but unable to advance. Looking directly across the street, I saw Frank Catalano's tan brick warehouse with its doors closed and no one in sight. This was one of the few old buildings still here since the era of the elder Schillinger, and it appeared to be very small and anachronistic and fuzzy as it stood in the midafternoon duskiness of this street now being polluted by passing motorists and dominated by soaring rows of white brick modern high-rise apartment houses that cast deeper and darker shadows than had been the case when elevated trains had hovered over Second and Third avenues. Thousands of people now resided on this block, paying high fees to live in terraced apartments as high as possible, and as remotely as possible, from the horn-honking traffic and grime below. There were no cafés, no dress boutiques, no fine shops of any kind on either side of the street, and therefore no incentives for window-shoppers nor diversions for strollers. The only person I saw on the sidewalk as I sat drumming my fingers on the steering wheel while inhaling the foul air that matched my mood was a uniformed doorman who stood some yards away, close to the curb, smoking a cigarette beyond the range of the security cameras posted in the lobby of his large apartment building at 205 East 63rd Street, near the corner of Third Avenue.

Then I heard a voice calling out to me, coming from somewhere behind my car. Turning, I saw a short, round-faced man standing near the rear fender, the one with the smashed taillight cover. He was wearing a yellow peaked cap and a dark windbreaker, and in his left hand he was carrying a fishing rod. It was Frank Catalano.

"You gotta take it *easy*," he said, slowly shaking his head, but he spoke in a manner that was more avuncular than admonishing. Embarrassed by the thought that he had seen me at my worst, foolishly enraged because someone had cracked an inexpensive and replaceable piece of plastic, I sat and said nothing.

"You're young yet," he went on. "Whatever it is, you shouldn't let it get to you. . . ."

Carefully laying down his fishing rod near the edge of the sidewalk, Frank Catalano walked in front of my car and assumed the posture of a crossing guard, raising his arms high and gesturing with his hands for the traffic to halt. After it did, he nodded in my direction.

"Okay," he said, keeping both arms raised, "it's your turn."

As I pulled out into the street, spun to the right, and passed him, I heard him say, "I like your car."

"Thanks, Frank," I replied, calling him by name for the first time.

In 1973, as Frank Catalano anticipated turning sixty, although it would not happen until the following year, he decided to quit the moving business. He and his wife, who had served as his bookkeeper, had more than enough money to live comfortably in Florida for the rest of their lives, and their two college-educated children were now both self-supporting, married, and residing far from New York City. Their daughter, Luanne, was a homemaker in Michigan, and their son, Frank Catalano, Jr., was an attorney in Oklahoma. What the elder Catalano now wanted to do was not retire from work but, rather, embark upon a new career that would allow him to do full-time what he liked to do best—go fishing. He would operate a charter-boat business in Key West, Florida, and spend his days as a seafaring captain and fishing guide. For many years he had regularly taken time off from the warehouse to drift in the currents of the East Coast and the Caribbean, and one day while angling in the Point Judith fishing grounds near Galilee, Rhode Island, he struggled with his catch for nearly two hours before hauling in a 746-pound, ten-foot-long tuna. A photograph of him posing next to the hanging fish appeared in *Movers News*, a publication sponsored by the New York City Movers Association, which had elected Frank Catalano to serve three terms as its president.

Although he terminated his business on Sixty-third Street in 1973, it was never his intention to sell the building outright; he would retain it as a rental property, and eventually it would be inherited by his daughter and son. Meanwhile, he turned over the empty warehouse to a real estate firm, which in turn leased it to a lanky, blond, wealthy twenty-seven-year-old land developer from Sarasota, Florida, J. Z. Morris, son of multimillionaire Robert Morris, who had financed the construction of many shopping centers and condominiums in western Florida after making a fortune in the grain business in his native Indiana.

His son J.Z. (for Joseph Zol) grew up in New Harmony, Indiana, where he was flying solo in his own plane at sixteen. Following his graduation from Indiana University in 1969, he moved to the Caribbean island of Jamaica, where in the early 1970s he completed a development project along the six-mile beachfront of Negril. In 1973, during a prolonged stay in New York, and while ambling along Sixty-third Street one day, he noticed the rental sign on Frank Catalano's warehouse and telephoned the leasing agent. After receiving permission to inspect the premises, he detected a not unpleasant equestrian fragrance rising through the dank and hollow interior of the building, and he observed the sheen that had been formed by horses' bodies rubbing along the wooden sides of the freight elevator that carried him from floor to floor. He was charmed by the place. And since he could obtain possession of it for an initial sum of $65,000, plus an annual rent of $20,000 to Catalano that guaranteed a long lease and a renewal agreement—and since J. Z. Morris also had no pressing financial problems at the time—he assumed control over the property in a leisurely manner, making little use of it for the next two and a half years except when parking his Rolls-Royce behind the paneled doors of Catalano's onetime garage on the ground floor.

In 1976, J. Z. Morris hired a construction crew at a cost of about $700,000 to gut the interior of the property and make the upper three floors rentable as offices or studio apartments. He sublet the lower two floors and basement to a restaurant partnership for an annual sum of

$46,000; the partners had the intention of transforming it into an elegant Art Deco dining duplex they would call Le Premier. The restaurant partnership was also committed to spending an additional $1.5 million on reconstruction, renovation, and the removal of the freight elevator, which it would subsequently replace with a kaleidoscopic brass-railed staircase that would connect the upper and lower dining areas. The main dining room on ground level—once having borne the weight of trucks and horses—would eventually become resplendent with polished mahogany floors, and the room would be enclosed with salmon-colored walls and a five-tiered ceiling emitting soft beams of pinkish light. Delicate lace curtains embroidered with peacocks would cover the large front window that faced the sidewalk—a window as wide as the paneled doors it had replaced—and the tables would be surrounded by pearl gray suede-covered chairs and banquettes. An antique hand-carved bar imported from Paris would be positioned along the eastern wall behind the laced peacocks, while other walls would be adorned by female figures posed coquettishly within stained-glass Art Deco mirrors.

Upstairs, the theme would be replicated, with Art Deco pendant lights hanging from the ceiling, and the walls decorated with murals including one showing a loose-gowned eighteenth-century woman frolicking in the woods with a satyr and other mythical creatures of obviously lecherous intentions. There would be fewer tables upstairs than on the floor below because the second floor was to function as a kind of club, with dues-paying diners having access not only to more privacy but also to a small room in which they could play backgammon or cards, and that would contain humidified lockers in which members could store their cigars and smoke them in the second floor's piano bar.

After the freight elevator had been removed, J. Z. Morris was obliged to install an enclosed staircase along the western edge of the building, to be used by his tenants who were renting space on either the third, fourth, or fifth floors. He himself temporarily moved into the fifth floor, establishing a small office and a pied-à-terre, and decorating it in a style that unavoidably drew attention from many of his Sixty-third Street neighbors. A delivery truck arrived one afternoon carrying a glass cockpit and the wingless silver fuselage of a World War II naval fighter plane that he had purchased from a salvage company in Maine with the idea of utilizing the truncated plane as a combination objet d'art and telephone booth in his office. Among the observers who stood watching along the sidewalk as the fuselage was hauled up by cable along the front of the building to the roof, from which it was lowered through a large hole onto the fifth floor, was a beautiful young Chinese woman who decided that she now had a neighbor who was sufficiently eccentric and financially well-off to justify her interest.

Her name was Jackie Ho. She occupied a penthouse apartment in a modern building a few doors east of the warehouse. She was a slender, athletic woman of twenty-six who spent two hours of every afternoon in an East Side gym when she was not spending similar amounts of time in a gym in Hong Kong. She regularly traveled back and forth between the two cities. She had been born in Hong Kong in 1950 to a Chinese family from Canton, and from her hillside home in Hong Kong, overlooking the harbor, she was within walking distance of her rental properties, from which she earned a hefty income. When she was not in Hong Kong or New York, she often indulged her passion for skiing and the après-ski life—in Austria, Switzerland, and Chile—in the company of such men as the son of a leading German industrialist, a jet-setting French financier, and King Hussein of Jordan. An occasional dinner companion of hers prior to her dating J. Z. Morris was the onetime vice president of the United States, Spiro T. Agnew, who often visited Asia as a business consultant after leaving office. She had dined in New York with Agnew at La Grenouille on the evening before she had seen Morris standing on the sidewalk with the truck men as they unloaded the fuselage. Jackie Ho was subsequently introduced to J. Z. Morris at a cocktail party held in the Sixty-third Street apartment of an Argentine woman who helped run Valentino's shop on Fifth Avenue, where Jackie bought her dresses. Two years later, in 1979, Jackie Ho and J. Z. Morris were married. At the same time, since he continued to conduct most of his business from Sarasota, Jackie Ho became his rent collector and manager for the building at 206 East 63rd, where, should anyone be tardy with the rent, she would react with the cantankerous temperament for which Cantonese women are renowned and dreaded.

When Le Premier held its gala opening in mid-September 1977, Jackie Ho was in Hong Kong, but J. Z. Morris was there along with two hundred other guests, including myself. While I did not meet Morris on this occasion, I did shake hands with the restaurant's principal owner, a suave and handsome dark-haired man of twenty-eight from Grenoble named Robert Pascal. The latter stood in the front of the main dining room, posing for photographers with an arm around his girlfriend, the Princess Yasmin Aga Khan, daughter of Aly Khan and the movie star Rita Hayworth.

"Oh, this is going to be a *massacre*," Robert Pascal called out to a crowd of well-wishers, and by this he meant that he was about to slay New York's dining public and his rival restaurateurs with the seductive power of Le Premier's cuisine, and the allure of its ambience, and surely the presence of such appealing women as his current companion. Robert Pascal, as I would get to know him in the weeks and months ahead, was never lacking in assuredness and audacity.

But the "massacre" he had envisioned on opening night was hardly what he later got when the reviews by the food critics began to appear in print. They generally castigated the work of the cooks he had hired and accused his waiters of being haughty and negligent, and, in the words of the *Times*'s Mimi Sheraton, the female figures depicted in the wall murals were "whimsically pornographic" in a way that some patrons "may well find embarrassing if not downright insulting." Invoking the *Times*'s four-star rating system, she gave only one star to Le Premier, calling its wine list "outrageously overpriced," the cold fish pâté "rubbery and bland," the quail "slightly overcooked," and the poached bass "strangely dense and hard," having "a slight petroleum oil taste that came through despite its excellent sauce." She also criticized the restaurant's policy of serving dinner either at 7:00 or 9:30 p.m. This "tyranny of two seatings," she said, was being imposed for the convenience of the proprietor rather than that of the patrons, and she also observed that the proprietor and a few of his waiters were in need of a closer shave. Robert Pascal's choice in table appointments also disappointed her; instead of drinking wine in glasses with rounded edges, she would have preferred cut-edged goblets that were more expensive but more delicate and harmonious with the restaurant's high prices. "Sugar was also presented as wrapped cubes and in paper packets," she noted, and while "tidier perhaps for waiters," it was unacceptable in a place where "elegance is obviously the name of the game."

The unfavorable review in the *Times* disturbed as well as surprised Pascal, for among his satisfied customers during Le Premier's first month of operation was the publisher of the *New York Times,* Arthur Ochs Sulzberger, and the publisher's special assistant, Sydney Gruson. Gruson had first met Pascal while patronizing the latter's older restaurant farther uptown—Chez Pascal, at 151 East 82nd—and it was Gruson who had introduced Sulzberger to Le Premier; and since Mimi Sheraton at this point had not yet reviewed it, Gruson promised Pascal that he would see her in the office and put in a good word about Le Premier's food and the decor and suggest that she stop in at her earliest convenience.

During the ensuing weeks, she appeared on three occasions, once for lunch and twice for dinner. Since the table reservations had always been made in the name of one of her accompanying friends, neither Robert Pascal nor his staff was aware of Mimi Sheraton's presence, nor did Pascal have any idea what Gruson might have said to her, if indeed he *had* actually gone ahead and approached her. As Robert Pascal later explained to me—a few days after the printing of her review—he could well understand her resentment *if* she had gotten the impression from Gruson that he had been trying to influence her integrity as a critic.

In any case, her review in the *Times* did great damage to his restaurant, cutting business in half almost immediately, and prompting his partners—who now saw their huge investment going down the drain of Le Premier's newly installed pipes—to sue Mimi Sheraton for slander. She had overstepped her legal rights with regard to fair comment, they concluded, and now no amount of advertising on their part could offset the effect of what she had written in the all-powerful *Times*. Robert Pascal, however, vetoed their proposal to sue. It would only draw more attention to her review, he said, and furthermore, he believed that Le Premier could survive, as Broadway shows sometimes survived, the initial wrath of even critics from the *Times*.

But as his business failed to improve throughout 1977 and 1978, and as Gruson and Sulzberger no longer came to dine, and as the Princess Yasmin Aga Khan drifted out of his life amicably but forever, and as he could not attract additional customers even after reducing the food and beverage prices and removing the most erotic of the "whimsically pornographic" murals from the walls, Robert Pascal finally decided, in December 1978, to relinquish his authority over Le Premier. He and his backers agreed, for a sum of $800,000, to turn over the restaurant, its fixtures and its furniture, and the eight years that remained on its ten-year lease, to a new group of investors headed by a specialist in tax shelters.

The restaurant would be renamed Bistro Pascal, with Robert Pascal expected to stay on as a greeter and consultant; but he would show up infrequently after the change in management had been completed in January 1979. Never one to linger long in places where he was not in charge, and always convinced that he would sooner or later meet new risk-taking financiers who would be swayed by his irrepressible optimism and would bankroll his next bold adventure, Robert Pascal was suddenly back in the money in 1980 with a hit restaurant in New York. It was located on the site of a former steak house at 334 East 74th Street, and, like the French play and the film that had inspired its name—*La Cage aux Folles*—its theme and artifice were centered on transvestism. Pascal's waiters wore dresses, and the male singers who entertained the dinner crowd were female impersonators representing well-known movie actresses and other show business personalities.

The idea of starting such a restaurant occurred to Pascal one afternoon when, not long after the closing of Le Premier, he was alone in a New York movie theater seeing the French farce for the third or fourth time (it had been voted the best foreign film of 1979 and had earned an Oscar nomination for its director). Each time he saw it, Pascal was overwhelmed by the hilarious and zany performances of the two leading characters on the screen—one of whom, the French actor Michel Serrault, portrayed an aging transvestite, while the latter's young drag queen partner was played by the Italian movie star Ugo Tognazzi.

After Pascal had urged some of his affluent New York friends to see *La Cage aux Folles*, and after they had reported back their enthusiasm for the film's wit and wisdom, he sold them on the idea of backing his restaurant rendition of *La Cage aux Folles*. It opened in New York in November 1980, and during the following spring, encouraged by the restaurant's success, the Pascal partnership launched a La Cage aux Folles in the West Hollywood section of Los Angeles. Subsequently, there would be La Cage restaurants in San Francisco, Toronto, Atlantic City, Las Vegas, and Miami Beach.

Pascal was active only in the Miami Beach franchise after selling out his share in the Los Angeles Cage in 1982. At this time he was suffering from throat cancer, and his doctor warned him that if he did not eschew cigarettes (Pascal was smoking three packs a day), he would be dead within a year. Though he was then in his early thirties, he decided that he liked cigarettes more than he feared dying young; so he kept smoking and he lived on for decades, entering the twenty-first century with a raspy voice but otherwise as talkative and persuasive as ever.

After relocating himself permanently in Miami in the mid-1980s, he would meet and marry a wealthy divorcée who was a designer of flashy fashion (best known for her crystal rhinestone sweatshirts), and Pascal would also find financing for several new restaurants in and around Miami Beach—Villa Pascal, Pascal's Pascal, and, among others, La Voile Rouge (The Red Sail), which he named in honor of La Voile Rouge in Saint-Tropez, a topless beach club where he had begun his career as a teenage waiter.

Meanwhile, the New York restaurant at 206 East 63rd Street that bore his name, if not his presence and interest—the Bistro Pascal—had gone out of business in July 1983. I had patronized it once or twice after Pascal had sold it, and I assumed, since there was little else to recommend it, that it had remained open for two and a half years because it satisfied the hunger of its tax-shelter partnership for write-offs. Then, in the late summer of 1984, after the Bistro Pascal floor space had been vacated for about a year, my friend Nicola Spagnolo learned about it—and, over the angry and anguished reaction of his wife, Linda, he decided it would become the locale of his forthcoming Gnolo.

"Linda says the place has bad karma," Nicola told me over the phone in the fall of 1984, five weeks before Gnolo's scheduled opening. "I made the mistake of letting her see the place before we fixed it up." I later learned from Linda that she had gone several times to 206 East 63rd Street while it was being renovated and repainted, pleading constantly with her husband and his partners to cancel their plans, to annul the lease and thus avoid the financial disaster that she foresaw there.

"What do *you* know about restaurants?" Nicola had asked with irritation after she had interrupted one of his meetings with the decorators.

"I'm telling you, I have premonitions about this place," she said.

"Well, why don't you go upstairs and get a job with the fortune-tellers on the third floor?" he responded, adding, "Look, I've been in restaurants all my life, and you *don't* know what you're talking about. . . ."

While it was true that she could not articulate her trepidation, it was also true, as she explained to me, that she had never been more sure about anything in her life: Her husband was headed for a fall, and she had sensed this almost immediately after her initial visit to 206 East 63rd. Although it had been a sunny afternoon as she and her husband had stepped out of the taxicab, the old brick building itself was overcast in the shadows of the high-rises; and while he and his workmen gathered around the bar to examine the floor plans, she wandered off by herself through the aisles of the dust-covered dining room, which was dimly lit by low-wattage bulbs and was reflected murkily in the smoked-glass mirrors left hanging by the departed souls of the Bistro Pascal. All around her were upturned chairs stacked atop tables, crate boxes filled with plates, and, on the upper rung of a wooden ladder, a white telephone with its cords cut. No amount of remodeling or renovating would alter her low opinion of this place, and what also bothered her was what she had seen outside—the sun-blocked sidewalk, the scarcity of shops, the sterile architecture of the modern buildings that lined the street, and the reckless pace of the speedy motorists heading west along Sixty-third Street toward Third Avenue; one of them had nearly crashed into the back of the taxicab that she and Nicola had ridden in on their way here. Unlike her residential area in the East Eighties, this part of Sixty-third Street lacked neighborliness, and, as she asked herself, how could her husband expect to establish a successful restaurant on a one-way street that was a motorists' speedway and was unappealing to pedestrians?

She had questioned Nicola about this on the way home, but he had paid little attention. He insisted that 206 East 63rd represented a rare opportunity, and he reminded her that many of New York's most appealing restaurants existed in unappealing neighborhoods. He recalled that when Elaine Kaufman introduced her place on Second Avenue near Eighty-eighth Street, it was said that she would fail because it was in a remote and run-down area, along a heavily trafficked one-way street. He also pointed out that a family-style Italian restaurant called Rao's had prospered for more than eighty years in *Harlem*. It is not the *neighborhood* that influences the fate of a restaurant, he instructed his wife, but, rather, the *neighborliness* of the restaurant, the welcoming personality of the owner, and the romantic aura exuding throughout the premises while dinner is being served. Yes, Linda had agreed, but what if that romantic aura is star-crossed or jinxed? What if there is something inherently *wrong* with 206 East 63rd Street that no restaurateur can fix?

"Oh, she won't let up," Nicola told me on the phone a few days before Gnolo's opening. "Linda's Jewish, but she sounds like those Italians I grew up with and left behind in the Old Country. They were always seeing the dark side, always having bad premonitions. Except for people like Linda, the Italians are the most pessimistic people in the world."

"Yes," I said, "my father used to say that," explaining that in his part of Italy the people are so concentrated on the possibility of adversity, are so spooked by the idea of this powerful spirit of misfortune, that they have a name for it. They call it the *Jettatura*. It is their "patron saint" of bad luck. It is the prophet that nobody prays to, that everyone loathes, and that remains omnipresent in their lives.

I was probably telling Nicola more than he wanted to know, but since he did not interrupt, and since I myself was not so emancipated from my Italian heritage to risk debunking the stature of the *Jettatura*, I related more of what my father had told me about this odious spirit. It had risen to prominence during the Dark Ages in southern Italy, evolving out of medieval Catholic mysticism, and it easily perpetuated itself through subsequent centuries marked by plagues, earthquakes, droughts, famines, barbarous invasions, and other abominations and vexations that gradually established a gloom-ridden, amulet-addicted society that dreaded nothing more than more of the *Jettatura*.

"Okay, enough of this crap," Nicola finally said, cutting in. "It's all nonsense. And I won't let you or Linda mess up my head with this stuff."

"That wasn't my intention," I said.

"I don't care," Nicola said. "I'm in America now, and I couldn't care less about your *Jettatura*, or Linda's Jewish *Jettatura*. All I know is that within a few days I'm opening up my new restaurant on Sixty-third Street. And everything's going to be great."

10

WHILE IT LACKED THE FLAMBOYANCE OF THE INTRODUCTORY party to Le Premier that I attended in 1977—a black-tie event where most of the guests arrived by limousine—the first-nighters who went by taxi or on foot to Gnolo in early December 1984 were, in my opinion, a less trendy group of restaurantgoers, who were beyond being dictated to by food critics and who, having a long-standing relationship with Nicola Spagnolo going back to his days at Elaine's, would now support him in his quest for a bright future in this darkly shadowed building at 206 East 63rd Street.

Nan and I had a good time at the opening of Gnolo. I was particularly impressed by how cheerful Linda seemed to be, smiling as she stood next to her husband near the entranceway, welcoming more than one hundred old friends and acquaintances. Nicola could barely contain his excitement, vigorously shaking hands and often kissing people on both cheeks; and yet, energized as he undoubtedly was by the surrounding goodwill and merriment, I doubted that he would ever allow himself to be carried away by excessive confidence and repeat the mistakes that Robert Pascal had previously made at 206 East 63rd Street.

Shortly after Pascal had opened Le Premier in 1977, someone had stolen the restaurant's name plate from the front of the building, signaling the beginning of Pascal's identity problems at this address. He gave the impression not only that his establishment aimed to please the city's epicureans and the beautiful people but that it was probably beyond the appreciation and means of the neighborhood's residents. He was also presumptuous in labeling Le Premier a top-notch restaurant *before* the food critics had gotten around to judging it for themselves. In his opening-day advertising he boasted that Le Premier was "the finest restaurant on this side of the Atlantic," and he pointed out as well that the second-floor dining area was "designed to cater to the tastes of only 500 preferred customers," who would have access to the reservation manager's unlisted phone numbers. When these preferred customers started going to Le Premier, they usually did so in limousines driven by chauffeurs who were used to double-parking and waiting for hours while their employers had dinner. This caused much congestion, of course, inciting endless horn honking from other motorists backed up in traffic jams and disturbing the dwellers in the apartment buildings, prompting their angry calls to the precinct house and their growing disenchantment with the existence of Le Premier.

But the crowd that Robert Pascal catered to—the perk-privileged CEOs, the international financiers, the jet-setters whom he could flatter in any of four languages, and regularly did—also required the reassurance that they were dining in the right place, and when the *New York Times* critic condemned the restaurant, they abandoned it. I felt sure that the Gnolo crowd would not have reacted in this manner; they were more intellectual, more independently minded, more like the customers Nicola had gotten to know at Elaine's. If Mimi Sheraton had written that Elaine's served the worst food in New York and that rats were running loose in the kitchen, I doubt that she would have drawn away a single customer. In fact, I recall reading a news article in the *Times* about Elaine's being cited for violations by New York City health inspectors, and that night every table was occupied.

The decor of Gnolo was as simple and basic as that at Elaine's, although Nicola refrained from adorning his beige-colored walls with photographs of writers or other people he had first met at Elaine's. He did not want to hear again from Elaine Kaufman's attorney. The opening of Gnolo in late October was sooner than Nicola might have preferred, since not all the remodeling had been completed. But at the suggestion of one of his partners, he pressed the workmen to get the place ready for the holiday season in the interest of drawing diners from among the Christmas shoppers and also to make Gnolo available for the office parties that some of his partners' acquaintances in the business world had promised to hold on the second floor.

The pre-Christmas opening turned out to be a very profitable decision. The restaurant was filled to capacity almost every night, being patronized frequently by many of Elaine's regulars, including myself; and Nicola's wife, Linda—who could gauge the restaurant's success because she kept the books—was ready to forget her premonitions and concede that her husband seemed to know what he was doing. By mid-December, however, a week or so before Christmas, Linda was not so sure. The first of what would be a number of unfortunate incidents occurred when a drunken man, while attending an office party on the second floor, toppled through the open door of the dumbwaiter—which was in the process of being rebuilt—and came crashing down through the chute onto a tile counter in the first-floor kitchen. He broke a few bones and damaged his spine, and on the following morning his attorney informed Nicola of an impending lawsuit for negligence.

That night, the holiday spirit was further dampened when a Gypsy fortune-teller on the third floor, after turning on her bathtub water, forgot about it and left her apartment to do an errand. During her prolonged absence, the building's side-wall staircase resembled a waterfall, and as one of Nicola's soggy-shoed waiters banged loudly on her locked door, water began to stream down from the second floor onto the first floor of the restaurant. As the moistened customers in the main dining room hastened from their seats, hollering and gesturing, a kitchen worker who did not understand English activated the fire alarm and sprinkler system, and so torrents of additional water were released, forcing everyone outdoors, including Nicola and Linda. The arrival of the fire trucks on Sixty-third Street led to mile-long traffic jams, much horn honking, residential unrest, and, subsequently, the eviction of the Gypsy fortune-telling family, which had been occupying the third floor at night illegally. The cost of the many unpaid-for dinners was probably the least of Nicola's expenses, since he lost considerably more as a result of having to close Gnolo for several days while the damage was dealt with, depriving the restaurant of what was left of the holiday business.

In the interim, Linda tried to encourage her husband in his desire and efforts to overcome these deterrents. The walls were repainted in brighter colors. Newly bought modern-art posters replaced those that had been ruined. The chairs that had been broken by the exiting crowd were repaired or replaced. When Gnolo reopened in January 1985, most of the usual crowd of customers returned, but not with the ongoing fidelity that Nicola had anticipated. He confided to me that he was now more guardedly optimistic about his restaurant's chances to succeed.

One night in late January 1985, after Nicola and Linda had returned to their apartment from Gnolo, they found their fourteen-year-old son feverish and trembling from what would soon be diagnosed as meningitis. The boy underwent days of intensive care at Lenox Hill Hospital, followed by weeks of recovery at home before returning to school. Since he had occasionally helped out as a busboy at Gnolo, Linda saw this as additional evidence of her earlier apprehensions, and from this point on she refused to appear in the restaurant, doing Gnolo's bookkeeping in the apartment. Nicola told me that he and Linda were now quarreling constantly, that she was threatening to leave him if he did not say good riddance to the restaurant; but he, in turn, demanded to know: *What's my next move if I sell out? Until this place succeeds, who'd want to buy it? And where do I find another restaurant to run? Am I supposed to go crawling back to Elaine Kaufman and beg her for a job waiting tables? Or stop in at Elio Guaitolini's new restaurant and ask this man, who had worked under me when we both worked under Elaine, if I could now work under him? Or return to the Eighty-fourth Street place that's named after me and ask favors from my ex-partners, who'd always thought I couldn't succeed without them?*

Considering these and other options, Nicola decided that he was forced to remain where he was. He had already sunk $150,000 of his own money into Gnolo, and while this was considerably less than his partners' investment, they nevertheless recognized him as the restaurant's boss; they voiced their opinions, strongly at times, but permitted him final authority. And furthermore, he told Linda, there was no way that this run of bad luck would continue. He challenged her to rise above her negative feelings and convince herself that better times were ahead.

But they were not. Business did not improve and the restaurant remained a magnet for misfortune and misadventure. One evening in February 1985, a prominent business executive and frequent customer, while dining at Gnolo with his inamorata, was spotted through the restaurant's front window by a private detective. Nicola soon received a subpoena that required him to take a few days off from work in order to be available as a courtroom witness in an adultery suit filed by the executive's wife. In March 1985, a customer tripped going down the staircase en route to the bathroom, and Nicola was again legally notified, this time for liability. In May, having survived the winter, Nicola looked forward to warmer weather, to more people strolling through the side streets, to more walk-in customers. His business did, in fact, seem to be picking up slightly. At the end of May—on May 30, to be precise—he was delighted to review his reservation list and notice that Gnolo was entirely booked for the evening ahead. All the tables on the main floor were reserved, and a private party numbering close to one hundred guests would be assembling on the second floor.

Early in the afternoon, as Nicola was overseeing his staff's preparations for the upstairs event, he became aware of the sounds of fire engines in the near distance, and the shouting of many people gathered outside. Then his chef, who had been tuned in to the news on the kitchen radio, hurried into the dining room to announce what he had heard: A woman was now pinned under a construction crane that had capsized just west of the restaurant, on Third Avenue north of Sixty-third Street. The woman had been walking on the sidewalk on the west side of the avenue, adjacent to an open lot on which a forty-two-floor apartment house was being erected, and, as the crane collapsed against a plywood barrier while hoisting a load of steel rods, she fell under the barrier. She was alive but immobilized. Both of her legs were partly severed below the knees.

Throughout the afternoon and into the early evening, Nicola stood among thousands of onlookers along the barricaded Third Avenue, hoping that the rescue squads would be able to remove the woman without her sustaining further injury. Many spectators watched from the windows and rooftops of nearby buildings. Hundreds of media representatives were on hand to film and recount the ordeal of the forty-nine-year-old woman, who remained conscious and lucid while restrained for nearly six hours under the weight of the fallen barrier and the crane. Finally, after patiently digging through the debris and pulling away the last of the impediments, the rescuers slowly lifted the woman onto a stretcher and placed her in a nearby ambulance. Some spectators applauded. Others watched in respectful silence. The police, having already banned all motor traffic from the area except for official vehicles, now closed off a mile and a half of the FDR Drive to facilitate the speedy delivery of the woman downtown to Bellevue Hospital, where a team of surgeons awaited her. They would later devote five hours to the repair and reattachment of her crushed bones. At the conclusion, a hospital spokesman announced that it was uncertain if the woman would ever regain the full use of her legs.

Nicola returned home that night with much sympathy for the woman, but also a little sympathy for himself. The day and night blockage of Gnolo's neighborhood had nullified what would have been a lucrative occasion for the restaurant. When I walked into its near-empty dining room a few nights later, Nicola told me that he and his wife were barely communicating, and that his partners were pleading with him to close the place down. The crane accident had cast a pall along the street, they said, and with summer approaching and New Yorkers often out of town, the future for Gnolo was hardly auspicious. I and my good friend A. E. Hotchner—well known as the author of *Papa Hemingway*, a biography describing the adventurous life and suicidal death of the Nobel Prize–winning novelist Ernest Hemingway—contacted many of our fellow writers and acquaintances in the hope of rallying support for Gnolo. Very few people were swayed by our appeal. It is difficult to lure customers into a restaurant reeking of foreclosure. Still, Hotchner and I agreed to dine there together at least once a week, taking turns telephoning ahead for reservations, maintaining the courteous illusion that Gnolo was yet capable of having crowds of customers.

Shortly before 6:00 p.m. one day in early June, returning to Gnolo after a brief stroll in Central Park, Nicola was pleased to see that all the tables were set for dinner and to hear the sound system dispensing up-tempo music. But there was not a single waiter in the dining room. After proceeding into the kitchen, Nicola realized that, except for the young Peruvian dishwasher, he was alone on the premises. The dishwasher, struggling with his English and clearly discomfitted, explained that the entire staff had walked out about a half hour before. They had been gath-ered in the kitchen, sampling what the chef was preparing for that night's menu, when suddenly one of the waiters proposed that they resign en masse, leaving at once this moribund atmosphere of unoccupied tables and deficient gratuities. They could easily find better jobs elsewhere, the waiter declared; moments later, having retrieved their clothing from their lockers, the six-man staff was out the door, leaving the key with the dish-washer and instructing him to pass it on to Nicola with their salutations.

Nicola was stunned. He watched silently as the dishwasher untied his apron and, after laying the key on the wooden counter, said good night and followed in the path of his colleagues. Putting the key in his pants pocket, Nicola slowly walked out to the bar and made himself a drink. He sat on a stool, staring out at rows of white linen-covered tables, each properly set with silverware, glasses, and folded napkins. He had opened Gnolo only eight months ago, and nothing that he had experienced in more than forty years of restaurant work could bring clarity and under-standing to this moment. He would be sixty in less than two years, and, having invested the last of his savings in this debacle, his retirement was out of the question. He would have to keep working. But where?

Glancing through the big front window, he thought he spotted the novelist John Irving walking briskly along Sixty-third Street with his girl-friend, Rusty, who had an apartment a few blocks west on Park Avenue. The two of them had eaten a few times at Gnolo, but on this occasion they did not even pause to turn their heads to glance in; Rusty, dabbing her eyes with a handkerchief, appeared to be very unhappy. Nicola swung around on the stool and made himself another drink. Displayed on the backbar was a framed photograph inscribed to him by a renowned Holly-wood comedian: *To Nick, my best . . . Bob Hope*. Hope had come in one night while visiting New York, and Elaine Kaufman could definitely not claim him as one of her own. Next to the picture of Bob Hope were sev-eral others taken during Gnolo's joyful inaugural month of October, including those of the Halloween Champagne Gala hosted here by Peter Rockefeller, Christina Oxenberg, and other social figures. Every inch of the restaurant, upstairs as well as downstairs, was packed that night with young swells dressed in fairy-tale costumes, and nobody seemed eager to leave. This was a night when Nicola thought that owning Gnolo would make him rich.

Nicola heard the telephone but let it ring five or six times before getting up to answer it behind the bar.

"Gnolo's Restaurant," he said in a loud voice.

"Hi, Nick, this is Gay," I said, "and I need a table tonight."

He began to laugh.

"What's so funny?"

"Oh, nothing much," he replied after pausing for a second. From his end of the phone I could hear slightly what sounded like ice cubes clicking in a glass.

"How many you gonna be tonight?" he then asked.

"Just two," I said. "Hotchner and myself."

"When you want to come in?"

"Eight-thirty."

"Fine," he said. "See you at eight-thirty."

When we arrived, we were greeted in the entranceway by a smiling Nicola, who escorted us to a table next to the front window, seating us with our backs to the rest of the dining room. As Nicola went off to get a gin and tonic for Hotchner and a dry gin martini for me, not having to be told what we wanted to drink, I sat for a moment staring directly across Sixty-third Street into the brightly lit tunnel leading down into the garage where I used to keep my '57 TR-3. Now I secure it, along with my equally pampered '71 Triumph Stag, in the dent-free garage of my home in southern New Jersey. The car that I then kept in New York, parking it in a different underground garage nearer to Lexington Avenue—and not caring how often the attendants might bang it up—was a Chrysler station wagon that my wife saw as ideal for transporting our daughters back and forth to college, until they came of age to borrow it and could nick it up themselves.

While waiting for our drinks, Hotchner and I conversed, as we invariably did, about the difficulties of our work and the fact that so many underachieving professional athletes are so highly paid. Neither of us commented on the desolateness of Gnolo's dining room because we had long been aware of and were sensitive to Nicola's difficulties, and also because Nicola decided, after delivering our drinks, to join us for dinner. He had actually proposed making our food selections for us, imploring us to leave everything to him, including the cooking; we agreed on the condition that he sit and eat with us.

The dinner was delightful, and Nicola's demeanor, especially after he had consumed more than his share of the bottle of Chianti Classico that he had uncorked with the effortless flare of a professional, was as upbeat as the music flowing from the speakers. I was actually not aware that the three of us were the only individuals in the entire restaurant until, after completing our main course, I stood and turned to go to the men's room—and *that* is when it hit me: the glare of white linen rising above rows of empty tables before me, and more white material dangling from the sides of the front tables on the second floor, and suddenly I was able to identify with a phrase I had read in a *Times Magazine* article that I had clipped and filed away years ago. It was a piece by Gilbert Millstein, in which he described walking into an empty New York nightclub after 2:00 a.m. and becoming "snowblind from the tablecloths." *Snowblind from the tablecloths!*—but exactly; and after Hotchner and I had walked home that night, we both guessed that we had attended the last supper at Gnolo.

The next afternoon, after I had telephoned Nicola to see how he was doing, he confirmed it.

"Me and my partners have decided to shut the place down," he said. The restaurant history of Gnolo would conclude after only eight months. "Linda was right all along," he added. "That building on Sixty-third Street is cursed."

11

SHORTLY AFTER THE CLOSING OF GNOLO, NICOLA MOVED WITH HIS family to Florida, never to return to New York. In Palm Beach, he found backers to finance another restaurant, but I did not visit it. To be perfectly frank, though frankness has never been my style, I made little effort during this time to remain in close contact with Nicola. I had grown weary of collecting information about restaurants; all that research, and no story to show for it. Bad luck had apparently infested Nicola's restaurant in Palm Beach as it had on Sixty-third Street. I did not know the details, and did not *want* to know the details, but he was obliged to go out of business and other investors later took over the space and turned it into a nightclub called Au Bar.

In 1991, while lodged at a small hotel in Calabria, working on the final sections of *Unto the Sons*, I heard references to Au Bar many times on Italian television, and it was also mentioned in newspapers, all in connection with a scandalous situation in the United States. A nephew of the late president John F. Kennedy had met a young woman one night at Au Bar, and, according to what she later told the police, he escorted her back to the Kennedy estate and raped her. Perhaps because I was in southern Italy, the spawning ground of the *Jettatura*, I began associating Au Bar with the jinx dust that seemed to cling to my friend Nicola no matter where he was. And during my returns to New York, whenever I passed 206 East 63rd Street, a site that Nicola's wife believed was "cursed," it seemed to me that she was onto something. Each of the half dozen restaurants that would follow Gnolo at that address would encounter hard times. It was as if the building were carnivorous, devouring whatever restaurant tried to succeed on that spot.

After *Unto the Sons* was published in 1992, I thought of resuming my inquest into the restaurant world, but resisted. I needed a respite from research, I believed; perhaps I should try writing more from memory, less from the vantage point of an observer and interviewer. Soon I was outlin-

ing an account of my college experiences during the years 1949 to 1953 at
the then lily white University of Alabama, a memoir that I saw as continuing into 1965, when I returned as a *Times* staffer to interview the
school's first black graduate, twenty-two-year-old Vivian Malone, and
also to file stories about the civil rights demonstrations in the old cotton-
growing community of Selma. I tried to re-create in my imagination the
kind of person I had been back in the early autumn of 1949, a shy and
uncertain teenager who, after being driven by his parents to a rail terminal in Philadelphia, embarked upon a twelve-hour journey through the
Shenandoah Valley of Virginia, and then into the Carolinas and Ten-
nesseee and the northwestern tip of Georgia, and finally into Alabama. I
had never before been far from home, and had no idea where Alabama
was until my letter of acceptance from the University of Alabama
prompted me to consult a map.

In the train, I sat alone in the back behind rows of young men and
women who chatted amiably among themselves and laughed often, and
who traveled with their tweed jackets and camel's hair coats folded carelessly up in the overhead racks next to the suitcases with stickers
announcing DUKE, GEORGIA TECH, SWEET BRIAR, LSU, and TULANE. I did
not see any luggage labeled ALABAMA, but I did not do a lot of strolling up
and down the aisles during the trip, nor do I recall speaking to anyone,
even when I visited the crowded club car in the rear of the train to
get something to eat. There were many middle-aged men back there in
business suits, communicating loudly among themselves as they stood
drinking and smoking at the bar or while seated at one of the small
bolted-down tables; and behind them, along a money-strewn floor, was a
crap game being conducted by several shouting and crawling casually
dressed men in their mid-twenties who were students on the GI bill. I
learned that the dice players were ex-GIs because I later overheard two
black porters complaining about the ruckus but suggesting it might be
unpatriotic to stop it; so the crap game continued through all the hours I
remained on board.

I spent most of my time at my seat, staring out at the rolling landscape
and trying to memorize some of the strange and faintly stenciled names
that appeared on the trackside shacks of the small towns and hamlets we
passed. I imagined that my father must have felt some of what I was now
feeling when *he* was seventeen, twenty-five years before, and had left
home in uneasy anticipation of a new life in a new land. Alabama, to me,
was foreign territory.

Since I could not sleep, I read a few chapters from the novel I was carrying, *The Young Lions*, by Irwin Shaw, and I also perused the Alabama registration catalog that had been mailed to me in New Jersey a few days before my departure. I planned to major in journalism. Although I was still not convinced that this would become my career, I believed that taking journalism courses would challenge me the least in an academic sense. I wanted every chance to remain in school and protect my student-deferment status from the clutches of my draft board.

After the train had arrived at a city in central-western Alabama that was called Tuscaloosa, where I was the single departing passenger, I handed the two cracked leather suitcases I had borrowed from my father down to a top-hatted black man who drove a jitney, and who soon transported me into what could have been a movie set for *Gone With the Wind*. Stately antebellum buildings loomed wherever I looked from the jitney's windows; mansions, and smaller homes with columns, and all with sprawling lawns, lined both sides of the wide tree-lined boulevards of Tuscaloosa, which had been the capital of Alabama until the 1840s, when it had been succeeded by Montgomery. The campus of the University of Alabama, founded in 1831, adjoined Tuscaloosa, and while it conformed to it architecturally, many of the older University of Alabama buildings had been renovated many times since being attacked and torched by the Union soldiers who had advanced through the campus during the Civil War.

My dormitory was half a mile beyond the main area of the campus, and it stood in wretched contrast to all that I had seen earlier from the jitney. It was one of several unadorned single-story wooden barracks that had been hastily built on the lowlands, near a swamp, to serve as temporary housing for some of the freshmen within the overly populated student body that was still crowded with veterans on the GI bill. My quarters consisted of a small room with a single cot, a wooden table, a chair, and an armoire with a lower drawer. As I would soon discover, my surroundings would be penetrated throughout the day by a windblown musky odor emanating from a paper mill located beyond the campus near the main highway. My dormitory was also invaded by the nightly return of ex-GIs from the beer halls that flourished beyond the "dry" county that encompassed the campus—serenading revelers ready to begin playing cards and shooting dice with the vigor I had seen exhibited by those other veterans in the club car.

But far from being disturbed by the nightly commotion—though I contributed very little to it even as I began making friends during the succeeding weeks—I became drawn to these older students more than to my contemporaries. In my comfortable role as an observer and listener, I liked watching the veterans sitting around a card table in the dormitory's common room playing blackjack and gin rummy, and hearing their war stories, their barracks language, their dirty jokes. Up half the night, and rarely cracking a book, they rose daily to attend classes, or cut classes, with no apparent fear of ever failing a course—an attitude that left some of them open for surprises. Not all of the survivors of the war were academic survivors in their classrooms.

I, of course, did not follow their example, lacking the confidence at this point to take anything for granted. But being around these older men loosened me up a bit, spared me from having to compare myself exclusively and perhaps unfavorably with my age group, and it seemed to have a favorable effect on my health and schoolwork. My acne had all but vanished within six months of my arrival, a cure I could attribute to the friendly and diverting spirit that pervaded my dorm. I earned passing grades in all of my freshman courses, and near the end of the term I had my first coffee date, then movie date, then my first French kiss from a Birmingham-born blonde who was studying journalism, but later transferred into advertising.

As a journalism student, I was usually ranked in the middle of the class, even during my junior and senior years, when I was the college weekly's sports editor and "Sports Gay-zing" columnist as well as campus correspondent for the daily *Birmingham Post-Herald*. The faculty tended to favor the reportorial style of the conservative though very reliable *Kansas City Star*, where some of them had previously worked as editors and staff writers. They had definite views of what constituted "news" and how news stories should be presented. The "five W's"—who, what, when, where, why—were questions they thought should be answered succinctly and impersonally in the opening paragraphs of an article. Since I sometimes resisted their approach, and might try instead to communicate the news through the viewpoint of the single person who observed it from the sidelines, or might adopt some other narrative technique learned from reading fiction, I was not a faculty favorite. But unlike my English teacher in high school, the journalism faculty at Alabama complimented me at times for the outside writing I did for the college newspaper and the Birmingham daily. One story they liked was my interview with a lumbering seven-foot-tall student from the hill country of northern Alabama who, in spite of many pleas from the school's basketball coach, refused to try out for the team. He explained to me that he preferred devoting his out-of-class time to trimming trees. Another article that my teachers praised was my profile of an elderly black man, the grandson of slaves, who was the football team's locker room attendant and was also considered to be the players' good-luck charm; before each game, as they lined up to trot onto the field, they would take turns stroking the black man's head. Without overstating the situation, it was evident to most of my readers that I was describing one of the rare examples of interracial physical contact that then existed within the segregated world of Alabama athletics.

The admission of black students in 1963, ten years after I had graduated from Alabama, did not mean that black athletes were immediately accepted into the school's sports system. The football coach, Paul "Bear" Bryant, was advised by the alumni's reactionary element to abstain from any kind of "race mixing" within his team, and between 1963 and 1968, Coach Bryant did not offer a single scholarship to any graduating high school football star who was black. Either the leading black prospects were considered insufficiently gifted to make the team or the players themselves decided to accept scholarships to play football at more hospitable colleges in the Midwest or the far West. But in 1969, after the color line had long been broken by football-playing colleges in Kentucky, Tennessee, and Florida—and as Alabama's interstate rival, Auburn, had also recently accepted a black player—Coach Bryant received permission to follow the trend, and thus in mid-December 1969 a black schoolboy star named Wilbur Jackson from Ozark, Alabama, was invited to the campus and was issued a uniform.

But since freshmen players were not eligible for varsity competition in those days, Jackson was sitting in the stands with more than 72,000 other spectators in Birmingham's Legion Field on Saturday night, September 12, 1970, when the all-white Alabama team was overwhelmed, 42-21, by a University of Southern California squad led by a 215-pound black fullback named Sam "Bam" Cunningham, a nineteen-year-old sophomore reared in Santa Barbara, California. Also in the Southern California backfield that night was a Birmingham-born black player named Clarence Davis, who scored two touchdowns. But most of the damage was done by Cunningham, who scored three touchdowns, rushed for 212 yards, and almost single-handedly demoralized the pro-segregation faction among the Alabama fans, who up to that point had believed that Bear Bryant could continue to be a winning coach of an all-white team that resisted the emergence of black athletic power. Through the annals of Alabama football there has never been much tolerance among its fans, including its fans affiliated with the Ku Klux Klan, for unsuccessful seasons on the gridiron, and in the aftermath of the trouncing by Southern

California, a sportswriter later suggested that the state's best-known racist, George Wallace, had privately vowed that Coach Bryant's team would never be "outniggered" again.

There was little doubt that Sam "Bam" Cunningham's awesome performance against the Alabama defense accelerated the pace of black recruitment at the University of Alabama. Three years later, when Coach Bryant's team completed the 1973 season with eleven victories and only one defeat—it lost by a single point to Notre Dame in the Sugar Bowl—one-third of Alabama's varsity starters were black.

"Cunningham," said Coach Bryant, "did more for integration in Alabama in sixty minutes than Martin Luther King did in twenty years."

12

HAD I MYSELF POSSESSED AN ADMIRABLE SOCIAL CONSCIENCE AT the University of Alabama, I might have honored my student days there with a valiant denunciation of racism that would have predated by several years the appearance of civil rights activists in the state; but whatever egalitarian sensibilities I possessed as a student were stifled by the gratitude I felt toward the university's administrators, who had allowed me access to the only campus in the United States that agreed to have me.

I am not saying that I was immediately welcomed everywhere with open arms, or that I could have joined one of the better Christian fraternities (I joined the worst, Phi Sigma Kappa, the one most accepting of students from the North), or that I could have fulfilled my senior-year ambition to become the editor of the student newspaper. I guess I knew but was not yet ready to accept the fact that the most prestigious positions for which students vied at the ballot box would go to one of the southern-born students affiliated with the leading fraternities that had the most influence within the political "machine" that controlled the campus. When I applied to become the editor, I was told by one student political leader that the job I wanted had already been promised to someone else; furthermore, if I did not immediately withdraw my application, I might not be able to continue as the paper's sports editor and columnist during my senior year. So I complied without delay or argument. I knew my place. I was an outsider, a token Italian Yankee. On this campus not yet ready to accept blacks, it got its "diversity" and "affirmative action" quotas from people like me and other olive-skinned out-of-staters whose ancestry might be Jewish, Arab, or Greek—students whom the Tuscaloosa chapter of the Ku Klux Klan saw as borderline whites. And yet I also believed in those days, and I would continue to believe after I had graduated and moved to New York, that racism in many unacknowledged and unreported ways was as present in the North as it was in the South.

It had been so casually accepted in my hometown on the New Jersey shore during the 1930s and 1940s that I grew up virtually unaware of it. At our Village cinema on the boardwalk, it was customary for black people to view movies from seats in the balcony, and, without any directional signs or signals from the management, they did so without objecting. While black students joined the whites in our town's public schools, there was little social contact between the races outside the classrooms and athletic fields. The racial divide in real estate was maintained from one generation to the next by various rental and home-loan banking policies that, no matter what laws might exist, ensured black residents were essentially banned from white neighborhoods, thus creating a century-old black quarter in my hometown that was decrepit with decay and deprivation.

In my hometown and in other cities throughout the state and in New York as well, there were secret chapters of the Ku Klux Klan. Except in my town, at least during my boyhood in the late 1930s into the 1940s, the Klan's presence was sometimes quite obvious. I remember seeing white-sheeted figures gathered in public for such ceremonial functions as the installation of new members, or the mourning of older members, and, for whatever reason, there they were, all in white, assembled on the greensward of the Methodist Tabernacle Society's campgrounds, or on the boardwalk, or along the beach, doing their thing—which was mostly standing around and conversing among themselves as casually as if they were a group of chefs discussing menus for an outdoor cooking class.

The general public paid little attention to them. Pedestrians would stroll by, blacks included, and keep walking. My father told me with certainty, without ever explaining why he was so certain, that he knew the identity of three of our town's Klansmen. He said that two of them were local firemen, and the other individual, a graduate of the Philadelphia College of Pharmacy, owned our leading drugstore. This man and my father attended once-a-week dinners together as members of the Rotary Club. While my father conceded that there were no conversational references to the Klan at these dinners, he went on to suggest that he and the other Rotarians behaved toward this pharmacist with the same unobtrusiveness that is often adopted by residents of large cities like Philadelphia or New York when they have a neighbor who is in the Mafia. As long as the violent activities of organized crime remained outside the neighborhood—or, parenthetically, as long as white-hooded men did not burn crosses on our beach or hang blacks from our trees—it was possible in such places at such times for good and evil citizens to coexist closely.

As I ponder this now, more than half a century later, it is remarkable only in a contemporary context that in those days white-sheeted men, doing next to nothing in public, could be so persuasive for so long in maintaining the status quo in towns like mine, while the rest of my townsmen acquiesced. Perhaps a majority of these townsmen were interchangeable with the people under the sheets. But then again, I recall seeing newsreels in the 1930s showing crowds of Klansmen marching unchallenged through Washington, D.C.; and while the capital of the United States in the 1930s was very different in its democratic spirit and its racial consciousness from what it would be in the 1960s when it welcomed the words of Dr. King, I am reminded by Coach Bryant's later comment that it was Sam "Bam" Cunningham who made the most meaningful impression on people who might otherwise have remained in step with the Klan. In any case, when I left home for college in 1949, I did not find Alabama to be as foreign as I thought it would be from what I had known. I, as an Italianate outsider, attended classes with fellow students whose family history in the American South was in many ways similar to my own family's history in southern Italy. In fact, when I first explored the southern Italian countryside, beginning in the spring of 1955 while on furlough from my army unit based in Germany, I often thought that I was traveling through rural Alabama. It was not only the similarity in climate, the simple beauty of the land, the slow pace of the country people trekking along dusty roads amid the surrounding sounds of farm animals, and the sedate though occasionally festive town squares with their centerpiece statuary—built in Italy to memoralize martyred saints as in Alabama to commemorate fallen Confederate soldiers—and their rows of old men who sat in the shade wearing peaked caps and holding canes, and who with their sun-creased faces stared in quiet wonderment whenever a stranger passed before them, a stranger who was at times myself; no, what most connected these Italian southerners with American southerners was, in my opinion, their lingering sense of separateness.

When the American South was under attack from Northern armies in the 1860s, the southern part of Italy was also under seige from northern militants led by Gen. Giuseppe Garibaldi, who had planned his strategy in northern cities with northern money and troops and then sailed south into the Mediterranean Sea to launch his invasion through the island of Sicily up into the southern peninsula, penetrating my father's native province and finally conquering the southern capital city of Naples. General Garibaldi achieved victory with such expedience that President Abraham Lincoln tried without success to enlist him to lead some of the Union's divisions in their continuing campaigns against the Confederacy.

The capitulation by the people of southern Italy and those of the

American South in the 1860s was followed in both places by periods of military occupation that spawned rabid and ruthless bands of local resisters (led by the Mafia in Italy and the Klan in America) and that in the end did nothing but reinforce the disparity and disunity between the South and the North because natives whose homeland is governed by conquerors are guided by a spirit of defiance. In Italy nearly a century and a half has passed since General Garibaldi's invaders and their northern civilian leaders took over the south, but during my many visits to Italy since the first one in 1955, I have found the average southerner to be stubbornly resistant to change, to be relatively poor and deprived and generally pessimistic. The southern dialect spoken in my father's region during his boyhood lacked a future tense. General Garibaldi's lasting achievement was not national unification but, rather, the destruction of the southern kingdom's autonomy and the resulting departure from Italy of southerners fleeing to America. As they embarked from the port of Naples, they left behind a city distinguished for its chipped and tarnished baroque palazzos built by the aristocracy that Garibaldi drove from power in the 1860s. Many of these buildings have since been renovated and maintained by later generations of old-family southerners who have remained in Naples and who are the spiritual cousins of those Americans in Alabama and elsewhere in the South who continue to restore and revere their antebellum mansions.

When I saw Walker Evans's Depression-era photographs of some of Alabama's poor white sharecropping families—several of these photos appeared in a book that Evans and his collaborator, the writer James Agee, published in 1941 under the title Let Us Now Praise Famous Men—I thought I was seeing some of the same grim, gaunt faces that I had seen while traveling around my father's area of southern Italy. These faces in Alabama reflected what Agee called "the lives of an undefended and appallingly damaged group of human beings." While the publishing effort of Agee and Evans presented a memorable and compelling portrait of their subjects, their book, which Lionel Trilling reviewed enthusiastically, did receive a bit of his criticism for its failure "to see these people as anything but good," and for its underemphasizing the "malice or meanness" that often accompanied the racism that was omnipresent in the sharecropping community as it was throughout the state.

The lowly whites of Alabama needed someone lower than themselves, and this distinction befell the blacks. The miserable lives that both races shared as neighbors in equally shoddy pine-board shacks did not blur the discrimination that gave white people the upper hand, allowing them to retain whatever set them apart from the blacks. Evans's photographs documented the democracy of white failure in Alabama, and the pale and freckled faces in his book—faces that were somber-eyed, tight-lipped, and lined—were offered as expressions of enduring strength, stoicism, and indifference to suffering. But I have seen similar expressions in news-magazines on the faces of lynch mobs, such as the mob in the Alabama town of Scottsboro that wanted to hang nine young black men and boys following questionable charges of rape brought against the accused by two white women. Indeed, the physiognomy of the lynch mob prefigured the white faces of law enforcement that I observed as a journalist in 1965 while they stared impassively at black marchers moments before the latter were clubbed and beaten into submission along a highway in Selma, Alabama.

The marchers were in the forefront of Martin Luther King, Jr.'s civil rights movement, and their attackers—wearing helmets and carrying billy clubs, cattle prods, and gas canisters—were members of the Alabama state police and the sheriff's posse. They could have been the sons or grandsons of the old sharecroppers Walker Evans photographed, for they were products of the same deprived and undereducated upbringing, and their facial expressions were similarly austere. But in the mid-1960s, these helmeted men personified Alabama's frontal assault against the Reverend Dr. King's demonstrators, and the city of Selma had been deliberately chosen by King because there was no place in the South more likely than Selma to become enraged if invaded by out-of-town black marchers advo-cating change, and the inevitable clash would draw the attention of the media and further publicize his mission. The Atlanta-born and -based Baptist minister knew Alabama very well, having been a pastor in Mont-gomery and having often traveled through the state preaching against its inequities, doing so once behind bars in a Birmingham jail.

In 1955, after a black seamstress named Rosa Parks had refused to yield her seat to a white passenger on a bus in Montgomery, the Reverend Dr. King used the incident to denounce the city's policy of segregated public transportation, and his subsequent 381-day bus boycott inaugurated the civil rights movement in America. A decade later, as he planned to refo-cus on Montgomery as the source of the state's strategy that was depriv-ing black people of their voting rights, he decided to make his case in Selma, an old plantation town of ingrained southern traditions and abuses, located about fifty miles west of Alabama's capitol building in Montgomery.

Selma was a serene city in south-central Alabama, perched on a high bluff on a bank of the muddy Alabama River. More than half of its approximately 27,000 residents were black, many of them related to the slaves who had been brought here by planters during the 1820s. By 1840, Selma was the heart of Alabama's booming cotton economy, and there were considerably more slaves than whites. In 1848, three hundred German immigrants, many of them ironworkers and mechanics, went to Selma and introduced iron casting and gun making, and as the city was served by both river and railroad, it became a major supply depot and industrial center for the Confederate states just before the outbreak of the Civil War. Thus it also became, in the spring of 1865, a key military objective of the Union army. On April 2, Selma was attacked by nine thousand Northern soldiers, who overwhelmed the almost four thousand Confederate defenders and destroyed the city. They burned homes and public buildings, molested women, butchered horses, torched thousands of bales of cotton. Perhaps no part of Alabama was more ravaged by warfare, and was more controlled by its conquerors during the ten postwar years of armed occupation, than Selma, and the town's white residents cultivated a deep and abiding resentment that extended well into the following century.

As a result of the United States Supreme Court's school desegregation decision in 1954 in *Brown v. Board of Education*, Selma became the first Alabama city to organize a White Citizens Council to resist the ruling. The town's prevailing attitude helped shape the racial views of such local products as Eugene "Bull" Connor, the public safety commissioner who led dogs and directed fire hoses against black demonstrators in Birmingham; Leonard Wilson, the University of Alabama undergraduate who in 1956 spearheaded a campus uprising that discouraged the matriculation of the school's first black student, Autherine Lucy; and James G. Clark, Jr., Selma's sheriff and its most stalwart segregationist, who, when asked at a news conference if he had a hero who had influenced his thinking, unhesitatingly replied, "Nathan Bedford Forrest." Forrest was the Confederate general who tried to defend Selma against its Civil War invaders—and a hundred years later, in 1965, Sheriff Clark claimed a similar aspiration in trying to block the Reverend Dr. King and the latter's "outside agitators" from crossing the Selma bridge and marching on to Montgomery.

I was among many dozens of out-of-state journalists and one of a three-man *Times* team who flew into Alabama during the first week of March 1965 to cover the demonstrators' five-day procession from Selma to Montgomery, which was scheduled to begin on March 7. Unlike most of the arriving media, I was quite familiar with Selma, having driven through it many times during my college days, and on occasions I had paused to look at its restored white mansions with their wide verandas and fluted Corinthian columns, and its waterfront hotel, erected in the 1840s with French-style ornamented iron filigree balconies, and, across the street, its deteriorating warehouses and other old buildings that had once been the site of Selma's slave-auction center.

Most of the slaves' descendants who had chosen to remain in Selma after their so-called emancipation found work as white people's domestic servants, farm laborers, or store clerks, and by the 1950s a few had risen to join a middle-class contingent of black doctors, dentists, morticians, businessmen, teachers, and preachers who catered to their community. But while there was no shortage of black clergymen in Selma, there was not a single black lawyer working in the city when the U.S. Supreme Court ruled in 1954 that segregation by color in public schools was unconstitutional. And among Selma's approximately fifteen thousand black residents, fewer than two hundred possessed the right to vote, and none of these had ever been asked to serve on a jury.

This latter situation had been unsuccessfully challenged a year earlier by black people attending a county court trial in which a black defendant stood accused of sexually molesting white women. One woman was the wife of an airman stationed at Craig Field, six miles outside the city. She claimed that her attacker had climbed through the window of her home and, with a knife at her throat, had raped her one night in March 1953. Although he'd worn a mask, she testified that she had been able to see his eyes and knew he was black. A month later, a young married woman whose father was Selma's mayor reported that a knife-wielding black male with a white towel over his head had entered her bedroom. But she had fought him off, she said, grabbing his knife before he fled. Soon other Selma women were telephoning the police at night and suggesting there were black prowlers near their homes, and suddenly Selma was smitten with some of the hysteria that had characterized Scottsboro two decades earlier.

A few months after the allegations by the airman's wife, a black man who lived thirty miles outside Selma, in a small town called Marion, where he had a wife and four children and worked in a gas station, was seen walking one night in an alley near a white neighborhood in Selma. He was detained by two white men, who soon notified the police. The suspect's name was William Earl Fikes. He was described by a black acquaintance as a barely articulate man who was possibly feebleminded but not inclined to criminality. The man's white employer also doubted that Fikes was the culprit. But the police, without allowing Fikes to consult with a lawyer, drove him fifty miles away to a prison in Montgomery, claiming that it was necessary to get him out of Selma for his own protection. While in custody, Fikes was interrogated repeatedly for several days, until he produced what the police called a "confession." He was said to have admitted raping the airman's wife and of trying to rape the daughter of Selma's mayor. Each offense in Alabama could have subjected Fikes to the death penalty.

When he was returned to the Selma area and later appeared in the county courthouse for the first trial, the one involving the airman's wife, he was defended by two white lawyers and confronted a jury consisting of twelve white men. He was found guilty. But since one member of the jury opposed the death penalty, Fikes received a prison term of ninety-nine years. This provoked protests from many white people in Selma, who wanted him dead, but it also aroused an outcry from within the black community because the verdict reaffirmed what until then they had more or less been resigned to—the lack of justice for black defendants in a racist courthouse. So they rallied around Fikes prior to the second trial, knowing that *this* white jury might bury him if the mayor's daughter had her way; in addition to the money raised in Selma's black churches for Fikes's legal defense, the National Association for the Advancement of Colored People arranged for two black lawyers from Birmingham to go to Selma and function as Fikes's counselors.

The trial was well publicized within the state. I had read about it in the Alabama newspapers during the end of my senior year in college, and the trial was mentioned in some of the phone conversations I had with Alabama friends after I had graduated and moved to New York in the summer of 1953. But I was then not overly interested in William Earl Fikes. I was preoccupied with my work as a news assistant at the *Times* and was also anxiously awaiting notification of when and where I would begin my two-year military obligation as a second lieutenant in the tank corps. I was twenty-one, had rented an L-shaped room month to month in a Greenwich Village brownstone, and was living a narrowly defined existence on a day-to-day basis, wondering more about where I was going than where I was, or where I had been. Several years would pass before I would be reminded of the name William Earl Fikes and learn that his trial in 1953 had been a prelude to the national civil rights movement begun in Alabama by Martin Luther King, Jr.

I would be made aware of this through my subsequent interviews with, and from the published writings of, J. L. Chestnut, Jr., a black attorney who was a native of Selma and whose law practice there, beginning in 1958, would in time become heavily engaged in freeing from jail and defending in court a large number of black civil rights activists.

I first met Chestnut after I had been sent to Selma by the *Times* in 1965 to help cover the King-led demonstrations. Although I did not then know it, this would be my final year in journalism, and the Selma story my last major assignment as a *Times* man. I had been a reporter for ten years, having been elevated from news assistant to the writing staff in 1955 shortly after I had returned from Germany upon completing my military tour. A month before arriving in Selma, I had turned thirty-three. I had been married for six years to Nan, then an associate editor at Random House, who was about to publish her first best-seller, *Papa Hemingway*, and my wife and I were residing in a rent-controlled apartment within a dilapidated East Side brownstone in Manhattan that we would one day buy, sharing space at the time with two Siamese cats, a one-year-old daughter, and her buxom young red-haired governess from Bavaria, whose charms were not lost on the neighborhood's delivery boys and doormen.

While I had loved working at the *Times*, after ten years I was no longer adapting well to the daily space limitations, to the deadline pressures, and to feelings that whatever I had finished writing was not really finished— there was so much more to be learned and written about than what I had researched and published in the *Times*. This fact frustrated me throughout the weeks of my prolonged assignment in Selma, perhaps because here I was in a familiar part of my past that was no longer so familiar, and I was very curious about why and how it was changing; and here I also realized—and my acquaintanceship with J. L. Chestnut, Jr., heightened this realization—how incomplete had been my education at the University of Alabama and how little aware I had long been of the common struggles and adversities known to Chestnut and the rest of the black people of my generation who had been born in Alabama and been thwarted by the traditions that had dominated southern social life well into the middle of the twentieth century.

I referred previously to the "lingering sense of separateness" endemic to my southern Italian forebears and the families of my southern classmates at the University of Alabama, but what I did not take into account was the separateness in the extreme that had been historically inherent in the lives of black southerners in such places as Birmingham, Montgomery, Selma, and my old college town of Tuscaloosa. If J. L. Chestnut, Jr., and I had been born a generation later, we might have been classmates at the University of Alabama. After meeting him in 1965, and continuing to correspond with him and visit him after I had left the *Times*, it was apparent to me that he and I had much in common, had many shared aspirations and standards, and had we been classmates and friends, my education at the University of Alabama would have been less deprived and I would have no doubt been a wiser reporter and writer than I was when I arrived to cover the Selma story in the spring of 1965.

Chestnut was then nearly thirty-five, the only black attorney in Selma—a short, stockily constructed, somewhat remote, and always formal man invariably dressed in a manner appropriate to the court, meaning mainly white shirts with dark suits and ties and well-shined black shoes. He gave the impression that he was taller than his five-foot-eight-inch frame because of his broad chest, his commanding demeanor, and his booming baritone voice. His close-cropped kinky head of shiny black hair was receding to the crown of his head in a way that resembled a skull cap; however, his penetrating bright-eyed expression, ever inquiring yet withholding judgment, was his most salient characteristic. Though he was less than two years older than myself, I privately deferred to him as if he were much older and more mature, a situation that had nothing to do with our respective ages and everything to do with who he was, and what he had been forced to overcome in order to become who he was. He was well known only in Selma, where the black people admired and depended upon him and the white people saw him as a notoriously irrepressible force in their legal system. He was nevertheless the only black man in Selma who thought highly enough of himself to write about himself, and his memoir—*Black in Selma*, coauthored with Julia Cass—takes the reader inside the head of a native son who was influenced by Selma's traditions but whose perceptions were altered by the circumstances of the Fikes trial, and who finally lived out his life in Selma long after the city had ceased to attract national headlines and had been abandoned by the last procession of out-of-state demonstrators singing "We Shall Overcome."

When the case of the attempted rape of the mayor's daughter was brought to trial in 1953, J. L. Chestnut, Jr., was a twenty-two-year-old law student attending classes at Howard University, a black college in Washington, D.C.; but he returned home to witness the performance of Fikes's defense counselor from Birmingham, Peter Hall, a black attorney whose impressive prior efforts with NAACP-sponsored cases were known to Chestnut and to his fellow students and the faculty at Howard. Chestnut stayed at his parents' home in Selma. His father formerly owned a grocery store in the black quarter. His mother performed many chores for white people, and knew how to maneuver herself socially and productively without ever seeming to be crossing the color line. She had scrupulously set aside her savings for the college education of her son and only child, J.L., who had inherited his only-initials name from his father, J. L. Chestnut, Sr., who had been so named by *his* mother because she had once been acquainted with a prominent white banker in Selma who had these initials.

J. L. Chestnut, Jr., did not intend to resettle in Selma after getting his law degree, assuming that to open a practice in his hometown would lead only to frustration and starvation. Other black professionals in Selma—physicians, dentists, educators—could make a living catering to the needs of their own kind, but blacks in trouble with the law were better off having a white attorney, inasmuch as they would be appearing in front of a white jury and judge. So Chestnut thought he would hang up his shingle in Harlem or Washington, D.C., or somewhere else far from Alabama, and he would return to Selma primarily for family visits—or, as in this instance, to see how William Earl Fikes's lead lawyer, Peter Hall, would fare in a courthouse where people were accustomed to seeing black men working only as janitors.

On the eve of the trial, at a social club for black people in Selma, Hall sat on a bar stool, slowly sipping whiskey and explaining to the well-wishers who surrounded him (in the crowd was young Chestnut) how he intended to attack Selma's rigged legal system and its policy of blocking black residents from serving on juries. Hall was a handsome, slim, light-skinned, mustachioed man in his late thirties. He wore a well-cut suit, which Chestnut admired up close, wondering what it had cost. "I don't know if Fikes is guilty," Hall was saying, speaking in a clear and authoritative voice without a trace of a southern accent, although he had been raised in Birmingham, "but it is damn certain that the system is guilty. And I intend to try the system while the circuit solicitor is trying Fikes."

These were very bold words coming out of a black man's mouth in Selma in 1953, and it occurred to Chestnut that Hall was maybe emboldened by what he was drinking and might turn into a shrinking violet when facing the white judge and jury. But on the following morning, it was the same Peter Hall—stouthearted, articulate, and clearly confident—who entered the courtroom a few minutes late, and then at his own pace headed toward the elevated desk of the judge to introduce several pretrial motions that advocated, among other things, the dismissal of the jury due to their prejudicial selection and the freedom of Fikes, since his confession had been extracted via "Gestapo-like tactics."

Perhaps because the judge was so bedazzled by the presence of a pertinacious black attorney, he neither censured nor interrupted him, and as J. L. Chestnut, Jr., would recount many years later in his book:

> . . . it was obvious that Peter Hall was the smoothest, most competent lawyer in the room—and Peter Hall knew it. He dominated the

white judge, the white lawyers. . . . Blacks who packed into the courtroom watched with delight as Peter questioned white county officials—the circuit solicitor, the circuit clerk, the jury commissioners, and others—in a polished, polite way that masked the aggressiveness of what he was doing. The officials testified that, indeed, no blacks had served on juries in modern times, but that didn't mean they were being systematically excluded. A few had been in the pool of potential jurors over the years, they said, but black people had to be more carefully screened than whites because of their higher percentage of illiteracy, venereal disease, and felony convictions. . . . Peter's mode of defense—or offense—was new to me. Naturally, Peter did not succeed in getting a white judge in Selma to allow any blacks on the jury. This was an argument geared for appeal to higher courts outside Alabama. The judge also denied Peter's motion to prevent the prosecution from using Fikes's confession. . . .

But Peter Hall did succeed in saving Fikes's life. After the three-day trial had resulted in Fikes's conviction and the death sentence, Hall got the conviction overturned by the U.S. Supreme Court on the grounds that his client, a man of deficient mental and verbal capabilities, had been wrongly queried by the police and had also been improperly sequestered. While Fikes would remain in jail for the next twenty years, the trial itself, as Chestnut wrote, "rallied the black community as it had never been rallied before." Black parents had brought their children into the courtroom to get a look at the valorous attorney, Hall, who was not "Uncle Tom-ing" in front of the white legal establishment. This valor was also in evidence two years later, in 1955, when Rosa Parks refused to surrender her bus seat to a white passenger in Montgomery, bringing Martin Luther King, Jr., to her aid. What Dr. King and Peter Hall were doing in the South convinced J. L. Chestnut, Jr., that he should return home after getting his law degree in Washington in 1958. He would become Selma's first full-time black attorney. He would join the courtroom battle against a legal system that fostered racial injustice. He knew he was needed and the timing was right.

"Rumblings of change were coming from the South," he wrote. "Alabama was where the action was."

13

It was a sunny but chilly Sunday morning as more than five hundred civil rights demonstrators made their way through the main business district of the city, ignoring the stares of the white people and defying the court order of a local judge as they headed in the direction of the bridge and the highway, marching two abreast and carrying satchels filled with extra clothing and shoes for the fifty-mile journey to the governor's office in Montgomery.

I stood with other reporters along the grassy edge of the highway, beyond the bridge, watching the oncoming procession and also the helmeted white men from the state police and the sheriff's posse who had set up a roadblock two hundred yards in the distance. Except for the sounds of the clacking hoofs and the baying of the posse's horses, the prolonged silence hovering around us was interrupted now and then by catcalls coming from behind me just as the first pair of marchers had descended from the bridge.

"Here come the niggers" was what I heard, and, turning, I saw about thirty white male spectators gathered in front of a small drive-in restaurant, most of them wearing dungarees with plaid shirts and peaked caps, and one of them, a scrawny teenage boy who was the heckler, waved a long pole on which was attached a faded Confederate flag.

On the other side of the road, paying no attention to the flag-bearer, was J. L. Chestnut, Jr. He was wearing a black suit, white shirt, and blue tie. He stood on a flatbed truck that was parked near a ditch, and he was stretching up on his toes to get a better view of the marchers. A few other black people, whom I did not recognize, watched from behind him. I had introduced myself to him earlier in the morning in the black part of town, where the marchers had lined up in front of Brown Chapel, a redbrick church that since the early 1960s had been the gathering place for civil rights organizing and protesting. When Chestnut had returned home with a law degree in 1958, he lived in a housing project across the street from Brown Chapel, and in time he became the legal adviser to the preacher and others who had the will and energy to challenge the existing order.

Although I had not yet intruded myself into Chestnut's busy schedule for an interview, I already had collected information about him from journalists who specialized in civil rights coverage, and I was impressed with his unique status as the only black officer in a white man's court. When he had started his practice in Selma seven years before, earning a meager livelihood dealing mainly with black people's wills, divorces, bar fights, and petty crimes like shoplifting, he had been socially ostracized by nearly all of Selma's white attorneys and had been welcomed to the courthouse with stern words from the probate judge.

"I want to get one thing straight with you now," said the judge after summoning Chestnut into his office. "I want you to be respectful of and treat accordingly each of the ladies in my office. I will not tolerate any abuse of them in the slightest, do you understand?"

"I understand what you're saying," Chestnut replied. "What I don't understand is why you're saying it." Chestnut was offended by the judge's presumptuousness and embarrassed as well to be addressed in this way in front of the judge's secretaries and the other white women who observed from an outer office.

"I have never been disrespectful of a lady in my life," Chestnut replied boldly, "and, unlike you, I also respect black women."

Chestnut knew immediately that this remark would escalate the situation and result in his being ordered out of the office by the judge, which is what happened. Chestnut also assumed that he had just made a new and important enemy, although he was not greatly concerned. The judge had been his enemy even before he had met him, as were most of the legal authorities in the courthouse. Chestnut was sure that any obsequiousness on his part would have gained him nothing. Courtesy and fairness from white people toward black people was never extended without a struggle. Frederick Douglass had written this, and Chestnut often quoted it: "If there is no struggle, there is no progress. . . . Power concedes nothing without a demand. It never did and never will. . . . Men may not get all they pay for in this world but they must certainly pay for all they get."

Chestnut later in 1958 found himself facing a judge named George Wallace—who was then four years away from becoming the governor of Alabama, and eventually America's leading symbol of racism—but on this occasion Chestnut discovered Wallace to be surprisingly polite. Wallace was the first judge ever to address him as "Mr. Chestnut." Prior to this, other judges reserved "Mr." for white attorneys, referring to Chestnut in the courtroom simply as "J.L.," when they were not ignoring him completely. Chestnut had traveled from Selma to the courthouse in Barbour County—Wallace had been elected there as a district judge in 1953—to represent a group of black cotton farmers involved in a financial quarrel with their white overseers. In addition to calling him "Mr. Chestnut," Judge Wallace insisted that the overseers' white attorneys identify Chestnut's clients as "plaintiffs" rather than the term they were using—"those people." At the conclusion of the case, Judge Wallace ruled in favor of Chestnut's clients, awarding them even more money than Chestnut had hoped for. "Wallace was for the little man, no doubt about it," Chestnut wrote in his book, recalling his early impressions of the district judge in Barbour County, when Wallace might rightly have been seen as a populist, or a New Deal Democrat, or a "politician of inborn gifts," which was how the New York Times described him editorially before his career became "blighted by his opportunistic alignment with bigotry."

The transformation was apparent in 1962 when Wallace, eager at any cost to become the governor, marketed his message to exploit a time when growing numbers of white people in Alabama, as well as elsewhere in the nation, were becoming increasingly concerned that the advancements of blacks were threatening the well-being of whites—especially those poorer whites whose property values were declining as their neighborhoods were darkening and who could not afford to enroll their children in private schools in order to escape integrated public schools, where the student body was becoming predominantly black. George Wallace catered to the fears and fury of white people who could not buy their way out of the problems induced by a federal government altering rules and traditions that Wallace believed were the prerogatives of states righters like himself, and as a first-term governor in 1962, he represented himself as a small but determined defender against the aggressions of big government. He furthermore suggested that black people living in the North had it worse than those in the South, and he touched upon this in a Times interview that I did with him on June 2, 1963, during his brief visit to New York prior to appearing on NBC's Meet the Press.

I had arranged to see him through his press secretary, Bill Jones, an acquaintance of mine and journalism classmate a decade earlier on the Alabama campus. (Wallace had entered the University of Alabama as a freshman in 1937, receiving his law degree there in 1942.) While in New York, Governor Wallace was staying in a penthouse suite in the Pierre

Hotel on Fifth Avenue, a few blocks from where I lived, and although he was initially very cordial as Bill Jones introduced us—Wallace himself walked across the room to get me a cup of coffee instead of asking Jones or one of his other aides to do it—he was soon agitated after we had sat down and I began to wonder aloud why he was trying to prevent black students from attending our alma mater and why, in his inaugural address as governor, he had declared, "Segregation now, segregation tomorrow, segregation forever."

Governor Wallace denied that he had a racist hatred of black people, claiming that his position on segregation derived from his reading of the Bible and the Constitution and his own belief that segregation augmented most naturally a biracial coexistence. He had always lived in peace with black people, he told me, going back to the days of his youth in the dirt-road town of Clio; and throughout his life he had known and identified with individuals experiencing poverty and deprivation. He had been a nonfraternity member of the Alabama student body, and he helped to support himself there by working as a waiter and cabdriver; as the governor of Alabama, he reminded me, he was living in quarters surrounded on all sides by black residents. Wallace then stood and took me by the arm, leading me to a window that overlooked Central Park and the rows of elegant apartment buildings lined along the east side of Fifth Avenue, and he announced, "*Here* we have a citadel of hypocrisy in America."

There were no black people living in these buildings or anywhere within a mile of this place, he asserted, adding that this very hotel in New York was as segregated as any hotel in the Deep South. "Oh, I've been in these northern hotels," he went on, nodding in a knowing way, "and I hear these clerks telling Negroes, 'Now, let me see. Oh, yes, we're full up,' or 'Doesn't seem your reservation is here.' Down South, at least, we shoot straight across the board; we tell you how we feel. Here, you practice subterfuge and hypocrisy."

As I took notes, I guessed that the governor was rehearsing some of what he intended to deal with on *Meet the Press*, but I did not interrupt because I had assured Bill Jones earlier that the *Times* intended to allow Wallace to have his say, and I also was in agreement with some of what Wallace was saying about racism and hypocrisy in New York. As a long-time resident of this area, I had never had a black neighbor, and this would continue to be the case into the twenty-first century.

Returning to his seat, the governor lit up a cigar. "And then there's the northern press," he went on. "They come down and blow up everything to sell papers. You can have gang killings in New York, but it's immaterial."

Holding up a May 14 copy of the *Chicago Tribune* from the coffee table, he pointed to a headline. "It says, '5,000 Stone Cops in Shooting' after the police shot and wounded a fourteen-year-old Negro boy. But they don't send no federal troops into Chicago. And in Washington, D.C., after that Thanksgiving Day football riot—there were 485 hurt, and they used dogs to control the crowd. Yet when *we* use dogs in Birmingham, they make it sound like using dogs is a terrible thing. . . .

"After the Civil War," he said after a pause, "our land was burned down to the ground, and every chicken and every cow and every mule was slaughtered. And instead of getting Marshall Aid and Lend-Lease, we got carpetbaggers and scalawags. We got the Reconstruction. And in the Alabama legislature, they were all black folks or carpetbaggers. The South then was treated just the opposite of Japan, Italy, and Germany after World War II. Now don't get me wrong—I'm glad we rehabilitated Italy, Germany, and Japan because they've become Western friends and are against communism. But the South after the war was stripped down, and we had to pull ourselves up all alone—greatest comeback in history—hell, we pulled ourselves up, and pulled the Negro up with us. He lived. He ate. Who else pulled him up? We did. Or else he'd have starved to death."

The next day's *Times* printed what he had told me, together with his photograph and a headline that read WALLACE SCORNS CITIES OF NORTH. Within a week, his photo was on front pages nationwide after he had traveled to the University of Alabama campus to voice his opposition to classroom integration, even though President Kennedy had already federalized the Alabama National Guard and had made it clear that nothing would now delay the registration of black students. Although Governor Wallace would finally yield, knowing that he would go to jail if he defied a federal court order, he insisted on making a speech in which he condemned the ruling as a "trend toward military dictatorship in this country," and before he departed with his entourage, he declared, "I am returning to Montgomery to continue working for constitutional government to benefit all Alabamians—black and white."

But his definition of what was constitutional was unrelentingly challenged in Washington, and he was never able to condone the annoying black voter-registration program that the federal government was then encouraging in the old plantation lands of Alabama, and especially in Selma, which had been co-opted by Martin Luther King, Jr., in 1964 as the launching site for his national voter-registration campaign.

Dr. King's Atlanta-based Southern Christian Leadership Conference was actually not the first civil rights group to adopt Selma as its stomping ground. The first activists in Selma were affiliated with the Student Non-violent Coordinating Committee, also based in Atlanta, but inspired in Greensboro, North Carolina, where, in 1960, four black college freshmen had refused to vacate their seats at the Woolworth's lunch counter after being denied service. This highly publicized incident substantiated the tactical use of the sit-in style of protesting, and it was followed in other college towns by black students who soon banded together under the identity of the Student Nonviolent Coordinating Committee—commonly referred to as SNCC, and pronounced "Snick." While it professed to be influenced by the tranquil tactics of Mohandas Gandhi, SNCC was nonetheless motivated by what one of its leaders, John Lewis, called a "moral urgency," which manifested itself at times in an impatient and confrontational approach to problem solving that went beyond what was deemed prudent by many white liberals in the North and on the West Coast, whose financial contributions underwrote so much of civil rights work in the South. The young and idealistic members of SNCC were cause-led, not clergy-led; and as the writer Diane McWhorter described them in her Pulitzer Prize–winning book about Birmingham (*Carry Me Home*), the people at SNCC played "picador" to the "sluggish matador" of Martin Luther King, Jr.'s Southern Christian Leadership Conference.

It was an activist from SNCC, not one from Dr. King's SCLC, who had entered Selma in 1963 to assume a leading role in the black people's voting-rights drive. He was twenty-two-year-old Bernard Lafayette, from Nashville, and not long after he arrived he was ambushed one night by two white men, who beat him over the head with a rifle butt and left him bleeding along the road. After he had recovered days later and rejoined his fellow demonstrators on the steps of the town's courthouse—wearing his bloodstained clothing—the voting-rights campaign in Selma attracted longer and louder lines of protesters, and this, in turn, drew more television coverage, which added to the resentment being felt by Sheriff James G. Clark, Jr., and others in law enforcement and the white community at large.

While the town's newly elected mayor, Joseph T. Smitherman—a political acolyte of Governor Wallace—was not privately enamored of Sheriff Clark's manner in dealing with protesters, the mayor offered no counterstrategy and therefore succumbed to the whites who supported Clark's aggressiveness. Clark was a large burly man in his early forties who was six-two and weighed 220 pounds, and he had blue eyes and a pale-skinned round face that was fleshy and soft. Except for a brown curl just below his forehead, he had lost most of his hair, but he usually covered his head with a snap-brimmed fedora or a military-style cap with a scrambled-egg bill. His gold sheriff's badge was always highly polished, as were his shoes, and the trousers of his tailored brown uniform were sharply creased and his shirt was tapered at the waist and triple-pleated in the back. He had been born on a farm in the Alabama hamlet of Elba, and after joining the army air force and serving during the 1940s as an engineer-gunner, he returned to Alabama and a career in law enforcement that brought him quick notoriety when he began having altercations in public with black demonstrators.

"Look, I'm a peace-lovin' guy ordinarily," he once explained to me during an interview in Selma, "but some of these people'll stop at nothing." He then removed from his desk a wire-service photograph in which he was shown wrestling on the ground with an obese black woman. "I'm really mad about this," he said, holding it in front of me. "This shows Annie Lee Cooper, and she hit me *first*, caught me unaware. She'd stolen a club from one of my deputies and all I was doing in this picture was trying to get it out of her hand. Those damned newspaper fellows made it look like I was beating *her*. She's *bigger* than me. That Annie Lee Cooper's two hundred and twenty-six and a half pounds, six and a half more than me. I know this because, after we arrested her, I had her weighed."

Since becoming the sheriff in 1955, Clark would be reelected regularly through the mid-1960s by the area's southern whites, who saw Selma as a city under siege and saw themselves as needing to be defended against the statutory incursions of the federal government, and against such outside agitators as those sent in by SNCC, and against the national media, which seemed to be sympathetic to the blacks, and against the money changers in distant places who bankrolled the civil rights movement, and against the array of black celebrities, ranging from the comedian Dick Gregory to the writer James Baldwin, who visited Selma on many occasions to encourage the protesters and endorse a list of proposals and demands to which Sheriff Clark had a one-word reply: "Never." He wore a NEVER button on the lapel of the jacket he wore to church, and he displayed it on the front of his brown uniform as he stood guard with his men at the courthouse door, sometimes shoving aside and waving his club at those blacks who moved too slowly after he had ordered them to retreat.

Dr. King knew that he would be crowding in on SNCC if he ventured into Selma at this time, but by the summer of 1964, as the constant disturbances were regularly being reported in the national press, King knew he had no choice but to affiliate his organization with the struggle. He was *the* messiah of the movement in America. He had been *Time* maga-zine's Man of the Year in 1963, and he received the Nobel Prize for Peace in 1964. He had also been visited in Atlanta by a delegation of local lead-ers from Selma—J. L. Chestnut, Jr., among them—urging that he take over the leadership of the town's voter-registration campaign.

Chestnut had initially approved of the SNCC-led contentiousness in and around the Selma courthouse, but now he was inclined toward a more lawyerlike approach, and he thought that Dr. King, as a proponent of nonviolence, would approve of what he had in mind. Chestnut's plan was to comply with the latest ruling by a local judge, James A. Hare, that banned future street demonstrations and stand-ins; at the same time, Chestnut would change the battle site from the sidewalks to the court-room, within which he would file lawsuits against those white officials whose stalling tactics and edicts had so far minimized the number of black registrations. Instead of having four or five hundred black people standing in line and making noise, Chestnut favored selecting four or five black people who were among the better educated and qualified, and after *they* had been prevented from registering to vote, they would become test cases to prove the denial of their constitutional rights. Any of these cases could be directed up to the Supreme Court if necessary; and since Chest-nut was now an attorney representing the NAACP Legal Defense Fund in New York, he knew that there was money available to cover such an undertaking.

But Chestnut failed to persuade Martin Luther King, Jr., who saw Chestnut's approach as excessively time-consuming, and King reiterated that there were occasions when it was morally right to disobey unjust laws, and that such laws now existed in Alabama. He also told Chestnut, "You have neglected to pursue one of your strongest arguments," and King summarized this argument in two words: "Sheriff Clark." Chestnut was surprised to hear this. Until now, Chestnut had underestimated, as appar-ently King did not, the importance of a violent white man to the cause of black liberation. Chestnut knew, of course, that violence easily got the media's attention, but he also saw Sheriff Clark as a low-level thug, and to elevate his importance by making him a catalyst in the cause of black people was perhaps demeaning to the high purpose of the cause. The power that was oppressing black people in Selma, Chestnut told King, was not the sheriff but, rather, a man who was one of the leading members of the town's blue-blooded gentry, namely Judge James A. Hare. Chestnut had gotten to know Judge Hare fairly well in recent years, and as Chest-nut would later comment in his book:

Judge Hare was a sort of 1960s version of an 1860s plantation owner. Jim Clark was his overseer, the lower-class white man who ran the fields and controlled the slaves . . . the judge had upper-class contempt for "white trash" [and] once he told me: "Mongrelization would improve some of these people." He thought something was wrong with a man, especially a white man, who couldn't make it in America. He was capable of throwing the book at a poor white thief and giving a black thief a light sentence. One day as a skinny, scraggly-looking young white man was being led out of Hare's courtroom, Hare seriously commented to me: "I don't know why you're pushing integration. You're going to have to be with them."

Another reason that J. L. Chestnut, Jr., had misgivings about using Sheriff Clark to generate publicity was Chestnut's continuing belief that the most civilized means of addressing injustice in America was through the court system and not through commotion in the streets. In order to change the system, one should work within the system, he thought. Just because a person loathed a certain law did not give that person the moral right to disobey the law. Dr. King's thinking regarding Judge Hare's injunction differed on this point. Chestnut would not concede even to such a sagacious spiritual leader as Dr. King the farsighted and clearheaded capacity to know which law was just or unjust. This was for the courts to decide, although Chestnut might acknowledge King's wisdom in wondering where the justice was if people were expected to wait patiently for years and years until some superior court might finally, *maybe,* overturn an unjust ruling issued by such a racist judge as James A. Hare. But even in American cities where black people had long held the right to vote, there was not yet full justice, Chestnut reminded himself, elaborating in his book: "The white powers let blacks have some power and influence so long as it was kept on the south side of Chicago or Harlem in New York. At best, I thought we might make some sort of arrangement like that in the South. But as far as envisioning black people sitting on county commissions and city councils making decisions that affected white people, that was fantasyland."

Chestnut's view of himself was that of a realist who was interested in results and also committed to making a success of himself in Selma. He was now thirty-four, the husband of a local black woman with whom he already had four children, and his home, for better or worse, was in Selma. He and his family were part of Selma's full-time population, while Martin Luther King, Jr., and the other endowed activists were transients who "came and went [while] we faced the problems without letup. When King went to the boondocks, he'd stay a few days, then fly off to Atlanta, Washington, or Los Angeles where he was around people who appreciated and understood what he was doing. The Freedom Riders had each other, and they often went to Atlanta to recharge. We were sunk, by ourselves, in Selma." When SNCC sent in young Bernard Lafayette in 1963 to jump-start the voter drive, and after Chestnut's mother learned that J.L. had volunteered his support, she told her son, "That boy ought to go home. He's gonna get the white people all stirred up, then he'll run back to Atlanta and we'll be picking up the pieces . . . stay away from that mess. You can get yourself killed."

In late February 1965, a black voting-rights marcher named Jimmie Lee Jackson was shot to death one night by a state trooper in Perry County, thirty miles outside Selma. At the funeral, his angry friends insisted that his death be memorialized by a rally that would magnify the outcry against this latest atrocity, and then someone suggested, "Goddamn it, we ought to carry his body over to George Wallace in Montgomery." This soon was modified into the plan to walk from Selma to Montgomery to deliver an ultimatum to the governor, insisting that he abandon his racist policies toward black voter registration. The petitioners were to commence in Selma sometime during the first week of March, but there was disagreement as to when precisely they should proceed, and who exactly would be going, because there was ongoing disharmony between some members of SNCC and Dr. King's SCLC, and there were also rumors that the Klan would be waiting to ambush the marchers along the highway.

After huddling with his SCLC staff, some of whom feared that he himself might be the main target in an ambush, Dr. King vacillated for a few days in Atlanta, undecided as to whether he should go to Selma to lead the fifty-mile, five-day march to Montgomery, or urge instead that it be temporarily postponed until he had a clearer sense of the situation. The logistical problems alone made it an awesome undertaking—the security arrangements, the campsites, the requisition of food, tents, latrines, medical vehicles, ambulances—and adding to all of this was King's uncertainty about the mental state of the protesters, specifically whether they could restrict themselves to nonviolence after their passions had been inflamed by the murder of Jimmie Lee Jackson and while they would be facing an equally impassioned cross section of whites.

When I arrived in Selma on March 5, 1965, two days before the start of the tentatively scheduled procession to Montgomery, there was no sign of Dr. King mingling among the crowds that had been visible for days in and around Brown Chapel, nor was King necessarily missed by the younger activists who were more in sync with the soft-spoken but tenacious twenty-five-year-old chairman of SNCC, John Lewis, who stood ready to lead the way toward Montgomery.

Lewis was a former Freedom Rider who, while adhering to his definition of "moral urgency" in the early 1960s, never once backed away from the fists, baseball bats, or the guns of the white mobs and the police who objected to his traveling around the South on interstate buses with his fellow activists and then parading through terminal buildings to denounce the signs he saw reading WHITE MEN, COLORED MEN, WHITE WAITING, COLORED WAITING, and other designations of discrimination that were an affront to his dignity and his pursuit of an interracial democracy. Lewis had been born in 1940 into an impoverished Alabama sharecropping family in Pike County, nearly eighty miles southeast of Selma, where he attended a rural segregated school when he was not required to labor in the fields, earning less than thirty-five cents for every hundred pounds of cotton he picked. As a teenager, he was inspired by the news of Rosa Parks's assertive behavior on a bus and by the sermons of Dr. King that he heard on the radio. Because the tuition was free at the American Baptist Theological Seminary in Nashville, John Lewis applied there with the intention of becoming a preacher. It was while studying comparative religions that he learned of Gandhi's philosophy of nonviolence, and he was later guided by this when he joined with other students in desegregating lunch counters in Nashville and then helped to found the Student Nonviolent Coordinating Committee. In 1963, he was one of the main organizers of the Washington march and also a keynote speaker, along with Dr. King and four others then acknowledged to be national leaders in the civil rights movement (Roy Wilkins, James Farmer, Whitney Young, and A. Philip Randolph). But since Lewis was and would remain an unassuming individual, one who never sought personal attention from the press, he stood off to one side as the photographers in Washington asked the six men to pose together before the start of the parade. When the pictures were published, and Lewis's grave face and diminutive figure were almost out of the frame, one of Lewis's associates at SNCC, James Forman, admonished him: "You've got to get out *front*. Don't let King get all the credit. Don't stand back like that. Get out *front*."

In 1964, John Lewis was in Mississippi, actively engaged in the statewide voter-registration campaign, and a year later he was similarly involved in Alabama, where he found himself one day marching with twenty other demonstrators toward the Selma courthouse and into a barricade of state troopers and members of the sheriff's posse, led by Jim Clark himself.

"This is as far as you can go," said Sheriff Clark. "Turn around and go back. You are *not* going in the courthouse today."

"The courthouse is a public place," Lewis replied, "and we have a right to go inside. We will not be turned around."

"Did you hear what I said?" Clark asked in a louder voice. "Turn around and go back."

"Did you hear what *I* said?" Lewis countered. "We are *not* going back."

Lewis stared impassively up into the big reddened face of the sheriff, who then reacted by moving his jutting jaw down closer and closer, until it was nearly resting on the ridge of Lewis's small bulbous nose. Neither man spoke for several seconds, retaining their positions as the tension built within them and within the men who stood rigidly around them— the black marchers gathered anxiously behind Lewis, and the phalanx of helmeted armed men standing shoulder-to-shoulder behind the sheriff. The only sign of movement anywhere was the twirling of the billy club that the sheriff held in both hands at chest level, below his jaw and above Lewis's nose.

Then a door opened in the federal building across the street, and out walked J. L. Chestnut, Jr. He had been inside arguing motions all morning and most of the afternoon, knowing nothing of Lewis's intentions to lead a parade on this day; he was now stunned to be seeing what he was seeing, and even doubting that he was seeing it: the fearless, runty chairman of SNCC confronting the monstrous sheriff of Selma. Oh, John Lewis is crazy, Chestnut thought, and now he's going to get hurt. A week ago, almost on the same spot, Chestnut had seen the sheriff knock down an elderly black man who had been part of a march; Chestnut wanted to yell out words of warning to Lewis, to urge him to back away from Clark's billy club, but Chestnut was too transfixed to say or do anything but wait and watch—and what he next saw he would later identify as a "born again" moment, a "kind of conversion" that helped him to understand what Martin Luther King, Jr., had meant earlier about the moral right and the Godly might that at times guided one's resistance to unjust laws, and about how, if there's nothing for which you are willing to die, you are not fit to live.

Clark must have sensed, too, that John Lewis was crazy, or so recklessly righteous that he was dangerous, or at least too confusing to deal with at this time. Clark took a step back, turned toward his troops, and signaled with his club in the air for them to separate their ranks. Then he faced his nemesis once again, and, after nodding his head toward the courthouse door, he said in a voice that was surly but soft, "Goddamn it, go on in."

Saying nothing, showing no gesture of gratitude or even making eye contact with the sheriff, John Lewis proceeded toward the steps of the courthouse with his followers trailing solemnly behind him—and J. L. Chestnut, Jr., continued to watch with amazement, reminding himself, There's no way Lewis could not have been scared to death, but he stood his ground and won! And he didn't have any pistols. He didn't have any troops. He just had about twenty resolute folk there in a little line. Yet he stood face-to-face with the power of Alabama and refused on moral grounds to give in . . . and Alabama blinked . . . and to hell with Hare. . . .

But on the next occasion when Chestnut would observe John Lewis in such a situation, leading a line of black people across the Selma bridge on the Sunday morning of March 7, 1965, he would see Lewis's body flattened along the highway, his bones battered, his head bleeding, and his skull fractured, and Sheriff Clark and dozens of other law-enforcement figures chasing the retreating marchers back to Brown Chapel, leaving seventeen of them strewn along the road in pain and coughing from the gas until they were hauled away to a segregated hospital. The police attack had been so quick that even Lewis, with all his experience in the front lines of SNCC and as a Freedom Rider, had not foreseen this calamity, this vengeful rampage by the police, which Lewis would come to know as one of the worst and best days of his life.

Until a few minutes before his concussion he had been walking as casually as if he were on a Sunday stroll through a park, guiding a merry gathering of picnic-bound kinfolk. There were songs coming from behind him, the harmonizing of black men and women allied in their solidarity, carrying together with their satchels the burdens of their beliefs and a sense that they were on the right road to some form of redemption. Keeping pace with Lewis was King's representative, Hosea Williams, and behind them were a pair of voting-rights organizers from nearby Lowndes and Perry counties (the latter being the locale of Jimmie Lee Jackson's murder); behind these men were two veteran female activists from Selma—one a dental hygienist, the other a Tuskegee-trained agrarian economist who worked with farming families and was striving to get them registered; and behind them came the pastor from Brown Chapel, together with an educator who taught science at the black high school; and trailing them, in tandem, were hundreds of others, men and women of various occupations and ages and also many students, nearly all of them wearing their Sunday best and obeying their elders' instructions that they walk only on the sidewalk through the business district and behave in a modest and orderly fashion, even though every black person in this long procession was guilty of what Judge Hare termed "disorderly conduct."

Still, the police did not stop them as they proceeded through Selma's shopping area, nor were they impeded by anyone among the cranky crowds of white people who stood watching along the storefronts. But after the marchers in the lead had begun crossing the arched center section of the bridge, they could see that the highway ahead was blocked by lines of helmeted men. As John Lewis got closer, he recognized some of the blue-uniformed officers of the state police and the khaki-clad mounted members of the sheriff's posse, and, of course, Jim Clark himself. Lewis intended to keep walking until he reached the roadblock, and then he assumed he would be told that he was under arrest and would be sent to jail until J. L. Chestnut, Jr., bailed him out. This had become rather pro forma for John Lewis as a youthful but highly experienced civil rights worker. He had already been arrested more than thirty times since he had begun sitting in at Tennessee lunch counters five years before, and while as a Freedom Rider he had been slapped, kicked, spat upon, and pistol-whipped by white mobs and the police, he did not anticipate any physical harm coming his way today on the highway to Montgomery. Clark's recent timidity at the courthouse possibly contributed to Lewis's thinking, and so he continued to move ahead without concern as he got to within three hundred feet of the police and heard one of the officers begin to shout through a bullhorn, ". . . I give you three minutes to disperse and go back to your church. This is an unlawful march. It will not be allowed to continue."

From where I was positioned, on the side of the highway across the road from where Chestnut stood atop a flatbed truck, I observed that many members of the sheriff's mounted posse did not appear to be fully controlling their horses. The animals seemed to be nervous, even delirious as they raised up on their hind hoofs and jerked their heads spastically while uttering loud seething sounds that were interrupted by the cursings of their riders, who pulled tightly on the reins while struggling to remain in the saddles. I know little about horsemanship, but I had seen the mounted police of New York controlling crowds of demonstrators on many occasions, and I was sure that what I was seeing here was a situation in disarray, either because the men had been assigned to rowdy horses they were unfamiliar with or because the horses themselves were reacting to the currents of bellicosity that their riders were transmitting to them down through the saddles. But the sheriff seemed not to notice, walking by himself away from the barricade toward the side of the road where I stood with other members of the media. He was wearing his tailored uniform and the cap with the gold-braided bill, and as he came nearer to us, swinging his billy club as he walked, I could see his broad face brighten and his eyes twinkle as the lights of many cameras flashed upon him.

To my right was a television crew from NBC; to my left, a freelance photographer named Norris McNamara, who had driven over with me earlier in the scarlet red Chevrolet coupe that I had rented from Avis two days ago when I had flown into Montgomery. I would have preferred a less conspicuous vehicle, hoping to draw as little attention as possible in this place that I assumed had already had enough of out-of-towners who were here to highlight Selma's discord, but the red coupe was the only car I could get. On this Sunday morning, I had parked it on a side street in the business district because the police had closed the bridge to motor traffic after learning about the march. And as I then walked across the ramp toward the highway with McNamara, hearing the insults that some young white men were directing toward us as newsmen—McNamara was wearing two or three cameras around his neck—I began to resent McNamara. I wondered why he had to walk around in this feverish city flaunting all those cameras. But I said nothing, and Sheriff Clark was clearly not offended when McNamara pushed in front of me and began snapping his picture. After the trooper with the bullhorn had issued his three-minute warning, the sheriff turned away from us and returned to the barricade near his posse and their jittery, foaming horses.

Now the front rows of marchers, having reached the barricade, paused and stood silently for some seconds facing the lawmen, as if waiting for further instructions or some form of dialogue. But the sheriff and the chief officer of the state police just stared at them, and especially at John Lewis, who reacted by steadfastly exhibiting the same passive mode of defiance that he had shown at the courthouse. It was a posture devoid of provocation, leaning toward nonchalance. Meanwhile, the trooper with the bullhorn raised his left hand to glance at his watch. At least a minute remained before the end of the time limit. Behind him the other troopers and the posse were busily donning their gas masks, and about thirty seconds later, without any signal or order that I was aware of, they prematurely went into action by tossing the first of many gas canisters high in the air, out toward where the demonstrators were lined up—and suddenly, as people began to scream and scatter, the canisters exploded with gun-pop percussion on hitting the highway, emitting stinging swarms of smoke that soon enshrouded the black people and burned their eyes and sent them tumbling blindly backward in panic before they tried to get up quickly and distance themselves from the punishment of their onrushing uniformed attackers.

The lawmen charged ahead on foot and horseback, swinging their clubs and cattle prods and rifle butts down upon every recoiling black figure they could vaguely see in the swirling masses of smoke. As I stood watching next to the camera-clicking McNamara, aghast and speechless while taking notes along the shoulder of the highway, I could hear rising out of the haze a few hundred feet away the howling cries and almost songlike sighs of black women, and the swearing and moaning of many men, and other sounds, too, that I had never heard before—namely, that of wooden clubs and rifle butts pounding with muted audibility the demonstrators' clothes-covered flesh and at the same time nicking the rims of some of the lawmen's steel-lined plastic helmets—*clap, cluck, clop; clap, cluck, clop!* I also heard the sounds of NBC's three-man television crew standing in a grassy patch nearby recording the whole scene, soon to be spun around the world and come boomeranging back to Selma.

"Let's get out of here," I shouted to McNamara, smelling gas and lifting my pocket handkerchief to my face. I wanted to follow the hundreds of fleeing marchers and their uniformed stalkers whom I now spotted through the smoke as they crossed over the bridge back to Selma, running in different directions along the waterfront and through the business district. Hoping I could easily relocate my car, I thought ahead to visiting Brown Chapel, and then the police station, in search of information about the extent of the injuries and the number of arrests, and perhaps I could get statements from the mayor, the sheriff, and some of the marchers and their organizers. Then I planned to drive to my hotel, the gilded old slave-built edifice in the center of town where many newsmen were staying, and begin writing my article. I would have to finish it by 6:00 p.m. in order to meet the *Times* deadline.

As I now ran along the shoulder of the road toward the bridge with McNamara, thinking about how I might begin my story, I saw the highway littered with shoes, hats, handkerchiefs, umbrellas, toothbrushes, and other items abandoned by the marchers; there were also several prostrate bodies of black people on the roadside receiving medical assistance, and a single ambulance had just been waved across the ramp by a policeman— an ambulance whose passengers would include, I later learned, the bleeding and barely conscious John Lewis. I had not seen him get hit, but I would hear that he had been the first target, no doubt the primary target of Sheriff Clark and his henchmen.

Relieved that my car had not been stolen or vandalized, I quickly unlocked the doors as McNamara, with his cameras swinging around his neck, ran to the other side. Black people were dashing through the sidewalks on both sides of us, sometimes disappearing into alleys, or ducking momentarily behind billboards or the fences and walls of residential buildings and stores, eluding the reconnoitering lawmen who galloped back and forth on their horses or cruised through the street in their patrol cars. After I had started up the engine and was slowly pulling out from the curb, I noticed that some of the white people who stood watching from their second-story windows and front porches were gesturing to get my attention, pointing toward the rear of my car. I then felt myself rocking from side to side and heard pounding along the car's trunk and back fenders, and suddenly my door was pulled open by a stocky red-bearded white man in his thirties who was breathing heavily, kicking up his legs in a backward motion while holding on to the outside handle of the extended door of my slow-moving car.

"Hey, nigger lovers," he yelled in at McNamara and myself, "where you off to?" Before we could answer, two of his friends came running alongside to join him and grab onto the door, and one of them spat what I think was tobacco juice in my direction as they continued to rock the vehicle while I kept my hands on the steering wheel and inched ahead.

"*Hurry*, give it gas!" McNamara whispered urgently, flapping forward the lapels of the bulky cotton jacket he wore, covering up his cameras. I thought of racing ahead and dragging this trio with me if they hung on, but it also seemed too risky at this moment in this turbulent place—me speeding through downtown Selma in a red coupe with three angry and possibly armed hooligans hanging on while the raging lawmen around us were hunting down black people in flight. I stopped the car completely but kept the motor idling, and then turned toward the three intruders, and it was then that I recognized them. I had seen them earlier standing behind me along the highway, near the drive-in restaurant; they had been in the forefront of the group of white men led by the heckler brandishing the Confederate flag.

"How'd you like it if we broke off yo' fucking door?" one of them now asked me, a lean, glint-eyed individual in his early twenties wearing a baseball cap and showing a missing front tooth.

"I hope you won't do that," I replied. "I rented this car in Montgomery."

"Then how'd you like it if we broke off yo' fucking head?" asked the red-bearded older man who had spoken to me first.

"I hope you won't do that, either," I said. I tried to speak in an even tone, not wanting to seem intimidated but also not wanting to stir up these people any more than they already were. They are probably half-drunk, I thought. They spoke in a slurred manner and stood unsteadily, as if relying on the door to maintain their balance. If any of them let go of the door and headed toward me, I knew I would slam my foot on the gas pedal and take my chances. But they remained where they were, swinging and pulling upon the outstretched door and its fully extended hinges, holding on even as a Selma city police vehicle pulled up next to us.

"Hey, you're blocking the road," an officer said to me from the open window of his vehicle. "Move that damned car of yours. . . ."

"We're trying to, Officer," McNamara replied, leaning across me as he spoke in a loud voice, "but these guys are stopping us."

The policeman looked at the three men but said nothing. The red-bearded man was grinning at the cop in a way that told me they were acquainted. Then the bearded man and the two others slowly backed away from the door and, as if on cue, suddenly ran toward it and slammed it shut with their booted feet and the palms of their hands so forcefully that McNamara and I went reeling sideways, careening against each other on the other side of the car.

"Now you can get your damned car out of here," the police officer said.

After I had readjusted myself behind the wheel and shifted into the driving gear, I began to move forward. As I pulled away, heading toward Brown Chapel, I heard the red-bearded men yelling after us, "We shoulda kicked yo' ass. You come down here, you start all this trouble, and you don't know shit about Alabama. . . ."

14

by Gay Talese
Special to The New York Times

SELMA, Ala., MARCH 7—The long line of Negroes walked slowly and silently to the main sidewalk of Selma's business district on this quiet Sunday. There were 525 of them, walking two abreast, and they were headed for a small concrete bridge at the end of the street. . . .

AFTER I HAD TYPED AND RETYPED MY ARTICLE, COMPLETING IT two minutes before the end of the deadline, I dictated it by telephone from my hotel room to one of the recording transcribers in the *Times* news department in New York, dissatisfied, as I so often was, with what I had written and wishing that there had been more time for me to interview more people, to rephrase my sentences and think of better words to describe what I had seen—even though, in a fully understood and enduring sense, I was not really sure what I had seen, beyond the sadism and suffering along the highway, which the television networks had made the most of, interrupting their prime-time Sunday-night programs to show film clips of the lawmen clubbing people amid the screaming and the excruciating smoke, scenes that were rebroadcast on the following day and throughout the week, prompting thousands of appalled white and black citizens from all parts of the nation to accept Dr. King's invitation to visit Selma and accompany him on the next march, one that he likened to the pilgrimage of the ancient Israelites out of Egypt.

With all respect for the magnetism of Dr. King, I believe that most of those people who came pouring into Alabama did so because they were horrified by what they had been shown on television and felt compelled to register their disapprobation and disgust personally. I also believe that these film clips from Selma, so starkly vivid in their depictions of inhumanity and so uncomplicatedly clear in their differentiation between good and evil—black angels and white devils engaged in five minutes of graphic interaction culminating a century of post-Reconstruction wrath—reaffirmed how persuasive television news reporting had become in projecting imagery and attitude in ways that could immediately mold and mobilize public opinion. Television's influence was being discharged not only from Alabama but from all parts of the nation in 1965, a polemical year, in which advocates and detractors—appearing in television studios or in front of cameras on campuses and in the streets—debated such subjects as whether leading athletes should compete in South Africa while its government continued to practice apartheid, or whether First Amendment protection should be extended to the vociferous students of Berkeley's Filthy Speech Movement, or whether the United States should withdraw its military forces from Vietnam. Whatever the topic, the television news shows strived to be succinct, pictorially graphic, and ingrained with whatever might induce people to stay tuned; and the newsmakers themselves (the people the news cameras focused upon) often performed for the cameras in order to accommodate the cameras' need for visual expression and animation and their *own* need to be seen and heard on television and thus spread their message far and wide to the masses. It was not that television was slanting the news but that the newsmakers were slanting *themselves* to television, were falling to the ground as the police broke up their demonstrations and thereby forcing the police to drag them to patrol wagons, prolonging the scene for the cameras and illustrating at greater length their willingness to suffer for their cause.

I had been reared within the perimeters of print journalism, and when television reporters first entered the field during my early years on the *Times*, they were scorned by my older colleagues as a breed of illegitimates who were embarrassing to the profession. They were said to be superficial in outlook, all surface and no substance; and save for such notable exceptions as Walter Cronkite (who had worked as a foreign correspondent during World War II for the United Press), the television anchormen and assignment editors lacked the training and experience to properly evaluate and to comprehensively communicate in a balanced and reliable manner the serious events of the day. The preeminent figures in American journalism when I joined the *Times* were men who augustly personified the power of the printed word. Among this group of individuals was the venerable syndicated columnist Walter Lippman, not a *Times* man, and also my elder colleague at the *Times*, James Reston, the paper's Washington bureau chief and its top writer (and a man so famous that he was once the subject of the lead story in *Time* magazine, with his photo on the cover); in addition, there were at least half a dozen star nonfiction writers on the staff of *The New Yorker* whom I admired and whose articles I clipped and filed away as examples of journalism that was both literary and historically relevant.

One article that I saved was a reprint of a piece that had totally occupied the editorial space of *The New Yorker* issue of August 31, 1946. It was an article by John Hersey entitled "Hiroshima," and it described the devastation of the first atomic bomb from the viewpoint of six people in Japan who had survived the blast a year earlier. Hersey conducted hundreds of interviews with these survivors and other people in Japan and then produced a work of art that re-created for me the horror of that moment (8:15 a.m., August 6, 1945) in human terms so riveting and transcending as to soar beyond what I could imagine while viewing the film clips of the poisonous cloud mushrooming on the horizon.

The *New Yorker* issue featuring Hersey's article sold out hours after reaching the newsstands, and on four successive nights the American Broadcasting Company canceled its regular radio broadcasts so that "Hiroshima" could be read to millions of its listeners. I was thinking about that piece and its effect on the pretelevision public while I was on assignment in Selma, and I wondered what examples of great contemporary reportage in magazines and newspapers were currently being filed away by young students of nonfiction in this video age, when the television newsmen were zooming in and communicating to the home audience an intimate sense of being at the red-hot center of history. It was not that I was foreseeing the obsolescence of the print media due to the mobile cameras and the more competitive initiatives of television newsmen, and I certainly could not conceive of a day when my own newspaper would no longer stand as America's "paper of record"; moreover, I believed, and would continue to believe, that what the *Times*'s editors each day saw fit to print would be the dominant daily guide for the assignment editors at the networks. But at the same time, the general public was now receiving most of its breaking news from television, and this inveigling visual medium was to some degree heightening or altering or reflexively relating reality as it offered pictorial evidence of its existence, and it was impacting upon the public more immediately and dramatically than the print journalism I was practicing in Selma.

After I had finished filing my story, I went down to the hotel bar to rejoin McNamara, and a *Newsweek* correspondent named William J. Cook, and also the television crew from NBC, the latter being in a gleeful and self-congratulatory frame of mind.

"Oh, what great stuff we got today," one of them was saying, having already heard from New York that the film clips of the highway bludgeoning had been terrific and would be featured during prime time. When I saw the clips that night on television and again the following morning, I had a closer visual sense of the lawmen's ferocity and the victims' capitulation than I'd had when watching from the highway. Still, I was surprised by how quickly these film clips caused Selma to be singled out and condemned nationwide for the atrocities of its lawmen. Police brutality, after all, could be found almost anywhere. I would live to see the day when policemen in New York would bring a black suspect into a precinct house for questioning and then sodomize him with a broomstick. But Selma in the spring of 1965 was demonized like no other place in America because the most abominable moments of its lawmen had been exposed on national television; and President Lyndon Johnson called attention to Selma's notoriety as he urged Congress on March 15 to pass a new voting-rights bill. It would, among other things, suspend literacy tests, install federally appointed registrars in places like Selma where black registrations were customarily obstructed, and it would impose federal scrutiny over all election procedures in order to ensure that blacks would no longer be subjected to racist tactics of intimidation, discouragement, and delay.

"At times history and fate meet at a single time in a single place to shape a turning point in man's unending search for freedom," President Johnson told Congress. "So it was at Lexington and Concord. So it was at Appomattox. So it was last week in Selma, Alabama."

It seemed to me that President Johnson's reference to Appomattox, Virginia, was an overly optimistic comparison to the situation in Selma; at Appomattox the Confederate army had surrendered in the spring of 1865 to their northern conquerors, whereas at the time of Johnson's speech the civil rights demonstrators were still being blocked from advancing along the highway to Montgomery, and Dr. King's main accomplishment since arriving in Selma within hours of hearing about the "Bloody Sunday" incident was in promoting his cause before the television cameras. When he led his people from Brown Chapel through downtown Selma across the bridge on Tuesday, March 9, it was essentially a media event, a situation staged for the cameras, rather than an authentic follow-up to the first attempt to reach Montgomery two days earlier. Although his rank-and-file supporters were unaware of it, Dr. King on

March 9 was operating in accord with a privately agreed-upon deal with federal and state authorities that would permit him to move forward but not beyond the point on the highway that had been barricaded on Bloody Sunday and was still being blocked off.

Dr. King's marchers in Selma now included, or would soon include, hundreds of out-of-state white people who were responding to his appeal for added companionship along the "highway up from darkness." Among the respondents were ministers from New England, hippies from San Francisco, postdebutantes from Philadelphia, labor leaders from New York, a blind man from Atlanta, a one-legged social worker from Saginaw, Michigan, the wife of a U.S. senator from Illinois, the widow of a senator from New Hampshire, and a thirty-nine-year-old mother of five children who was married to a Teamster agent from Detroit. Few of these people had ever before walked arm in arm with black people, or had joined in the singing of Negro spirituals, or had been overnight guests in the homes of black families (such hospitality was necessary, since the town's few hotels and motels were fully booked), or had felt safer and more secure in black neighborhoods than in those where the residents were white. When Dr. King's integrated mile-long parade approached the barricade on March 9, a police officer with a bullhorn proclaimed that the march was illegal, being in violation of an injunction upheld by a federal judge in Montgomery. King then halted his people and asked them to kneel with him on the highway and join him in prayer. Moments later, as television crews memorialized the scene, he gestured for his legions to rise and withdraw and return with him to Brown Chapel.

"This is what happens when we get white people involved," a young black minister named James Bevel told me as I walked with him and a few other black activists back over the bridge into town. The lean Alabama-born Rev. James Bevel, wearing an Iranian skullcap and neatly pressed overalls, was essentially saying that Dr. King had been restrained because of his concern for the well-being of these white newcomers to his ranks. While disappointed with King's reticence, Bevel was not as critical of the civil rights leader as were many members of SNCC, who declared that King had lost his nerve, and they later referred to this day, frequently and facetiously, as "Turn-Around Tuesday."

But J. L. Chestnut, Jr., King's local legal consultant in Selma, thought that King's strategy was wise and proper. Another bloody day in this town would achieve nothing. Evidence of Selma's racism had already been exposed on national television, and Chestnut believed that now was the time for King to reassert his image as a proponent of peace, as a law-abiding man of God patiently awaiting the day when the injunction would be lifted and the marchers would be allowed to proceed beyond the outskirts of Selma and onward to Montgomery.

The day of advancement finally occurred on March 21. But even though the federal judge had now provisionally sanctioned the march, the continuing rumors of violence and death to the participants meant that President Johnson felt obliged to provide them with a vast and heavily armed escort. One of Dr. King's white supporters had already lost his life in Selma. A Unitarian minister from Boston, James Reeb, had been clubbed by a white mob on the evening of March 9 after leaving a restaurant reserved for black people, and he died of head injuries two days later. And so President Johnson was unstinting in the security arrangements that he authorized for the procession to Montgomery that commenced on the afternoon of March 21—500 soldiers from Fort Bragg, North Carolina, and hundreds more from other military installations in the South, plus the 1,863 members of the Alabama National Guard. In addition, there were 100 FBI agents, 75 federal marshals, and a pair of military helicopters that hovered over the 2,500 blacks and the 500 whites who walked eight abreast through downtown Selma and across the bridge before reducing their numbers as they left town and headed southeast toward the old country roads adjoining what had once been slave-laboring plantations.

Along the way, the marchers, dressed in motley multicolored clothing—denim, khaki, clerical black, cashmere turtlenecks, toggle coats, ponchos fashioned from plastic garbage bags—were occasionally greeted by small groups of roadside hecklers: "You can't vote, you son of a bitch—you ain't human yet"; "Get the hell off the grass!"; "Hey, black boy, gettin' any from that Yankee girl?" I also saw, mingling among the onlookers, some sullen-faced members of the Selma police force and the sheriff's posse, including Jim Clark, who was dressed in a business suit and fedora and displayed a NEVER button on his lapel.

In compliance with the federal judge's ruling, the fifty-four-mile trek from Selma to Montgomery was to be completed within a five-day period, and no more than three hundred civil rights demonstrators were supposed to occupy the highway in areas where it was limited to two lanes, and they were also directed to stay to the left, keeping the right lane open for motor traffic moving in the opposite direction. Due to the marchers' late start on the first day, and the fact that Dr. King and many others developed foot blisters, only seven and a half miles had been covered when they stopped for the night in a prearranged place—a cow pasture owned by a black farming family that had asked me not to write about them, hoping that in maintaining a low profile they would minimize the risk of reprisals from Klan members or their cohorts.

I drove on ahead of the marchers throughout the day in search of feature stories or other sidebar material, joining some of my media colleagues as they filed hard news accounts from motels or hotels in Montgomery or its vicinity; and then I returned in the morning to the march route, which moved past farmlands, swamplands, piney thickets, and tall trees densely clustered with Spanish moss. While on the road, Dr. King slept at night in a well-guarded camper, while other security personnel posted themselves in front of the tents that sheltered the rest of the marchers and the volunteer workers who provided water, food, and medicine. Those marchers who were too exhausted or were otherwise unable to remain with the group were transported back to Selma and replaced by those who were physically able and eager to participate.

On the second day, the marchers got an early start and managed to travel seventeen and a half miles before nightfall. King left his followers in the late afternoon in order to catch a flight to Cleveland, where he was the scheduled speaker at a fund-raising event. His place as the march's leader on the following day was taken by the man whose skull had been fractured on Bloody Sunday—John Lewis. It rained heavily on this day, and also during a part of the next, limiting the march's progress to eleven and twelve miles, respectively. But toward the end of the fourth day, as the roadway expanded from two lanes to four and as the marchers' numbers soared from three hundred to more than one thousand, the capital of Alabama was in view. At the campsite that evening on the edge of the city, the marchers' tents and vehicles were arranged to make room for a stage. It was a jerry-built stage formed by borrowed coffin crates, and on them that night were several renowned performers who had come to Montgomery to entertain the crowd—such stars as Harry Belafonte, Mahalia Jackson, Tony Bennett, and Sammy Davis, Jr. Other show business people in New York were planning to support the cause with a one-night theater benefit entitled "Broadway Answers Selma."

On the fifth and final day of the march, an estimated 25,000 supporters of the civil rights movement had arrived in Montgomery from near and far to participate in the concluding ceremony, which was a massive rally scheduled for noon on the steps of the colonnaded capitol, on the dome of which were flags representing the state of Alabama and the old Confederacy. Adjacent to the building, dangling separately on a staff of its own, was a flag identifying the United States. Anxious municipal authorities, hinting of likely riots or other disturbances, urged all students, black and white, to remain in school throughout the afternoon and avoid the capitol area, while state employees were given the day off and many downtown shops decided to remain closed until the demonstrators left the city. In response to the mounting concerns of President Johnson, added numbers of federal troops were flown into the city beginning at 4:00 a.m., six hours before Dr. King was to start the march, and members of the city's police force were stationed at each of the 104 intersections that King's legions were to pass as they advanced from their campsite to the steps of the state building. Governor Wallace had no intention of coming down from his office to greet them.

He remained in his executive suite throughout the afternoon, relaxing and joking with his aides and a few trusted southern journalists, not seeming to care that he was loathed by the clamorous crowds who presently jammed the sidewalks and streets that surrounded him and were directing their insults up toward him through their loudspeakers. He was indebted to these people for helping to make him what he had become—a contrarian whose opposition to their proposals had found appeal in Middle America and had propelled him into the limelight as a Democratic presidential contender. White voters in Alabama and throughout the country, and increasing numbers of working-class ethnics in the urban areas, were finding themselves in accord with Wallace's stand on "law and order," his quarrel with college students protesting the war in Vietnam, his "little guy" feistiness in the face of the nation's corporate elite and intellectuals, and his continuing defense of racial segregation. And even these masses now assembled in Montgomery were inadvertently lending testimony to his stature. How else could one explain that 25,000 people had taken the trouble to come here in order to take issue with him? He interpreted it as a form of flattery, and as he stood behind the venetian blinds of an office window, holding a pair of borrowed binoculars and squinting as he poked them between the slats, he remarked lightly to his companions: "That's quite a crowd."

The demonstration lasted four hours, featuring many speakers but highlighted by the remarks delivered by Dr. King, who stood on the back of a flatbed trailer parked among the throngs in the street. "[T]oday," he cried out, "I want to say to the people of America and the nations of the world that we are not about to turn around. We are on the move now. Yes, we are on the move and no wave of racism can stop us . . . not even the marching of mighty armies can halt us. . . . Let us march . . . on segregated schools . . . on poverty . . . on ballot boxes until all over Alabama, God's children will be able to walk the earth in decency and honor. . . ."

After Dr. King and the other speakers had left the site of the demonstration along with their armed escorts and the media, and as the municipal authorities expressed relief that this tense and muggy afternoon had ended without any instances of the disorder and property damage that they had anticipated, several hundred marchers lined up to be transported back to Selma and other destinations in the buses, vans, and other vehicles driven by dozens of civil rights volunteer workers.

One of these volunteers was a thirty-nine-year-old blond woman from Detroit named Viola Liuzzo, who had left her five children and husband at home a week earlier so she could travel to Selma and partake in the march. Within a few hours of its completion on March 25, Mrs. Liuzzo had delivered one carload of marchers to Selma and was on the way back to Montgomery to pick up a second group, when her car was passed by another vehicle along a slight curve on the two-lane road within the swamplands of Lowndes County. A nineteen-year-old black male civil rights worker sat next to her, but only Mrs. Liuzzo was hit by their gunfire, and she died instantly of head wounds as her car swerved off the road and became entangled in a barbed-wire fence.

The next day, President Johnson announced on national television that Mrs. Liuzzo's murderers were four white men from the Birmingham area who were members of the Ku Klux Klan. "They struck by night," Johnson said, "for their purposes cannot stand the light of day," and "because I know their loyalty is not to the U.S. but to a hooded society of bigots," Johnson said he was forthwith declaring war on the Klan in the form of intensified surveillance and proposed legal punishments that would induce Klan members to quit "before it was too late." The four Klansmen under arrest were a forty-three-year-old steelworker, a forty-one-year-old retired steelworker on a disability pension, a thirty-one-year-old individual who was unemployed, and a twenty-one-year-old mechanic. Although in the Klansmen's subsequent trials the jurors were unable to come to terms on the issues of murder, the men were ultimately convicted on federal charges of violating Mrs. Liuzzo's civil rights and were sentenced to ten years in jail—all except the thirty-one-year-old. He went free. For six years he had been an informant on the payroll of the FBI.

15

TWO MONTHS AFTER THE MARCH, IN MAY 1965, I RETURNED TO Selma to write a follow-up story for the *New York Times Magazine*. I was curious to see what, if anything, had improved for the local black people in the wake of Dr. King's campaign and while the cause of civil rights continued to command the highest priority in the Lyndon Johnson White House.

After registering at the old Albert Hotel, where I had stayed before, I drove around town in a rented blue Ford sedan amid familiar sights and unfamiliar circumstances—the bridge without marchers, the highway without civil rights music and tear gas, the chapel in the black ghetto without camera crews posted on its front steps, and no hecklers standing downtown along the wide globe light–lined sidewalk of Broad Street. Now on Broad Street there were white teenagers pedaling bicycles, mothers pushing babies in carriages, truckers unloading supplies, traffic cops routinely ticketing improperly parked cars. The business district was crowded with mostly white but also some black pedestrians strolling in and out of two-story office buildings and warehouses and retail shops—the whites and blacks not pausing to chat with one another, or to acknowledge one another with a nod or a smile, but at least they were not insulting and glaring at one another during this undefinable period of cessation approximating an interracial truce.

The white people whom I interviewed told me that, thanks to the departure of Dr. King and his followers, the city was gradually returning to "normal." They reminded me that Joe Smitherman was still the mayor, Jim Clark was still the sheriff, and Governor Wallace was making no promises to the small group of black petitioners whom he had finally admitted into his office on March 30. And so segregation was still the policy within Selma's school system, its police department, its jailhouse, its public pools and other recreational facilities, and in most of its churches. The restaurants and hotels did not officially list themselves as segregated, but the white management and staff made black people feel so unwelcome that the latter tended to stay away. "You can't legislate how people feel," I was told by a white man named Carl Morgan, the president of Selma's all-white city council.

The black people I consulted with said it was yet too early to gauge the civil rights demonstrators' impact on interracial developments in Selma. Even as Congress was about to pass President Johnson's voting-rights bill, and as the black people of Selma remained dedicated to doubling and tripling their registration numbers, it could nonetheless take years for Selma's black population to organize itself politically in ways that would challenge the entrenched white power structure. J. L. Chestnut, Jr., was satisfied meanwhile that the "reign of terror" was over in Selma, and he believed that the successful completion of the five-day march had been a symbolic triumph that would inevitably inspire black people and encourage them to go further because, as he had heard Dr. King phrase it in Montgomery, "We are not about to turn around." Before the march, Chestnut had admitted to having concerns that the promotion of black people's rights was being politically exploited by the Democrats in the White House in order to allow President Johnson to singularly dominate the daily headlines, and Chestnut was then bothered by the possibility that "King was no longer the number-one civil rights leader in America; Lyndon Johnson was . . . and we'd been outfoxed and were in danger of being co-opted"—and Chestnut was further discomfitted by the question he asked himself: If President Johnson "became recognized as the man responsible for our civil rights victories and allowed to set our agenda, did this mean the end of the movement?" But the successful completion of the Selma to Montgomery march allayed all of Chestnut's earlier anxieties, and it most particularly made him proud of the fact "that no white person had decided there would be a march or where or how far it would go. These were black decisions. A white judge said, 'Well, okay, it's legal,' and a white President federalized the National Guard, but they were reacting to a situation created by black people. Blacks were in charge, and there were whites in the march who clearly agreed with this arrangement and were there to play a supporting role. The march to Montgomery was the first enterprise I'd ever seen involving black and white people where the black people set the agenda and ran the show."

But during my stay in Selma for the *Times Magazine*, I saw no signs of black people running anything; all I saw was evidence to the contrary. Without the presence of King's forces and the media, it seemed clear to me that the situation here had reverted to what the white locals called "normal," meaning that *they* were controlling things and the traditionally subordinate local blacks (with certain rare exceptions, such as the optimistic J. L. Chestnut, Jr.) were sitting back and hoping that entitlements and their prayers and the higher conscience of the nation would eventually liberate them from their bondage.

Perhaps I was reacting with impatience and insufficient insight into the uplifted souls of these postmarch black residents of Selma, and yet as an exploring journalist I was influenced by what I saw, and what I now saw on display in the black quarter was an absence of energy and direction, a laid-back attitude everywhere I looked—teenagers lounging around within a housing project's social center, listening to pop music on a jukebox; women with their arms folded, chatting casually among themselves across their front porches or near the curbs of unpaved streets; men seated around a table behind a Coke machine in a corner grocery store, playing cards.

I was accompanied through the area by a black deacon whose church basement was filled with boxes containing hundreds of as-yet-undistributed care packages sent from all parts of the nation by civil rights supporters. Most of the boxes had been opened and picked through by church volunteers who were supposed to make lists of what had been sent, and then to record the names and addresses of those donors whose uncommon generosity the pastor might want to acknowledge with a note of gratitude, and finally to see to it that what was in the boxes was made available to the community's more impoverished families, which might make the best use of the articles of clothing and various items, including a share of the cash donations and checks that had been designated for Selma relief and been sent in care of the church.

In my visits to the church, however, I never saw anyone actively engaged in the process of sharing what had been received (the deacon explained that the volunteer committee had not yet had the time to implement the procedure fully); piled high along the walls of the basement were cardboard cartons with their tops torn off and some of the contents draped over the edges, or sprawled along the floor, or stacked haphazardly—hundreds of cans of Campbell's soup, bars of soap, bottles of soft drinks, shampoos, detergents; cellophane bags of Fritos and pretzels; sacks of rice, sugar, flour; children's toys, toasters, radios, books, and many piles of footwear: sneakers, slippers, men's and women's shoes, the latter having high heels, low heels, no heels, some shoes being unmatched, and there were seven pairs of ice skates. On wire hangers, dangling from long lines of rope extending high across the rear walls of the room, were countless dresses, blouses, suits, pairs of trousers, shirts, jackets, overcoats, and some fedoras and other brimmed hats attached by clothespins to the sleeves of the coats.

Seeing all this clothing, some of it new, most of it used, reminded me of my boyhood days in the mid-1940s, when I would often accompany my father to the post office to help him carry the care packages that he and my mother had addressed to their relatives dwelling in poverty in a part of Calabria that had been overrun and bombed by the Allies near the end of World War II. Although the boxes were bound with heavy rope and further secured at the seams with sealing wax, I knew what was inside because I had earlier participated in the packing: There were suits and coats that my father no longer wore, some of my mother's old dresses and also new ones that she had been unable to sell in her boutique, and various articles of attire that my parents' customers had left unclaimed for a year or more in our dry-cleaning plant and storage vault.

Ten years after the war, when I visited my family's ancestral village in Calabria for the first time while on furlough from Germany in the spring of 1955, I was reintroduced to much of this clothing as it appeared in ill-fitting form on human figures for which it had never been clearly measured or fashioned; and yet as I embraced these people and brushed against the familiar scratchy fabric of my father's hacking jacket, and the soft silk, long-sleeved, slightly faded primrose yellow dress that once had been among my mother's favorites, I felt reconnected to my past and allied as well with these strangers and foreigners whose lives had long been distantly interwoven with my own.

I had come to the village unannounced, having two days earlier hopped an army transport plane in Frankfurt that was headed for Rome, and then I hitched a ride on a military bus that was escorting naval officers from the Rome airport to the American base in Naples, and on the following day I decided to purchase a third-class rail ticket at the Naples terminal on the overnight Rapido, which would carry me down the Tyrrhenian coastline into Calabria—a journey I would make with many passengers I assumed to be farmers, a few of whom sat and slumbered through the night on wooden benches with rope-leashed baby goats and pigs sitting at their feet, while our belching Rapido chugged along at no more than twenty-five miles per hour (when it moved at all), and it took us about fourteen hours to traverse less than three hundred miles of track.

Wearing my lieutenant's uniform and carrying a small canvas overnight bag that had served as my pillow, I stepped down from the railcar after the train had hissed to a halt along a sand-covered platform in front of a sturdy granite-walled, soot-stained station house bearing the sign

SANT' EUFEMIA, which I knew was my final stop. My father had often mentioned this place as his departure point on leaving home in 1920, taking all his belongings because he did not plan to return. He described the station in those days as hectic and bustling, teeming with tense young men like himself who were eager to leave, and who bumped into one another as they advanced while grappling with their luggage and hoisting their steamer trunks, all the while being surrounded and assisted by relatives and family friends who did not want to see them go, especially the expectant brides, who traditionally wore maroon skirts and brown shawls and who, as the train pulled away, could only hope that the promises made by the men would be met.

My father had been taken to the station from his hillside village by an uncle who had cautiously guided a donkey-led wagon down a winding rocky road for three miles until they had reached the flatter coastal region and the railroad tracks that bordered the Gulf of Sant' Eufemia. The gulf and its environs—and eventually its rail terminal—had been named in honor of an eleventh-century martyr who died near Constantinople during the anti-Muslim crusades and whose head had been returned to southern Italy by the governing Normans so they could deposit it in the foundation of a Benedictine monastery they were then constructing south of where the rail terminal now stood. Although the old monastery was completely destroyed during the earthquake of 1638, my father told me that some of the rocks from this disaster had later been utilized in constructing the terminal—an unremarkable fact, it seemed to me, but one that my devout father, reared in a religion extolling relic worship, saw as signifying the enduring essence of the Church. He told me that he had paused to kiss one of the stones of the terminal's wall as he entered the building, praying for guidance, hoping he had made the right decision in disregarding his earlier inclinations toward a priestly life and choosing instead to abandon his widowed mother and his younger dependent siblings on the assumption that he could help them more if he were far away earning money. He was seventeen when he boarded the train, leaving behind an austere and indigent youth that, insofar as he recounted it to me, was so devoid of romantic longings and dalliances, there was not a chance that there might be standing among the waving onlookers on the platform a young woman lamenting his departure.

Arriving in Naples, he transferred to a train headed north to Milan, and then into France, toward an apprenticeship in a Paris tailor shop owned by an older cousin—all the while anticipating his future career as a custom tailor with a shop of his own in America. After he had achieved this in 1922, and had enlarged upon it with a dry-cleaning plant and my mother's dress shop, he was sufficiently well-off financially to support his kinfolk overseas on a regular basis; he mailed them money orders every week, and gifts for special occasions, and boxes of well-cut suits and brightly colored frocks and blouses that, while perhaps slightly out of fashion or otherwise deemed dispensable on the New Jersey shore, nevertheless represented new-world modernity in southern Italy, where most of the people—as I observed from the window of my sluggishly progressing train during my lengthy ride from Naples to Calabria—were attired in the mode of the Middle Ages.

I saw men strolling along nearby roads wearing conical hats, pantaloons and waist-length tunics belted with rope, and turbaned, black-cloaked women balancing boxes or jars on their heads, and other women, sitting sideways on mules, enshrouded with dark scarves similar to the yashmaks worn by the Muslim women who had come here during the tenth-century Saracen invasion. This antiquated area of southern Italy, extending down through the hills and plains of Naples into Calabria, is often referred to by northern Italians as "part of Africa," emphasizing that it is primitive, backward, and arid, its lowlands swept by sands from the Sahara, its highlands inhabited most naturally by mountain goats, and everywhere within its boundaries a characteristically slow-paced population and an ambience changing little from century to century.

The Sant' Eufemia station that I saw on arriving in 1956 was undoubtedly as my father remembered it on leaving thirty-five years before. There were the terminal's dark wooden benches and the thick, dank stone walls derived from what he had told me was the rubble of a medieval monastery. But there was also a hollowness and quietude about the terminal's interior that contrasted greatly with the crowded and active place that my father had pictured for me. Indeed, after I had stepped down onto the platform at Sant' Eufemia and entered the terminal in a vain search for an attendant—hearing at the same time the rattling departure of the southbound Rapido, which was scheduled, sooner or later, to reach the tip of the Italian boot—I realized that I was now entirely alone.

This surprised me even though I had been riding for a few hours in an almost empty train. Most of my fellow passengers, including all of those traveling with animals, had gotten off earlier at stations upcoast, nearer to the more fertile countryside of towns founded by feudal landlords and still plowed by peasant farmers only slightly risen from serfdom—while I, on the other hand, now found myself stranded in a dry, lifeless part of Calabria, marooned in the midday heat with flies buzzing around me in this forsaken rail terminal that owed its identity to a thousand-year-old decapitated martyr.

I noted that a shutter had been lowered behind the bars of the ticket window, and that the toilet door was padlocked, and the fact that the premises lacked a drinking fountain, although this was probably a sign of prudence. As writers of Italian guidebooks have long warned their readers, this region is renowned for its stagnant and malarial lagoons and tributaries. Fortunately, I had ample water left in my canteen from the bottle I had purchased in Naples, and, since there were dried biscuits preserved in my bag in an army-issued tin container, I had no immediate fear of starvation. But I was worried about getting out of here, and I berated my impulsiveness in coming here and the bargain-motivated mentality that had propelled me to board the cost-free army flight from Frankfurt to Rome. It had all come about very quickly: On the day of my furlough I had been tipped off about the empty seat on the plane by a lieutenant who worked with me in the Frankfurt-based headquarters of the Third Armored Division—this lieutenant being a tireless procurer of whatever perks and marginally legal freebooting opportunities might exist within our grasp as young information officers who had previously dealt directly in Fort Knox with our highly decorated and eminent commander, Colonel Creighton W. Abrams, a World War II combat veteran who would eventually earn four stars and be appointed chief-of-staff for the entire army. I arrived in Italy without speaking a word of Italian. It was a language I had never been inclined to learn, it having been the mother tongue of Mussolini during my wartime boyhood. Even if I had hired an interpreter in Italy, I doubt it would have made it easier for me to get around; on the contrary, it would have imposed a sense of structure and directness antipathetic to what I prefer to believe was my improvisational nature. I had no idea what I wanted to do, nor where I wanted to go, nor did I want anyone to accompany me and suggest my itinerary. Even before I knew the meaning of the word *serendipity*—traveling without a specific destination, discovering things by chance—I was intrigued by the idea of aimless wandering, not committing myself to anything in advance, wanting to leave all options open, never wanting to be pinned down. This attitude had often brought me into conflict with my overly controlling father, and I had deliberately not telephoned him to inform him I was in Italy. He would have proceeded to tell me what to do, where to go, and he surely would have insisted that I visit Calabria. He himself, as I already indicated, had never revisited his homeland, using as an excuse the argument that he could not afford to take the time away from his business, being obliged to work incessantly in order to earn sufficient sums for the continued well-being of his mother and the others in Italy. My father's responsibilites toward his business, however, did *not* prevent him from visiting his sartorial cousin in Paris for four weeks in 1938, sailing to and fro on the luxury liner *Normandy*. But when it came to revisiting his humble origins in Italy, my father seemed to be capable of sending everything back to his village except himself.

I dislike being critical of my father, and perhaps I am more familiar with his faults than my own. But I knew that he would have *ordered* me into Calabria had I called him, presuming that he had no less authority over my life than did Colonel Abrams; my father would also have arranged for his relatives to be awaiting my arrival—all of which I told myself I wanted to avoid. And yet here I was in Sant' Eufemia on my own terms, a solitary figure standing in a godforsaken terminal at the exact time of day when southern Italy was idle and indolent, when the local people and their farm animals were sleeping, resting, or otherwise partaking in the reposeful rite of their daily siesta. I read somewhere that the siesta is subscribed to more seriously in Calabria than anywhere else in Italy, and that between noon and 4:00 p.m. the only sign of life thereabouts is provided by the flies. Since I got off the train shortly before noon, it was possible that I could be there by myself for another four hours, unless in the interim a northbound train should arrive to offer me a wearisome ride back to Naples, an option that seemed even more dreadful than remaining where I was.

Removing my jacket and leaving it next to my bag on a bench, I walked out into the bright sunlight and began to pace back and forth along the platform, feeling on my face the dry heat and sometimes the light sting of the coarse-grained sand carried by the inland wind blowing between the jagged hills standing about three miles away from the railroad tracks. As I looked up to the highest of the hills, I saw my father's village, nestled like a soap dish into the cliffside, the white stone houses clustered together and crowded around a larger structure, which I guessed was the turreted Norman castle that had served as a prison when my father was a boy.

Turning my back to the village, I looked across the tracks toward miles of barren beach, dotted here and there by huge rocks that had probably been transported by the force of earthquakes. There was also lodged along the beach one of the concrete cone-shaped bunkers built by the Germans during World War II for the encasement of their heavy guns and the support of their defense of the Italian coast against the Allied invaders sailing in from North Africa. I had seen several other bunkers of this type positioned upcoast along the train route, and I remembered seeing photographs of them in newsmagazines, but I now resisted whatever urge I had to trudge out into the sand and closely inspect this bunker that stood about one hundred yards away from me. I was not that interested, nor that foolishly venturesome, certainly not here in this isolated place where I was unable to speak the local language and where there was no telling what impression I might create if seen climbing in or out of this Nazi-built bunker.

I thought I was alone, but there was always the possibility that someone was secretly watching me, some farmer or vagrant crouched behind the cornstalks and the overgrown oleander shrubs that lined the lower hillside road overlooking the terminal, or some hunter with binoculars and a shotgun who might have been a Nazi sympathizer. What I was wearing had been the uniform of Italy's enemy not too long ago, and, while I was required to wear it while flying gratis on military planes, now I would have not minded being in mufti. I recalled the embarrassment I had felt as a boy when flipping through our family album and seeing the snapshots of my father's brothers wearing their Italian army uniforms. I kept the album out of sight whenever my classmates were visiting after school. My father had left Italy two years before Benito Mussolini had brought the country under his fascist control, and while my father had been outwardly pro-American throughout World War II, I never recall having heard him say anything in the privacy of our home that was condemning of Mussolini. My father believed that the Italians required a strong leader, being disorganized and undisciplined as a people. He often quoted to me Mussolini's line: "Governing the Italian people is not impossible, merely useless."

I think my father left Italy with great misgivings about his homeland, disappointed with its low status as a world power, lower than that of the French, barely higher than that of the Greeks, its government in Rome unstable and inefficient and unable to adequately feed and shelter its people, and having no social conscience—driving people like himself, among the most ambitious and restless members of his generation, out of the country forever. Despite all his piety and sense of obligation to those dearest to him, my father was, in my imagined way of thinking, an inwardly angry and very selfish man when he left home, and I further believe that when he came to live in America, he blended his anger and self-centeredness into the melting pot of a nation motivated by millions of men like himself, dissatisfied and driven, coming originally from Europe, Asia, the Middle East, South America, wherever—a diverse group of newcomers who had in common a quarrel with where they had come from and who, unlike many of their relatives who remained behind, had the gall and gumption to say good-bye.

It surely must not have been easy for these departing people to say good-bye to everything that until then had been so familiar, so understandable, so encoded in their consciousness. No matter how intolerable the situation might have been, leaving demanded a certain hardheartedness, a survivor's mentality, a lack of sentimentality about those they loved. All good intentions and rationalizations aside, these travelers behaved little differently than deserters. I know this word would hardly resonate well within the storied walls of the immigrant museum at Ellis Island, but nonetheless I think that within the DNA of the mass migration to America there is an unromantic and primal pursuit of a better life, a propensity to extricate oneself from losing causes, a capacity to look ahead, not back, and accept new customs, a new language, and sometimes a new name. Whenever I hear America singled out for its aggressiveness and pragmatism, its mercenary zeal, its meddlesome foreign policy, or its market for violence with reference to its taste in popular culture and entertainment, I think these things are genetically linked to the passion, defiance, and anger that was brought to these shores first by the Puritans and then by the multitudes of emboldened boat people who followed them.

After I had waited at the Sant' Eufemia terminal for a little more than two hours, alternatively strolling around the platform and sitting down to read Graham Greene's *The End of the Affair,* I heard an odd metallic sound coming over the hill; I would later learn this came from the engine powering the one and only automobile then operating in this part of Italy. It was a battered gray prewar Fiat owned by the stationmaster. And as I saw it make a sharp turn off the hillside and head down the rocky road toward the terminal, I quickly stepped off the platform and ran toward the vehicle with my right hand waving in the air. The driver slammed on the brakes and, lowering his window, poked his head out and regarded me with narrowing eyes and complete silence.

"*Americano-Calabresi,*" I announced, pointing to the gold lieutenant's bar that was pinned to the collar of my khaki shirt. He continued to stare at me, saying nothing. He was an elderly man with wizened dark facial skin, and he wore a black visored cap down over his bushy white eyebrows. I tried again to introduce myself, this time I hoped more favorably by stressing the second word: "*Americano*-Calabresi." I knew from my father that people in this region identified themselves as Calabrians, not Italians. Even my mother's immigrant parents, having left Italy half a century ago, invariably emphasized their separatism and their provincial insularity within their Brooklyn Italian neighborhood by calling themselves Calabrians—*Calabresi*.

"*Calabresi!*" he finally repeated, his voice rising and his head nodding with what I took to be a sign of his approval. He got out of his car and slowly came closer. He was a short, slightly stooped man, whose white shirt without a tie was buttoned tight under his Adam's apple, and he wore a frayed black cutaway from which the tails had been cut off.

"Philadelphia?" he asked.

"New York," I replied, relieved and pleased that we were able to communicate.

"Me a coma from a Philadelphia," he said.

I then tried to inform him of my surname, pronouncing Talese as it had always been pronounced in my home and in my parents' store in New Jersey—*Tal-lease*. The old man looked at me quizzically. Then I pronounced my name as I used to hear it pronounced by the Naples-born maître d' and the waiters who worked at an Italian restaurant in Atlantic City that my father frequently took us to on Sunday evenings. *Tal-lay-zeh*.

"My name is *Tal-lay-zeh*," I said, "I have come to visit the family *Tal-lay-zeh*." Pointing toward the village on the hill, I continued: "They are up there."

"Ah, *Tal-lay-zeh*." He nodded with familiarity, suddenly genial and enthusiastic. "*Si, si, si*," he said, waving me toward his car. "I take you."

I hurried to get my bag and jacket, and, after placing them in the car's backseat—atop a stack of freshly cut logs, and as far away as possible from a partly opened sack containing coal—we slowly proceeded up the narrow, winding three-mile road; and as we bumped along, zigzagging and at times almost stalling, I began to see various signs of human activity that I had not seen from below: people casually riding mules close to the edge of a cliff, women walking gracefully with objects on their heads, a shepherd leading a herd of sheep and his dog into a meadow.

My driver's name was Lucio. If I understood him correctly, he had been the stationmaster at Sant' Eufemia since the war's end, having replaced a nephew who had died in the Italian army. Lucio said he had lived in Philadelphia for four years during the 1930s, and then was deported. I did not ask him why. I did not probe deeply into his background, fearing that my curiosity might lead me beyond what he wanted me to know. I was attuned to the guarded nature of Calabrians, a distant demeanor that I also associated with some of the hill people I had met in northern Alabama and West Virginia while driving to and from home during my later years in college. And yet Lucio was surprisingly forthcoming. Perhaps this was due to his having been born and reared along the Calabrian coastline, where he had often been in contact with seafaring travelers and transients at the terminal. He said he was not personally acquainted with my relatives, but he reminded me he was aware of my name. He added that he knew people in the village who could easily arrange for my introduction.

He stopped the car when we arrived at the town square, parking it next to a large circular fountain with a cherubic figure in the center but with no water flowing. The cobblestone square was lined with large Baroque-style houses, most of which had cracked walls and chipped ornamentation, and on the balconies of some of the buildings were women wearing shawls, who stepped forward and leaned over the rails to get a closer look as Lucio got out of the car. I remained seated, as he had suggested, watching as he walked toward a group of men who sat along the edge of the square, playing cards on a wooden table under the tattered awning of an unattended café.

The men stood to greet Lucio, and as he spoke, they turned and looked in my direction. One of the men then gestured up toward one of the women on the balcony, calling out to her in a loud voice. Soon a boy in his early teens came down to join the men, and, after being spoken to, the boy ran swiftly across the square toward a narrow road that led uphill, in the direction of a high-tiered row of small stone houses that seemed to be leaning against one another and clinging precariously to the side of the cliff.

Lucio returned to the car smiling, explaining that the boy had been dispatched to get my relatives. I got out of the car and for the next fifteen minutes I stood waiting with Lucio next to the fountain. He was smoking one of the cigarettes I had picked out of a pack in my pocket and had bought at the PX in Frankfurt. I had an unopened pack in my bag that I intended to give him later. I noticed that the men had now resumed playing cards, but the women on the balcony were still directing their full attention toward us, leaning over the rails and regarding us rather boldly, I thought, not looking away when I glanced up at them but, rather, gazing back with the unflinching expressions of fixated crows. I wished that they would go away. I was feeling a bit uneasy now, awkward about being in this public place, awaiting a personal meeting with kinfolk whose language I could not speak and around whom I was not sure how to behave. I again thought I had made a mistake in coming here, misguided by my impulsiveness. It's not *me* who belongs here, I told myself, it's my *father*, my gift-giving, unsentimental father. I was merely a tourist traipsing through his past, on a furlough into antiquity, waiting in this languorous place to meet some of these strangers whose pictures were in my parents' photo album, the album I'd kept hidden from my school friends.

"Ah, they are coming," said Lucio, squinting into the distance while puffing on his cigarette. Soon I recognized the boy. He was leading a few dozen men and women down the winding road toward the square, and there were also some teenagers and children trailing behind. I shifted about, readjusted my olive drab military cap lower over my brow, and peeked at my wristwatch. It was nearly 4:00 p.m. The sun was blazing, and there was hardly a breeze sweeping across the square. Although it was a spring afternoon in Calabria, it felt like a midsummer heat wave in Manhattan. The flies were everywhere, and as I looked up, I again observed the crowlike women watching me from their balconies.

"When is the next train going back to Naples?" I asked Lucio.

"After seven o'clock," he replied.

"I *must* be on it," I said.

"*Si, si,*" he said, "I take you."

Now the approaching group was so close that I could see their faces and could recognize some of the clothing they wore. As I forced a smile, two gray-haired women in the front pushed ahead of the boy and ran toward me with their arms outstretched, calling out words that I did not understand, and they proceeded to kiss me with such enthusiasm that my hat was knocked to the ground. These women were the wives of my father's brothers, Lucio explained to me, and one of them was wearing my mother's old primrose yellow dress. Soon my father's brothers, my uncles—the soccer-playing ex-soldiers in Mussolini's army—had advanced to embrace me, kissing me on both cheeks, grazing me with their stubble, and I noticed that there were tears in their eyes. They resembled my father more in person than they did in the snapshots, having the same lean features, high cheekbones, and profiles; and yet, though they were several years younger than my fifty-two-year-old father, they seemed to be older, having skin that was lined and weathered, and both men were missing a few front teeth.

After them came the others, a clutching encirclement of nephews, nieces, and varying grades of cousins—I was not sure who all of them were, although Lucio questioned them and tried to identify them for me. But no matter if they were closely related or distantly related, they *all* assumed the same ardent and immediate sense of familiarity with me, kissing me and pulling me toward them and placing their arms around my neck and shoulders with a firmness and presumptuousness that I found excessive and unwanted and unseemly in this public place. My instinct was to back away, but I was positioned against the ledge of the fountain, and I was also fearful of giving offense by appearing to be unresponsive to their heartfelt openness and exuberance. I was simply unaccustomed to this, not having been reared by parents who were demonstratively affectionate. While I had seen my parents greet my mother's family in Brooklyn with Italian-style kisses during our holiday visits, such expressions of endearment were never exchanged in public, and on those rare occasions when a relative or an Italian-born friend from Brooklyn or Philadelphia came to see us at the Jersey shore—my mother, incidentally, always tried to discourage such visits, claiming she had no time for houseguests because she was preoccupied with her dress boutique—I saw only the most perfunctory form of salutation extended by my parents, such as a handclasp, a light hug, or, at most, a quick kiss on the cheek. Cold and uncordial as this may characterize my parents as being, I should explain that public kissing was considered to be unacceptable by most standard-bearing Americans in the mid-twentieth century. The Hollywood films that I saw during my high school years did not contain scenes showing kissing couples even when the actors portrayed married people; in 1954, the picture editor of the *New York Times* lost his job because he permitted the publication of a wedding-day photograph showing Marilyn Monroe and Joe DiMaggio revealing their physical attraction to each other while standing in front of City Hall in San Francisco—she with her head back and her mouth slightly open, and he with his lips puckered and his eyes closed.

Since public kissing was a mark of unrefinement in conservative communities like my hometown, and since my parents effortlessly blended in with this conservatism, I came of age in a time and place where well-bred Americans were epitomized by their reserved manner and their taciturnity, their sobersidedness and other qualities that were at variance with all that was now surrounding me in Calabria and that, had I been able to manage it, I would have shunted and fended off. But my relatives would not let me go, holding on to my arms, pulling me forward, guiding me in the direction of the rows of houses higher on the hill, wanting (Lucio explained to me) to show me where they lived. And so we left the square, a procession with Lucio and I following my uncles, with my aunts flanking us, and the rest of them following us, chattering cheerfully and waving at the women who stood watching from the balconies of the big houses.

It took us about ten minutes to climb the narrow, uneven roads. As we walked along over loosely embedded rocks, and sometimes up the stone steps that led us past the crumbling Norman castle, I considered slowing the pace a bit because of my fatigue and dehydration. But none of the others, neither the younger people nor my older uncles and aunts, seemed in the least daunted by our journey, and so I kept going and resisted the temptation to fetch my canteen, which Lucio was carrying in my bag. He had insisted on carrying it, along with my jacket. I also thought I should preserve my water for the train ride back to Naples. Lucio's car was, naturally, of no use on these roads, and he'd left it parked next to the fountain. The doors were unlocked and the key was in the ignition. Lucio told me that nobody in this area would try to steal his car because he was well known and respected, and also nobody around here knew how to drive.

We reached a flat part of the road and this led us into another square, which was architecturally less formal than the one below—no fountain in the center, no Baroque manors along the sides—but it was more vivacious and colorful in a helter-skelter way, with many pedestrians and footloose farm animals vying for the right-of-way while maneuvering around donkey-drawn wagons and children chasing chickens. A goat was walking down the steps of a tiny two-story house overlooking the far side of the square, and the smell of sausages rose from a coal-burning grill at the other side of the square. The church bells rang. The siesta was over, and farmers were returning to their land downhill. Several small shops that lined the square were now open for business. I wondered if it had been in one of these shops that my father began his apprenticeship, and if it had been in this square that his brothers and their friends used to play soccer after school. I thought of asking Lucio to pose these questions to one of my uncles but decided against it.

After turning a corner and heading up a wide cobblestone path, we entered a large house that had an ornate but shattered stone plaque engraved on the lintel above the main door. Even before Lucio had confirmed it, I thought this building had been the residence of my great-grandfather Domenico Talese, a landowner of some consequence who, according to what my father had once told me, had acquired this baronial property from an impoverished nobleman in the 1880s. While my father spoke admiringly of Domenico, he did concede that the latter was a man with a minimum of friends, and when he died, he had been mourned by few people except his family, and not all of them. However, they still owned the property, and on this day of my visit I would learn that some members of the extended family lived here, including an elderly woman whom I had been brought to visit.

She was bedridden, and as I was ushered into her room on the second floor, I was told that this was my father's mother. The shutters were closed and it was so dark that I could barely see the face of this white-haired woman who lay under the covers wearing a high-collared white nightgown, and who, as I approached, reached in my direction with her frail arms and then, with a surge of energy that surprised me, rose from her pillow into a sitting position and began to cry out toward me again and again in a shrieking voice, "*Peppino! Peppino!*"

I stepped back, bumping into my aunts and uncles, who were close behind me. I was startled, unprepared for this moment. She was calling me by my father's name! My father, Joseph, was often referred to as "Peppino" by our relatives in Brooklyn, and this nickname was undoubtedly how he was known here in Italy. But now it seemed that my father's mother believed that *I* was her son! I thought maybe she was becoming senile, or perhaps she was going blind, or possibly she had misunderstood or been misinformed by the messenger boy who had come here earlier. I turned toward Lucio, who was standing near the foot of the bed. I hoped that he would offer a word of advice, but he merely shrugged and remained silent.

"*Peppino*," she repeated, softly now, beginning to cry. One of my aunts then walked hurriedly to the other side of the bed, comforting her while beckoning me closer. Awkwardly, I leaned across the bed to embrace my grandmother and hesitantly kissed her on the cheek.

My uncles then spoke tenderly to her, as did some of the other people who stood behind them. There were a dozen people in the room now, some that I was seeing for the first time. My eyes were adjusting to the darkness, and I noticed on my grandmother's bureau, next to a crucifix and statue of Saint Francis, some wood-framed photographs, one of which showed my parents at their wedding reception in Brooklyn. As my grandmother sank back onto her pillows, we were ushered out of the room by my aunts and led downstairs, where coffee that had been poured in small cups, and a tray containing cookies and fried pastry, awaited us.

A man of about my age, carrying a child in his arms, called out to Lucio and told him to tell me that he was my first cousin—his father was one of my father's brothers—and that we had the same first name. He was my height, just as slender, and had dark brown hair and eyes similar to mine. He was wearing overalls, a cotton shirt, and boots crusty with dried mud. After I had embraced him, he asked Lucio to apologize for his appearance, explaining that he had been working in the fields and had come here directly on learning of my visit. He said he was excited and pleased to be meeting me. Then, seeing his young sons standing near the door among a crowd of adults, he waved them over and presented the two of them, ages seven and five. They raised up on their toes so I could kiss them, and the older boy introduced himself in English.

"I am Peppino," he said.

Later, I met their mother, a cheerful young woman with a round face, who was wearing a slightly oversized faded brown dress that I believed had been on sale a few years before in my mother's shop. The woman said that her house was next door, and that her grandmother and my grandmother were sisters. She also said that she and her husband were expecting their fourth child in early autumn, adding that they were both very happy about this.

They *are* happy, I thought, and this impression accompanied me down the hill to the train station. My kinsmen in Italy—so poor, living so simply, so accustomed to hand-me-down clothing—were at peace with themselves, were resigned to their circumstances, were contented in ways that my family in America rarely seemed to be. This was particularly true of my father. He hardly ever smiled and was often contentious. I recall how sensitive and defensive he seemed to be whenever the issue of his failure to revisit Italy arose, and how he took every opportunity to suggest that his homeland was a hopeless and uninhabitable place, fixed in its ways and at fault for making him incompatible with it. Once when a customer in the store was commenting critically about the polluted industrial air hovering over Pennsylvania and New York, my father replied, "Well, if it's pure air you're looking for, you'll find plenty of it in my part of Italy, where the people are practically starving to death!"

On the way back to Naples, I thought about the consequences of leaving home forever: boarding a train, sailing across the ocean, and never returning to one's country. Lives of succeeding generations were changed forever by this single decisive journey. Were it not for my father's restive nature and willfulness, I might have ended up working in the fields of southern Italy with my cousin and kinfolk, eagerly anticipating the birth of a child and finding joy in simple pleasures.

You people must get out of here! You must pack your bags and bid good-bye to this place!

I was saying this under my breath to the seemingly complaisant black people I saw shuffling along the sidewalks and the dirt roads of Selma as I explored the ghetto with the deacon from Brown Chapel, collecting impressions for the magazine piece I was writing for the *Times* in May 1965. As a reporter, I had been trained to be objective, not to become emotionally involved, but in Selma, inwardly at least, I could not help myself—I was reacting critically, even angrily, toward many of these blacks who appeared to be reconciled to their surroundings. On my notepad I made comments that would remain private, but they reminded me of my no-fun father and, alas, myself, and how I had felt about my relatives in Calabria. But I toned it all down for the *Times*, and in the Sunday paper of May 30, 1965, I wrote:

The rain has stopped in Selma, the storm is over. It is now May and it is a bright hot sun that beats down on Sylvan Street and makes pie crust of bumpy dirt roads, bakes the concrete pavement, scorches the grass. All along Sylvan Street are lined red brick houses, identically designed, and within them live the Negroes who, back in March, were hosts and hostesses to hundreds of whites who came to "make witness" in Selma. . . .

They are passive Negroes, by and large, and if they are going to make advances, they must be led, must be mobilized, must be marched by civil rights leaders. And today most of the leaders and civil rights freedom-fighters—both black and white—have abandoned Selma. They have either returned to New York, Los Angeles, Chicago, or Atlanta; or perhaps they have found a new cause in another town . . . in any case, they are not in Selma, as any tourist who wanders into the Negro quarter of this town can see.

On Sylvan Street, that famous street of so many crowds ago—that street in which Negro and white demonstrators, nuns and S.N.C.C. boys and Radcliffe girls and labor leaders joined hands and stood all day and night in a driving rainstorm and sang "We Shall Overcome"—that street today, deserted except for a few small Negro children playing in the gutter and some adults who slowly come and go, is a street where the Movement is now crawling.

16

LTHOUGH I HAD LEFT THE STAFF OF THE *TIMES* AT THIRTY-TWO in 1965, I had since written an occasional book review for the Sunday edition, or an article for the sports section, or an essay for the op-ed page, which welcomed outside contributions; and when I learned in 1990 that the black leaders of Selma were marking the silver anniversary of Bloody Sunday with a large demonstration and a parade, I contacted a senior editor whom I had known from our days together as reporters and asked if he would help get me assigned to cover the story.

I was then fifty-seven and lost in the languor of my book about my Italian ancestry. What I thought I needed was a quick fix, a jolt of journalism to stimulate and motivate me with its urgent expectations, and finally to reward me, however briefly, with a sense of satisfaction and reassurance that a good piece printed in the *Times* can bring to a long-unpublished writer.

While the ephemeral gratification of daily journalism had not long sustained me even in the early days of my career, it was equally and lastingly true that I had never had so much fun as a writer as when working on daily assignments, hastily leaving the *Times* building to cover late-breaking events in and out of the metropolitan area, accompanied sometimes by a *Times* photographer and being joined at the site by my journalistic rivals from other newspapers. Some of these reporters I liked personally, drank beer with on weekends, competed with assiduously on stories, and later shared rides with back to our respective newsrooms to face the deadlines and struggle with our leads and constructions. We were one-day wonders, or so we believed; never before, or since, had I had so many friends and colleagues among my contemporaries with whom I had so many common interests and complaints.

We grumbled constantly about our copyreaders, who were the first people in the newsroom to read what we had written, and they had the authority to arrange our articles and to trim them or rewrite them extensively without consulting us and without removing the bylines that identified us as the authors. We suspected that these desk-bound deprecators and grammatists, these humorless scriveners and censors of our work, privately envied the freedom and the modicum of fame we enjoyed as news gatherers in the outside world; I ordinarily returned home from the newsroom at 8:00 p.m. fearing that one of the heavy-handed copyreaders had mangled my lead, had blue-penciled most of my favorite phrases. Three hours later, I was likely to be found standing on the sidewalk in front of my neighborhood newsstand awaiting the *Times* delivery truck bearing bundles of the first edition, which would reveal to me whatever butchery had been imposed upon my prose. Even at a distance of many blocks, I could spot the hulking dark truck coming closer and closer through the traffic, its roof rimmed with tiny lights. As it pulled into the curb and as the wire-bound bundles of the *Times* were tossed onto the pavement and were clipped open by the news vendor, I stepped forward to buy the paper and flip through it until I found my article and saw how it had survived the scrutiny and judiciousness of the copyreader.

If it had been changed to blunt my meaning or had otherwise been manhandled, I would hurry to a sidewalk telephone and dial the director of the copydesk, asking that my byline be removed from the article. After he had digested my disgruntlement and reviewed what had been done, he would usually say that my work had been *improved* by the copyreader's changes and that it might be appropriate for me to be communicating my thanks rather than my displeasure. If I remained adamant, insisting that what had been printed in the first edition under my name was unrecognizable to me—a statement I would shout above the street noise while quoting from a carbon copy of the original, which I had pulled from my pocket—the director would sometimes agree to restore what I had written, and these words would appear hours later in the second edition. If, however, he decided to reprint the copyreader's version in the second edition, then my byline would be removed.

But this would not be the end of it. A memo describing my agitation with the editing would be placed by the director in the overnight box to be perused on the following morning by the city editor, who disliked hearing about the remonstrations of his reporters against what he assumed to be the emendations of the paper's standard-bearers on the desks, although such quibbling had become increasingly common among the younger reporters in the newsroom during the late 1950s and early 1960s. The top editor of the *Times*, the Mississippi-born Turner Catledge, had made it known that he hoped the newswriting would become livelier, saying that the era of just-the-facts journalism was insufficient now that television was the first to reach the public with the text and pictures of late-breaking news. I had been transferred at Catledge's suggestion from sports to general news in 1958 to become part of his plan to emphasize writing as well as reporting in the main section. But changes occurred slowly at the *Times*, he once told me, adding that the paper often reminded him of an elephant. It was huge, reliable, and stubborn. It was slow to learn new tricks and was clumsy. If it was expected to dance, it had better dance well; otherwise, it could look mighty foolish in public. He therefore knew that a considerable amount of practice, patience, and time would be necessary to make an impression upon the tradition-bound mind-set existing within the paper's nerve center, which was its sprawling block-long newsroom occupying the third floor of the fourteen-story *Times* building on West Forty-third Street. Catledge would sometimes survey the newsroom through the pair of binoculars he held while standing outside the door of his corner office, and what he saw in front of him were endless rows of gray metal desks and multitudes of people seated or strolling about—dozens of senior editors and mid-level editors, and battalions of copyreaders flanked by desk clerks and other supernumeraries, and hundreds of reporters of varying ages and specialties, some of them newly appointed to the staff, like myself, others being senior citizens adhering to the rather fusty, formulaic style of reporting that had been in vogue when the publisher had been Adolph Ochs, who died in 1935. Although the present publisher—Arthur Hays Sulzberger, who was married to Ochs's daughter and only child—was fond and supportive of Catledge, the old guard in the newsroom were stalwart shrine keepers who believed it might be perilous to tinker with the Ochsian formula (straight facts, no frills) and encourage instead a stylish flair that more properly belonged in the newsroom of the *Times*'s near-bankrupt rival, the *New York Herald-Tribune*.

The latter was long known as a *writer's* paper, led in the early 1960s by such stars as Tom Wolfe and Jimmy Breslin. The *Times* had always been a *reporter's* paper, a *recorder's* paper, one that each day published a record of every fire in New York, the arrival time of every mail ship, the names of every official visitor to the White House, the precise moment the sun set and the moon rose; in its long history, the *Times* had never hired journalistic stars with a marquee status that made them indispensable to the paper in a box-office sense or any other. The *Times* was an ensemble. It was a gigantic gray institution of subdued luminosity. And the aging traditionalists, sharing few of Catledge's concerns about the future impact of television journalism upon the newspaper's readership, were certain that the continued prosperity of the paper was secure as long as its top executives and its proprietors remained faithful to Mr. Ochs's dictums.

Allied with this conservative and cautious mode of thinking was my city editor, a stout, stern old-time reporter named Frank Adams, who did not welcome me to his staff with a handshake after Catledge had maneuvered my transfer, nor offer me a raise during the nearly four years I worked under him. But the main enforcer of tradition on the *Times* was one of its assistant managing editors and its premier deskman, a lean, fastidious, and deceptively ingratiating tyrant named Theodore M. Bernstein, who concealed his disesteem of Turner Catledge with a convincingly gleeful response to the banter and aphorisms that Catledge delivered during editorial meetings—typical Catledge sayings: "Never plow around stumps." "Don't overrun more than you can overtake." "The time to fire a man is when you hire him." "There is only one indispensable man on this paper, and modesty prevents me from mentioning his name."—and who revealed his indifference to Catledge's desires about newswriting by slicing and surgically removing from the paper any turn of phrase, indeed any article in its entirety, that did not conform to what *he*, Theodore M. Bernstein, believed was properly printable in the *Times*.

In all my years on the paper I had never once heard it said that Turner Catledge had arrived in the morning expressing any dissatisfaction with what Bernstein had done there the night before. Catledge never revealed himself openly, being characteristically circuitous. He was a tall, ruddy, carefully groomed, chubby southerner who favored dark pinstriped suits and preferred to communicate inferentially through hints, gestures, and what his friends called "Catledgisms." On those occasions when he felt compelled to redress office misdeeds that he deemed intentional or otherwise an affront to his authority, his form of retribution was typically so subtle that his targets were often the last people to know that they had become his victims. He had risen through the ranks as a political correspondent in Washington, and he had learned at the feet of the capital's leading wheelers and dealers how to manipulate people, how to stroke and assuage and cajole and eventually achieve his objectives.

Before I left the paper in 1965, my frosty boss Frank Adams had been eased out as the city editor by Catledge, and Theodore Bernstein had been marginalized following the appointment of two newly elevated editors who outranked him and were answerable to Catledge. However, when I first joined the newsroom in 1958, such stratagems were a long way from reality; Catledge was operating slowly and patiently, as befitted the choreographer of an elephant. And young reporters like myself were meanwhile left to fend for ourselves, to complain at our own risk to the copydesk, knowing that our grousing would sooner or later come to the attention of Frank Adams and might result in our not getting an assignment for a few days, or perhaps an entire week. This had sometimes happened to me and to others among my more querulous young colleagues—we were "benched," as athletes often were by their discontented coaches; in our cases it meant that we sat at our desks for prolonged periods without hearing our names announced over the city editor's microphone, which was how we were summoned to learn the locale and the subject of our story *if* Adams had included us on the daily assignment sheet. There were always many more reporters on duty than there were stories to appear in the next day's paper (management believed it was better to be overstaffed than shorthanded when major incidents unexpectedly occurred) and so having one's name bellowed through the third-floor sound system was usually music to a reporter's ears—it signaled that one was chosen, one was in the day's starting lineup. And while it was considered bad form to ever exhibit an outburst of merriment, satisfaction, or relief, it was nonetheless a common sight in the newsroom for beckoned reporters to rise quickly from behind their typewriters and to stroll friskily up the aisle toward the big front desk, where the city editor stood waiting, sometimes holding the microphone in front of his chest, as if it were a trophy he was about to award to a worthy recipient. As I sat watching from a rear row in the newsroom, listening intently, hoping that the next name I heard would be my own, I was often reminded of televised scenes from Hollywood on Oscar night, and I also thought back to my boyhood days as an altar boy at High Mass on the Jersey shore, standing at the rail while a priest hoisted his aspergillum in my direction, sprinkling me with holy water ritualizing the renewal of my baptismal vows. Reporters could well believe that they were in a state of grace when facing Adams to receive their instructions; they were true and trusted *Times* men, and most of them had habitually subordinated themselves to the judgment of the copydesk and were therefore in his favor.

We who were not in his favor rarely reacted with inner feelings of gratitude on those occasions when we were called before him to receive an assignment; far more frequently than otherwise, we commiserated with one another in the back of the newsroom before dispersing ourselves to our appointed destinations, being collectively convinced that each of us had been assigned to cover a story that was uninteresting, inconsequential, and ultimately destined to be cut to shreds by the copydesk, if not killed entirely by Bernstein. When we were proved wrong—that is, when our assignments ended up as page-one stories, drawing letters of approval from readers—then, of course, we took full credit. It had been our writing skills and creative approaches to these assignments that had transformed what had been ordinary to something extraordinary. On the other hand, if our assignments had proved to be as pointless and unpublishable as we had predicted, then all the blame belonged to our superiors. How could any reporter write about something so bereft of substance, so ill-conceived and banal?

In recounting my days under the aegis of Frank Adams, I do not mean to represent myself as an insubordinate, know-it-all newcomer to the newsroom. It is true I wanted to see my work published pretty much as I had written it; and I believed that newswriting could be both literary and factually reliable; I understood that my being transferred from the sports section to the main section at Turner Catledge's behest was rightly disturbing to Frank Adams, who had not been previously consulted. This I learned later from one of Adams's clerks. Still, it was hardly unprecedented for the newspaper's top editor to occasionally influence the placement and redeployment of personnel without always clearing it beforehand with mid-level management. What was the point in being at the top if it required getting permission from those below? Politesse had its place in maintaining harmonious intermanagement relationships, of course, and Catledge normally might have been expected to notify Frank Adams in advance about my transfer. But in this instance, he apparently had not. It might have been an oversight. Or maybe it was his way of indicating fatigue with Adams's intransigence and hinting that the latter's job was in jeopardy. Or perhaps Catledge was merely exercising his prerogative, as powerful people sometimes do to prove that they possess power, to shift an employee from one section of the paper to another. I was pleased by the move. I had been promoted from journalism's "toy department," which is how the *New York Post* columnist Jimmy Cannon referred to sports, to the *Times* main section, populated by full-fledged reporters. I hoped and believed that I was worthy of Catledge's confidence.

Still, I knew that merit was not all that mattered. There were then about four thousand individuals working within the building in various white-collar and blue-collar capacities, and so autonomous were the various departments—including the advertising department, the circulation department, the promotion department, the news department, the typesetting department, and the Sunday department—that the heads of each department routinely indulged in nepotism, cronyism, and other forms of favoritism when it came to hiring or advancing people within their spheres of operation. The issue of merit *was* taken into account, but because there were always more applicants of merit as well as qualified employees for every available opening or advancement within the organization, the final selection tended to be determined subjectively by those holding positions of influence.

The man at the very top of the *Times*, the publisher Arthur Hays Sulzberger, got his job because he was married to the late Adolph Ochs's daughter, Iphigene. When I joined the newsroom, I believe there were at least a dozen jobholders on the paper who were family relatives of the *Times*'s first lady and her husband. Among the more prominent of these was Arthur Hays Sulzberger's cousin, who was the Paris-based chief foreign correspondent of the *Times*, and Iphigene's cousin, who headed the editorial page and presided over a staff of opinionated pontificators on the tenth floor. In other departments within the paper, and in the disjointed nooks and crannies of the Gothic building's cavernous interior, or within offices owned or leased by the *Times* outside the city or abroad, there were sons and daughters, nephews and nieces, brothers-in-law, uncles, and cousins galore who were collateral descendants or intermarried kinsmen of the Ochs-Sulzberger alliance. Not all of these relatives held important executive positions. Most, in fact, were mid-level bureaucrats. I am alleging, however, using one of journalism's favorite words, that *all* of these people—whether it was Iphigene Sulzberger's nephew, who assisted the advertising manager, or her niece, who clerked for the drama editor, or her other niece, who was an associate editor in the Sunday department, or her son-in-law, who would eventually succeed her husband as the publisher and who, in turn, would be succeeded by her son, Arthur Ochs Sulzberger, and eventually by her grandson, Arthur Ochs Sulzberger, Jr. (the latter in 1992)—*all* of these were on the *Times* payroll in part (if not *entirely*) because of their consanguinity or their conjugal affiliation with the Ochs patrilineage.

The *Times* was a family enterprise. No major decisions regarding the paper's policies and practices could be implemented without the imprimatur of the ruling faction of the Ochs-Sulzberger family. It alone decided which male heir would ascend to the title of publisher. And the publisher was thereafter open to the opinions and recommendations of the family, and to certain intimates of the family, and, more often than acknowledged, to the top public figures of the day. Ochs himself had been influenced in 1929 by President Herbert Hoover's efforts to have a reportorial job on the *Times* offered to young Turner Catledge.

Prior to gaining the White House in 1928, Hoover had been the secretary of commerce, and it was in this capacity, while observing the damage caused by the overflowing Mississippi River, that he had become friendly with the affable and diligent twenty-four-year-old Catledge, then covering the flood story for the *Memphis Commercial Appeal*. Hoover recommended Catledge to Adolph Ochs; but it was not until after Hoover had won the presidency that Ochs hired Catledge away from the *Baltimore Sun*, to which Catledge had gone in 1927 after leaving the *Commercial Appeal*. Catledge was brought onto the New York staff for five months, and was then told by one of Ochs's senior editors that he was being sent to the paper's Washington bureau so that he might capitalize journalistically on his connections with the president.

Catledge did very well during the Hoover administration, but he did equally well during the years of Hoover's successor, President Franklin D. Roosevelt. In 1936, when Catledge was thirty-five, he was named the paper's chief news correspondent in Washington. At the same time, he was told by his bureau chief, Arthur Krock—whom Ochs had brought to the *Times* in 1927 at the suggestion of the financier and statesman Bernard Baruch—that within a year or so he, Arthur Krock, would probably retire and Catledge would take over the bureau. Krock held on as the bureau chief for another seventeen years. So Catledge resigned in 1941 to work for the *Chicago Sun*, being at first a roving correspondent and then the editor in chief. But after seventeen months with the *Sun*, a paper of limited prestige that would soon merge with the *Chicago Times*, becoming the *Chicago Sun-Times*, Catledge accepted an offer in 1943 from Ochs's son-in-law and successor, Arthur Hays Sulzberger, to return to the *New York Times*.

Catledge was assigned to the New York staff for a while and was then sent overseas on special assignments. Near the end of World War II, as a passenger in an overcrowded military transport flying bumpily through a storm in the Burma-India theater, Catledge saw his life careening toward a disastrous conclusion, and, having been the last man aboard, he stood against the door, feeling nauseous and nervous, anticipating his having to leap from a burning wreckage after the plane had crashed into the desert. The pilot, however, did manage to land the plane safely; and, as the aircraft was brought to a halt, a British officer opened the door from the outside and announced, "Gentlemen, you are in New Delhi, the capital of India. You will please leave the plane by rank."

"Guess that means the American taxpayer first," declared Catledge, thrusting himself unsteadily down the steps ahead of everyone else.

After the war, Catledge was appointed by Sulzberger to serve as an assistant in New York to the managing editor of the *Times*, Edwin L. James, and on James's death in mid-December of 1951, Catledge took over as the managing editor. Catledge had been residing in various hotel apartments since his separation two years before from his first wife, whom he had met and married in Baltimore in 1931. The couple had two daughters, neither of them driven to become journalists, but Catledge did bring to the *Times* some friends who had served with him on other newspapers. One of these individuals was a tall, broad-chested, gregarious native of Louisiana named John Randolph, who had briefly attended the University of Alabama, among other colleges, and who, because he had served effectively as Catledge's picture editor at the *Chicago Sun,* became the picture editor at the *Times* in 1952, remaining in that job until he offended Iphigene Sulzberger by printing that picture in 1954 that showed Marilyn Monroe on her wedding day French-kissing her husband, Joe DiMaggio.

Catledge would have preferred overlooking the incident, and probably *would* have if the complaint had not come to him from the publisher's office, prompting him to demote his old friend to a copydesk position for a couple of years until Randolph was transferred to sports in 1956 to write the hunting and fishing column. This allowed Randolph to travel around the country on a liberal expense account, writing about what he most liked to do: hunt, fish, relax on a boat, and escape the clamor of big-city life—a dream assignment, as Randolph saw it. For the next five years, until he died of lung cancer in 1961, his column was one of the most readable features in the paper. I got to know Randolph quite well while we were coworkers in the sports department, and it was he who had identified Iphigene Sulzberger as the one who had reacted negatively to the Monroe-DiMaggio photo. Mrs. Sulzberger, then in her early sixties, was rarely seen in the *Times* building except when walking through the lobby on days when the board of directors met on the top floor, but it was generally believed by veteran *Times* men that she stood constantly behind her husband with gloved hands, reenforcing her late father's definition of what constituted good taste within the paper.

"I'm all for good old Victorian and French hypocrisy," she later admitted in a book about the Ochses and Sulzbergers called *The Trust,* written by Susan E. Tifft and Alex S. Jones with the cooperation of the families. What Iphigene did not exactly say in *The Trust,* but what its authors suggested, was that she was more protective of the propriety of the *Times*'s news columns than she was openly censorious of the infidelity of her husband, Arthur Hays Sulzberger, who was known for his extramarital affairs and most particularly the one with his longtime mistress, a movie star during the 1930s and 1940s named Madeleine Carroll. One evening when Carroll was on her way up to visit Sulzberger in his executive suite, a reporter from the drama department, who was surprised to see her riding in the elevator, posed the question: "What brings you to the *Times*, Miss Carroll?"

"Don't ask," she replied.

When Arthur Hays Sulzberger was close to sixty-five, in the middle 1950s, he was involved with an actress named Irene Manning, and he once saw to it that Turner Catledge got a photograph of her into the paper's theater section. At around this time, the publisher's thirty-year-old son, Arthur Ochs Sulzberger—who would take over as publisher in 1963—was being charged in a paternity suit with impregnating a staff reporter named Lillian Bellison, whom he would refuse to marry and who, in turn, would not accede to an abortion. "She was sleeping with other people in the news department," he was quoted as saying in *The Trust*, but he went on to explain that since a blood test in connection with the paternity suit "couldn't prove that it wasn't mine," he agreed to long-term financial assistance, although he would always avoid personal contact with Lillian Bellison's son. "I've never seen him," Sulzberger said in the book. "It's a piece of history, it's over, it's done." Many years later, when Lillian Bellison's son was in his twenties, he would sue his presumed father and eventually settle for an undisclosed portion of the Ochs-Sulzberger inheritance. His mother kept her job on the *Times* despite her differences with Arthur Ochs Sulzberger, and she was never shy about bringing her boy into the newsroom, introducing him to her reportorial colleagues, including myself, as George Alexanderson, the surname being that of her onetime husband, who died two years prior to the birth. The prevailing view in the newsroom was that young George was a "spitting image" of Arthur Ochs Sulzberger. And while most of the news personnel on the third floor seemed to be quite blasé about this unusual situation—quoting from the lyrics of a saloon song they attributed to the late Stanley Walker and other staffers on the *Herald-Tribune*: "Drink is the curse of the *Tribune*, and sex is the bane of the *Times*"—I had naïvely joined the *Times* in 1953 thinking that the private lives of the people who owned or worked for the organization would reflect the conventional standards and restraints that prevailed each day in the paper's news and editorial pages. But after being on the paper for a while—and especially after the Sulzberger-Bellison revelations—I realized that I was working in a place of appearances. It was as if the walls of the *Times* building were made of one-way glass that gave us a view of the outside world and prevented those on the outside from looking in and judging us. As long as we journalists did not despoil the image of Ochsian propriety in the columns of the paper—which John Randolph had apparently done—then we could presumably deal with our dirty linen in private and cope as best we could with whatever problems we caused one another.

Still, recalling those long-ago years, it is noteworthy that during the supposedly dowdy days of the Eisenhower fifties there existed such a high tolerance for risqué behavior within the *Times,* and it was certainly not limited to the activities of Sulzberger *père* and *fils.* A married man who was a Pulitzer Prize–winning reporter on the third floor had a mistress who worked on the eleventh floor in the promotion department. Seated near the Pulitzer winner's desk was the best female general-assignment reporter on the *Times,* and she was having an affair with one of the senior editors who assisted Theodore Bernstein. In the middle of the newsroom sat a male reporter who was married but was also privately involved with a young woman who wrote "Talk of the Town" pieces for *The New Yorker.* For some reason, he kept a diary during his free hours in the office, describing in vivid detail his extramarital activity; he updated the diary during his free hours in the office and kept it locked in the bottom drawer of his desk. But when he suddenly died due to an allergic reaction to a doctor-prescribed drug following minor surgery, one of the clerks cleaned out the reporter's desk and mailed home to the widow all the contents, including the diary.

Shocked to learn that she had not only been betrayed by her husband but also by *The New Yorker* staffer, whom she had felt close to, the widow wrote a book about the episode and entitled it *Such Good Friends.* Although it was published as a work of fiction—no real names were used—it was nonetheless an accurate account of the adulterous life of her late husband, and yet neither the book nor the movie version of the book, which was directed by Otto Preminger, in fact, none of the sexual indiscretions of any of the other individuals affiliated with the *Times,* tarnished the reputation of the newspaper. The public posture of the *Times* was able to coexist contradictorily with the private lives of those who owned it and were employed by it.

On those rare occasions when what we did was newsworthy but was also embarrassing to us, we could count on collegial coverage within the media, even from our journalistic rivals and the least discriminate of the tabloid columnists. While we journalists disliked hearing "No comment" from elected officials and other public figures when they were connected to controversies—and they were often criticized editorially for their evasiveness—our spokesmen were just as likely to say "No comment" when members of our profession were entangled in delicate situations, such as when a publisher was at odds with a striking labor union, or when a television anchor or syndicated columnist, balking over a contract, was in the process of quitting one employer for another. We in the media espoused double standards, and, as it suited us, we alternated between being "insiders" and "outsiders." We were outsiders in that we were uninvolved personally with the insiders we cultivated as sources, and we were insiders in the sense that we lived within the protective shield of the First Amendment and justified invading other people's privacy in ways that, were it done to us, we would have resented. We were ephemerons. Most of what we wrote was encompassed in a single day, and as professionals we lived vicariously through the ups and downs of other people. Our feelings were filtered, our sensibilities secondhand. With seeming sympathy and understanding, we encouraged the cooperation of those we pursued; but inwardly we were removed from the reality we recounted and the objects of our passing interest.

We were courtiers, wooers, ingratiating negotiators who traded on what we might provide those who dealt with us. We offered voice to the muted, clarification to the misunderstood, exoneration to the maligned. Potentially we were horn blowers for publicity hounds, trial balloonists for political opportunists, lamplighters for theatrical stars and other luminaries. We were invited to Broadway openings, banquets, and other galas. We became accustomed to having our telephone calls returned from important people, and being upgraded as airline passengers through our connections with their public-relations offices, and having our parking tickets fixed through the influence of reporter friends who covered the police department. Whatever we lacked in personal ethics and moral character we might rationalize by telling ourselves that we were the underpaid protectors of the public interest. We exposed greedy landlords, corrupt judges, swindlers on Wall Street.

But nothing published was more perishable than what we wrote. This bothered me when I first joined the newsroom. As a Catholic, I had been conditioned to think in terms of the hereafter. Once as I sat sweating over a story, fearing that I might miss the deadline, I heard a veteran reporter calling to me from across the room: "C'mon, young man, be done with it! You're not writing for posterity, you know." I did *not* know. I was habitually late in delivering stories because I constantly rewrote them, believing that what I wrote would be preserved eternally on microfilm in the archives of Ochs's enduring paper of record. I imagined myself as a monk illuminating the Book of Kells, a prideful scribe hoping that my polished prose would make a lasting impression. We journalists, in my view, were the preeminent chroniclers of contemporary happenings, the foot soldiers for the historians.

With time, however, I begrudgingly acknowledged my older colleague's remark. We were not writing for posterity. We journalists seemed at times to be allied with the fast-food industry, being the short-order cooks for consumers of often half-baked information and ideas. What we wrote in haste was frequently incomplete, misleading, inaccurate. While our editors sought to amend these shortcomings by printing correction notices, such notices were never so lengthy or prominently featured as had been the flawed articles that prompted the corrections. Our editors advocated objectivity and impartiality, the presentation of different positions in a manner that was fair and equal to all parties concerned. But achieving this goal was unlikely, if not impossible. Our editors—*all* editors— subjected the news coverage to *their* understanding of what was fair and balanced, of what was very important, or not very important, or of no importance. Their fingerprints were on every article, every headline, every photograph, every layout in the newspaper. Everything that was published, or not published, was traceable to their subjective selves, to their private values, their vanities and battle scars, their ancestral histories, geographical origins, and whatever influence that politics, race, or religion had over them.

I was told that the *Times* newsroom during the 1930s was dominated by Catholic editors—it was then commonly said among staff members that "the *New York Times* is owned by Jews and is edited by Catholics for Protestants"—and it was also said that the Catholic editors slanted the Spanish Civil War coverage in ways that favored the Church-supported Spanish dictatorship over the Communist and socialist-led rebel opposition. During my time in the newsroom the two top-ranked editors were both small-town southern Protestants—Turner Catledge from Ackerman, Mississippi; and his favorite underling, Clifton Daniel, from Zebulon, North Carolina, who was the first editor that Catledge elevated to a level higher than Theodore Bernstein's. Although I would be hard pressed to document it, I believe that my having gone to the University of Alabama did me no harm with the two gentlemen from the South. The socially aloof and dandyish Clifton Daniel, disliked by most staffers, was particularly cordial and accommodating toward me; it had been under his influence—with Catledge's support, no doubt—that I was able to be transferred quite often from the city staff to out-of-town assignments that I desired, such as going to Cocoa Beach, Florida, in 1960, to describe the crowd scene as the first American astronaut was being launched into orbit, and to be in Chicago in 1962 to report on the Patterson-Liston heavyweight bout, as well as a prefight literary debate in a Chicago auditorium between writers Norman Mailer and William F. Buckley; and to revisit my alma mater at various times between 1963 and 1965 to report on the changing policies and politics on campus, and to write about the voting-rights clashes in Selma and finally the long march of Dr. King and his followers into Montgomery.

My stories from Alabama brought forth notes of congratulation from Catledge and Daniel, both men commending what they called my "objectivity." But what I really think they approved of was the fact that I had not followed the lead of most northern journalists in blaming only the South for racist practices that existed nationwide. I had also not failed to mention the sacking and burning of Selma one hundred years before, when nine thousand Northern troops overran Selma's nearly four thousand defenders who were serving under the Confederate general Nathan Bedford Forrest. In General Forrest's ranks was a soldier named James Turner, the maternal grandfather of Turner Catledge.

17

TURNER CATLEDGE AND ALL THE SENIOR EDITORS OF HIS GENERA-
tion were either dead or retired from the *Times* when I returned to
the newsroom in March 1990 to receive my credentials and airplane tickets for my single-story trip to Selma. Catledge had died in 1983,
while in his early eighties. The editor currently holding Catledge's old
title was an ex-reporter and contemporary of mine, Max Frankel. My
assignment was to write an article of about 2,500 words recounting the
changes in Selma since the massacre had prompted Congress to pass the
Voting Rights Act of 1965, and to describe as well the silver anniversary
festivities and other public events scheduled to take place in Selma,
such as the ceremonial march across the bridge, and the reenactment of
Bloody Sunday in an unbloody manner that would nonetheless call
attention to the suffering sustained by civil rights demonstrators a quarter
of a century ago. Using machine-blown smoke to simulate the tear gas
that had been inhaled by black protesters, and tape recordings that would
reecho the sounds of brutality and anguish that marked that violent time,
this 1990 occasion was supposed to make vivid to young blacks what their
elders had endured in gaining access to the ballot box.

Among the honored guests would be Coretta Scott King (widow of the
civil rights leader assassinated in Memphis in 1968), the Reverend Jesse
Jackson, who currently saw himself as a viable Democratic candidate for
the White House, and John Lewis, who as a twenty-five-year-old agitator
from SNCC had been flattened on the highway but who now returned as
a fifty-year-old member of the U.S. Congress, having been elected as a
Georgia Democrat in 1986.

From my preliminary research, I learned even before arriving in Selma
that most of the city's white residents saw little merit in reviving memories of a situation that had brought such shame and infamy to the community. They wished that the blacks would look ahead rather than back.

Much interracial progress has been made since 1965, the whites pointed out in comments to the local press, and *this* is what should now be remembered and advertised. It would improve the city's image. It might attract more outside investment and result in the construction of more shopping malls and chain stores, more jobs for black people and economic gains for everyone.

All the roads in black neighborhoods were now paved. There were also new streetlights, sewer lines, trees, and hundreds of new housing units that were built as part of a multimillion-dollar federal assistance program. About five thousand dollars went to the restoration of Brown Chapel, which the city enshrined as a historical site and listed as a tourist attraction along with a number of antebellum mansions. The principal street in the black quarter, Sylvan Street—which also extended for three blocks downtown into the territory of white shopowners—had been renamed in honor of Martin Luther King, Jr. Selma's public schools had been desegregated since 1970, and five black appointees served on the eleven-member school board. There were black jurors and police officers, firemen and sanitation workers. Four blacks were on the nine-seat city council, and three of the five seats on the county commission were held by black candidates, and a black resident of Selma, Henry "Hank" Sanders, a partner in J. L. Chestnut, Jr.'s law firm, was now a member of the Alabama state senate.

There were now about 7,500 registered black voters in Selma, which was hundreds more than the whites (although a higher percentage of the latter went to the polls), and while the mayor of Selma in 1965 was *still* the mayor of Selma in 1990, Joseph Smitherman's political advisers were quick to say that he had learned from his past mistakes, and that the city no longer deserved to be smeared by references to Bloody Sunday. That unfortunate incident had largely been provoked by Sheriff Jim Clark, they claimed, adding that he was no longer among them; he now lived in the Birmingham area and worked in the mobile-home business. The other leading local segregationist from that era, circuit court judge James A. Hare, was now dead. And while former governor Wallace was still alive, at seventy—though ailing and paralyzed since being shot by a twenty-one-year-old white man during Maryland's 1972 Democratic primary—he continued to say that he had never been the enemy of black people. He boasted instead that it had been the large turnout of black voters that had helped to reelect him repeatedly to govern the state from his wheelchair in the 1970s through the 1980s, and among the people in Selma who had supported him (liking the fact that he had given raises to schoolteachers and free textbooks to students, and had not seemed to be as offensive as the white candidates running against him) had been the mother of J. L. Chestnut, Jr.

But Chestnut himself had never been swayed by what he saw as George Wallace's desire to reinvent himself, dismissing him as a political opportunist nowadays matched in Alabama only by Joseph Smitherman, the latter being a longtime Wallace follower who had brought his own folksy style, and the persuasive talents he had earlier developed as the town's leading appliance salesman, to the mayoral campaign in 1964; with the help of black voters whom he had impressed with his cordiality and satisfied with small pieces of the political pie, Smitherman had remained in office for seven straight terms. In Chestnut's view, the mayor adhered to the political adage: "If you give just a little, you won't have to give a lot."

I first interviewed Smitherman for the *Times* in 1965, when he was a skinny, blond, six-foot country boy in his mid-thirties who weighed 145 pounds and wore clothes that always seemed a size too large and who looked as if he had not had enough to eat. This had indeed been the case during his upbringing, he told me, since both of his parents had died before he had reached his teens and since those kinfolk who took turns raising him were as dirt-poor as any of Selma's blacks living in the city's nearby shacks or in the boondocks of the county. He worked as a Southern Railway brakeman after graduation from high school, and then moved on to become an appliance salesman at the local Sears, Roebuck, selling vacuum cleaners door-to-door and impressing customers as a trustworthy individual who would personally guarantee whatever he sold. Years later, he was a partner in an appliance shop on the main street, selling many refrigerators and washing machines with equal ease to black and white customers, and at the same time selling himself to them as an electable candidate for a seat on the city council. This he would achieve in 1960, and four years later, when he was thirty-five—and living with his wife and three children in a neighborhood near black people in a single-story house without a burglar alarm—he would win an upset victory in the mayoral campaign, defeating an incumbent who had establishment political connections and old-family status.

The Joseph Smitherman I had met in the mid-1960s, and would see again at times in the 1970s and 1980s while revisiting Alabama, was very adroit in presenting himself as Selma's middleman mayor, the only officeholder capable of being a buffer between the city's disenchanted black and white residents. Comfortable among black people, he would casually enter their social clubs and churches to discuss with their ministers and leading members the many favors he intended to bestow, hinting that with their continued support his gratitude would be shown in the form of political appointments to them, and city jobs for their friends, and prompt road repairs and whatever else was needed to improve the quality of life in their neighborhoods. Then the mayor would privately meet with various groups of white people and suggest that the money and efforts he was directing toward the blacks was the minimum amount necessary to encourage their goodwill and forbearance, and their disinclination to protest in the streets in ways that might attract the networks and bring more bad publicity to Selma.

Most of the money that Smitherman was dispensing for allegedly promoting peace and prosperity in Selma was actually federal money that had been earmarked in Washington primarily for the benefit of black people, these funds being authorized by Congress after Bloody Sunday and continuing to filter down into Selma for years thereafter. There were white politicians in the South who shied away from Washington's War on Poverty largesse because it came with many federal controls and restrictions, mandating that black people should share heavily in the benefits, should be employed at all levels of U.S. government-assisted building projects, training initiatives, and reforms, and should enjoy equal opportunities in a social environment devoid of racism. This federal money was thus "tainted," in the view of some southern politicians, but it was certainly not so regarded by Smitherman, who welcomed every federal dollar he could get his hands on, claiming that the only thing "tainted" about it was there "t'ain't" enough of it—even though the federal sums allocated to Selma during Smitherman's many terms was reportedly close to $40 million. He was therefore well endowed to influence numbers of voters through patronage and to modernize the city in ambitious ways that created many jobs while appearing to conform to government regulations aimed at promoting racial harmony.

Smitherman replaced the slave-built Albert Hotel with a new city hall, and he oversaw the construction of a library in which both races had equal access to books, lecture series, and other services. The downtown shopping area was renovated with brick sidewalks and refaced storefronts, and blacks and whites were now accustomed to drinking out of the same fountains, patronizing the same restaurants, and using the same rest rooms in public buildings and terminals. Smitherman saw to it that his office door was open to all visitors, even those without appointments, and near his desk he kept a small refrigerator filled with cans of Coca-Cola and other soft drinks, which he popped open before serving them to his guests.

Even reporters who had portrayed him negatively in the past were welcomed into his office. He believed that the more they saw of him, the more likely they were to write favorably about him. He was invariably candid with the press; and in an interview with William E. Schmidt of the *New York Times* in 1985, he took issue with the white people of Selma who preferred to blame Sheriff Clark for most of what had gone wrong in 1965. "Our hands are just as dirty as his," Mayor Smitherman said. He also conceded in conversations with other newsmen that racism was often central to his political strategy, adding, however, that it was other people's racism, not his own. He went on to say that many contemporary black candidates were also guilty of exploiting the issue of race whenever they believed it would advance their political careers.

The man in Selma who seemed to be the most determined to undermine Smitherman's efforts to serve as the town's intermediary between black and white residents was J. L. Chestnut, Jr. When Chestnut got his law degree in the late 1950s, there were only five black lawyers practicing in all of Alabama; by the late eighties, Chestnut had five black partners in *his* office alone—it was the largest black firm in the state—and his clients were located not only in Selma but throughout the region. These included many black-influenced county boards and school boards and other entities that received and apportioned sizable sums in order to operate. When four of Selma's black men first gained membership on the city council, they met in Chestnut's conference room for discussions with Chestnut and his partners *before* they walked across the street to join their five white colleagues at the council meeting. Whenever the Smitherman administration deviated from what Chestnut strongly advocated, especially when it concerned the policies and federal sums being directed toward Selma ostensibly to keep the blacks happy and off the streets, Chestnut would sue the city. In the opinion of the mayor, J. L. Chestnut, Jr., would never be happy until *he* ran the city, not by sitting in Smitherman's chair in City Hall but through ongoing behind-the-scenes maneuverings and utilizing the litigious power of the Chestnut law firm in launching discrimination suits and other actions that threatened or blocked the flow of federal funds into the coffers of the Smitherman administration.

Chestnut's most demonstrative and politically ambitious partners were a husband-and-wife team who had earned their law degrees at Harvard. They were Henry "Hank" Sanders, a member of the state senate since the early 1980s, and his wife, Rose, who had been a student activist at Harvard, calling for more black professors on the faculty, and also a black dean. She was also committed to working with black youth groups in

Cambridge and later Harlem and still later in Selma, after she and her husband had joined Chestnut's firm in 1972. The couple had spent a year in Africa before going to Selma, and Rose Sanders in her off-hours from the firm sought to inculcate in the black ghetto an element of African pride, especially among younger people. She presented street fairs that introduced them to African art, music, and dance, she wrote and staged plays that were relevant to black history, and she also used such occasions to warn teenagers against drug abuse and pregnancy.

A lean and petite woman who had an Afro-style haircut and whose wardrobe was decidedly African, and who could barely abide black women who indulged in heavy cosmetics and who straightened their hair, Sanders was not without her detractors in the black community; but when she began meddling in the political affairs of the city, which she did with increasing vigor after becoming a law partner, she quickly emerged as Smitherman's new nemesis, an outrageous little woman who was willful in manner and whose public speeches attacking his policies and his personal character greatly offended him, unsettled him, and yet also confounded him.

White men in the rural areas of the South, even brutes like Sheriff Clark, sought within themselves a measure of lenience and restraint whenever they came into public contact with loud and assertive black women. With black men, it was another matter. Their aggressiveness might be a prelude to a physical challenge, or something worse; but black women were not perceived to be threatening, and so just as long as their black male kinfolk did not join in any of the cantankerousness toward white men that black women could seemingly get away with, the South usually allowed these women a free-speech prerogative perhaps equal to the conversational liberties commonly heard at highway diners favored by interstate truck drivers.

With the arrival of Rose Sanders in Selma, however, the boundaries of bold-talking black women were extended even further than southern tradition had heretofore condoned. Because of her African clothing, her tribal-crafted accessories, her Harvard credentials, and the self-assurance she seemed to exude as she strode around town on errands or en route to appointments, Rose Sanders had become an object of curiosity and discussion throughout the community even *before* she began uttering unflattering comments in public about Mayor Smitherman. Thus when she *did* begin to criticize Smitherman in her prepared speeches and impromptu remarks, her words were destined to carry weight, to be reported in the local newspaper, to be read and debated by factions within the black and white communities. Rose Sanders instantaneously became a public figure of potential persuasiveness beyond that of any bad-mouthing black woman in the history of this onetime plantation area of Alabama, and the white men of Selma, and particularly Joe Smitherman, did not know exactly how to react to her. She was a black *woman*, after all, and so he should logically react as if her words did not matter. She was *noise*. Were he to issue statements refuting her own, it would create big headlines in the *Selma Times-Journal*. This is surely what she wanted. Furthermore, the public had *already* heard her list of complaints—her boss, J. L. Chestnut, Jr., had vented them every time he sued the city: The mayor was a closet racist; the mayor was Machiavellian; the mayor helped only those blacks who were his lackeys. Chestnut, however, communicated his chagrin in a relatively formal manner, showing some respect for the office of the mayor, if not for the mayor himself. Chestnut was of the old school, a wily wordsmith with years of experience in southern courtrooms. His partner, Rose's heavyset husband, Hank, was also a smooth speaker. Hank Sanders was reflective. He was quietly determined and rarely abrasive. He had overcome a few political setbacks in his quest for a seat in the Alabama senate before he finally prevailed. But his wife, Rose, was a rant. Smitherman did not know how long he could continue his strategy of avoidance toward her, his crossing to the opposite sidewalk if he caught a glimpse of her approaching, his raising the windows of his car whenever he saw her standing at the curb glaring at him, her mouth moving in ways that made hearing unnecessary. And yet *how* could he continue to avoid her when she practically resorted to stalking him on the steps of City Hall? She also invited black students and other followers to join her in front of the building and led them in roars of disapproval as they waved signs reading JOE MUST GO, and SMITHERMAN MUST GO.

Then in early February 1990—a month before the silver anniversary remembrance of Blood Sunday, of which *she* was the project director—Rose Sanders and two of her cohorts barged into the outer office of the mayor and refused to leave, blaming him for his role in the ongoing crisis that had long beset the city's public school system.

There was little doubt in Smitherman's mind that serious problems did exist within Selma's public schools. But these problems were exacerbated, he believed, by Rose Sanders herself. No matter what efforts were made to give all of Selma's students an equal opportunity to reach their full academic potential, she would find fault with something and start a public ruckus. Though the schools had been desegregated for decades, she insisted that there was still segregation. In one of her interviews with reporters from the *Selma Times-Journal*, she declared, "Blacks and whites go in the same school door, but once inside they go to separate and unequal classes." She was referring to the local trilevel scholastic rating system, whereby pupils who were judged to be the brightest were grouped together, while the supposedly less gifted students were taught separately in classrooms recognized as representing the second or third level. But these levels were prejudicially designated, she insisted, being the result of such factors as unfair testing measures and the tendency to further favor the privileged students (nearly all of them white) with the best teachers, while these white students' parents reinforced segregation in the classrooms by applying pressure on the schools' administrators and the faculty to continue the leveling procedure. Although there was a black superintendent at the helm, and an abundant number of black teachers in the system, the city's board of education was still controlled by white people, Rose Sanders reminded everyone, adding that her young daughter in elementary school had already been subjected to the prejudiced practice of leveling. Her girl would come home after school complaining that she belonged in a higher level, being unchallenged by the classroom work and the undemanding standards of her teachers. After her daughter was privately tested, Sanders said, it was determined that she was an academically advanced student. There were many black parents with similar stories to tell, Sanders went on, but when the black superintendent of schools, Dr. Norward Roussell, finally began to pay attention to these stories, and even indicated that it might be equitable and just to modify the leveling policy, many white parents suddenly became enraged. They saw him—though phrasing it more delicately—as dumbing down academic standards in order to pacify black parents who wanted their children seated in top-level classrooms. In late 1989, there were rumors that the white-majority school board was leaning toward *not* renewing Dr. Roussell's contract, which was to expire in June 1990.

Smitherman was pleased to hear this, although a few years before, in 1987, he had welcomed the arrival of Dr. Roussell as the city's first black superintendent of schools. Smitherman then believed that it would bring pride and contentment to the black people while calming things politically throughout the community; and the fact that Dr. Roussell was coming to Selma from New Orleans meant that he was not part of J. L. Chestnut, Jr.'s local clique of troublemakers. Chestnut himself made no secret of disliking the appointment. Norward Roussell was probably an Uncle Tom, Chestnut thought at the time, an opportunist beholden to the white-majority school board that had hired him. Chestnut had always resented the fact that the people on the board were not elected. They all were appointed, blacks as well as whites, by the white-controlled city council. And it had been a white-led search committee that had eagerly recruited this high-profile educator, presenting him with a fee that was five thousand dollars more than the fifty-thousand-dollar annual salary of Mayor Smitherman himself, and they undoubtedly offered other benefits and concessions to Dr. Roussell in the interest of luring him to Selma, hoping that his presence would perpetuate the myth that the city was becoming progressive. Chestnut saw through it immediately. What they really wanted, he said, was a "black superintendent to hide behind."

But what they got was something else, although in the beginning no one could quite agree on what they had gotten because the citizens of Selma—black as well as white—had never before encountered a dark-skinned pedant with the majestic dignity of Dr. Roussell. He spoke English eloquently, quickly but politely emphasizing that the proper pronunciation of his surname was *ROU*-ssell. He was a slender gentleman of about five-eight, with close-cropped kinky hair and an angular face with deep-set eyes and a mustache; and while not foppish, he dressed in a way that suggested he was comfortable in front of mirrors. Everything about him was *just so:* His hair and mustache were tidily attended to, his vivid-toned silk ties were carefully knotted and centered within the collars of his shirts, and his suit jackets fit him snugly at the shoulders and were never wrinkled. He hardly ever appeared in public without a jacket, a tie, and a genteel manner. Like Rose Sanders, he attracted much curiosity and comment from people throughout the community; but while she was known for stirring things up and causing disorder, he was perceived as an orderly individual who would create an atmosphere within the school system and the city that would foster biracial cooperation and advance the idea that headline-making activism was detrimental to Selma's economic growth.

After a group of white businessmen had invited him to join the local Rotary Club, offering him an opportunity that had never before been extended to a black man, Dr. Roussell accepted. But when there was talk around town that he might be a candidate for membership in the Selma Country Club, Dr. Roussell took the initiative to remove his name from consideration. He knew that it was perfectly fine for him to dine and fraternize with white male professionals at Rotary meetings, but he was under no illusion that the elite white men and women gathered around the pool of the Selma Country Club would respond with glee to the sight of his three children splashing and thrashing in the water next to *their* children, nor would they necessarily enjoy watching him practicing on the putting green while his tan-skinned, freckled wife sat in the shade of the veranda sipping iced tea. Selma's color line in 1987 was most definitely drawn along the greensward and the chlorinated waters of the country club, and

Dr. Roussell did not have to be the scholar that he was in order to understand that, no matter how well-intending those few white folks who contemplated sponsoring his membership might be, it was a bad idea to do so. It would thrust him and his family into the limelight in a way that would distract from his purpose in coming to Selma.

"I do not want to pay $2,500 to play golf," he finally announced to the local press, bringing immediate relief to the membership committee of the Selma Country Club—which, incidentally, would continue its whites-only policy into the next century. Dr. Roussell also told reporters, "I did not come to Selma to claw down racial barriers."

When Norward Roussell went to Selma in 1987, at the age of fifty-three, seeing the city for the first time, he was put in charge of a system much smaller than his earlier jurisdiction in New Orleans, but it was nonetheless more challenging. Here in Selma he would be entrusted to educate an interracial student body in a very polarized and peevish community, one in which white pupils were a dwindling minority but in which white parents and other adults were striving to maintain, as had long been their custom, a controlling interest in the school system. Except now they were being questioned by black parents, by concerned mothers like Rose Sanders who wanted to be sure that their children were not receiving an education that was second-best. At the same time, Dr. Roussell was politically sensitive and, whenever possible, he would try to avoid, or to compromise or attenuate, the implementation of policies that might drive away from Selma's schools what was left of the white classroom population.

White students represented barely 25 percent of the total enrollment of about six thousand youths attending public schools in 1987. On school days, these 1,500 whites intermingled with 4,500 black students in the corridors, cafeterias, gymnasiums, and classrooms of the eleven buildings that constituted Selma's public school real estate. The largest building was occupied by the fourteen hundred students attending Selma High School. There were also two middle-school buildings, one on the east side of town, the other on the west side, which had a combined enrollment of thirteen hundred students who were taught in the sixth-, seventh-, or eighth-grade classes. Finally there was a scattering of eight elementary school buildings that accommodated the more than three thousand younger students who attended classes ranging from kindergarten to the fifth grade.

Isolated from the public school system were two private schools in Selma that catered only to white children, at an annual cost to their parents or guardians of about two thousand dollars, and the combined number of students attending these two institutions was slightly more than eight hundred. Roussell wanted to prevent this figure from increasing, as it surely would if heightened racial tensions in his schools prompted white parents to transfer their children into one of the private schools. And there were also other places that might attract them. There were public schools in the county that had a higher percentage of white pupils and there were a few private schools (whites only) in the outer boroughs that were less expensive than the two in Selma and were at a convenient driving distance from the city. But where these schools existed was unimportant to him—he saw them all as sites of "white flight," and this term and its possible consequences both disheartened and perturbed him.

He had not come to Selma to oversee buildings in which the student body had once been exclusively white, and had then been integrated, and had then become exclusively black. His position would be reduced to that of a ghetto administrator, and it would also be a setback for the civil rights movement, which he had benefitted from and identified with. The movement had finally succeeded during the mid-1950s in enrolling black students in white classrooms, providing young blacks and whites with an equal opportunity for a broader education, and also a chance as classmates to learn more about one another and ideally promote greater understanding and tolerance. What a pity it would be if the victory over school segregation in the 1950s were followed at century's end by school segregation of another type. He would strive mightly against this happening, wanting neither to see his white students defecting from his schools nor their families relocating their homes to other places, depriving Selma of taxpayers, consumers, and white parents with a vested interest in his school system.

Having said this did not mean he would allow himself to be subverted by his white supporters, who might raise the issue of white flight as a threat to justify reining him in, to exert pressure on him to behave in accord with the will of white parents in the hope of retaining their children. He knew he could not become the white folks' hostage. He must maintain his independence from the town's white leaders as well as the black ones. He was an educator, not a mediator in race relations. He had been summoned to Selma to deal with the city's troubled schools, which had a 36 percent dropout rate prior to his arrival. He had been assured by the white people who hired him that they believed in integrated public schools as much as he did, letting him know that they could well afford to place their children in private schools but that they nonetheless saw public schools as essential pillars in the pluralistic community they preferred and wished to cultivate. He had been provided with an annual operating budget of $18 million, larger than any agency in the city; and so with this substantial sum of money, and with the biracial backing of many city boosters, Dr. Roussell was confident in the fall of 1987 that he could succeed in upgrading Selma's schools academically and could create within them a desirable environment that would reduce truancy and encourage a higher degree of prideful participation from the parents and students of both races.

A year later, his efforts had earned him a praiseworthy report from the school board and congratulatory comments throughout the community. Parents were pleased that he had quickly introduced their children to the new technology, installing computer labs in the schools, thanks to a $1.2 million federal grant he had requested and received not long after he had assumed his duties. He also brought professional counselors into the schools to meet and assist the needs of pupils whose low or failing grades and habitual truancy were thought to be linked to their crises at home, or their drug use, or their dyslexia or other physical disorders and personal problems. In a move intending to improve the efficiency of the members of his faculty, he often granted them free time so they could attend workshops and lectures that were held outside the city and featured prominent educators. While he kept abreast of the latest teaching methods being advocated elsewhere, Dr. Roussell kept a vigilant watch over what was going on within his jurisdiction, and the people of the town became accustomed to seeing him driving around in his maroon Cadillac, visiting one school after another. After greeting his principals he would make the rounds, observing his teachers at work in their classrooms, and he noted how the students were responding.

At the completion of the first year, some teachers were transferred from the high school to one of the middle schools, or from the middle schools up to the high school, although it was not always made clear to them why they were being moved. These teachers began to complain among themselves. There was also some grumbling being expressed around town by the proprietors of those businesses that had long done work for the schools—as printers, as maintenance contractors, and as providers of other services—and now learned of other firms taking over these contracts. Roussell was making changes, decisively but arbitrarily, it seemed to some people. Their criticisms were muted, however, until his popularity began to wane, which it did during the middle of his second year, when certain unfortunate happenings within the schools began to call into question the autonomy that he had assumed was his due.

Among these incidents were a number of publicized interracial quarrels involving students, one of which began after a group of white youths took exception to those black classmates who appeared in school wearing African medallions, and a fistfight erupted after a white was overheard to say, "Hey, nigger, go back to Africa." There were also allegations of unfairness in the amount of punishment that a white faculty member had meted out against the black boys on the track team who were accused of boisterous "partying" as compared to what the whites on the debate team had received for a similar offense. After a white member of the school board had become displeased by Dr. Roussell's tardiness in replying to an inquiry relating to the curriculum, which the latter believed was beyond the former's right to review, the board member began to circulate a memo indicating that Dr. Roussell was showing signs of "arrogance" and "excessive independence"—and this opinion soon drew concurring nods in the black community as well as the white. Members of the town's leading black businessmen's club had already been unpersuaded by his explanation that he was too busy to attend one of their social functions and deliver a speech. And the white couple who had held a cocktail party in his honor at their home had been offended when he arrived one hour late.

His difficulties in Selma came to the forefront, however, when he decided to discontinue the schools' trilevel scholastic rating system, which Rose Sanders had been complaining about. It was not that Dr. Roussell had chosen to ally himself with the Chestnut-Sanders anti-Smitherman faction, but, rather, that after the eleven-member school board had decided not to renew his contract (six white members had voted to replace him; five black members voted to retain him) the Chestnut group saw Roussell's plight as a racial issue that might arouse black passion and promote unity in the ghetto. Roussell himself was not pleased to find himself in this situation, being caught in the middle of a polarized community, and yet it made him more receptive to those who might possibly help him hold on to his job.

J. L. Chestnut, Jr., was clearly *the* ascending black power broker at this time, one who was starting to pull the political strings in the ghetto so effectively that he had all but delegitimized the black leaders who were accepting patronage from Mayor Smitherman; and Chestnut had already demonstrated that he had the influence to help black candidates overcome white incumbents at the polls. This had happened in the recent countywide election, which saw his choices garnering enough votes to gain control of the county government, setting the stage for his own triumphant entrance into the courthouse on January 16, 1989—Martin Luther King, Jr. Day—to congratulate those commissioners whose campaigns his law firm had helped to manage. One of the newly elected commissioners was, in fact, the office manager of Chestnut's law firm—Perry Varner, who earned his law degree at Boston College and was a brother-in-law of Rose Sanders. What was additionally gratifying to Chestnut on this day was the festive and spruced-up presence of those many black men who had brought their wives and children to observe the swearing-in ceremony. It reminded Chestnut of the crowds of black families he had seen in this same courtroom back in 1953 when they had assembled to watch the performance of Peter Hall, the first black attorney ever to try a case in Selma. That was the rape case involving William Earl Fikes—the one that had influenced J. L. Chestnut, Jr., to return to Selma in 1958 after getting his law degree. The Fikes case had convinced Chestnut that "Alabama was where the action was," and this action would engage him for the rest of his working life, bringing him in 1989 into open conflict with Mayor Smitherman and the school board that was trying to oust his new friend, Norward Roussell.

Not only did Chestnut file a lawsuit against the board, claiming that its six white members should not continue to function while its five black members were absenting themselves in support of Dr. Roussell, but Chestnut's law office proceeded to become the nerve center of many demonstrations and confrontations that would disrupt the city for nearly six months. During this period—from September 1989 into March 1990—there was a high school sit-in, a boycott against the business interests of the white board members, several pro-Roussell rallies in the streets, and a brawling invasion of the office of Mayor Smitherman. This last incident, which occurred on February 5, 1990, had been the handiwork of Rose Sanders.

Chestnut had not been with her at the time, but she was accompanied by two other individuals from his firm. One was his office manager, Perry Varner, and the other was Carlos Williams, one of the five partners at Chestnut, Sanders, Sanders, Turner, Williams & Pettaway. After Mrs. Sanders, along with Varner and Williams and a half-dozen younger followers, had entered City Hall and settled themselves in the hallway near the mayor's office, Joe Smitherman himself came out to explain that he was too busy at this time to invite them in, but he said that he would try to see them later. After offering them soft drinks, which he laid on the receptionist's desk in his outer office, which on this day was guarded by a police officer, Smitherman returned to his inner office, where a second policeman was on duty, and closed the door.

Sanders and her group waited in the hallway for the next hour, sitting or standing in or near the outer office's door while singing civil rights songs or chatting among themselves, and occasionally bantering with some of the city employees who strolled through the corridors. When Rose Sanders saw the city attorney, Henry Pitts, walking in her direction and then quickly turning and heading unhesitatingly through the outer office to within a few feet of the mayor's door, she yelled out, "I've had it"—and immediately she and her people ran forward and fell in line behind Mr. Pitts, doing so with such force that they knocked him head-first over the outer office's reception desk. While a police guard bent down to assist him, Rose Sanders and the others slipped past them and proceeded to open Smitherman's door, pressing it against the buttocks of the three-hundred-pound police officer who was posted inside, and who now turned around, with his elbows raised high, blocking and shoving aside Sanders and her fellow intruders.

As they pushed forward into the office, bodies tumbled to the floor, furniture began to splinter, and the alarm system signaled for the arrival of more security. Joe Smitherman rose angrily from behind his desk and, pointing a finger at Rose Sanders, declared, "You're going to be charged with obstructing governmental operations and anything else we can come up with. . . ." She regarded him contemptuously but did not respond. She continued to glare at him in silence as more police officers entered Mayor Smitherman's office and began to handcuff her colleagues, including Carlos Williams and Perry Varner. Refusing to leave on foot, both men were carried away by the lawmen, with Varner exiting headfirst, and facing the ground, as he was hauled through the corridor of City Hall and then raised into a patrol wagon that was parked at the curb and was headed for the prison.

Rose Sanders also refused to leave voluntarily, kicking and screaming as the lawmen picked her up and shoved her into the backseat of a police vehicle. She would claim that she sustained injuries as a result of her arrest and that the white male officer who had accompanied her in the car to prison had "brutalized" her, committing such offenses as placing his club between her legs. Her condition required immediate medical attention, she insisted; days later, at a news conference that she held in her room at the Vaughan Regional Hospital, she appeared before the press wearing a rose-colored gown and a neck brace. She sat in a wheelchair guided by her husband. Her left arm was in a sling and hooked up to tubes attached to an intravenous trolley. A black physician, her gynecologist, told the press that while she had not broken any bones, she was unable to use her left hand and also suffered from chest, neck, and arm pain. She herself added that the mental anguish and the sexual violation she'd experienced had been equally damaging to her well-being, and she took the opportunity to insist on the dismissal of the white policeman and to emphasize that Mayor Smitherman was the sort of man who "doesn't give a damn about a black woman" and had handled her "the way slaves were treated by their masters two hundred years ago."

After the conference, two white reporters who were assigned to the story—one was Alvin Benn of the *Montgomery Advertiser*, the other Adam Nossiter of the *Atlanta Journal-Constitution*—were told by one of the hospital's nurses that Sanders was exaggerating her injuries and performing for the cameras. Within a few hours the reporters had returned to the hospital and, without knocking, opened Sanders's door. They saw her sitting comfortably on the bed, without wearing her neck brace or her sling or being attached to the IV device, smiling as she spoke on the phone, holding it in her left hand, the one that her doctor said was so weak she could hardly grip anything with it.

Rose Sanders's mother, seated in a chair near the door, was the first to see the reporters peeking in, and she quickly jumped up to slam the door shut. Sanders and her supporters were enraged by the reporters' initiative and the articles they subsequently wrote describing what they had seen. Days later, when Alvin Benn was covering a rally honoring Dr. Roussell in a black church, Benn was threatened and shoved out of the building by some black men; and a black woman—not Rose Sanders, but one of her close friends—was overheard referring to him as an "evil Jew."

After the church event had been concluded, a pro-Roussell parade was formed outside, and soon more than 2,500 black people—led by Rose Sanders, wearing a neck brace—were marching through town singing, chanting, and denouncing the mayor. This routine was repeated in the days and weeks that followed, but, unlike the situation in 1965, the lawmen who surrounded this crowd controlled their tempers and did nothing in public that could expose them to incrimination either by the demonstrators or the media.

"C'mon, beat us, beat us," a black marcher taunted a white state trooper one evening as the parade proceeded past the middle school on the east side of town. The trooper pretended he did not hear. He and the other state troopers (some of whom were black) wore soft hats instead of riot helmets. They came with pistols but not clubs, gas canisters, or flak jackets. When the marchers would pause in the street to kneel and pray, the troopers would remove their hats and lower their heads. These black marchers were now unaccompanied by the villains of law enforcement who had helped to create Bloody Sunday, and in order for the protesters to make the national headlines at this time, said one observer, "they're going to have to find another Jim Clark." This comment was made by Bryan Woolley, a fifty-two-year-old senior reporter for the *Dallas Morning*

News who was in town to write an updated story about Selma after having come in 1965 as a Harvard divinity student partaking in the voting-rights march to Montgomery. "What happened then appealed to the conscience of the country, including white Southerners like me," Woolley said in an interview published in the *Montgomery Advertiser* in mid-February 1990. The demonstrators in 1965 "were led by ministers," he emphasized. "This one is being led by lawyers."

When I arrived in Selma during the first days of March 1990, it was a foregone conclusion that Dr. Roussell would soon resign. Despite the support he had received from Rose Sanders, J. L. Chestnut, Jr., and the others, he saw his situation as untenable, his purpose in coming to Selma no longer practical nor possible. He had aspired to guide and improve upon an integrated school system; but due to the political infighting and the interracial rancor, his worst fears had been realized: White flight had swept through his classrooms like a windstorm, and in recent weeks approximately five hundred white students had left his system to attend one of Selma's private academies or the private or public schools outside the city. The ratio of black students to whites had been 75:25 when he arrived in 1987; it would be 90:10 when he resigned in 1990, agreeing to a $150,000 contract buyout and surrendering his position to a local black educator, Dr. James Carter, who would distance himself from local politics but would nevertheless see additional numbers of white students abandoning his schools.

At century's end, Dr. Carter's public schools, and the city as well, would be as segregated in many ways as had been the case before Bloody Sunday. Although current law made it possible for blacks and whites to dine in the same restaurants, to register in the same hotels, and to send their children to the same public schools, it could not prevent white flight, nor legislate goodwill and trust between the races, nor integrate the guest lists at private dinner parties and social events, nor mandate what had been advocated long ago by Booker T. Washington and W. E. B. Du Bois, which was full inclusion by black people in the American experience. The color line was perhaps more opaque than it had previously been, but it was still discernible in twenty-first-century Selma and throughout the United States, and national surveys reflecting this uneradicable separatism between black and white people, a separatism most clearly and immediately evident in the lives of the school-age children of both races, would be regularly reported in the press. In an article in the *New York Times*—under the headline SEGREGATION GROWING AMONG U.S. CHILDREN—a sociologist named John R. Logan, from the State University of New York at Albany, was quoted as saying, "The problem for minority children is that, on average, they're growing up in neighborhoods where they are the majority, and that's not the world they will live in."

But what interested me most after I had arrived in Selma for the *Times* in March 1990 was not the exodus of white children from the city's school system, nor the intensified estrangement being experienced by black and white adults; it was, rather, that in the middle of this tumultuous mingling and discord there was in progress a private love affair between an attractive white woman who had worked in one of the town's interior-decoration shops and a black man who was employed in City Hall as Mayor Smitherman's director of personnel. And this couple planned to publicize their romance with a wedding ceremony that would take place on Saturday, March 3, in the groom's home, during a weekend when, some blocks away, Rose Sanders and J. L. Chestnut, Jr., would be overseeing a number of programs and a parade that would hark back to the racial hatred that had prevailed here twenty-five years ago on Bloody Sunday.

18

I LEARNED OF THE LOVE AFFAIR WHILE INTERVIEWING JOE SMITHER-man, although it had not been his intention to tell me about it. I had gone to his office shortly after arriving in Selma, walking past two policemen who were posted on the steps of City Hall to keep an eye on the picket line of black teenagers who were strolling along the sidewalk and the front lawn, singing civil rights songs and carrying signs reading JOE MUST GO.

"It don't bother me a bit," Smitherman assured me as he rose from his chair to shake hands and then waved me into a seat across from his desk. Behind him was a Confederate flag as well as one representing the United States, and hanging on the walls were several photographs showing him discharging his official duties, which in 1988 included greeting the black Democratic candidate for president, Jesse Jackson, and presenting him with a key to the city. Smitherman was now sixty, a compactly built six-footer wearing a tan suit and a white shirt with a maroon silk tie. He had a full head of sandy gray hair that was carefully groomed and parted on the side, and his blue eyes were framed by tortoiseshell glasses that rested high on his straight nose. He had gained more than fifty pounds since taking over the job, but I thought he appeared to be in better shape now (though I knew he smoked three packs a day, and liked his vodka at night) than he had been as an undernourished 145-pound newcomer to City Hall in 1965. After offering me a Coke and a cigarette, he removed his jacket, loosened his tie, and sat down.

"No," he said, "this protesting don't bother me because I know there's some people you'll *never* satisfy, no matter *what* you try to do. But the blacks are doing the same thing we did twenty-five years ago. We hollered for 'segregation,' and played on the white people's fear of integration—and this got us elected. Now, twenty-five years later, the black elected officials, and black leaders not elected, are hollering 'white racism' and 'de facto segregation' and 'economic oppression' to get elected, and they're doing a good job."

His tone was one of equanimity, not stridency. He had spoken in this tone earlier in the day while appearing on a network morning show to discuss that weekend's memorial march. Marching was fine with him, he had said; he'd be on the sidelines watching. The march would also be a sign of Selma's progress, he added, pointing out that the town's police force was 35 percent black, and the fire department was 25 percent black, and the postmaster was black, and that several important jobholders within his administration were black.

Smitherman expanded upon this in his interview with me, and while I took notes, wanting to give the impression that I was interested, I was not. This was recycled material that I had read and heard before, and I wanted to change the direction of our talk toward something I might like to write about. As yet, I had nothing specifically in mind, but I knew that I did *not* want to write about what I was hearing from the mayor. Still, it is not always easy to redirect conversations when dealing with individuals who are very experienced and skillful in using the press as their sounding boards. The technique I have occasionally used to derail such people's trains of thought is to politely but abruptly ask them a question that they might initially think is stupid. Or, if not stupid, so completely out of context and surprising that they are rendered momentarily speechless.

During such times they may stare at me, indicating bewilderment, and I can imagine them asking themselves, Is this interviewer serious? Is he really expecting an answer to this ridiculous question? Some people become quite irritated, and they not only refuse to answer but immediately terminate the interview, which is one way of answering. Other people request that I repeat the question, which I always do in my customarily sincere and respectful manner, even though I know that what I am posing is intended to fluster them, to catch them off guard, to confront them with an unanticipated question that might be awkward for them to respond to.

It seemed to me that it would be very awkward for Mayor Smitherman to address questions concerning interracial sex and the possibility that secret liaisons were currently taking place somewhere within his polarized city, and that it might be commonplace in future decades for Selma's black and white people to marry one another and be accepted socially by the community at large. I had probably been thinking along these lines ever since I'd recently read in a magazine, or had heard on the radio, that Alabama was one of only two states in the entire nation (South Carolina being the other) that still outlawed interracial marriages. The Alabama constitution, as written in 1901, not only prohibited a black person from marrying a white person but it ruled against the *descendants* of black people intermarrying with whites.

"Mr. Mayor," I began, "I don't want to seem frivolous, but you've been saying that the blacks and whites of Selma are more integrated than ever, and you gave Jesse Jackson a key to the city, and I'm wondering how far this will go and whether you see good things happening if black people and white people could get married without a hassle and settle down in Selma."

The mayor's face assumed a look of disgruntlement, as if I'd hit him over the head with a piece of fruit. Saying nothing, he glanced over my shoulder toward his office door. We two were alone in the room, but the door to the outer office was open slightly. A policeman was posted out there, and so was the mayor's secretary, a middle-aged woman who liked to eavesdrop while seated at her desk.

The mayor turned back to me. In a soft voice he asked, "Are you bringing all this up because of Randall Miller?"

"Who's Randall Miller?" I asked.

"He's the black fella that's my director of personnel. He's got an office in this building that's bigger than mine. He's getting married tomorrow. . . ." After a pause, Smitherman added, "To a white woman."

Now *I* was silent. I had heard nothing about this.

"Was this in the papers?" I asked.

"No," said the mayor.

"Where's the wedding going to be?"

"Few blocks from here, at Randall Miller's house."

"Do you think he'll talk to me?"

"I don't know," the mayor said, reaching for his phone. "I'll call him."

The secretary in personnel said that Randall Miller was in Montgomery and would not be returning until later in the evening. After hanging up, the mayor obliged me with Miller's home address and phone number and told me a few things about him. Randall Miller was a very capable individual of about fifty, tall and well mannered. His late father, Ben Miller, had opened a funeral parlor in the black quarter many years ago, and Randall, after acquiring a mortician's license, inherited it and still oversaw it, in addition to holding down his position in personnel.

The mayor said that he had first hired Randall Miller in 1972 to work in Selma's urban renewal office. At the time, Miller was married to a young black woman who was a schoolteacher, and the couple had a daughter. But ten years later, Miller became involved with a white married woman who had two daughters. Miller had met her in the shop where she worked. Smitherman would learn about the affair because Miller's angry wife complained to him about it, hoping that he might persuade Miller to end it. Smitherman decided not to become involved. It was a private matter. It was also a subject that Mayor Smitherman did not now wish to discuss with me further, he politely made clear. So I stood up, thanked him for his time, and said that I would see him on Sunday afternoon at the parade.

I planned to drive directly to the address he had given me, 209 Alabama Avenue. I thought that perhaps the bride-to-be might be in the house, getting things ready for the next night's wedding. I did not consider telephoning ahead. I would just show up, and, if she was there, I would introduce myself and hope to get my foot in the door. I had not revealed my intentions to the mayor. Since he used to sell vacuum cleaners door-to-door, I assumed that he would understand.

The house was a mauve-toned single-story frame Victorian structure with a beige picket fence, located on a quiet tree-lined residential street in an integrated neighborhood that existed beyond the purview of Selma's antebellum pride. There were no mansions on this street, not even large houses. It had been a lower- to middle-income white area until recently, and the whites who now remained among the newly arrived black residents were mainly elderly people, retired teachers, office workers, and other pensioners with no children to attend to and with lots of time on their hands. As I parked my car behind another car at the curb in front of the Miller home, I noticed that I was being watched from across the street by a frail-looking woman with unkempt white hair who was holding on to the wooden railing of her front porch. I could also hear echoing loudly in the near distance, coming from the direction of the river and bridge, a forceful female voice calling instructions over a loudspeaker. That voice might belong to Rose Sanders, I thought, rehearsing her people for one of the programs.

I knocked only once before the door was opened by a tallish, blue-eyed, strawberry-blond woman in her early thirties who was carefully coiffed and attired and was appealing both in a physical sense and in her friendly manner. Smiling, she accepted my congratulations, even though as I offered them I was not sure that she was the bride-to-be.

"Thank you," she said, extending a hand. "I'm Betty Ramsey. Tomorrow, I'll be Betty Miller."

She led me into the living room and introduced me to her teenage daughters. One was blond, the other brunette. They had been watching television, but, without being told, they turned off the set and left the room, as if aware that their mother wished to speak with me alone. I guessed that the mayor had telephoned her from his office, warning that I might be stopping by. She hardly seemed to mind. She offered me something to drink and then sat across from me for the next hour, answering all my questions, while also adding information of her own. It was one of the easiest interviews I had ever conducted—or rather, it was *she* who conducted much of it, perhaps seeing me as a convenient and timely means of spreading the nuptial news to the general public, from which she, until now, at least among most white people in Selma, had more or less remained isolated by choice, or necessity, or a bit of both.

As I sat listening to her description of her nearly decade-long relationship with Randall Miller, jotting it down as quickly and fully as I could on the folded sheets of hotel stationery that served as my notepad, I began to see Betty Ramsey as a kind of renegade, a radicalized romantic who tomorrow, wearing an off-white satin gown and standing in front of a black Baptist minister, would be coming out and crossing over, ceremoniously affiliating herself with a minority more separate and segregated probably than the one she was marrying into. Willingly, she was entering into a sector of society in which grandparents white or black did not always easily recognize, or want to recognize, their grandchildren. *Miscegenation*—the very word suggested a nation of misplacement, misalliance, and misery. Even though the state of Alabama was apparently not enforcing its statute against interracial matrimony—there was even talk of a proposed amendment that would remove the language from the law books—Betty Ramsey must be a most intrepid and inner-directed woman, I told myself, or else she would have avoided becoming intimate with a black man in Selma and would not be discussing it so openly with me now.

She said that prior to meeting Randall Miller—which she had done in 1981, shortly after moving to Selma from her native Arkansas with her husband and children—she had never been acquainted with a black man, nor had she been accustomed to having black people as part of her community. She had been born, reared, and educated in a segregated town that was not even half the size of Selma. When her husband's income as a rural schoolteacher proved to be inadequate for the support of the family, he accepted a position managing a three-hundred-acre farm in Selma owned by an Arkansas businessman. The job paid one thousand dollars a month, plus free housing, a food allowance, a vehicle to drive, and forty acres that he could sharecrop or farm himself. Betty Ramsey, who had a degree in education but did not teach, accompanied him with their daughters, aged nine and seven, and enrolled them in the local public school, where the student body was equally divided between blacks and whites. The girls adjusted easily and enjoyed the new experience; but Betty, unhappily married in Arkansas, was just as unhappy in Selma until she fell in love.

The first time she saw Randall Miller was when he had walked into the Carpet Mart, accompanied by his wife, Winona. Betty, who had taken a job there, stood watching from the other side of the store as they were attended to by the owner, a middle-aged white man who was friendly with Randall Miller because the latter was a regular customer, having formerly purchased many items needed by the various city-supervised agencies. In addition to carpets, the store sold wallpaper, window shades, floor tiles, and paint. On this occasion, Randall and Winona Miller were there to select a particular shade of gray paint with which to cover their home's cornice and other exterior embellishments. A few days after the paint had been delivered to their home, Randall returned alone to exchange it. He explained to Betty, who was then the only one on duty, that the gray paint he and his wife had selected contained a greenish tinge that he had not noticed earlier, and so he wondered if he could make another selection.

Overcoming her initial shyness as a new employee assisting for the first time a black man whom she found attractive, she was pleased to help him find precisely what he said he had been looking for when he had walked in. After he had thanked her as he carried away the paint, and waved to her from his car as he drove off, she continued to have thoughts about him during the afternoon, without imagining that she would be hearing from him a day later and many times more in the weeks and months that followed.

"He started by telephoning me at the store, and then stopping in—not to buy anything, just to chat—and yet it took me quite a while before I'd attached any significance to this," she told me. "Whether he telephoned or just walked in, he'd always start the conversation by asking to speak with my boss. But my boss never seemed to be in at the time. Later I did begin to wonder if Randall knew beforehand that the boss wasn't in. If you drove past the store, you could see that the boss's car wasn't parked in its usual place along the side of the building, and you could also see when I was working in there alone—there was a big plate-glass window in front. And yet, as I say, it took me a while. Randall was always respectful and nice," she went on. "He impressed me as a real friendly type. He was interested in how I was getting along in Selma, and how my daughters were doing in school, and what I thought about this or that. Even when his talk started getting a little more personal, you weren't sure exactly how to take it. It could mean one thing. Or it could mean something else."

The fact that Randall was black also contributed to Betty's early doubt that he was pursuing her. He had been born more than forty years ago in Selma and had surely grown up hearing about the horrible history of black men in the South who had so much as looked twice at a white woman. While lynching was a thing of the past, this was still Selma, a town in which gossip, scandal, and maybe worse might result from any interracial intimacy that Randall might have in mind; and Betty continued to ask herself, Why would he risk it? He was a prominent political figure. He had many friends and associates among the city's blacks and whites. He was married to a schoolteacher, they had a daughter, and he owned a lucrative funeral business that catered exclusively to black people. If he betrayed his wife and took up with a white woman, wouldn't this cause resentment in the black community and encourage people to take their business to another funeral home? And finally, didn't Randall foresee big problems if something *did* develop between the two of them and her husband learned about it?

Betty did not share her concerns with Randall, she told me, because during the first six or eight months of their acquaintanceship, she had no proof that her concerns were legitimate. She might be misinterpreting or imagining his ultimate purpose. She was therefore contented to leave things as they were. She had someone to talk to who was interesting and different. If there were no customers in the store, and her boss was away—she soon became aware of her employer's daily routine, his golf schedule, his other outside appointments—she and Randall could talk at length, either in person or over the telephone. She looked forward to his calls and visits. In the beginning, their discussions were centered mainly on her—since he did most of the questioning—but gradually it was she who took the lead. She was very comfortable with and very curious about Randall Miller.

Whatever preconceived notions she might have once had about black people living in the Deep South—that is, their inclination to be subordinate, indolent, or a bit stoical—certainly did not apply to Randall Miller and his kinsmen in Selma. Randall's father, Ben, had been born poor but was smitten with ambition and resourcefulness, and while in his early forties he simultaneously owned or co-owned a restaurant, a real estate business, a barbershop, a working farm, and a funeral parlor. He would sire seven children, all of whom received an advanced education, even while contributing to Ben Miller's labor force, learning the value of a hard-earned dollar under a demanding taskmaster. The emancipation of

Selma's slaves long ago did not necessarily make life easier for the progeny of Ben Miller.

The second-born child, Randall, rarely knew leisure. When he was not attending classes in grade school, he was shining shoes in the barbershop, or scrubbing pots in the restaurant, or digging dirt on the farm, or washing limousines prior to a funeral. He had thoughts of one day becoming a doctor, but his father saw his future in embalming. Ben's other children would go on to become teachers and school administrators, but Randall's fate was sealed in 1958 when he was nineteen and a premed student attending a black college, Stillman, located in Tuscaloosa, not far from the University of Alabama. Inasmuch as the last of his father's licensed morticians had just quit after a quarrel, and since Ben himself lacked the proper credentials to prepare a corpse for burial, he thought that it would be an excellent idea for Randall to transfer from Stillman to the Atlanta College of Mortuary Science. Charming when he had to be, Ben cajoled and gradually convinced his son that the latter had been born to succeed in a grand way in the funeral trade: Randall possessed a consoling nature, he was patient and personable, and, since he was tall and good-looking— he had been a basketball star at Stillman—he would cut a dashing figure as he appeared wearing a dark suit with a boutonniere on his lapel, and his broad shoulders would offer comfort and support to bereaved widows.

In 1959, Randall graduated in Atlanta with a degree in mortuary science. He then returned to Selma to work in the funeral parlor under his father. A year later, when Randall was twenty-one, he married his high school sweetheart, Winona, and the following year the couple had a daughter. While not a civil rights activist when Selma first began making the news with its voter-registration drives in the early 1960s, Randall did join Dr. King's procession from Selma to Montgomery in mid-March 1965. He drove a hearse behind the last row of marchers. It was a tail-finned 1960 Cadillac with a blue body and a white top, and Randall had a dome light that he could attach to the roof when using the vehicle as an ambulance.

In addition to the black persons' hospital in Selma, the only other medical facility in the city that accepted black patients was the Catholic hospital, Good Samaritan. But in the event that Dr. King was shot or otherwise harmed along the highway during the five-day journey, Randall was instructed to take the civil rights leader to Craig Field, six miles outside Selma, where a United States Air Force jet stood ready to fly King to Washington for treatment at the Walter Reed Hospital. The hearse that Randall was driving was one of several black-owned vehicles that had been loaned to the march's organizers, and at night, while the marchers rested at a campsite, the hearse served Randall as his sleeping quarters. On the fifth and final day of the march, following the highway murder by the Klan of Viola Liuzzo, Randall was dispatched to pick up her body, but the Alabama state police did not permit him to pass their roadblock.

In 1974, Randall became his father's partner at the mortuary, and in 1983, following his father's death—and after Randall had bought out the inherited interests of his siblings—he assumed sole ownership of the Miller Funeral Service, subsequently expanding it within Selma, and also within the neighboring community of Marion, into a flourishing business that fueled nearly twenty Cadillac limousines. His marriage to Winona was not a happy one, but the combined demands of his business and his responsibilities within the Smitherman administration gave him little time and not much incentive to worry about his domestic situation *until* his relationship with Betty Ramsey was no longer restricted to the store, and he began to anticipate the day when Winona and Betty's husband learned about it.

Betty and Randall became lovers after knowing each other for a bit more than a year. It began with his suggestion that they meet after work and perhaps go to a motel situated at some distance from downtown; as she had already decided that her marriage was over, and that she was in love with Randall, she agreed. They were as cautious as they could be, parking in the motel's back lot and registering under the name of one of Randall's friends, a man who had paid for the room earlier and then delivered the key to Randall prior to the couple's arrival. But within a month, several people in Selma were aware of the relationship. One afternoon, Betty was approached on the sidewalk by a female staff member of the *Selma Times-Journal,* who warned, "If you plan to stay with *that* man, you'd better get out of town." "I'm not going anywhere," Betty responded. In the paint shop after her boss had commented, "That Randall Miller is one black man who sure believes he's white," Betty replied sharply, "No, Randall Miller is one black man who sure believes in working hard." Randall's wife telephoned Betty at times, threatening bodily harm if the affair did not end; but it continued without interruption until Betty's exasperated husband removed their daughters from school, gave up his job, and, with Betty accompanying him, returned to Arkansas. She remained there for nearly ten months. Then in late 1985, anticipating her divorce, she returned alone to Selma, rented an apartment, and resumed seeing Randall Miller, this time doing so with more openness.

They walked together in the streets, dined together in restaurants, and stood waiting together in the ticket line outside the local cinema. Whatever unfriendly curiosity or hostile comments they encountered from white people, and occasionally from blacks, they ignored. In this divided town they cut their own path. The mayor distanced himself from the situation while retaining Randall on the municipal payroll, and the Miller Funeral Service did not appear to suffer financially, even though Winona Miller gained allies in the black community as she expressed outrage over her husband's behavior. He, meanwhile, moved out of their home, was proceeding toward a divorce, and was residing temporarily in living quarters that he had established for himself within the funeral property. Sometimes he would visit Betty at her apartment, on the second floor of a building in an integrated neighborhood. Later he acquired the house at 209 Alabama Avenue, where I had gone to interview her.

Having spent an hour with her, and aware that Randall Miller might be walking in at any minute—it was now nearly 6:00 p.m.—I thought I should soon be leaving. He might not be happy to find me speaking to his fiancée about intimate matters that involved him. I had been lucky in finding her at home and in a receptive mood, but I had been calculating as well in pursuing her after being told that Randall Miller was in Montgomery. I instinctively felt that she would be more forthcoming without him being there. Were he in the room, he might have interrupted her thoughts or attempted to prevent her from telling me things that he believed should remain private. My talk with Betty was "on the record," as evidenced by my taking notes in front of her. I could only hope that when Randall returned home, he would have no misgivings about the interview, for I later wanted to spend time with him and get his version of the relationship. I also wanted to attend the next day's wedding. After I had proposed this, requesting that I bring a photographer, Betty voiced no objection but recommended that I clear it directly with Randall. She said that about twenty people had been invited, split evenly between blacks and whites; in addition to her daughters and one of her nieces from Arkansas, and a few of Randall's siblings and cousins, the list included Randall's old friends, and Betty's new friends, who had been the most supportive of the couple.

I stood and shook hands with Betty, and as she escorted me to the door, I told her that I would be calling back within a few hours, at around 8:00 p.m., hoping that I might then return and introduce myself to Randall Miller and take the two of them out to dinner at the Tally Ho, a popular restaurant on the outskirts of town. Betty said that they had gone there in the past and liked it, and she hoped that Randall would be home when I called and would be willing to meet with me.

19

As I drove through downtown Selma onto Highway 80 toward the Holiday Inn, which was where I and most of the out-of-town media who were here for the silver anniversary conclave were staying—along with Jesse Jackson and the other honored guests and speakers—I continued to think about the wedding and how coincidental it was that Betty Ramsey and Randall Miller would be formalizing their union at a time when civil rights proponents would be memorializing the disaffection that had led to Bloody Sunday.

Most of what I read about race relations in the Selma paper that week focused upon the tension and differences of opinion that made the chances of cooperation between the town's blacks and whites seem highly unlikely in the near future. There was a police report that a bomb might be planted at the base of the bridge over which the twenty-fifth anniversary participants were scheduled to march. There was an interview with Jesse Jackson in which he described the bridge as symbolizing "Calvary" for black people, explaining, "We carried the cross of oppression and suffered the crucifixion so that all would have a new hope." But this hope, according to a white councilman named Carl Morgan, was being undermined by the contrariness of such black leaders as Rose Sanders. Her well-publicized accusations that a racist grading system prevailed within the classrooms of Selma's public schools was a manufactured controversy, Morgan suggested, one that kept Rose Sanders in the headlines and provided her and her anti-Smitherman friends with a lively issue to rally around. It was noted elsewhere that Sanders was currently raising funds for the establishment of a voting-rights museum near the bridge; it would display artifacts and memorabilia associated with the 1960s era of Dr. King, the Freedom Riders, and the rampaging posse of Sheriff Jim Clark. There was also a guest column on the editorial page of the Selma paper by J. L. Chestnut, Jr., in which he asserted that he and his parents had been receiving many threatening phone calls at night from white people who were part of a "planned conspiracy to assault and harass."

With these and other articles concentrating on the grievances and ill-feelings that were said to characterize the city, it seemed to me all the more important that I emphasize in my story for the *Times* what was apparently *not* deemed to be newsworthy here in Alabama—the fact that, despite all the local reports of contentiousness, it was nonetheless possible in today's Selma for a black man to walk arm in arm with a white woman along the sidewalks without being physically impeded. Did this not say something about changing attitudes in Selma? Was it not a step forward along the path of what Dr. King called the "highway up from darkness"? Did this not exemplify a black man's right to choose? In this state still associated with the notoriety of the Scottsboro trials, and in this city still marked by its own prejudicial prosecution of William Earl Fikes, was not Randall Miller newsworthy for having flouted what in these parts had long been a taboo?

The William Earl Fikes conviction, following testimony by white women about his sexual transgressions, had led in 1954 to the creation of an antiblack organization in Selma called the White Citizens' Council, which, according to the historian J. Mills Thornton III, in his book entitled *Dividing Lines,* motivated white people to adopt an "unusually aggressive and unanimous commitment to an extremist racial position during the coming decade"—the decade that produced Bloody Sunday. And yet what influences had emerged in Selma since then that might explain Randall Miller's bold and confident pursuit of a white woman? He had wooed her, had won her, and had finally obtained a license to marry her—and, except for some snide commentary uttered within the community, he had fulfilled his intentions without being challenged. He had cuckolded a white man in Selma and had gotten away with it. Betty's then husband had returned to Arkansas feeling anger and humiliation, but, insofar as I gathered from talking to her, he had held *her* accountable for what had happened and not her suitor, and he had never contemplated seeking revenge upon Randall Miller.

I thought about this as I continued to drive through the early-evening traffic toward the Holiday Inn. In my ancestral part of Italy, a husband who had been cuckolded would often get a gun and shoot bullets at his unfaithful wife and her lover, and then elude a prison term because it was a "crime of honor." I wondered how Betty's ex-husband was now getting along in rural Arkansas? What did his friends and neighbors say and think about the situation? Was losing one's wife to a black man doubly deflating to Mr. Ramsey's ego? Or did it provide him with the excuse that the failed marriage had nothing to do with him—wasn't it obvious that Betty had to be crazy and out of control to leave her family and cohabitate with a black man in Selma? But since I had no intention of going to Arkansas to explore this matter further, I returned my attentions to my area of interest, which was Selma.

Selma was *the* reason that the interracial affair represented a story to me. I would not have considered writing about it had it occurred in Toledo, Sarasota, Wichita, or Buffalo, or in any of a thousand other places, including such southern cities as Atlanta, Birmingham, Montgomery, or Memphis. Memphis was where Dr. King had been murdered in 1968 by a white man, and yet that city had not been demonized as Selma had been after Bloody Sunday, even though on the latter occasion not a single demonstrator had been killed. But the widespread media depictions of the staggering tear-gassed protesters being pummeled to the ground by law-enforcement authorities were so riveting and revolting that Selma thereafter represented the national nadir in narrow-mindedness, the last lingering remnant of the Civil War South and of white-columned bigotry and enslavement. This city that had been identified with prejudice was presently on the receiving end of prejudice from the press.

Even now, twenty-five years after Bloody Sunday, reporters from around the nation, including correspondents employed by news organizations in England and Germany, were here to cover the silver anniversary memorial, and Rose Sanders was raising funds in order to enshrine the area as the hallowed grounds of a quasi-Holocaust; and I was considering using the anniversary as the backdrop for the story about a local black man who had ventured across the color line into the arms of a white woman. Was I misinterpreting its significance? Was I trying to turn Randall Miller into a connubial Jackie Robinson? Would I be doing a disservice to this weekend's civil rights gathering if, instead of producing a story that would remind readers of the black anguish preceding the congressional passage of the Voting Rights Act, I introduced into my coverage an almost contradictory scenario that focused on interracial love and was *not* what the *Times* editors in New York were expecting? How come the local newspaper had not already published something about the couple, especially after the two of them had divorced their spouses and let it be known that they intended to marry? It seemed to me that if the *Selma Times-Journal* had sought them out for a feature story, or had at least printed an item on the social page about their forthcoming wedding, it might have been picked up by the national media and been presented around the country in a way that would have put Selma in a good light—giving the impression that the city, in being the locale of such a ceremony, was deviating from its image and was no longer supporting principles that denied African-Americans full equality with regard to opportunities and choices.

I considered driving over to the *Times-Journal* building and questioning the editorial bosses about why they had ignored this story, but I doubted that they would tell me much. Decision makers at news organizations are characteristically guarded when asked to explain why they have *not* published something, usually responding that it is nobody's concern but their own. Maybe the *Times-Journal*'s business office had advised the editors to stay away from the story, arguing that to do otherwise could indicate editorial tolerance of interracial sexual intimacy, and this might prompt some of the newspaper's leading advertisers to withdraw their financial support. Or maybe the editors shied away for reasons of their own, perhaps out of concern that a printed story might offend readers who were hard-core segregationists, resulting in a rock or a bomb being hurled through the window of Randall Miller's home before or during the wedding—an incident that would surely bring forth protests from black activists and *more* unwanted attention to Selma from out-of-state media. And, furthermore, there was no proof that the African-Americans of Selma or elsewhere in the United States liked reading about their people marrying whites any more than white people liked reading about interracial marriages with blacks.

While U.S. census data pointed to a substantial increase in black-white marriages in the aftermath of the civil rights movement's challenges to segregation in schools and the workplace—in 1960, there were approximately 50,000 black-white marriages; in 1990 the estimate was about 300,000—there was no evidence that this rising number had broadened or hastened the general acceptance of blacks into the white social world. And advocates of black pride could well resent such marriages, reasoning that they contributed nothing to the movement's cause and might lend credence to the idea that a solution to racism was achievable via the gradual eradication of the black race, the watering down of black blood into the white mainstream through the repeated and prolonged process of miscegenation. The birth of millions of mulattoes before and since the Civil War had failed to have a positive impact on the historical problem of racism in America—and, more often than not, black separatists and white segregationists were generally in agreement on the undesirability of marital relationships between black people and white people. Oddly allied on this matter was the Black Muslim leader, the Honorable Elijah Muhammad, and the onetime sheriff of Selma, James G. Clark.

In the early 1960s, former president Harry S. Truman spoke out against black-white marriages when I interviewed him as a *Times* reporter. It was then customary for Truman to permit the press to accompany him when he visited New York and seek his comments on topical subjects during his postbreakfast walks along Park Avenue near his hotel; and on this particular morning, since interracial conflicts were dominating the headlines, I asked him whether he thought that racial intermarriages in America might become widespread in the future.

"I hope not," Truman said unhesitatingly, maintaining his quick stride while I and three other journalists tried to keep pace while taking notes. "I don't believe in it," he continued. "What's that word about four feet long?"

"Miscegenation," I replied.

Neither slowing down nor seeming to be impressed that I knew the word, Truman turned toward me and asked, "Would *you* want your daughter to marry a Negro?"

"Well," I said after a pause, surprised that this interview had now turned personal, "I would hope that a daughter of mine would marry the man she loved."

"You *haven't* answered my question," Truman replied sharply.

I said nothing, walking next to him with my eyes lowered and my ballpoint pen scribbling notes along the folded sheets of paper I held in my left hand.

"Well," he went on more softly, "she won't love someone who isn't her color. You'll edit the man she goes out with. I did, and mine married the right man."

He was referring to the assistant managing editor of the *Times*, Clifton Daniel, who had married Truman's daughter, Margaret, in 1956. When I returned to the newsroom, I wondered how this story would be played, and if Daniel might hold it against me for asking his father-in-law such a question. But I heard nothing from Daniel nor from any other editor after I had turned in the story, and on the following morning the paper printed all of Truman's comments. It was not on page one, however, appearing well back in the news section—under a small-size headline: TRUMAN OPPOSES BIRACIAL MARRIAGE—and in the second paragraph of my piece some editor or copyreader had added a sentence explaining that Mr. Truman was "long an advocate of integration" in other respects.

"I don't want to marry the white man's daughter. I just want to get the white man off my back," I had heard James Baldwin say often during the early 1960s, either when he was speaking out as a black man on television or when he was my dinner guest in New York. In late September 1962, a few days before the Floyd Patterson–Sonny Liston heavyweight fight in Chicago, I drove Baldwin out to Patterson's training camp in Elgin, Illinois, where the two of them met for the first time. I was writing about the fight for the *Times*, while Baldwin was covering it for *Nugget* magazine. After we had spent an hour with Patterson, Baldwin presented him with two of his books—*Another Country* and *Nobody Knows My Name*—inscribing them: "For Floyd Patterson—because we both know whence we come, and have some idea where we're going. . . ."

A year later, in *The Fire Next Time*, Baldwin wrote:

The only thing white people have that black people need, or should want, is power—and no one holds power forever. White people cannot, in the generality, be taken as models of how to live. Rather, the white man is himself in sore need of new standards, which will release him from his confusion and place him once again in fruitful communion with the depths of his own being. And I repeat: The price of the liberation of the white people is the liberation of the blacks—the total liberation, in the cities, in the towns, before the law, and in the mind. Why, for example—especially knowing the family as I do—I should *want* to marry your sister is a great mystery to me. But your sister and I have every right to marry if we wish to, and no one has the right to stop us. If she cannot raise me to her level, perhaps I can raise her to mine.

20

by Gay Talese
Special to The New York Times

SELMA, Ala., March 6—Twenty-five years ago, after borrowing a tail-finned Cadillac hearse from the mortuary owned by his family in this onetime plantation town in south central Alabama, a young man named Randall Miller joined hundreds of other blacks as a volunteer ambulance driver in a civil rights march that was soon scheduled to head east to the state capital, Montgomery. . . .

But now—a quarter century after the highway clash that was commemorated this past weekend by returning veterans of the march—Selma reflects much advancement in the quest for racial harmony. Not only interracial harmony, but also, on occasion, interracial love. Last weekend, the former ambulance driver, Randall Miller, now fifty-one years old, was married here to a thirty-eight-year-old white woman, Betty Ramsey. They were married in the presence of twenty white and black friends in Mr. Miller's house, in an integrated neighborhood within hearing of the cheers from the thousands who attended the commemorative ceremonies. . . .

THESE WERE THE OPENING PARAGRAPHS OF THE STORY I HAD typed in my motel room in Selma and then faxed to the national editor in New York, hoping that it would appear in the next morning's *Times*. I did not know until the following afternoon, after buying a copy of the *Times* at the Atlanta airport prior to flying home, that the editors had published exactly and fully what I had written, printing the first eight paragraphs across the lower half of page one, under a three-column headline: SELMA 1990: OLD FACES AND A NEW SPIRIT.

The rest of my 2,500-word article, which described the wedding ceremony and the reception as well as the twenty-fifth anniversary events occurring elsewhere in the city, was spread across a full page inside the paper. I was pleased by the amount of space given to my story, but disappointed that the editors had not used any photos from the wedding. The *Times* had sent a staff photographer from New York to work with me. On the night before the wedding, while dining with Randall Miller and Betty at the Tally Ho and thanking them for adding me to the guest list, I asked if I could bring along the *Times*'s photographer, Michelle Agins. An hour before, in the lobby of the Holiday Inn, I had met her for the first time; she was checking in as I was heading out to the restaurant. She was a personable young black woman who had once worked as a city hall photographer for Chicago's first black mayor, Harold Washington. I do not know if this impressed me more than it did Randall Miller, but, after I had mentioned it to him at dinner, he said that it would be okay if Agins came with her camera to the wedding.

She seemed to enjoy herself on the following night as she moved comfortably and unobtrusively through the living room while photographing the guests and the two people who commanded their attention—Randall Miller, dressed in a dark suit with a boutonniere, and Betty Ramsey, wearing a white satin suit of her own design and holding a bouquet of roses and carnations. After the couple had exchanged their vows while standing in front of the fireplace, the Reverend Charles A. Lett raised his arms and proclaimed their union "an act of divine origin." As Agins's busy camera recorded the ceremony and reception that followed, I was gladdened by the thought that her pictures would provide the *Times* with confirming evidence of what I was planning to write. It was my intention to suggest that even in this city that owed its identity to racial hatred, there was nevertheless space in which black and white residents might find a common cause, and this space and cause had converged on this particular night in this living room where the newlywed couple had been toasted by an interracial gathering of champagne-drinking guests.

Why had the *Times* not used a picture from the wedding? Inside the paper, where my article mentioned the silver anniversary parade and named a few of its prominent marchers and witnesses, the editors *had* run an Agins photo of John Lewis and Hosea Williams, two civil rights veterans, taking a nostalgic walk together across the bridge. They also printed her photograph of sixty-year-old Mayor Smitherman, posed at his desk with a row of flags hanging behind him, including one representing the Confederacy. But the main photo on page one, instead of visually complementing what I had written, depicted a black woman lying facedown on the highway, surrounded by helmeted white troopers equipped with clubs, guns, and gas masks. It had been taken in 1965 on Bloody Sunday by an Associated Press photographer, and as I looked at it in Atlanta, I wondered why this old wire-service image had been chosen over a wedding picture taken by the *Times* staffer who had been assigned to join me in Selma. Why could they not have shown the city in a nonracist posture for a change? Why continually represent the politics of victimization?

A week later, while attending a reception at the New York Public Library, I met a *Times* editor, who came over to say that he liked my story about the bridal couple in Selma.

"But why didn't you people run their picture?" I asked.

"Oh, I'll tell you sometime," he said.

"No," I insisted, "tell me now."

"Well, " he said, "some negative comment had been made about it at the editors' meeting by Gerald Boyd."

"Who's he?"

"He's in charge of the Metro staff," he said, adding that Boyd was a rising young African-American executive in the *Times* news department, and that it had been Boyd's lack of enthusiasm for the wedding photos that led his white fellow editors to agree with him.

I would not have pursued the matter further had I not accepted an invitation a few years later to participate in a noonday symposium about the *Times*'s news coverage, sponsored by the Center for Communication in Manhattan. With me onstage were four other members of the panel; two seats away from me, on the far side of the moderator, was Gerald Boyd. He was a soft-spoken, round-faced gentleman in his forties with a receding hairline, horn-rimmed glasses, and a thin mustache, and he wore a blue blazer with a white shirt and a dark tie knotted tightly under his throat. He was impressively articulate during his opening remarks, speaking softly and authoritatively in an unhurried manner. Toward the end of the program, prior to soliciting questions from the audience, the moderator invited the panelists to query one another; and that is when I turned to Gerald Boyd and asked: "Are you the man who blocked the photo of my Selma wedding story from getting onto the front page of the *Times*?"

He seemed stunned. There was rustling throughout the audience.

"Yes," he said finally.

"Why?" I asked in a raised voice.

"It was boring," he said.

"Boring!" I said.

"To show an integrated couple on the front page *wasn't* news," he explained. "The picture didn't represent anything *new*."

"In *Selma*?" I asked.

Gerald Boyd turned away from me, and the moderator, perhaps sensing Boyd's discomfort, changed the subject. Other topics were discussed and debated for the next hour or so, and then, at the conclusion of the program, after shaking hands with the moderator, Gerald Boyd headed directly for the exit.

21

IN LATE OCTOBER OF 1993, WHILE I AND HUNDREDS OF OTHER members of the alumni were gathered at the University of Alabama for the homecoming football game and other weekend festivities, I learned that an eighteen-year-old white female student from Selma had been abducted in her dormitory's parking lot days earlier by an armed black man, who, after driving her in her car six miles from the campus and then forcing her to the ground in a secluded area off the highway, had raped her.

A seven-paragraph account of this had been published in the *Birmingham Post-Herald* on the day I had flown into Alabama from New York, on Thursday, October 28. The story was unprominently displayed on an inside page under a quarter-inch headline: UA STUDENT TAKEN FROM PARKING LOT AND RAPED. The article did *not* mention that the female student was white and a native of Selma, nor did it specify the race of her attacker. In her testimony to the police, however, she did say that the crime had definitely been committed by a black man in his twenties, adding that he was approximately six feet tall and weighed two hundred pounds, and that he had used a handgun in gaining access to her car as she was parking it at about 1:15 a.m., upon returning to her dormitory. After he had driven her away and raped her, she said, he drove her back to the dormitory parking lot, left the car keys on the pavement under the rear bumper, and then disappeared.

The decision not to identify the race of the victim or the rapist in the *Post-Herald* had been made by the reporter and the desk editor who had written the headline. The two journalists were male and white. The reporter was actually a twenty-year-old journalism student from the University of Alabama, a blue-eyed, blond junior named Sean Kelley, who, in addition to his editorial role on the campus newspaper, *The Crimson White*, served as the college correspondent for the *Post-Herald*, which was a position that I had also held during my undergraduate days at Alabama forty years before.

My purpose in returning for the 1993 homecoming weekend was not only to join other old grads at a football game and enjoy their companionship at reunion parties but to participate in the centennial celebration of *The Crimson White* and speak at a banquet to be attended by past and present members of the staff. Since Sean Kelley wanted to interview me beforehand for a piece he was preparing for the college newspaper, he had met my flight in Birmingham, and, during our hour-long drive together from the airport to the campus in Tuscaloosa, I was able to interview *him* about how he had covered the rape story in that morning's *Post-Herald*.

I began by postulating that the *Post-Herald* management would have presented the story very differently had the incident occurred when I had been the correspondent. In 1953, instead of being buried inside the paper, it would have appeared on page one and would have revealed, rather than concealed, the fact that it had been an interracial rape, and this disclosure would have probably aroused the anger and fear of white readers in ways similar to what had been experienced in Selma in 1953 during the William Earl Fikes case.

"I won't argue with you that my story in this morning's paper was buried," Kelley said, steering his car along the highway. "But I still think it was properly handled." It was not a story about *race*, he insisted; it was a story about *rape*. He did concede, however, that his news judgment had been guided by his racial sensibility, by his reluctance to "stain the black race by identifying the rapist as a black man." He said that he took pride in being among the first generation of white southerners who had grown up in a desegregated society. As a boy, he had attended public schools with black youths, had joined them on athletic fields and in movie theaters, and had swum with them in public pools. He had been born in Birmingham in 1973—ten years after Dr. King had written his famous "Letter from a Birmingham Jail"; ten years after two black students, escorted by federal officials, had stridden past a displeased Governor Wallace to enter the University of Alabama—and while Sean Kelley's parents and grandparents had been forced to conform to changes imposed upon them by outside forces, he himself had no quarrel with his inherited circumstances. The troubled sixties were part of the past. He was part of the present. He had gone out on dates with a black girl in high school. He had many black female and male friends at the University of Alabama. There were black staff members working with him on *The Crimson White*. Although he acknowledged that a vast majority of his fellow students tended to socialize along racial lines in their private lives—the fraternities and sororities on the campus were either exclusively black or white—the dormitories were fully integrated, and of the school's nineteen thousand undergraduates, more than two thousand were African-American.

"But what if one of these African-American women on the campus had been raped by a white man from Selma?" I asked. "How would you have reported *that?*"

"That's a hypothetical question, and I don't really know the answer," he said. After giving it some thought, he said that if it *had* been a reversed situation— rapist white/victim black—it *would* probably have sparked a public protest led by black student activists, and this would have undoubtedly drawn outside media attention. He assumed this, he said, because of what he himself had seen during his freshman year on the campus, in 1991. Having heard that some white female students had attended a fraternity house costume party in blackface and had attached basketballs under their skirts to simulate pregnancy, Kelley decided to publish an account of this in *The Crimson White*. His story was picked up by the Associated Press and wired around the country. A camera crew from CNN soon appeared on the Alabama campus to film the black-led protest rally, which was also joined by several sympathetic white students. Hundreds of demonstrators marched past the Sigma Chi fraternity house where the costume party had taken place, and someone hurled a brick through one of the building's windows. The crowd also gathered in front of the offending girls' Kappa Delta sorority house, shouting words of condemnation up toward the darkened windows and locked doors of the white-columned manor, which was being guarded by a row of police officers.

This had been the first time that Sean Kelley had seen how his journalism could inflame and arouse the passions of other people, and the experience instilled within him a heightened sense of responsibility and even feelings of remorse. In bringing national attention to what he described as the "stupidity" of a few white sorority girls, he had unwittingly resurrected on the UA campus the specter of George Wallace, which was an association that hardly any of Kelley's contemporaries and elders desired or deserved. The behavior of those girls was not typical of the UA student body, he explained, and yet he had chosen to expose them in print because he sought the acclaim it would possibly bring him as a young investigative reporter. His story appeared on page one of *The Crimson White*, and it was also a worthy addition to his scrapbook when he applied to the *Birmingham Post-Herald* for the correspondent's position, which he obtained in 1992.

But now, as he spoke to me a year later in the car during my homecoming visit, he said that he was no longer entirely sure that he would pursue a career in journalism following his graduation. He knew only that, in his report about the rape in that morning's *Post-Herald,* he had been colorblind. He had not wanted to risk stereotyping black people any more than he had wanted to sensationalize the story by revealing that it had been a white woman from Selma who had been preyed upon.

During the days that I remained on the campus, the police had nothing further to say about the rape case. More security guards had been quickly added to the college's parking lots, and flyers alerting everyone to the occurrence had been posted on dormitory bulletin boards and elsewhere. But in the weeks and months that followed, the identity of the rapist would remain a mystery; and, according to what Sean Kelley would subsequently communicate to me via the mail or during our many exchanges over the telephone, there remained a palpably muted reaction to the rape on the Alabama campus. There were no "take back the night" rallies by white feminists, no interracial discussions initiated by any groups of student leaders, and no follow-up articles in the Alabama press. After having published a short piece in *The Crimson White* that was similar to what he had done for the *Post-Herald,* Kelley had been told by his editor in Birmingham that no further coverage was necessary. In essence, Kelley said, there was general agreement between the two of them that this was a one-day story.

I was able, with Sean Kelley's assistance, to arrange an interview with the young Selma woman during one of my later visits to the University of Alabama. She agreed to see me, with the understanding that I would not publish her name, but in our two meetings she basically told me what she had already told the police. She said that she hoped to forget as quickly as possible what had happened to her, and to concentrate on her studies and eventually graduate with a degree in education. Her father had also graduated from the University of Alabama, she said, and having been provided with her parents' address, I managed to see them when I was next in Selma.

Both her mother and father had been born into prominent old families. Her mother hardly spoke a word to me during our interview, but her father had plenty to say.

"I would have liked to have killed that man for what he did to my daughter," he said. "And I could have found out who did it, if I'd wanted to," he went on, indicating that the police were inadequate to the task of tracking down the culprit and rendering justice. "When I heard what had happened, I drove right up there so fast that it's a wonder I didn't kill somebody along the way. Oh, I could have sued the university," he declared, "and if I had done it, I would have won. They were negligent. The university was definitely negligent," he repeated, citing in particular having inadequate security in the freshman dormitory's parking lot. "But I had to back away from it. I *wanted* to get involved, to open up that case and get involved, but I had to back away. I just didn't want to put all of us through all the publicity and the rest of it. . . ."

He was speaking to me in his office, which was located within a large framed building that stood along the edge of a gravel road and led to the entrance of what had long been the family's cotton plantation. Adjacent to this land was the highway that Martin Luther King, Jr., and his civil rights followers had used in 1965 while traveling toward Montgomery.

22

PRIOR TO MY HOMECOMING VISIT TO ALABAMA, I HAD FREQUENTLY been in contact with the newly appointed editor of *The New Yorker*, Tina Brown, a forty-year-old British-born, Oxford-educated blonde who reminded me of my high school English teacher—a comely, decorous, and demanding taskmistress who was often at the center of my teenage erotic fantasies, and who was the first woman to personify for me the awesome combination of sex appeal and professional power.

In fairness to Tina Brown, I should explain that these dual qualities in her case were accompanied by a well-bred manner and a subtle sense of humor and also the capacity to influence people through a bit of flattery and a directive style that was never so ironclad as to seem unreasonable. I further think that Brown was particularly compelling and seductive when dealing with men of means or other assets who were close to the age of her father, George Hambley Brown, a film producer, whom she adored and who, in turn, stalwartly supported and encouraged her throughout her meteoric rise in the magazine business, beginning in London as the editor of the *Tatler* when she was twenty-five.

Two years later, in 1981, she married a man who was twenty-five years her senior, the celebrated fifty-two-year-old editor of the London *Times*, Harold Evans, who, when she first fell in love with him, six years before, had been married for decades to a woman with whom he had three children. Another important man in Tina Brown's life, and the same age as Harold Evans, was the American media entrepreneur Samuel I. Newhouse, who would agreeably lose millions of dollars while underwriting her career in New York, first installing her as the editor of *Vanity Fair* in 1984 and then transferring her in 1992 to *The New Yorker*. Notwithstanding her lavish spending on editorial production and promotion, and the high fees and liberal expense accounts she extended to her writers, photographers, and other contributors, she actually increased the market value of the Newhouse properties by adding to their name recognition and by tailoring their appeal to increasing numbers of readers and advertisers. She was called the "Queen of Buzz" by Judy Bachrach, author of a biography about Tina Brown and Harold Evans, and the writer and ex-editor of *The New Republic*, Andrew Sullivan, saw Brown as enthralled with "the crazed cult of contemporaneity," adding that she was a "woman of her time, acutely in sync with the delirious daydream of the 1990s and the media vanities it fostered and to which many of us fell victim." Although she drew much media scrutiny in the United States, as she had earlier in England, her detractors rarely seemed to rattle her to the point of discouragement. "The dogs bark," she said, "and the caravan moves on."

I first met her, along with Harold Evans, in New York during the late 1980s at a book party celebrating the latter's memoir, *Good Times, Bad Times*, in which, among other things, Evans wrote about his unpleasant experiences with the London *Times*'s owner, Rupert Murdoch, who had fired him in 1983, a year after Murdoch had become the proprietor. This was less than two years after the Evans-Brown marriage and two years before they would settle in New York—she as the thirty-year-old doyenne at *Vanity Fair*, and he as a fifty-five-year-old newsroom veteran with a distinguished past and an uncertain future.

But by 1990, he had been selected by S. I. Newhouse to serve as the president and publisher of the Random House trade division, and with her elevation to *The New Yorker* in 1992, Tina and Harold were generally recognized as the reigning couple in the capital of communications. Nan and I enjoyed attending dinners at the couple's East Side residence, occasions that brought together individuals from the worlds of entertainment, publishing, fashion, finance, and politics. And one day when I was having lunch with Tina Brown during the summer of 1993, seated next to her at her usual corner table at the Royalton Hotel on West Forty-fourth Street, a short walk away from *The New Yorker*'s headquarters, I was pleased and honored to hear her express the wish that I become a contractual contributor to her magazine. I could have my own office at *The New Yorker*, she said, and be identified as the "writer-at-large," which was the title she had bestowed upon Norman Mailer when he had worked with her at *Vanity Fair*.

What appealed to me about Brown's proposal was that it would offer me relief, at least during the one year's length of the proposed *New Yorker* contract, from my ridiculous life as a prolific author of unfinished manuscripts. Despite all time that I had spent in familiarizing myself with such restaurant personalities as Nicola Spagnolo, Elaine Kaufman, and Robert Pascal, and despite my delving deeply into the history of the

"Willy Loman" building of bad omens at 206 East 63rd Street—*and* all my research on the subject of Alabama—I had *nothing* that I could rightly point to as a book in progress.

I wondered if part of my problem was in choosing to write about people and places that changed little over prolonged periods of time, and about which it was difficult to draw conclusions. What could be concluded, for example, about the complex situation existing in present-day Selma? It was also possible that I was subjecting myself unduly to pondering and procrastinating because I tended to see each and every subject from different angles and varying viewpoints—a prismatic vision that is said to be commonplace among the people of Italy. I once read a historical novel by Peter Nichols about Italy's Cardinal Fabrizio Ruffo, a militant clergyman who was loyal to the Spanish Bourbon monarchy in Naples and led a popular late-eighteenth-century uprising against the invading forces of Napoléon, and one of the book's characters laments, "We Italians have suffered enough from being able to see too many sides at once."

If I worked for Tina Brown, I would not have that option, nor would I have much time for ruminating. I would become part of a fast-paced weekly magazine, directed by Brown's surefire instincts and youthful, though experienced, judgment. Still, she had tilted this magazine more toward topicality and "buzz," and I was not sure that I would fit in, especially if she assigned me to do profiles about people who had just entered the limelight or otherwise met the current definition of celebrity. Back in the mid-1960s, a year after leaving the *Times*, I had enjoyed working for *Esquire*'s editor, Harold Hayes, under the terms of a one-year contract, but *Esquire* was a monthly, and I believed that with Hayes I had been allowed more space and time than Tina Brown would presently permit, although in this matter I realized I could be wrong. It was true, however, that when I had written about famous people for *Esquire*, they were usually past their prime, or were dealing with the downside of success. In fact, I had contemplated writing *more* about obscurity and failure when I began meeting with Tina Brown, but, assuming that nothing would be of less interest to her, I hesitated discussing it. But I hesitated, too, about becoming one of her contractual writers, thinking that it was not a good idea at the age of sixty-one to do what I might have already done better when thirty years younger. Also, I was motivated by the notion I might rise above my state of indecision and discontent by writing about *other people's* discontent and despair, and I believed that I should do so *immediately* and lightheartedly in a short book that might be my homage to George Orwell's *Down and Out*, or rather my own "Profiles in Discouragement" or "The Loser's Guide to Living." It would deal with failure, perseverance, and more failure. Not an exhilarating subject for a publisher, obviously, but I thought that with so many books in the marketplace dealing with success, and how to get rich, and how to win, it might be instructive to read something about people who had perhaps developed a unique talent for losing, or for running businesses into the ground, or behaving in ways that inevitably led to foreclosures and bankruptcies, marital separations and divorces, misdemeanors and felonies.

Among the people that I had been reading about in the press the past summer were a pair of individuals that *Time* magazine identified as "America's most estranged couple"—John and Lorena Bobbitt, whose incompatibility had reached epic proportions early one June morning in 1993 when, after an evening of heavy drinking on his part, followed by the alleged raping of his wife, she had retaliated by climbing out of bed, getting a kitchen knife, and, while he slept, slicing off most of his penis. Since I was already engrossed in the aforementioned subject of losers, and since few people represented the subject with the distinction of the twenty-six-year-old former U.S. Marine named John Bobbitt—who, after losing contact with his male organ for two hours, perhaps lost the pleasure of its full use forever, despite his surgeons' best efforts in reattaching it—I was eager to meet with him before I attempted to interview his impetuous twenty-four-year-old wife, Lorena. But my interest in *her* increased after I learned that although she had been born in Ecuador and been reared in Venezuela, Lorena (née Gallo) Bobbitt claimed that part of her family's ancestry was rooted in southern Italy.

She had cut off two-thirds of her husband's penis early on the Wednesday morning of June 23, 1993. She did it shortly after 4:30 a.m., using a twelve-inch kitchen knife that she had carried into the bedroom of their apartment in Manassas, Virginia, a community of 28,000, located about thirty miles west of Washington, D.C. She later hurled the penis—having unintentionally kept it in her left hand as she ran from the apartment and drove off in her car—out the window of the car onto the grassy edge of a country road. Had it not been recovered there an hour and forty-five minutes later by the police, who promptly delivered it (packed in ice) to its owner and his doctors at the hospital, it might have been devoured by field mice or taken into the next county by a hungry high-flying scavenger bird.

Although the penis-cutting story was at once big news in and around the Washington area, it had for some reason not gotten much early attention in the New York press, and thus I had been unaware of it until twenty days after its occurrence. I first read about it on an inside page of the July 13 *Times,* in a column in the "Science" section written by the newspaper's medical specialist, Dr. Lawrence K. Altman. The column concentrated on the surgical skills employed in Manassas on June 23 by the two surgeons who had labored in an operating room for more than nine hours, often peering through microscopes as they slowly proceeded to reattach, stitch by stitch, the tiny torn tissues and the vessels of John Bobbitt's much-abused penis. A male friend of John Bobbitt had driven him to the hospital and escorted him into the emergency ward at 5:03 a.m. The medical personnel who witnessed Bobbitt's arrival were surprised that he had not already bled to death. Dr. Altman's column in the *Times* reported that the patient had walked in with a bloody sheet wrapped around his hand, which was covering his groin, and that the "two main arteries and a vein that carry most of the blood to and from the penis had gone into spasm spontaneously, and a large blood clot quickly formed over the stump." The urological surgeon and the plastic surgeon who had been awakened at their homes and were urgently summoned to the hospital to work together on the penile operation were, respectively, Dr. James T. Sehn and Dr. David E. Berman. Dr. Sehn got there first, and he was shocked as he surveyed Bobbitt's condition at bedside. In the *Times,* Dr. Sehn was quoted as recalling, "It was a horrific sight. He was on his back and there was just a clot left for where there should have been a penis." Since the police had not yet found the Bobbitt penis as Dr. Sehn and his colleague Dr. Berman had begun their preoperative procedures, and since it was then anyone's guess if the penis would *ever* be found, the surgeons were forced to consider, in the interest of the patient's survival, stitching him back together without a penis. "The surgeons would sew the stump closed in the type of procedure that is done for cancer of the penis," the Altman column explained. "After such an operation, a man urinates sitting down." Although this turned out to be unnecessary—thanks to a ferret-eyed police sergeant who spotted the penis in a clump of weeds at 6:15 a.m. and had it delivered posthaste to the hospital—there was no guarantee that Bobbitt would ever again attain a full erection. "Because the nerves were cut, the man at present has no sensation in the re-attached portion of the penis," Altman reported. "But his doctors said prospects for the return of sensation are good."

I was amazed by the story. I reread it a few times. If the optimism expressed by Bobbitt's surgeons did not entirely fulfill itself, I wondered, what sort of life lay ahead for this twenty-six-year-old onetime warrior? Would he be banished hereafter from the macho world that he had prob-ably identified with when he had enlisted in the Marine Corps? Would his wife, who had justified her act to the police as a proper payback for his habitually improper behavior toward her, now earn plaudits from within the battered women's lobby or win widespread admiration from multitudes of miserably married wives who might ultimately elevate her bloody deed to head-on-the-platter Holofernes status?

Even before Lorena Bobbitt had done what she had done, the media had been giving much attention to the issue of male attitude and conduct toward women. There had been many stories about Senator Robert Packwood, accused of harassing twenty-six women. There had been the congressional hearings on television focusing upon Anita Hill's allegations against Clarence Thomas. There had been the U.S. Navy's sex scandal, known as "Tailhook," and several other reports about American military men, including senior officers, who were facing charges of sexual impropriety toward their female colleagues in the service and toward civilian women, as well. Civilian feelings of patriotism toward the military were not at a high point at this time, it seemed to me, but perhaps this was understandable. Had these times been different, had America in the early 1990s been dedicated to defending itself against threatening foreign forces rather than to demilitarizing itself within a secure and stable peacetime economy, then there might not have been the federal cutbacks that prevented such grunts as John Bobbitt from reenlisting and which eventually led to his becoming, via his wife's knife, a battle-scarred veteran of the domestic front. Lorena Bobbitt's marital frustrations, as her testimony to law-enforcement authorities would soon make clear, had peaked after her husband had been released from the Marine Corps in 1991.

Although she earned all that she could as a nail sculptress in a Virginia shopping mall, her husband proceeded to lose, or to lose interest in, one job after another. He had failed to retain such positions as a furniture mover, a landscape laborer, a taxi driver, a cargo unloader at a trucking depot, a barroom bouncer, a 7-Eleven counter clerk, and a waiter in a restaurant located near the highly mortgaged home that the Bobbitts occupied for less than a year between 1990 and 1991. One of John Bobbitt's difficulties as a waiter was his slowness in operating the restaurant's computerized menu screen, which transmitted the customers' requests in the dining room to the printer in the kitchen. In any case, after he had been released from the regimentation and the predictable income of military employment, he proved to be insufficiently helpful to his wife in paying their bills. Still, I thought that losing part of his penis was a heavy price to pay under any circumstances, and I could not help feeling sympathy and compassion for this young man, nor could I avoid thinking about the many men whom I had read about or heard about whose genitals had been victimized by terrifying experiences, either deliberately inflicted upon them or due to other reasons.

I thought about the war-wounded and castrated Jake Barnes in Hemingway's novel *The Sun Also Rises*, and the character in Hemingway's story "God Rest You Merry, Gentlemen" who takes a razor blade to his penis in the interest of abating his sexual urges. In the John Irving novel *The World According to Garp*, a married woman unwittingly bites off her lover's penis while fellating him one evening in the front seat of an automobile that is parked in her driveway and that is rear-ended unintentionally when her carelessly driving husband returns home. The African writer Bessie Head wrote a story years ago in which a woman cuts off the penis of an acquaintance who had persistently preyed upon her. *Ms.* magazine would later reprint this story. And in Emile Zola's 1885 novel, *Germinal*, a group of French women vent their rage during a workers' riot by pouncing upon the dead body of a loathed ex-shopkeeper, Monsieur Maigrat, and after dismembering him, they parade around town with his penis on a pike. In Thailand, during the 1970s, there was a real-life situation in which nearly one hundred women took vengeance upon their philandering husbands by cutting off their penises at night. Dr. Altman had mentioned this in his *Times* column, adding that "reattachments were tried in about eighteen cases, with mostly poor results." I had read elsewhere about an episode that took place in Tokyo many years ago—a woman strangled her lover, then emasculated him—and was subsequently cited as inspirational in the creation of the critically acclaimed 1976 Japanese film *In the Realm of the Senses*.

While I was aware that in the annals of fact and fiction I was recalling relatively few of the myriad instances in which a penis is objectified, I could not imagine anyone surpassing the efforts of the late English author D. H. Lawrence in describing the vagaries and vicissitudes of the male organ in ways that are at once wise, explicit, and unblushing. I am referring to Lawrence's tenth and final novel, *Lady Chatterley's Lover*, which he completed in 1928. It tells the story of the sexually desirable Lady Chatterley and her impotent husband (paralyzed while serving on a French battlefield during World War I) and her husband's virile gamekeeper, who resides on the couple's estate. The gamekeeper not only gratifies Lady Chatterley during her furtive visits but also remains with her after she becomes pregnant and leaves her husband, her home, and her social class.

This work, which Lawrence himself called a "phallic novel," was quickly banned as obscene in his homeland and also in the United States and other nations. One critic in England referred to it as "the most evil outpouring that has ever besmirched the literature of our country. The sewers of French pornography would be dragged in vain to find a parallel in beastliness."

He was ashamed to turn to her, because of his aroused nakedness. He caught his shirt off the floor, and held it to him, coming to her.

"No!" she said, still holding out her beautiful slim arms from her drooping breasts. "Let me see you!"

He dropped the shirt and stood still, looking towards her. The sun through the low window sent in a beam that lit up his thighs and slim belly, and the erect phallus rising darkish and hot-looking from the little cloud of vivid gold-red hair. She was startled and afraid.

"How strange!" she said slowly. "How strange he stands there! So big! and so dark and cock-sure! Is he like that?"

The man looked down. . . .

"So proud!" she murmured, uneasy. "And so lordly! . . . But he's lovely, really. Like another being. . . ."

"Lie down!" he said. "Lie down! Let me come!"

He was in a hurry now.

And afterwards, when they had been quite still, the woman had to uncover the man again. . . .

"And now he's tiny, and soft like a little bud of life!" she said, taking the soft small penis in her hand. . . . "And how lovely your hair is here! quite, quite different!"

"That's John Thomas' hair, not mine!" he said.

"John Thomas! John Thomas!" and she quickly kissed the soft penis, that was beginning to stir again.

It was in Italy that Lawrence found printers who would set his manuscript into type. They were unable to read English, but after he had verbally explained to them what Lady Chatterley and her lover were described as doing in the novel's bedroom scenes, one of the printers remarked offhandedly, "We do it every day." The first few thousand copies of this underground edition (which would soon be smuggled into England, the United States, and elsewhere) were printed on creamy hand-rolled Italian paper and were finely bound and inscribed by the author. These editions would be followed by a variety of pirated imprints. Some were cheaply bound reproductions that had been copied photographically, and contained printed pages that were unfocused. Others were black-colored hardcover volumes that were designed to resemble hymn-books or Bibles, and these were usually more expensive than the original ten-dollar Italian edition that Lawrence had autographed two years before his death in 1930.

Nearly thirty years would pass before his controversial novel could be sold legally in the United States. In 1959, a federal judge, influenced by the less restrictive definition of obscenity that the Supreme Court had rendered two years earlier in the case of *Roth v. United States* (Samuel Roth being an imprisoned New York pornographer who had long trafficked in the sale of *Lady Chatterley's Lover* and other lawfully forbidden books), rescinded the ban against Lawrence's last work. But the liberation of the novel had actually been initiated by the courtroom efforts of a New York publisher, Grove Press, which had filed and won its case against the U.S. Post Office, which until then had assumed broad authority in banning "dirty" books and other objectionable materials from being mailed in America. The courtroom triumph of Grove Press was immediately celebrated by advocates of literary freedom as a national victory against censorship and an affirmation of the First Amendment.

I was assigned to cover this news story in 1959 as a staff member of the *Times,* and after the federal judge's announcement, I attended a party at the editorial offices of Grove Press, where all the guests received free copies of *Lady Chatterley's Lover,* after which I read it for the first time. In later years I reread it twice, and in 1980 I summarized its literary history in a chapter of my book *Thy Neighbor's Wife,* which included my personal appreciation and appraisal of D. H. Lawrence's achievement:

> Despite its adulterous theme, Lawrence was convinced that he had written an affirmative book about physical love, one that might help to liberate the puritanical mind from the "terror of the body." He believed that centuries of obfuscation had left the mind "unevolved," incapable of having a "proper reverence for sex, and a proper awe of the body's strange experience"; and so he created in Lady Chatterley a sexually awakened heroine who dared to remove the fig leaf from her lover's loins and examine the mystery of masculinity.
>
> While it has long been accepted as the prerogative of both artists and pornographers to expose the naked female, the phallus has usually been obscured or airbrushed, and never revealed when erect; but it was Lawrence's intention to write a "phallic novel," and often in the book Lady Chatterley focuses entirely on her lover's penis, strokes it with her fingers, caresses it with her breasts; she touches it with her lips, she holds it in her hands and watches it grow, she reaches underneath to fondle the testicles and feel their strange soft

weight; and as her wonderment is described by Lawrence, thousands of male readers of the novel undoubtedly felt their own sexual stirring and imagined the pleasure of Lady Chatterley's cool touch on their warm tumescent organs and experienced through masturbation the vicarious thrill of being her lover.

Since masturbation is what erotic writing so often leads to, that was reason enough to make Lawrence's novel controversial; but in addition, through the character of the gamekeeper, Lawrence probes the sensitivity and psychological detachment that man often feels toward his penis—it does indeed seem to have a will of its own, an ego beyond its size, and is frequently embarrassing because of its needs, infatuations, and unpredictable nature. Men sometimes feel that their penis controls *them*, leads them astray, causes them to beg favors at night from women whose names they prefer to forget in the morning. Whether insatiable or insecure, it demands constant proof of its potency, introducing into a man's life unwanted complications and frequent rejection. Sensitive but resilient, equally available during the day or night with a minimum of coaxing, it has performed purposefully if not always skillfully for an eternity of centuries, endlessly searching, sensing, expanding, probing, penetrating, throbbing, wilting, and wanting more. Never concealing its prurient interest, it is man's most honest organ.

It is also symbolic of masculine imperfection. It is unbalanced, asymmetrical, droopy, often ugly. To display it in public is "indecent exposure." It is very vulnerable even when made of stone, and the museums of the world are filled with herculean figures brandishing penises that are chipped, clipped, or completely chopped off. The only undamaged penises seem to be the disproportionately small ones created perhaps by sculptors not wishing to intimidate the undersize organs of their patrons. . . .

Each day the penis is prey to sexual sights in the street, in stores, offices, on advertising billboards and television commercials—there is the leering look of a blonde model squeezing cream out of a tube; the nipples imprinted against the silk blouse of a travel agency receptionist; the bevy of buttocks in tight jeans ascending a department store's escalator; the perfumed aroma emanating from the cosmetics counter: musk made from the genitals of one animal to arouse another. The city offers a modern version of a tribal fertility dance, a sexual safari, and many men feel the pressure of having to repeatedly prove their instinct as hunters. The penis, often regarded as a weapon, is also a burden, the male curse. It has made some men restless roués, voyeurs, flashers, rapists . . . its profligacy in high places has provoked political scandals and collapsed governments. Unhappy with it, a few men have chosen to rid themselves of it. But most men, like the gamekeeper, admit that they cannot deliberately kill it. While it may typify, in Lawrence's words, the "terror of the body," it is nevertheless rooted in a man's soul, and without its potency he cannot truly live. Lacking it, Lord Chatterley lost his lady to a social inferior. . . .

I had often wanted to write more about the penis since completing *Thy Neighbor's Wife*, but until I had read Dr. Altman's column about John Bobbitt, I did not see an opportunity. Now I thought about Tina Brown, and how I might persuade her to send me to Manassas, Virginia, to represent *The New Yorker* in the forthcoming courtroom appearances of John and Lorena Bobbitt. There would be two separate trials in the presence of juries. In one trial, Lorena would have to defend herself against the county prosecutor's charge that she was guilty of "malicious wounding." In the other trial, the same prosecutor would present Lorena's position that her husband was guilty of "marital sexual abuse." But John Bobbitt's penis would also be on trial, it seemed to me, and I hoped that these adjudications in Manassas would help to clarify what I thought was still unclear despite all the media coverage of the so-called Gender Wars. In this time of expanding women's rights and demands, was a married man's penis entitled to *no* privilege whatsoever within the lawful state of matrimony? Or, to explore the question further: Did a married man's penis enjoy any legal leeway or sexual concessions that might be denied rightfully to the penis of a young bachelor or an older divorced individual who had not remarried? If one's marital situation was not relevant to this question, then from the perspective of a penis, it might be fair to ask, Why get hitched in the first place? Why go through the trouble of hiring a justice of the peace and agree to be guided by the restrictive measures of the marital code and *still* run the risk of being sliced off in bed by a wife's kitchen knife and then tossed out of her car into the weeds?

The penises of married men were treated far better, I believed, during the era of my early adulthood in mid-twentieth-century America. Indeed, most men of my generation recognized many benefits in marriage, not the least being the almost effortless accessibility and the abundance of what the marriage manuals then preferred to call "coitus," and which under normal circumstances was readily and conveniently available within one's own home and usually within an arm's reach at most hours of the day and night—except when it wasn't. It would be misleading, I must admit, to convey the impression that husbands in the 1950s assumed sex-on-demand status while dwelling in close quarters with a spouse. It was understood in those days, as I guess it has been understood since the time when couples lived together in caves, that a woman possessed the irrefutable right to be ailing from a "headache" or to be otherwise excused from participating, now and then, in sexual intimacies with her mate. But I do not recall any woman of my generation ever lodging a litigious complaint of "marital sexual abuse" against her husband while she was willingly residing with him. And yet this is exactly what Lorena Bobbitt had done. Moreover, as she herself acknowledged to law-enforcement authorities, she had partaken in consensual lovemaking with her husband in their bedroom just two days before he had allegedly committed acts of "marital sexual abuse," prompting her to remove his penis.

In singling out Lorena Bobbitt's response to what she deemed to be her husband's unpardonable behavior, I am *not* discounting the probability that many women of my generation had also been frequent victims of "marital sexual abuse"—but the women of my day, as I have indicated, would not have been inclined to publicize it. Wives rarely discussed their private lives with anyone back then, and it was also tacitly understood that women of high moral character did not even think much about sex. Men often characterized such women as "frigid." This word is not in the lexicon of the 1990s, but it was commonly used a generation ago, and it was not necessarily meant to be pejorative. A frigid woman was imagined by men to be a wholesome virginal creature on the verge of becoming erotically aroused by the very men who were doing the imagining. Such women were more highly valued as trustworthy potential spouses than were those relatively "loose" women who had been cheerleaders in high school and dated star athletes, or who later in life tried to escape convention by working as airline stewardesses. Since sexual favors were less casually distributed by the bachelor girls of the pre-Pill 1950s than would be the case with the *jeunes filles* of the next generation, it was not uncommon for mid-twentieth-century men to welcome the prospect of marriage as a surcease to their unmet nightly needs, to their miscalculations and unrequited flirtations, and to the physical discomforts of having sex with their lovers in the seats of cars parked in the woodlands (while mosquitoes buzzed about, and Peeping Toms watched from the trees, and the patrolling policemen occasionally knocked on windshields while frowning within the glare of their upheld flashlights). Matrimony was supposed to mark the end of such gruesome experiences for unwed couples. It was supposed to offer them an emancipating alternative to borrowing and using friends' apartments as love nests, and arranging amorous meetings in third-rate hotels and motels—places where no self-respecting libidinous male was likely to sign his real name in the registration book.

The nom de plume that I sometimes used when registering in such hotels and motels on those occasions when I could convince my college sweetheart to accompany me overnight to attend football games or other events taking place far from the campus was "Johnny Lindell"—my favorite baseball player on the mid-1940s New York Yankees. He had also been the first player to ever give me an autograph, doing so when I was twelve and traveled daily by trolley to watch the Yankees' spring-training activities held in 1944 and 1945 in Atlantic City. I believe that I scribbled Johnny Lindell's name, together with various made-up addresses, five or six times on registration forms during the two-year period of my Alabama romance.

Some years later, while I was in the army and stationed at Fort Knox, Kentucky, I recall once using the name of another Yankee player, Jerry Coleman, on the registration card of a motel near the Louisville airport, where I was spending the night with a stewardess I had met earlier on the flight from New York. Although I admired Jerry Coleman's athletic abilities, I had never sought his autograph, nor had I ever met him personally until he had retired from the game and was working as a sports broadcaster. It was at an Old Timers game at Yankee Stadium during the middle or late 1960s that someone had introduced us, and I impulsively decided to tell Coleman about what I had done in Louisville. I thought he might be amused. But after hearing my story, his lips suddenly tightened, his face reddened, and, saying nothing, he turned and walked away from me. I would never see him again. I was surprised and sorry about what had happened, but at the time I had not chased after him and attempted to apologize, because I did not exactly know what had aggravated him. It occurred to me that Coleman's reaction was perhaps traceable to how he had been conditioned to feel as a ballplayer whenever a teammate had borrowed his favorite bat and hit a home run. Or maybe Coleman felt that my registering under his name had somehow put his personal reputation at risk, although this made little sense to me, because his name was very common—there were surely many similarly named men listed in every metropolitan telephone directory in America—and I could not understand why my belated confession about what I had done in Louisville during the mid-1950s would bother Coleman when I told him about it ten or fifteen years later.

Whatever Coleman's reservations were, this was a point in time when a majority of Americans were enjoying, and were *insisting* that they were entitled to enjoy, unprecedented access to freedoms and choices pertaining to how they conducted their private lives and how they exercised their constitutional rights within public spaces and accommodations. These were the years when the civil rights marchers were popularizing "We Shall Overcome," and when the anti–Vietnam War demonstrators were advocating "Make love, not war," and when the laws and moral standards of the nation were changing to such a degree that what had been prosecutorial and socially abhorrent in the not-so-distant past was now lawful and being longed for and being indulged in by masses of people. There were the bra-burning rallies of liberated women, and the frontal nudity of male and female dancers performing together on the stages of legitimate theaters, and the fact that nightclub comedians could get away with using words that in the fifties would have hastened Lenny Bruce into handcuffs. It was during the late sixties and early seventies that countless coeds helped to pay for their college tuitions and their supplies of marijuana by working in massage parlors, places where male patrons could remove all of their clothing and, uncovered by towels, recline on their backs and receive what was understood to be the *spécialité de la maison*— a hand job, or what the parlors' advertising brochures more discreetly described as "manual relief." These were boon times for penises from coast to coast.

But not all the permissiveness of this period would be accepted as desirable social behavior by younger Americans in the decades that followed. "When America is not fighting a war, the puritanical desire to punish people has to be let out at home," wrote the novelist Joyce Carol Oates, and I accepted this as one possible explanation for the burgeoning spirit of rectitude and correctness that seemed to pervade much of the country from the 1980s into the 1990s. This restrictive trend might also have reflected a newer generation's reaction against the perceived excesses of their parents' time—the drugs, the sex, the demonstrativeness, the dropping out. Or maybe it expressed as well a newer generation's fears and concerns about the well-publicized warnings of the existence of genital herpes and AIDS. It was a time when feminist activists campaigned against pornography as degrading to women, and when police departments' morals squads raided businesses in the sex industry that catered almost exclusively to men—strip clubs, peep shows, and massage parlors. In 1972, there had been at least thirty massage parlors operating openly along the thoroughfares of New York City—and nearly equal numbers in Los Angeles and some other major cities; but by 1992, whether I was on the East Coast or the West Coast or traveling elsewhere within the country, I could not find a single one. These were no longer boon times for penises.

Women's studies programs proliferated on college campuses and were well represented by female faculty members who ridiculed Sigmund Freud's concepts about penis envy, and Jacques Lacan's postulations about the penis as a "universal signifier," and the theories of biologists and brain specialists who suggested that physical differences between men and women, more often than not, produced sexually identifiable patterns of behavior. Such thinking was dismissed by most women as prejudicial, phallocentric, and sexist, and thus linguistic adjustments were made to conform to the new sense of correctness: *chairman* became *chairperson*, and *sex* became *gender*. With increasing frequency, women's hair was now seen under the hard hats of construction crews, the caps of police officers, the helmets of combat soldiers. The designers of military apparel were contemplating the creation of uniforms that would allow female troops in the field to urinate standing up. The stylishly uniformed young airline stewardesses who had once filled the friendly skies with the aura of their allure had now been replaced along the aisles of airplanes by gender-blended "flight attendants" who were employed more on the basis of how well they did the job than on how well they looked when doing it. Much of what had been described as masculine was now machismo and perhaps abusive. With so many highly educated and motivated women currently established in the legal profession as prosecutors and judges, it was unlikely that untoward male behavior would ever again be excused, or made light of, under the old adage that sometimes "boys will be boys." And with younger women joining their male contemporaries as editors and reporters in the print media and television news departments, there was heightened and unrelenting coverage of stories that an earlier generation of primarily white male editors would have dismissed or downplayed as gossip, innuendo, or too difficult to prove. The extramarital interests of John Kennedy, Robert Kennedy, and Martin Luther King, Jr., had not been seen as headline material by the mainstream editors of the sixties. These editors generally believed that individuals of such prominence were entitled to a life of privacy as long as it did not interfere with their effectiveness as leaders—and editors who thought otherwise usually worked for one of the trashier tabloids. But what separated the journalistic judgment of mainstream editors from that of their sensationalist colleagues was not always discernible in the 1990s. Much of what had been "scandal" was now "social history," and the practitioners of journalism high and low were equally aggressive in pursuing stories about the prowlings of politicians and high-profile cases dealing with sexual harassment, acquaintance rape, date rape, and marital rape.

I had never read about marital rape until I came across Dr. Altman's article in the *Times* about the Bobbitt couple, and since I was having lunch that day with Tina Brown, and assumed that she had also read it and would want to know more about the incident and how it would be resolved in court, I added this story idea to the list of proposals that I intended to discuss with her. But after I had joined her at her table at the Royalton Hotel and we had made our selections from the menu, and I had asked about her reaction to the piece, she replied, "I haven't had a chance to get through the paper yet. What's it about?"

"It's about a man whose penis was sliced off by his wife after he'd supposedly raped her, and about the two surgeons who operated on him and sewed his penis back together."

"This is making me sick," said Tina Brown.

"It's all in today's *Times*," I said, urging her to read it when she returned to her office. I also suggested that it might be the basis of a major article in *The New Yorker* because it showed how hostile some women were capable of becoming and it escalated the already heated debate about the Gender Wars—and furthermore it would remind men about the vulnerability of their penises.

"Oh, please," Tina Brown interrupted, pushing aside her salad, "this is *really* making me sick."

So I dropped the subject and we discussed other ideas during the duration of our lunch. But on the following morning, I faxed her a letter:

Dear Tina:

Thanks for the wonderful lunch yesterday, and I'll have more to say early this week on the ideas we discussed. One of those ideas— the one that twice turned your stomach—continues to fascinate me. This is the tale about the angry wife who severed her husband's penis. Did you read that on C3 of the Tuesday *Times*?

Yesterday we discussed the anger that prevails between men and women, a difference of views that smolders in the aftermath of the Anita Hill–Clarence Thomas clash. This latest incident involving the penis-cutting wife (a manicurist by trade) against her husband (an ex-Marine!) is a story I'd very much like to pursue. A trial is coming up this summer, and I'd like to cover that for *The New Yorker* as part of the piece—if I can convince you I have an interesting approach. . . .

This case promises to be a forum for much of the wrath exuding from American bedrooms these days, and with me doing the reporting and writing, I think it can be dealt with in a dignified and literary manner, while at the same time capturing all the sordid and fascinating details that characterized the work Capote did in *The New Yorker* in *In Cold Blood*.

A day later, Tina Brown replied:

Dear Gay,

Okay, you're on for the penis chopper. I took a penis poll in the office and you were absolutely right—men groaned and writhed and mumbled about their atavistic fears. The trial would be phenomenal for you since it so drastically dramatizes, as you say, the particularly violent mood of the sex war. If the piece would be raising these bigger issues, it does become much more, and a short book besides. I'm excited. . . . I'm thrilled to be working with you,

Best, Tina

23

Beginning in mid-July 1993, I commuted regularly between New York and Manassas, Virginia, interviewing dozens of people who were directly or tangentially connected to the Bobbitt story: the couple's lawyers, their doctors, their media advisers, their relatives, their friends, their neighbors and coworkers—Lorena's female associates in the nail-cutting salon, and John's cargo-loading buddies who had been working with him at the depot on the day before his misfortune and who were known in the trucking trade as "lumpers." I also interviewed the police sergeant who had discovered John's penis in the weeds, and the female police officer who found the bloody knife that Lorena had tossed into a trash bin, and the detective who was overseeing the investigation.

The latter was forty-nine-year-old Peter Weintz, a gravel-voiced man of six feet three inches and 260 pounds who smoked four packs of Marlboros daily and whose antipathy toward lawbreakers once extended to his arresting and imprisoning his own son. Weintz's son, who had been sixteen at the time, had been heavily engaged in drugs, alcohol, and sometimes in stealing. After driving off one day with his father's car and two cases of beer, he was apprehended by Weintz and escorted to jail. Following his son's release, Detective Weintz invested about thirty thousand dollars toward his rehabilitation, which would turn out to be successful.

When I first made arrangements to meet with Detective Weintz, I anticipated a difficult interview. I had been told by a few local journalists that he disliked dealing with the press. But I found him to be approachable and candid, and since he had been the first official to interrogate Lorena Bobbitt after she had surrendered to the police on the day of the cutting, he had a sense of her state of mind and her deeply personal remembrance of what had occurred just before, during, and after her attack on her husband on June 23. Detective Weintz had tape-recorded what she had told him, and six weeks later, at the preliminary hearing on August 4, which I and dozens of other media representatives attended at the county courthouse, he read aloud to Judge Paul F. Gluchowski the transcription of Mrs. Bobbitt's statement.

The purpose of the preliminary hearing was not to address her guilt or innocence but, rather, to determine if there was sufficient evidence against her to support the prosecutor's claim that she had "maliciously" cut her husband "with intent to maim, disfigure, disable, or kill," and should therefore ultimately be brought to trial for committing a felony. The prosecutor summoned four police officers to attend the hearing and offer evidence against her. The first officer called to the witness stand, Cecil F. Deane, exhibited to the court the photographs he had taken of the bleeding and bandaged John Bobbitt as the latter lay on a gurney in the emergency room shortly after Deane's arrival there at 5:15 on the morning of June 23. The second officer, Michael Perry, testified that he had retrieved the severed section of the penis along the roadside at approximately 6:15 a.m., had placed it in a Ziploc bag with ice, and then delivered it by ambulance to the hospital. The third officer, Sindi Leo, confirmed that the red-handled fillet knife that was presently on display on a table in front of Judge Gluchowski's bench was indeed *the* knife that she had found at around 8:30 a.m. in the trash can in front of the nail salon that employed Lorena Bobbitt. And the fourth officer, Detective Weintz, recited from the transcipt of Lorena Bobbitt's testimony that he had obtained from her at the Manassas police station on the afternoon of June 23.

Weintz quoted her as saying that her husband had returned intoxicated to their apartment at around three o'clock in the morning. He had been accompanied by one of his boyhood friends from Niagara Falls, New York, who was staying over on the couple's sofa in the living room. After her husband had closed the bedroom door and had fallen asleep beside her for about an hour, he woke up and took off his clothes—and, despite her protests, he forcibly removed her panties and proceeded to rape her. "I tried to scream or do something, to push him," she told Detective Weintz, "but I couldn't because he's so heavy for me." Later, as her husband drifted back to sleep, she slipped out of bed, put on some clothes, and walked into the kitchen for a glass of water. Seeing a block of knives on the counter—"I was angry," she recalled to Detective Weintz—she took one of them, held it in her hand, and returned with it to the bedroom. "I asked him if he was satisfied with what he did," she said, "and he just— half asleep or something—did not care about my feelings. . . . He always has orgasm and he doesn't wait for me to have an orgasm. He's selfish. I don't think it's fair. So I pulled back the sheets, then did it."

As Detective Weintz continued with his reading of the transcript, squinting through the aviator glasses that framed his hazel eyes and rested high on the bridge of his bulbous nose, Lorena Bobbitt sat in front of him at the defendant's table, next to her attorney. She said nothing, although she occasionally lowered her head and wept, allowing her long wavy dark hair to hang down along the sides of her face, touching her shoulders, enshrouding her as if she were wearing a mantilla. I was getting my first look at her. She was delicate-boned and petite (five-two and ninety-five pounds, one hundred less than her five-eleven husband); she wore neither jewelry nor makeup, and had on a long-sleeved belted purple dress of modest design that was buttoned at the throat. When she was not weeping, she appeared to be praying—her lips moving slowly, her hands folded in her lap, her eyes cast down. She projected an image of innocence and vulnerability; and while I reminded myself that her small manicured fingers and her slender wrists had in a split second directed a knife through her husband's manhood, I believed that she would later prove to be convincing as a witness in her own defense, instilling doubt in the minds of the jurors that she could have willfully done what the prosecutor had charged her with doing.

I had often tried to interview her prior to seeing her at the preliminary hearing, but both her lawyer and her media adviser had been uncooperative. I later learned that her media adviser had promised her story exclusively to *Vanity Fair*, which would feature her in a photo spread done by the noted photographer Mary Ellen Mark, along with a lengthy article written by Kim Masters. The issue would be published in the fall or early winter, presumably coinciding with the start of Lorena Bobbitt's trial. Her media adviser had also come to an understanding with the producers at ABC-TV for her to be interviewed on the weekly 20/20 television program sometime in late September. In the meantime, her attorney announced that she had received dozens of phone calls and letters of endorsement, mostly from women, volunteering to contribute to her legal expenses and to assist her in other ways. An article in the *Washington Post*—under the headline A SYMBOL OF SHARED RAGE—described her as emerging into a "feminist folk heroine." It quoted a thirty-one-year-old dress shop worker in Washington, Rose Maravilla, as saying, "I will be livid if they put her away." Also expressing support for her in the article was thirty-six-year-old Evelyn Smith of Maryland, who had shot her cantankerous husband to death in 1991, had been acquitted by a jury in 1992, and had recently begun a foundation to assist battered women. In a column in *Newsweek* magazine, the author Barbara Ehrenreich wrote, "If a fellow insists on using his penis as a weapon, I say that, one way or another, he ought to be swiftly disarmed."

On the day before Lorena Bobbitt's appearance at the preliminary hearing, her husband had been indicted by a grand jury on the charge of marital sexual abuse, and, while awaiting the announcement of his trial date, he was released on a five-thousand-dollar personal-recognizance bond. His attorney, who accompanied him while he was being booked and fingerprinted, later spoke to the press and emphasized his client's quarrel with Lorena's version of the truth. "The only fact that is not in dispute is the fact that she committed the heinous crime of mutilation against my client," the attorney said; and Bobbitt's media adviser repeated the statement that had earlier been distributed in the name of John Bobbitt: "Contrary to a few published reports and the desperate excuses of my wife, Lorena, I did not attack her the night in question . . . she will have to answer for her actions in criminal court." Bobbitt's doctors, who had released him from the hospital a month earlier, explained that he was urinating without a catheter but remained numb below the cut. One of the doctors told me privately that Bobbitt had been given a copy of the porn magazine *Chic*, hoping that Bobbitt might be aroused by the photographs of erotically posed nude women. So far this had not happened. As John Bobbitt walked to and from the court building, a reporter from the *Potomac News* noted that he was taking "long strides." He was nevertheless trailing his wife insofar as gaining widespread public support.

Sidney Siller, the founder of the National Organization for Men, a thirteen-thousand-membership group begun in 1983, told a *Washington Post* reporter that John Bobbitt lacked demonstrative backers because men "don't come out and show support in the same way women do." Alvin S. Baraff, director of the MenCenter counseling firm that started in Washington in 1984, defined the pro-Lorena campaign to the *Post* reporter as the "ultimate in male bashing," and he added, "I think they are championing a true criminal. This woman does not deserve any support. This case is another indication of reverse discrimination and gender bias."

While I had so far been gathering information in Virginia for less than three weeks, and knew that my early impressions might be altered as I extended my stay and learned more about this case, which the syndicated columnist Charles Krauthammer called "politically correct revenge," I thought that at least some of John Bobbitt's image difficulty with much of the public and the press was due to his inability to speak out effectively in his own behalf, being hampered by a congenital disorder that prompted him to repeat his words again and again, often in a hasty and garbled manner. He was the son of a mentally deficient Polish-American mother who resided in Niagara Falls, New York, and a father from Oklahoma who was partly Native American and had abandoned the family when John was four or five years old. I also believed that John Bobbitt's physical appearance—his weight lifter's torso, his close-cropped haircut, his square-jawed, hazel-eyed, tattooed-armed, blue-collared, white working-class handsomeness, which had once appealed to the recruitment sergeant who had enlisted Bobbitt into the Marine Corps in 1987—was what lent credibility to the typecasting efforts of his wife's defenders to portray him in the media as a militaristic pretty-boy brute who had behaved so abominably toward his diminutive wife that she finally gave him what he had deserved. When he was out of work, which he frequently was after leaving the Corps, he had spent much of his time and money barhopping at night with other young, minimally educated, minimum-wage white males like himself. If there was a national poll seeking to identify America's least-cared-about category of men, this element would have probably headed the list. Unlike black men, who could attribute a lack of achievement to racial prejudice, there were no easy excuses for these whites who were frequently scorned as "trash" and who, unlike other minorities, lacked political defenders, affirmative-action qualifications, and the social concern of the larger population. They were an endangered species of misfits, obsolete American buffaloes ill-prepared to long survive in the quickly changing and highly technical climate of a nation in a period of ever-decreasing need for brawn except in contact sports, and in which the very nature of traditional masculinity as a worthy and singular definition was being debated, doubted, and often linguistically outmoded by the 1990s generation of young middle-class and upper-middle-class men and women from academia, politics, the law, and the media. As influencers of national policy and opinion, these professionals not only mocked but sought to remake and modernize the manners and morals of lower-class men like John Bobbitt, and they no doubt believed, unless he could prove otherwise in court, that he was as his wife said he was.

Lorena Bobbitt was cheered by crowds of women as she walked out of the courthouse at the conclusion of the preliminary hearing. The prosecutor's evidence against her was ruled sufficient by Judge Gluchowski to force her to stand trial at a later date; meanwhile, she was free on bail. She smiled slightly as she passed bystanders and camera crews, walking arm in arm with the two female friends who had remained close to her throughout her ordeal and had been helpful to her ever since she had come to live in the United States and study at Northern Virginia Community College in 1987.

One of her companions was her employer at the nail salon, an attractive thirty-five-year-old blonde named Janna Biscutti, who had initially hired Lorena on a part-time basis six years earlier to help care for Janna's young son. Lorena had then been seventeen and not very fluent in English. She had been in Virginia for only a few months, and had been boarding with a Latin American immigrant family, having left her own family behind in Venezuela. She had been born in Ecuador in 1969, moving to Venezuela at the age of five with her parents and a younger sister and brother. Her father had found work in Caracas in a laboratory that made dentures. After she had graduated from high school in Caracas and had arrived in the United States to enroll at the community college in Virginia, her main hope was to become a dentist someday.

When not attending classes at the college, Lorena worked as a daytime nanny in Janna Biscutti's large home in Fairfax, Virginia. Janna, who had been born in Louisville, Kentucky, as Janna Abell, had made considerable amounts of money operating nail-sculpturing salons in the Virginia suburbs of Washington, D.C. Janna had dropped out of two colleges in Kentucky and a third one in Tennessee after deciding that she no longer wished to become a plastic surgeon or a dermatologist. She opened her first salon as a nineteen-year-old in Vienna, Virginia, in 1977. In that same year she married a six-foot-four-inch civil engineer named Errol Biscutti, an Australian-Italian who had come with his family to the United States during his boyhood. One year after her marriage and now using her husband's surname, Janna Biscutti started a second salon in Georgetown, Virginia, and then a third in Great Falls, Virginia, in 1980. Janna would leave her husband in 1984 but would retain custody of their only child, Kyle Biscutti, who was four years old in 1988, when Janna employed Lorena to serve as the boy's nanny. Janna also taught Lorena how to drive, instructing her in a Mercedes 300-D sedan automatic so she could transport Kyle to and from his preschool activities. After Lorena had worked in this capacity for a little more than a year, and had improved her English—aided by regularly watching the children's TV show *Sesame Street* at Janna's home with Kyle—Janna released her from her child-rearing role (since Kyle had gone to live for a while with his father in California), and then, months later, Janna hired her to work in a nail salon.

Lorena had meanwhile met Lance Cpl. John Bobbitt one evening at a dance hall near the U.S. Marine Corps base at Quantico, Virginia. He had recently been transferred there from Okinawa. He was twenty; she was eighteen. She was a virgin and had never seriously dated anyone before, and John Bobbitt's vision of romance had previously been limited to seeing bar girls in the Orient. After going out with each other for less than eight months, and having a courtship that consisted mainly of weekend meetings and sharing fast food in shopping malls, John and Lorena decided to marry. This decision lessened Lorena's anxiety about her impermanent presence in America, since she was here on a student visa, and for John Bobbitt the advantages of marriage would include moving from his crowded barracks into an apartment and extending to his bride the medical care that was provided free by the military. Inviting neither family nor friends to attend their hastily arranged civil ceremony in Stafford, Virginia, John and Lorena stood in front of a magistrate on June 18, 1989, to be pronounced husband and wife.

It was four years later, shortly before 5:30 in the morning on June 23, 1993, that Lorena drove speedily to Janna Biscutti's home in Fairfax, Virginia, banging on the front door loudly and ringing the bell repeatedly until the door had been opened by Janna's second husband, a Saudi Arabian–born mortgage banker named Nizzar Suleiman. It was Suleiman who awakened his sleeping wife on the second floor. After Janna had come down and had finally understood what the hysterical and barely articulate Lorena Bobbitt was saying about what she had done with a kitchen knife, Janna immediately telephoned the police and escorted Lorena to the station house—as Janna would, six weeks later, on August 4, accompany Lorena to and from the preliminary hearing.

Lorena's other close companion at the courthouse—the person who had first provided Lorena with a home upon her arrival in America—was a stout, dark-haired, and conservatively dressed woman of fifty-nine named Erma Castro, who, like Lorena, had been born in Ecuador, but she was a full-time resident of Virginia and had been an American citizen for nearly twenty years. Erma lived with her husband, Jose Castro, an engineer, and their two teenage daughters, in a newly developed suburban community, and she was employed as an administrator within an agency that catered to the area's immigrant settlers and their children. She assisted these families in filling out government forms and often volunteered as a translator for Spanish-speaking people who were having difficulty reading instructions written in English.

In the early fall of 1987, as Lorena was preparing for college, Erma Castro met her through a mutual friend and soon offered her a rent-free room in the Castro home *if* she would promise to keep up with her studies and set a good example for Castro's daughters, who were a few years younger than Lorena. For at least a year, Erma was happy with the arrangement. But after Lorena had met and begun to go out with John Bobbitt, in October 1988, Erma Castro's attitude quickly changed. She was unimpressed with John Bobbitt, having spoken with him a few times when he had come to the house, and she was worried about what might happen to Lorena as a result of dating him.

I became aware of Erma Castro's feelings even though I never communicated with her directly—she neither returned my phone calls nor answered my letters, and she did not receive me when I showed up at her workplace without an appointment—but I *had* gained access to a transcript of a pretrial interview that she had been legally bound to give during the late summer of 1993 to John Bobbitt's attorney in order to allow the latter to better defend his client in the upcoming marital sexual abuse case. Not only Castro but others who would later testify in the Manassas courthouse—a group that would include Janna Biscutti, Nizzar Suleiman, and Lorena Bobbitt herself—had been summoned to appear individually for pretrial interviews in the office of John Bobbitt's attorney in Alexandria, Virginia. These interviews were actually depositions. People being deposed were under oath to tell the truth. They were entitled to bring their own lawyers for guidance, but it was John Bobbitt's defense attorney in this instance who directed the questioning from within his office in Alexandria, and the laws of perjury applied there as much as if the witnesses were being interrogated in court. A stenographer was present to record every word. A typed transcript was made of each and every deposition. And thus, after I had obtained copies of these depositions, I had as accurate an account as I was likely to get from the vantage point of those who were among the most qualified to comment on the maiming of John Bobbitt, and to explain why and how the incident had occurred.

No one had been more prescient than Erma Castro in foreseeing the incompatibility that was destined to doom the relationship between John Bobbitt and Lorena; and, as Castro declared in her deposition, she had urged Lorena from the beginning to stay away from the muscular marine. Castro was a traditional Latin American matron, a natural duenna rooted in centuries of trepidation toward visiting conquistadors. Were her own daughters ever to elicit the attentions of such men as John Bobbitt—men who mumbled, men of low income and rank, men who were ill-prepared to support a wife and a family and who yet sought sexual pleasure from women—Castro would have bolted every window and door of her home, would have prevented her daughters from receiving phone calls, and would not have allowed them out of her sight. Her daughters often referred to her as "old-fashioned," she acknowledged to Bobbitt's attorney during the deposition, but after Lorena had disregarded her advice and had married John Bobbitt—and had subsequently been abused by him and had ended up being arrested by the police for slicing off his penis—

Erma Castro recalled that she had gathered her daughters around her and declared: "This is what happens if you don't obey what your mother or your parents say or [when] some friend, some older adult person, tells you who has your good in her mind. And I told them to see this as an example that they should never disregard . . . and they should be respectful to—if they don't want to listen to the old-fashioned voice—at least to the commandment that God gives to us. Because God gives the freedom to think and to choose the right and the wrong, and it is their decision. I just tell you, see what happens when young people don't listen, don't want to listen to your parents."

After being asked by the attorney if Lorena had ever discussed her private life with Erma Castro prior to her eloping with John Bobbitt, Castro replied, "I'm very conservative and I don't like to talk about that, but one night she came to my bed and she said, 'Mrs. Castro, can I talk with you?' I say, 'Yes, Lorena, what happened?' She started crying. I say, 'Lorena, don't be upset, tell me.' " Lorena remained hesitant as she selected the words, Castro recalled, and she herself found it difficult to draw her out, because what Lorena was asking (and it took Castro some time to figure it out) was embarrassing to them both. Castro found it no less embarrassing *now,* at this deposition, to be queried about it by a male stranger, albeit an attorney in front of whom she had sworn to tell the whole truth. Finally, she acknowledged what Lorena had asked her: Was it all right for a married couple ever to have anal sex?

Castro had responded, "Are you *crazy?* No, you *never* do that! And don't let *him* do that even if he asks that!" Although Lorena had promised to follow her advice, Castro said again, "*Don't* let men do that!"

But with all of Lorena's good intentions, the discussion had troubled Erma Castro. While she had initially admired the young woman's courage in coming alone to study in the United States, she was now beginning to feel uncertain about wanting to continue as Lorena's guardian. "I took her in my home because she was very anxious to become a professional," Castro explained to the attorney, adding that during Lorena's first year in college she had been an "A and B student," but "when she was with John, she got an F." Not only was Lorena "seeing him behind my back," Castro continued, but he never seemed to have any money when they went out on dates. It was Lorena, using funds she was earning as Janna Biscutti's nanny, who picked up the checks when she and John Bobbitt went out for hamburgers, pizzas, or ice cream. Castro had learned this from one of her daughters, and it further diminished what little respect she had for him as a proper man for Lorena. "He was not responsible," Castro concluded when speaking to the attorney; John Bobbitt lacked the kindness and generosity that courting men traditionally bestowed upon their girl-friends, "at least in the beginning." Castro wondered what John Bobbitt did with the money he received from the Marine Corps, and why Lorena would tolerate his being so cheap when he was out with her. Was Lorena trying to buy his affections, seeing him as a means of marrying her way into America? Castro had once seen a young Russian woman on a television show who admitted that she had paid an American man to marry her in order to secure her residency in the United States, and it occurred to Castro that Lorena might be having similar thoughts. But when Castro had questioned her about this, Lorena immediately denied it, saying for the first time, "Oh, Mrs. Castro, I love him, I love him." After hearing this, Castro became even more alarmed, she told the attorney; she had an emotional girl on her hands who *thought* she was in love, but who was too young and naïve to know what love was, and who was soon likely to lose her virginity (if she had not already) to this American cheapskate who had seemingly won her heart by allowing her to wear his Marine Corps jacket. Castro believed that she should immediately share her concerns with Lorena's family in Venezuela, and so she placed a call and spoke to Lorena's mother. "I told her Lorena has a boyfriend, and I don't like it and I'm afraid something might happen," Castro recounted to the attorney; and when the latter asked how the girl's mother had reacted, Castro replied, "She was crying."

No matter how critical Erma Castro was of John Bobbitt, Lorena continued to go out with him, and to regard his shortcomings in a positive manner. He was habitually late when he came to the Castros' house in the early evenings to take her out—as he was admittedly late most mornings when reporting to his sergeant at the motor pool—but Lorena interpreted his tardiness as a sign of his independent spirit. And the fact that he had a speech problem—racing his words, repeating everything that he said two or three times—she also found agreeable; since she was still in the early stages of understanding English, she was often obliged to ask Americans to please repeat what they had said. With John Bobbitt, it was never necessary.

He was also very honest and open when talking about himself, not being reticent about discussing his painful boyhood in his native Niagara Falls. It did not seem to bother him when, after he had knocked on the Castros' door, intending to see Lorena, he was met instead by Erma Castro, who invited him in, sat him down in the living room, and then began to bombard him with leading questions: What did his parents now do for a living? How long had they been in America? What did his brothers do? How long did he plan to remain in the Marine Corps? If he could not reenlist at the completion of his four-year contract, what would he do next?

John replied freely to every one of Erma Castro's questions. He said that he had brothers who were drug users, that his mother was mentally unstable, and that his father, a mean-spirited drinker who had been a motorcycle mechanic, had abandoned his wife and three sons when John was about five. John recalled that his father used to store a few motorcycles in the living room of their second-floor apartment, and once, as the apartment house was being destroyed by a fire, his father had run down the steps carrying his motorcycles to safety *before* concerning himself with the well-being of his family. John confessed that he had done poorly in school, being hampered by what was later diagnosed to be attention deficit disorder, and as his mother's mental condition had deteriorated while John was in grade school, he and his two brothers had been sent to live in the small home of one of his maternal uncles, who resided nearby in Niagara Falls. His uncle and the latter's wife had three sons of their own, and so John and his brothers grew up with an abundance of young male companionship and competitiveness, and the bedroom that they shared was not unlike the barracks that he would later come to know as a marine. Except for being an outstanding weight lifter and swimmer—he was maybe the best swimmer among the marines at Quantico, he told Castro—he was unable to claim any other abilities or achievements.

Erma Castro did not interrupt him as he proceeded to tell her more about himself, although she knew enough already. She knew that if Lorena continued to date this man, she would have to live elsewhere. Meanwhile, Castro sat in her living room across from Lorena and John, nodding her head occasionally, or forcing a smile, as John rambled on. At other times, when Castro seemed to be confused or dismayed by what he was saying, she would raise an eyebrow and glance quizzically at Lorena. But Lorena, sitting close to her boyfriend with her head down, seemed to be totally absorbed within the folds of the big fleece-lined Marine Corps jacket that he had earlier draped over her slender shoulders.

24

AFTER THE COUPLE HAD GOTTEN MARRIED ON JUNE 18, 1989, and had rented a small apartment in Manassas, John Bobbitt spoke often about visiting Niagara Falls, New York, so that Lorena could meet the family who had raised him. After telephoning his uncle and aunt, it was decided that the couple should have a church wedding in Niagara Falls on July 4; but by the time John arrived at the church, it was July 5. John had gotten the date mixed up. When the pastor described how irritated all the guests had been and how his adoptive parents had left the church and gone directly to a trailer-park camp they frequented in Canada, John could respond only with stuttered and repeated apologies. Lorena, for her part, was too overwhelmed to speak.

Hoping to make amends to his relatives by apologizing in person, John led his bride to the car and drove directly toward the Canadian border. But there they were delayed. Lorena had not brought her passport. It would never have occurred to her that she would need a passport anywhere in North America. As the border guards ordered them to the side of the road, one of the guards followed and stood next to John's window. Lorena waited for John to plead their case, to *do* something. But he merely sat forward behind the wheel, staring silently through the windshield, not even facing the guard. Finally, she leaned over and, in the most convincing English she could muster, and in a forthright manner that was both charming and persuasive, informed the guard that they had just been married and that she was a Venezuelan wife of a United States Marine, and that this was her first time at the Canadian border, and that their honeymoon—and maybe their marriage—might all be ruined due to her ignorance of the regulations. There were tears in her eyes. The guard motioned for them to move through.

John's aunt and uncle forgave him, perhaps in deference to the bride. At the cookout, Lorena met others in John's extended family and responded sincerely to their good wishes. But when the couple headed back to Virginia, she was silently angry. Without consulting her, John had invited one of his brothers—a brother on drugs, who carried needles in his overnight bag—to drive with them back to Virginia and stay with them for a week or two, sleeping on their living room sofa. The couple's sex life, which had been on an at least once-a-day basis, was now minimized by Lorena's expressed misgivings that her brother-in-law, occupying the sofa, might become privy to their love sounds at night. John complained that she was trying to punish him for bringing his brother into the house, and, in any case, he professed not to care if they had sex or not. He called her "selfish" and "spiteful," and even "un-American." America had opened up its door to people from elsewhere like herself, he shouted, and where did *she* come off trying to ban his brother and deny him the chance to live for a while in a different part of the country?

Months later, during Thanksgiving of 1989, after John's uncle and aunt had decided to drive down to Manassas and stay with the Bobbitts for a few days, Lorena avoided them, moving into the apartment of a nail sculptress she had befriended at her job. In December, however, the couple's compatibility had been restored, perhaps influenced by their abandoning their small place in Manassas for a much larger apartment in Stafford that had two bedrooms, a dining room, and a living room with a balcony that overlooked a lake. It was also located close to the Marine Corps base at Quantico, meaning that John Bobbitt no longer had to endure a forty-mile drive to work every morning, a tense time, in which he feared being late and consequently received many speeding tickets and sometimes sideswiped the bodies of deer and dented the fenders of his car.

During the second year of the marriage, while the couple was still living in Stafford, Lorena discovered that she was pregnant. She was now twenty, John was twenty-two, and they both agreed that this was not the right time to have a child. She would get an abortion. She was preoccupied and pleased with her job, being one of Janna Biscutti's leading nail sculptresses. Lorena's list of regular clients at the salon in Centreville had been increasing constantly, and her annual income, with tips, was in excess of thirty thousand dollars—a third more than John was earning from the military and whatever work he was picking up during his off-hours. Lorena was also developing a close bond with Janna Biscutti, who was to her the personification of modern American womanhood. Janna had success, money, enjoyed an active social life, could ski well and sail a boat, and she owned a gorgeous house and now had a second child, a daughter, born of Janna's second marriage, to Nizzar Suleiman. Janna inspired within Lorena the will to want more out of *her* life; and one of the things that Lorena began to want was a house—nothing as grand as

Janna's, of course, but certainly more than the apartment in Stafford, which, after a year's occupancy, no longer satisfied her.

She convinced her husband that they were wasting their money on rent, that they should *own* a piece of America. And so they soon found a white frame one-family house with three bedrooms and two bathrooms, which stood on an acre of land in the Yorkshire section of Manassas— meaning that John would once more have to get up at dawn in order to be on time at Quantico, making him prone to the roadway pursuits of the police and the wanderings of stray deer. The price of the house in Manassas was $135,000, and the monthly mortgage payments would exceed $1,300, which John found intimidating; but Lorena explained that she could bear much of the expense from her earnings, and he said he would work longer at extra jobs when he was not on duty with the Marine Corps.

After the couple had moved in, John decided to install a satellite dish. He had given little thought about its price prior to ordering one. Owning a satellite dish had seemed to him to be *the* thing to do; if you owned a home with some land around it, why not decorate it with a dish? He had seen several of them sitting on the lawns of the homes he passed while driving to and from Quantico, and he had sometimes wondered what it must be like to own one. Now he would know.

One evening when Lorena was working late at the salon and he was sitting at home exploring the great variety of channels that were available on the screen, he happened upon a porn channel called Spice. He then became so engaged in watching a few bare-breasted rodeo girls romping around in front of a cheering crowd in an arena that he did not hear Lorena unlocking the front door and entering the living room.

"I wish you wouldn't watch that," she said.

He turned toward her, feeling embarrassed and irritated.

"Turn it off yourself," he replied loudly.

She left the living room, saying nothing as she headed through the hallway toward their bedroom and slammed the door.

The next morning, he left at dawn for the motor pool, but when he returned that night, she was not there. He drove off to a bar. Returning home later, he saw her standing in the kitchen, and she was furious. She had cooked dinner and now it had gone to waste, she declared; with tears in her eyes, she explained that what she had wasted could have fed a large and impoverished family for two days in Latin America. She was not going to cook for him anymore, she continued. She was tired of doing all the household work and paying most of the bills while he was either loafing at home watching television or was out drinking and carousing in bars. This was not the first time she had accused him of carousing. He had met a woman whom he fancied months earlier when he was working part-time at a restaurant, and later, during an agument with Lorena, he had said that if Lorena was dissatisifed with him, he was acquainted with a woman who might not be.

But the marital discord had accelerated in intensity. Whether this was primarily due to the increased costs of the house or to Lorena's aspirations to be more like Janna Biscutti, John did not know. What he did know was that he was frustrated. He had been unable to find extra work that paid enough to offset the increased costs of the house. His speech problems precluded his getting sales jobs. Indeed, his speech difficulties were compounding the frustrations he was feeling at home with Lorena. She was now winning every argument. She, who had struggled greatly with her English a few years earlier, had now—thanks to her ongoing dialogues at her manicurist table with processions of well-spoken American women—exceeded his ability to speak in his native tongue. When she spoke in the harsh manner that characterized their nightly exchanges, his only recourse was to outshout her and maybe give her a vigorous shove—but she had lately gotten into the habit of shoving back. Small as she was, she was combative, and once when he shoved her backward against the refrigerator, she responded by slashing him in the neck with her long sculpted nails.

The depth of his inadequacy against her verbal thrusts became sadly clear to him during one noisy fight they were having in late August 1990, a fight from which he abruptly retreated, picking up the telephone and dialing 911. He was asking the Manassas Police Department to come to his home and solve his marital problems. And they did come, although they solved no problems. They merely asked questions of him and the crying Lorena, who complained that he was abusing her but said she did not wish to press charges. The police checked the house for weapons. Finding none, they left.

In the latter part of November 1990, after the couple had become embroiled in an acrimonious exchange over a matter that in less stressful times might have not transpired—*this* confrontation, incidentally, took place in the presence of Lorena's mother, then visiting from Venezuela—Lorena quickly reached for the phone and dialed 911 on her own, and with similar results: a police visit, more interrogation, more searches for deadly weapons, no filing of a complaint. In the Manassas Police Department report, it was noted: "Mother-in-law is there and not helping much."

In January 1991, John Bobbitt was released from the Marine Corps. In a period of military cutbacks and relative world peace, he was a very expendable leatherneck. When he told Lorena about his release, she said nothing. Now he was a man without a predictable paycheck, and this at a time when their expenses were higher than ever. He assured her that he would get a job, and he did—driving a Yellow Cab in and around Manassas. He worked a late-night schedule that contrasted greatly with his routine in the Marine Corps, and sometimes he went days without seeing or speaking to Lorena—which was just as well. There had been another 911 incident at the beginning of the year, a few days after he had been released from the military, and this had provoked John to grab Lorena, to wrestle the phone out of her hand, and then to rip the cord out of the wall. The couple's shouting back and forth had alerted one of their neighbors, who, in turn, telephoned the police—who came again, as usual, and, as usual, left without obtaining a complaint from Lorena. No matter how angry she was, no matter how elaborately she described him as the villain in every altercation, when it was over, she was reluctant to file a complaint.

In late February 1991, John Bobbitt had returned late at night from his taxi job and turned to the Spice channel on television. He heard Lorena's voice complaining from the bedroom that the sound was too loud. He turned it down and resumed watching. Then Lorena, wearing a silk outfit she had bought from Victoria's Secret, entered the living room and, seeing what he was watching, turned off the set. He jumped up and gave her a shove, and turned it back on. She came forward and turned it off again. This time he gave her a harder shove, but she shoved back. He banged her on the shoulder with the palm of his hand. And she kicked him in the genitals. He jumped on her and tossed her to the floor. After a lively exchange of swings and slaps, Lorena emerged with a battered face, a split lip, and other bruises. This time when the police responded to her call, they told her she *had* to file a complaint. She refused at first. The police took photographs of her face and then *demanded* that she immediately affix her signature to a document. This time she did.

When John Bobbitt, who had been kept outside on the lawn of the house in the presence of another police officer, heard that he was now under arrest, he protested loudly. He showed the officers the scratches and blood on his neck and arms, and insisted that she had started it all by kicking him in the genitals. That afternoon, John Bobbitt went to court to file a countercomplaint against Lorena for "assault."

After two additional 911 calls that year, which led neither to arrests nor complaints, Lorena herself became a party to criminal incidents that did not involve her husband in any way, although in one instance it was *he* who had cited her—not to the police, but to Janna Biscutti, from whom she had been stealing some hundreds of dollars' worth of salon products, which she apparently intended to use at home, or elsewhere, in catering to some of her customers, thereby avoiding having to split her fee the customary fifty-fifty with her boss. John discovered the products and, threatening at first to return them to Janna's office alone, convinced Lorena to drive with him to Janna's place and return the stolen items. Janna admonished Lorena but did not dismiss her.

In late June 1991, in Nordstrom's clothing shop in McLean, Virginia, Lorena was caught stealing a $170 dress. She pleaded guilty before a magistrate, and, as a first-time offender for shoplifting, was directed to complete fifty hours of community service. And then, in October of the same year, as Janna Biscutti was reviewing her business records, her suspicions were alerted by what appeared to be discrepancies in Lorena's accounting. Lorena denied any wrongdoing. After a more thorough investigation, Janna Biscutti discovered that Lorena had embezzled $7,200.

"You lied to me!" Janna was heard to cry out from the back room of her salon, while the manicurists and customers in the front paused to listen. Lorena's howls and cries could then be heard throughout the workplace as Janna proceeded to pull Lorena's hair. Janna reported the embezzlement to the police, but, after pondering the effects of the punishment, she decided not to press charges. If she did, Lorena would perhaps be imprisoned, but Janna could not be assured of getting her money back. So she kept Lorena on the job but extracted a 60 percent, rather than a 50 percent, commission on her work until the $7,200 amount had been paid back. This took Lorena nearly a year.

With the foreclosure on the Bobbitts' house, and with Lorena and John Bobbitt deciding to separate, Erma Castro allowed Lorena to return to the Castro household. John Bobbitt slowly made his way back to Niagara Falls in October 1991. For the next twelve months, drifting between upstate New York and Canada, he marginally supported himself through a series of jobs (such as cleaning roof gutters) that he neither liked nor held for very long. The Marine Corps had been the place for him. He wished that he could reenlist, but he knew better than to try. One of the jobs he thought of seeking was employment in a police department. Many ex-marines ended up working for the police after military retirement, he knew; but that single arrest on his record in Virginia would not serve him well. Wherever he went, that might follow.

And yet the very person who had been most instrumental in getting him arrested back in February 1991—his once-loving wife, Lorena—sent him a Valentine's Day greeting a year later. When he opened the envelope that had been mailed to Niagara Falls and discovered what was inside, he was amazed. Inside was a charming color photograph of Lorena, who was wearing a brown off-the-shoulder dress and a brown hat with silk flowers sewn on the brim. Her dark eyes were focused directly at the camera and she was smiling demurely; on the back of the photo, she had written: "Have a Happy Valentine's Day, John!!!—Lorena, 2-14-92."

He decided to call her. He knew that it made no sense, but he called anyway, contacting her at the nail salon. Her voice was very friendly, so unlike the familiar stridence of her 911 calls. She was occupied with a customer when he telephoned, so he called back later, at her suggestion. By September 1992, he had returned to Virginia and the couple were embarking on the revival of their relationship.

John Bobbitt had hoped that Erma Castro would allow him to join Lorena in the Castro household for a while until the two of them could find an apartment to rent. Castro, however, had adamantly refused; not even for *one night* would she permit John Bobbitt to be under her roof, she made clear to Lorena, who had tried (and failed) to make the case that the Bobbitt marriage was worthy of preservation. Lorena was more convincing in her appeals to Castro's sister-in-law, Sondra Beltran, who was then married to, but was living apart from, Mrs. Castro's brother, Segundo. Mrs. Beltran finally agreed to rent part of her home (located in Stafford, not far from Mrs. Castro's) to Lorena and John, with the understanding they reside there harmoniously with her and her two teenage sons. But not long after the Bobbitts had moved in, it was obvious to Mrs. Beltran that she had been unwise in her choice of tenants. The couple was soon arguing on a regular basis. John was especially moody and disgruntled. The ex-marine was now wearing the white cotton uniform of Burger King employees, earning five dollars an hour at the only place in the area where he could find steady employment; and while he was never rude toward Sondra or her sons, he seemed to release some of his pent-up hostility upon the stray cat that Sondra had adopted as a pet.

When Sondra was not paying attention, Bobbitt would grab her cat firmly in both hands and take it outside and shove it headfirst into the sidewalk mailbox. After closing and securing the metal door to prevent the cat from escaping, Bobbitt would return to the house and call out, "Sondra, Sondra—I think you have mail." Unsuspecting at first, and infuriated as he persisted in doing this, Sondra would walk to the mailbox and slowly open it, hoping that she could gently reclaim her petrified cat without being scratched or without it leaping past her into the street and into the path of oncoming motorists. Sondra Beltran was pleased and relieved when Lorena told her, in March 1993, that the Bobbitts would soon be moving out.

Lorena had set aside enough money from her earnings to obtain an apartment in Manassas, which was much closer to her nail salon than was Sondra Beltran's home in Stafford. The apartment was situated within a modern three-story gray frame compound in the Yorkshire area of Manassas. The tenants had access to a swimming pool and an indoor recreation area adjacent to the parking lot, from whose borders small signs rising from the ground read HAVE A NICE DAY. The Bobbitts' dwelling, costing $570 a month, was on the second floor and had a balcony that overlooked the parking lot. It had a single bedroom, and a living room that was within view of the kitchen, which was tucked behind a fixed barlike counter. It was smaller than any apartment that they had rented since the one they had moved into as a newly married couple nearly four years before.

When John Bobbitt learned that a large new restaurant, Red Lobster, was scheduled to open soon on Manassas's main thoroughfare, Sudley Road, he drove over for an interview. Sudley Road predates the Civil War in this town, which had been the locale of the South's two great triumphs against the North at the battles of Bull Run. But Sudley Road in recent years had surrendered to the land developers, and it was now a long garish strip of low-level buildings and a stunted skyline of signs: advertising Pizza Hut, Dunkin' Donuts, Roy Rogers, Long John Silver's, Denny's, T.G.I. Friday's, Taco Bell, 7-Eleven, and Mike's Diner. The developers had all but paved and conquered the nearby legendary lawns where a number of Confederate cannons were on display along with a statue of Gen. Thomas Jonathan "Stonewall" Jackson, who in this city had taken his historic stand. The federal government in recent years had succeeded in sweeping the developers from the battle area, but Sudley Road has long been open to opportunists large and small. One of the latter, John Bobbitt, drove to Sudley Road and applied as one of five hundred applicants at Red Lobster. The female executive in personnel who had interviewed Bobbitt described him in the company's comment sheet as "clean-cut," "well-groomed," "All-Amer type male." Only 20 percent of the five hundred applicants would be hired. One of those was John Bobbitt.

Wearing a white button-down shirt and a maroon striped tie (the restaurant supplied the tie), John Bobbitt was assigned to a cashier's job that showcased his good looks near the entranceway, and held him accountable during an average seven-hour shift for transactions of between six thousand and fifteen thousand dollars in cash and credit cards. After three weeks, a male manager, noting that Bobbitt was "a little slow," offered him a new position as an "allied coordinator." This meant anything from making salads, to garnishing the plates, to assisting the waitresses and waiters in cleaning the tables. At a wage of six dollars an hour, and working approximately forty hours a week, he was earning between $200 and $240. This was fine with him. But business failed to reach management's early expectations, and orders came down to cut the staff and the hours. Bobbitt was reduced to twenty-two hours. He quit this job to take one with a landscaper, thinking he would match his earlier salary at Red Lobster, but he did not. He took part-time work at a 7-Eleven, and also went early in the mornings to unload trucks at the Atlantic Food Services platforms, where his earnings as a lumper depended upon the frequency of the arriving vans and other vehicles. He maintained this routine for a while, but was looking for something better.

Lorena continued as before to be the couple's principal wage earner. Her coworkers at the nail salon, accustomed to her earlier complaints about John, expressed surprise that she had reunited with him. Lorena responded that she was giving the relationship one more try, although she admitted that the marriage had not improved much since their reconciliation. Maybe it was the close quarters of their new apartment, or the fact that John had fallen behind in his car payments (Lorena would not allow him the use of her car), or that Lorena believed that John was spending excessive amounts of time on weekends around the pool, showing off his masterly swimming style and his muscles to the clusters of young females who could usually be found there. The Bobbitts had only been in their apartment for three months (they had not even subscribed for phone service), and already Lorena was hinting to John that they might both be better off if one of them moved out. She had heard from a customer at the nail salon that John was romantically involved with a waitress he had met at Red Lobster. He loudly denied it, which hardly surprised her. Anyway, in mid-June 1993, she told him that *she* would soon be moving out, and he said fine.

He later went out to a coin box to telephone a male friend from Niagara Falls—an engineering student named Robert Johnston, who had just completed his fourth year at the University of Buffalo—and invited him to spend the rest of the summer in Virginia. Johnston accepted without hesitation and said he could drive down on the following weekend, arriving most likely on Sunday, June 20. At twenty-one, Johnston was four years younger than Bobbitt, and had actually grown up with one of Bobbitt's younger brothers. But when Bobbitt had returned to Niagara Falls after separating from Lorena, the two men had spent much time together at night drinking and playing pool. Johnston was a tall, slender six-footer with blue eyes and precisely combed chestnut-colored hair and the same clean-cut features as Bobbitt. He was extremely shy, however, and it was this shyness that had fortified the friendship with Bobbitt. Bobbitt was comfortable with people who in social situations were more uncertain than he was. And Bobbitt knew from their earlier good times together that having Johnston in Virginia would mean more of the same. Bobbitt was also glad that Johnston would be coming down with his car. Bobbitt's vehicle had been repossessed.

Robert Johnston arrived in Manassas shortly before noon on June 20, but his knocks on the Bobbitts' apartment door went unanswered. Later he learned from Bobbitt that he had disturbed John and Lorena while they were making love. Bobbitt had explained that Lorena was a most unpredictable woman—she could hate you one day, love you the next. When Johnston had returned a second time to knock, Lorena had opened the door. "Come back a little later," she told him in an unfriendly manner; "John and I have some things to discuss." Johnston had recognized her from the pretty photograph she had sent to John on Valentine's Day, but at this moment she was carelessly dressed in a wrinkled T-shirt and a pair of shorts, her dark shoulder-length hair was very tangled, and her brown eyes, which had shone so brightly in the photograph, now reflected only her discontent. Johnston immediately turned away from her without introducing himself.

He returned to his car, a black 1966 Mustang that was packed with the things he thought he should have while spending a pleasant summer in Virginia, but as he paused in the parking lot, leaning against a fender, fatigued from a ten-hour trip, he wondered if he should drive off and register for the night in a motel. But when he returned to the Bobbitts' apartment building an hour later, a smiling John Bobbitt was waiting on the sidewalk to greet him and help him carry things out of the car, such items as Johnston's portable color TV, clothing, video games, and a bicycle. John told him that his own bicycle was currently being repaired, having been bent out of shape two days earlier after being sideswiped by a car driven by a twenty-six-year-old man who had emigrated from Laos. John said that after he had been thrown to the street, the driver and a young Laotian woman who was a passenger had rushed to his side and apologized and wanted to take him to the hospital. But he had only a few scratches, Bobbitt said, and he was grateful that the couple agreed to fix the bicycle and return it to him within a few days.

As Bobbitt led Johnston up the steps toward the apartment, he suggested that on the following morning they might head over to the Atlantic Food's loading docks to earn some pocket money unloading trucks; in the meantime, John suggested Robert take a nap on the sofa. But on entering the apartment, Robert saw that Lorena was lying down on it, saying nothing, her face to a wall. There were two cardboard cartons near her on the floor filled with dishes, bottles of lotion, and other items that Robert assumed she was taking with her. John had said on the phone that she would probably be gone before Robert's arrival—but here she was, on the sofa that was to be his bed, and John saying nothing.

Later that night, after visiting a few bars and getting something to eat, Robert returned with John and was disappointed to see that Lorena's things were still in the apartment, and, through the open door of the bedroom, he could see that Lorena was asleep on the right side of the bed. John placed some of Robert's belongings in the closet, and then, after pulling out the sofa bed and providing sheets and pillows, John said good night and joined his wife in the bedroom, closing the door softly.

Robert slept with difficulty that night, and then was awakened abruptly at dawn by John Bobbitt's voice. He was saying repeatedly, "Gotta go, gotta go, gotta go!" Robert shook his head, confused, as John went on to say, "Work, work, work, work, gotta go!" John Bobbitt, already dressed in a warm-up outfit with a T-shirt underneath, continued: "Atlantic Foods—come, come, come."

It turned out to be a very profitable day, with the two men receiving from the various truckers nearly ninety dollars each. After a sunny afternoon around the pool, John took Robert that night to a nearby discotheque called Legends, where John had worked irregularly as a bouncer during the past week. The job was easy, he had explained along the way, consisting primarily of checking patrons' age cards. John liked sitting in Robert's Mustang, admired its low-slung design and souped-up motor sound. They had a few drinks at Legends, went out to eat, and were home by midnight. Robert noticed that Lorena's things were still on the floor, and Lorena was asleep in the bedroom.

The next afternoon, Tuesday, June 22, while John and Robert were out shopping after another morning of work at the depot, an eighteen-year-old Laotian woman drove into the parking space below the Bobbitts' balcony with a ten-speed bicycle tied to the roof. She knocked on the door of the Bobbitts' apartment, and when Lorena opened it, she said, "I'm looking for John."

"He's not here," Lorena said coldly, closing the door.

But as the woman returned to the lot, she spotted John stepping out of Robert's Mustang, and she called out enthusiastically, "John, look what I have for you!" John Bobbitt saw the bike and broke into a cheer. After John and Robert had untied it—it was a sleek racer's model—they took turns bouncing its springy frame along the path of the parking lot, praising the bike's workmanship and style. The young woman stood next to them, smiling. Her name was Dawn—she had been a passenger in her cousin's car when it had bumped into John—and now, she explained, she was offering this bicycle for John's use until his own was ready for her to pick up at the repair shop. She also repeated what she had said days earlier along the highway—how sorry she and her cousin were about what had happened, and how relieved they were that he had been unhurt. She then invited John and Robert to attend a party that she was giving later in the week. John accepted immediately, and, hoisting the bicycle above his shoulders, he exclaimed to Robert, "A party, a party! We're invited to a party!"

Lorena watched from the balcony. Closing the door, she went back to her packing. She had earlier carried the cardboard boxes and her dresses into a lower-floor apartment of a woman she knew named Diane Hall. She said nothing as John and Robert came upstairs, with John placing the bicycle against the railing outside their door and Robert carrying some groceries he had bought for dinner that night, prior to their going out drinking. Although Lorena had slept with John each of the two evenings Robert had occupied the sofa bed, he was still perplexed by the arrangement. He had not included Lorena in his shopping plans. Robert liked to cook. Should he have invited her? he wondered. He thought not. They had barely spoken. And before he had begun preparing the food, she had left the apartment and driven off in her car. But Robert remained uneasy about being a guest in this apartment.

After Robert and John had finished eating, they headed over to Legends. John thought he might be needed later as a bouncer, but the owner predicted a slow evening. The owner bought them a drink—Robert wanted a beer; John asked for his favorite B-52 (a shot glass layered with Kahlúa, Bailey's Irish Cream, and Grand Marnier). Then, after John had spoken with some patrons he knew, he and Robert drove off to visit other bars in the area—O'Toole's in Centreville, and then Champion's and P. J. Skidoo's in Fairfax County.

During the course of the evening, the two men each had three or four more beers and John had a second B-52. Shortly before 1:30 a.m., John and Robert left P. J. Skidoo's, neither claiming to feel the effects of the alcohol but both admitting to being tired. They had risen at six o'clock that morning to unload the trucks. Before returning to the apartment, they stopped at an all-night Denny's on Sudley Road to have something to eat along with a pot of coffee. It was a little after 3 a.m. when they entered the apartment. Robert slipped out of his sneakers, removed his clothing, and tossed his peak-capped Buffalo Bills hat into the corner. John entered the bedroom, where Lorena was asleep. What he would recall days later—when he was physically able to speak with the police about his wife's allegations that he had raped her—was that he had set-tled himself to the right of his wife in the bed, and he vaguely recalled embracing her, and even attempting to remove her panties with his feet. But he insisted that he recalled no struggle on her part—knowing from past experience she was surely capable of scratching and kicking. In other interviews with the police, he conceded the possibility that they had had intercourse; but, again, he insisted that his sexual urges that night had been underwhelming because of his fatigue. He had been conscious at one point of his wife's left hand fondling his penis—trying to get it hard, he assumed. Then, suddenly, a piercing pain bolted him upward, and he caught a glimpse of Lorena, wearing shorts and a T-shirt, racing from the bedroom. She fled past the slumped figure of Robert Johnston on the sofa bed; Robert remained asleep (although he would later claim that she had at some point gone into his wallet and removed a hundred-dollar bill, and that she had stolen his Nintendo Game Boy handheld computer).

Barefoot, Lorena ran down the steps and across the parking lot toward her car. It was somewhere close to 4:30 a.m. She managed to open the door despite carrying the knife in her right hand and, not noticing it at that moment, most of her husband's penis in her left. She had heard him groan as she cut him, and she had sliced him off with one swipe, as adroitly as if clipping a cuticle at her salon.

Driving a quarter of a mile to the intersection of Maplewood Drive and Old Centreville Road, she stopped, and it was then that she became aware of the penis in her fingers. A 7-Eleven store with some lights glow-ing stood across the road to her left. To her right she saw a grassy field. She hurled the penis with her left hand in that direction, over the roof of the car. It sailed about fifteen feet and settled in grass and weeds that rose about ten inches.

Then she turned her steering wheel to the right and sped along Old Centreville Road five miles into Centreville itself, following the route she regularly took to the salon in the shopping center. Parking in front of the salon and getting out, she tossed the knife in a wooden-framed trash can at the curb. Entering the shop, she reached for the telephone, calling Janna Biscutti. But the answering machine responded. Running out again to her car, she drove nearly ten miles to Janna's home, in Fairfax, where her cries and pounding on the door awakened Janna's husband upstairs and brought him rushing to her side. She collapsed in front of him on the living room floor, flailing her arms, sobbing, making no sense. Janna has-tened down in her bedclothes and tried to comfort her, but it took fully ten minutes before she understood what Lorena had done to John. Janna dialed the police. It was 5:20 a.m.

The dispatcher at the police station—who had already received word from the hospital about the arrival of the bleeding John Bobbitt—heard Janna say, "I've got the wife here . . . don't know if she did what she said she did, but she said she cut a piece of his anatomy off."

"Who are you?"

"I'm her boss. . . ."

"Keep her there, and keep her calm. . . ."

"She's *not* calm."

"Well, try to do the best."

"I'm trying as best as I can."

"Yeah, do the best you can. Don't let her shower."

"Okay."

"Okay, don't let her change her clothes. . . ."

"Okay," Janna said, adding, "He's been bringing women to the apartment."

"Okay, just keep her, keep her as calm as you can, and don't let her shower, wash her hands, or anything."

Later, Janna received a call from the county police, this time instructing her to bring Lorena Bobbitt into the station house in Manassas.

John Bobbitt had been cut at approximately 4:30 a.m., and he had never seen the knife. As he jumped from the pain and saw Lorena running out, he felt the flowing of liquid between his legs and was not sure whether it was urine or blood. Staring at the wound, he could not believe it. Nothing was there but an emptiness—he could even feel an "emptiness," he explained after his release from the hospital. "You know, it's . . . sharp, uh, sharp, being amputated . . . then, then the pain's gone and you go mental, like a mental shock, like . . . like you're scared, you're, you know, like, uh, you know, you don't know what . . . what's going to happen. What's going to happen. What's, you know, what do I do next, you know. And I had to react quickly, you know, instantaneous."

While applying pressure into his groin with his right hand, trying to lessen the flow, he reached with his left hand for a gray pair of warm-up pants he had left on the floor and managed to slip them on. He stumbled into the living room, and began kicking at Robert Johnston. "Gotta go, gotta go, gotta go!"

Johnston lifted his head up, frowning, and said, "Okay," assuming that John Bobbitt was getting him up for work at the Atlantic Food Services depot. Johnston headed into the bathroom, and he was brushing his teeth when he felt Bobbitt pulling his T-shirt from behind, saying, "Gotta go, gotta go!"

"*All right*, okay!" Johnston said, and then, turning around, he saw blood coming from beneath the warm-up pants, falling on Bobbitt's unlaced black sneakers, and then Johnston saw the trail of blood that had traced Bobbitt's movements from the bedroom.

"God, man, *what's wrong?*" Johnston said, spitting the toothpaste into the sink.

"Been cut, cut," Bobbitt said. "Gotta get to the hospital."

"Let's *go!*" Johnston shouted, slipping on his sneakers and then helping Bobbitt by the arm and escorting him down the steps. Bobbitt, who was bare-chested, kept his right hand between his legs, and with his left, he opened the door to the Mustang and slipped in while Robert Johnston started the engine.

"Where we going?" asked Johnston, who was still unfamiliar with the area.

"Left," Bobbitt said, pointing.

Johnston motored out of the parking lot, spun the car around, and, when Bobbitt pointed to Highway 28, turned again and was soon speeding through a multilaned and virtually empty street, passing gas stations and fast-food shops with their colorfully lighted signs blazing and flickering in the mist of the not-yet-dawning light of Wednesday morning.

"What *happened?*" Robert Johnston asked, speeding ahead, his hands tightly gripping the steering wheel.

"She did it," Bobbitt said. "She cut me." But he did not say where, being too embarrassed—and still not entirely believing what had happened to him. "How could she have *pulled* it off?" he remembered asking.

"*Left,* I mean, right, *right!*" Bobbitt yelled as Johnston turned incorrectly off Sudley Road. Then, moments later, with the Prince William County hospital in sight, Johnston took another left and headed directly toward the emergency entrance and slammed his car to a stop next to two parked ambulances. Bobbitt ran ahead of Johnston, climbed the steps, and entered the emergency room from a back door not intended for the public. Then Johnston, trailing a few steps behind, began to yell to all the technicians and nurses he saw: "Hey, this guy's wife tried to kill him. Hurry, he needs help!"

"Where is he?" one of the technicians asked, and when Johnston looked around, he could not find him.

Bobbitt had run into the trauma room and then stopped, astonished, as he saw a male patient he recognized—the Laotian motorist who had hit his bicycle on the highway days before. The man's name was Vienkhone Khoundamdeth, or "Khone," as his cousin Dawn had introduced him at the accident site.

"Hey, Khone," Bobbitt said, "what're you doing here?"

"Had a motorcycle wreck," Khone said, stretching up to look at the bleeding Bobbitt, whose trail of blood extended behind him for several feet.

"How you doing?" asked Bobbitt, not feeling any pain. (A doctor later explained that Bobbitt was in shock.)

"I'm going to be okay," Khone said. "What are *you* doing here?"

"Oh," Bobbitt said casually, bending forward a bit, with his hands pressing into his groin.

"Hey, you there!" shouted the ER doctor, Steven Sharpe, entering the room and glaring at Bobbitt. Dr. Sharpe, a stocky man of forty-three, with thick, curly hair and green eyes, was squinting through his small circular glasses at the blood along the floor, "Come here! Let me see your wrists."

"What for?" Bobbitt asked.

"I want to see where you've been cut," said Dr. Sharpe.

"That's not where I'm cut."

"So, where *are* you cut?" asked Dr. Sharpe.

With several medical personnel peeking in and directing their attention toward him, John Bobbitt lowered the pants and heard sighs and murmurings from around the room. The scrotum was intact, but where the penis had been was now a clump of bloody flaps of skin.

"What *happened?*" Dr. Sharp asked.

"I don't know."

"Did your wife do this?" asked Sharpe, who had heard what Robert Johnston had been yelling earlier.

"Guess so."

"Do you need any pain medicine?"

"No, it doesn't hurt."

Dr. Sharpe hastened to the registration desk and called the home number of the urological surgeon, Dr. James Sehn, who resided some thirty miles away, near Middleburg, Virginia.

"Jim," said Dr. Sharpe, "I've got a guy here whose penis has been severed."

There was a pause on Sehn's end of the line. Then he asked, "How much of it is gone?"

"As far as I can tell, all of it."

"Where's the penis itself?"

"I honestly don't know."

"I'll be right in," said Dr. Sehn.

25

SHORTLY AFTER 5:00 A.M., AS POLICE OFFICER DAVID SAWYER WAS slowly driving his patrol car through a wide street in the historic section of Old Town Manassas, passing a gazebo and a bronze plaque marking this as a Civil War battle area, he heard himself being summoned aloud by his identity number (169) on the police radio and was told to go at once to Prince William County hospital to interview and file a report on a "male assault victim" who was currently undergoing treatment there.

But after Officer Sawyer had arrived in the emergency room and then began looking around, expecting to find what he usually found when searching for an "assault victim"—a moaning patient with a lacerated face, puffy eyes, and a bandaged head—he saw instead a handsome and unmarked young man who, seated calmly with a white sheet draped over his shoulders and midsection, was chatting with a male medical assistant and a female nurse as they went about checking his blood pressure and pulse.

"Where's my victim?" Officer Sawyer asked them.

"This is him," said the medical assistant, nodding toward Bobbitt.

"What's wrong with *him?*"

"His wife cut off his penis," the nurse said matter-of-factly.

Misunderstanding her—thinking she'd said "pinkie" instead of "penis"—Sawyer looked at Bobbitt's right hand, then his left, and replied, "His pinkie looks fine to me."

"No, *penis,*" said the nurse.

Sawyer felt a sudden pang in his groin. Then, turning to the male assistant, he said, "Show me the injury."

The assistant lifted up the sheet, and after Sawyer had gotten a mere glimpse of the damage, he turned away. "I nearly vomited," he later told me. After the assistant had put the sheet back over Bobbitt's body, Sawyer asked him to remove it once more. Sawyer was not pleased by his instinctive reaction a moment earlier. "I regrouped, looked at it again, was more professional this time." He asked the nurse to let him borrow a Polaroid camera, and he proceeded to take eight photographs of Bobbitt's condition to be included in the police report. Then he looked squarely into the eyes of John Bobbitt, searching for some clue that might explain the latter's apparent calm in the aftermath of this unspeakable situation, and he asked softly, "What happened?"

"All I can remember is I woke up in pain, and saw my wife running out of the room," Bobbitt said, "and I really can't believe this happened, can't believe this happened. . . ."

Sawyer saw this as a crime fraught with legal complications and pitfalls for those involved in the investigation. It was what the police called a "red ball" case. It was a "he said/she said" domestic donnybrook that the media would feed upon, that would swamp the police department with paperwork, that would demand courtroom testimony in the presence of competing attorneys, and that would surely threaten the careers of any law-enforcement officer who overlooked or misinterpreted even a tiny detail. Sawyer knew that a search warrant would be immediately necessary before the police could enter the victim's apartment, and so he took out his notepad and asked Bobbitt where the cutting had occurred. Bobbitt gave his address: 8174 Peakwood Court, Apartment 5, on the second floor, overlooking the parking lot. Sawyer knew exactly where this was, and he felt a sense of relief. The crime had *not* been committed in Sawyer's jurisdiction! Sawyer was with the Manassas *city* police department, whereas Bobbitt's apartment building was technically across the city line and was covered by the *county's* police department. While the city of Manassas was part of Prince William County, it nevertheless operated independently, and therefore Sawyer should not have been sent to the hospital in the first place.

Meanwhile, two other police officers from the city had arrived to join Sawyer at the hospital. Sawyer had already informed his superiors by radio that the crime had occurred in county territory, and had provided the address, but Sawyer and his two colleagues remained ready to drive to the apartment and begin searching for the penis *if* they were told to do so.

"Officers, we *need* that penis!" one of the nurses reminded them. "The surgeons will be here any minute to start operating."

Moments later a radio message came to Sawyer and his fellow officers from city headquarters: "Do *not* go to the Bobbitt apartment; let the *county* police go—it's a *county* problem." A police dispatcher within the city's headquarters (Robert Weaver) was at this time communicating via radio with the police dispatcher within county headquarters (Carolyn Walls):

Weaver: ". . . Need an officer to respond ASAP to go out to pick up some property that [the patient] needs to have immediately. . . . It's pretty nasty."

Walls: ". . . Has he lost a part of his body?"

Weaver: "Uh, you can't really say over the radio, but . . ."

Walls: "Okay, but I mean, is it a thing?"

Weaver: "Well . . . they have to get that once they get out there."

Walls: "Okay. All right. We have someone en route."

Weaver: ". . . How long for an officer to get there?"

Walls: ". . . Fifteen minutes."

Weaver: ". . . You know how this thing about being in the city, being in the county . . ."

Walls: "Yeah."

Weaver: "It's kind of crazy, but no problem. . . ."

Walls: "Yeah."

After Weaver had hung up, Walls received a second call from the city's police force, this time from Sgt. Beth Weden. "You might want to send out a couple [of officers to the apartment]," Sergeant Weden suggested, and she was less restrained than the dispatcher Robert Weaver had been in describing Bobbitt's injury. "This man's got his penis all cut off," Weden told Carolyn Walls, "and the hospital needs it ASAP to try and salvage this man's dignity."

As three county officers, plus a rescue squad with an ambulance, motored toward the Bobbitts' apartment, hoping to retrieve the penis, three other county officers arrived at Prince William County hospital to relieve from duty the three city officers who had arrived earlier. The city officers greeted them at the emergency entrance, and one city cop announced with a grin, "Oh, do we have a case for you guys! Yes, you've got a victim inside, a Mr. Less. His first name is Richard. You can call him Dick. Dick Less . . . ha-ha."

One of the newly arrived county officers was Cecil Deane, who had been in the hospital a few hours earlier, interrogating the Laotian motorcycle rider Khone, who had sustained injuries in an accident. Cecil Deane was now here for the county police to take photographs of Bobbitt's diminished penis. After the medical assistant had lifted the sheet that Bobbitt had been wearing, and just before Deane had raised the 33-mm Canon color camera and focused it down toward the patient's groin area, he made eye contact with Bobbitt and then asked Bobbitt a question he knew was inane, but he asked it anyway: "How you doing?"

Shrugging and forcing a smile, Bobbitt replied, "Be careful who you date."

While Cecil Deane was taking pictures, his fellow officer Dan Harris was getting permission from Bobbitt to investigate the apartment. Having obtained the key from Bobbitt's friend Robert Johnston, Dan Harris left the emergency room and went outside to hand the key over to Officer John Tillman, who was waiting in a patrol car. Tillman then drove with it a few miles to the Bobbitt apartment, where, joined by two other colleagues, who had been waiting for him in the parking lot, he unlocked the door and began the search for the missing part of the penis.

Stepping around the bloodstains on the beige carpet in the living room, and trying to avoid rubbing against the blood smears on the walls, Tillman led the way into the bedroom and began to shake out the sheets, thinking that this was the most likely place to find what he was looking for. But no such luck. Then he and the others looked under the bed, around the floor, and lifted up the nightstand. Then they went into the kitchenette, expecting, hoping, to find a little piece of flesh near the knife rack on the counter. One of the rescue workers, Mike Perry, ran his hand through the water in the bottom of the washing machine. The others were now in the bathroom, looking in the toilet, in the trash basket, under the sink.

"Find anything yet?" came the radio query from Sgt. William Hurley, who was downstairs in his car, parked below the porch.

"Not yet," said Officer Tillman.

"Keep looking," said Sergeant Hurley.

Tillman and the others continued for another five minutes, searching through the closet, the bureau drawers, under the sofa bed.

"It's just *not* here," Tillman declared to Hurley.

"Okay, then," said Hurley, "come on down and let's look around in the shrubs and parking lot."

It was getting close to 6 a.m. as the men came running down the staircase and began exploring the grounds around the building with the aid of their flashlights. It was then that a seventy-year-old tenant named Ella Jones poked her head outside the front door of her ground-floor apartment and called out to Sergeant Hurley: "Good morning, Officer, what you looking for out there?"

"Oh, we're looking for something somebody might have thrown here," said Hurley. Then he heard his car radio blaring forth with a message: Lorena Bobbitt had just turned herself in to the county police, and she told one of the lieutenants that she had thrown the penis into the grass near the intersection of Maplewood Drive and Old Centreville Road, across the street from a 7-Eleven store. This was only a quarter of a mile from where Sergeant Hurley's car was now parked, and so he and his men were able to reassemble at the intersection within a few minutes. It was daylight now, and while the men wandered around in the fields with their heads down and their eyes intently focused on the ground around their feet—one man was reminded of his childhood days on Easter-egg hunts—Hurley stood somewhat aloof at roadside, trying to conceal the sense of ridiculousness that he felt, along with a certain personal discomfort, at being in charge of a search party that was trying to track down a wayward penis.

Sgt. William Hurley was a shortish, compactly built, dark-haired man in his forties. He had been a policeman for fifteen years, and he was also a born-again Christian and a proper and somewhat old-fashioned individual who disliked being around people who used blasphemous language or told dirty jokes or made smirking or mocking references to lovemaking or to sex organs. It was characteristic of him on this particular morning to refer to the missing body part as an "appendage," and he was chagrined when he heard over his car radio the voice of Sgt. Beth Weden referring to Bobbitt's lost manhood in a jocular and blatant manner: "This man's got his penis all cut off. . . . [Let's] salvage this man's dignity."

Hurley never expected to hear a cop, and certainly not a female cop, talking like this on the police radio network, perhaps broadcasting to hundreds of officers and employees of the department within the 348-square-mile radius of Prince William County. Although he had tried to make newly hired female officers feel welcome in what had once been an exclusively fraternal order, he suspected that some women believed that the best way to gain male acceptance was to emulate unacceptable male behavior. Sergeant Hurley thought otherwise. Which was *not* to say that in his younger days he had not occasionally been indiscreet and foul-mouthed, an admission that he made to me during one of our interviews. But his life had changed radically since he came to know God in 1976, he explained, and as a consequence he gradually stopped swearing, gambling, smoking, drinking, and otherwise acting in ways that had caused his wife, Cheryl, to pack her bags one day and tell him that she was leaving their marriage.

But he had persuaded her to give him one more chance to reform; and he *did* reform, he told me, after he had met a charismatic Christian preacher who recruited him into the Reston Bible Church and inspired within him a righteous vigor that eventually caused him to quit his job as a golf pro and apply for a position as a police officer within the Prince William County correctional system. As he might have expected, the hiring officer conducted a background check and discovered that William Hurley had been arrested six times for speeding and once for reckless driving. But Hurley convinced the officer that whatever appeared on the computer screen was an out-of-date reflection of the born-again man he currently was; and so Hurley was tentatively accepted as a police recruit in July 1978. In the fifteen years since then, he had justified the faith that the officer had shown in hiring him.

Sergeant Hurley was now standing next to his car radio at roadside, listening to the repeated calls from the hospital staff to the dispatcher: *What's the latest report from the search party in the field? How close are they to finding the penis? WHERE IS IT? Time is running out. . . . The doctors are in the operating room. The patient is waiting. The operation will soon begin!*

Hurley watched with his own sense of urgency as his three-man crew rummaged through the grassy intersection, searching without success for the missing appendage. So far, John Bobbitt had been separated from his penis for at least an hour and a half. Hurley wondered how much more time was available before the doctors would have to sew up John Bobbitt without it. Hurley had thought that his men would have found it easily. Bobbitt's wife had said that she had thrown it into the grassy patch at the intersection of Maplewood Drive and Old Centreville Road, an area of only fifty square feet, and Hurley could not understand why his men had not already recovered it—unless the wife's information was inaccurate, or unless a rodent had run off with it prior to the arrival of the police.

It was now close to 6:15 a.m., and, as Hurley's radio continued to resound with the chatter being transmitted between the hospital and police headquarters, he decided to scrutinize the area himself, and so he slowly made his way through the grassy stretch of land with his head bent low and his eyes trained downward, assuming the posture of his golf-playing days when searching for a ball that he had hit into the rough. Within a few seconds, he had spotted it, poking up through the weeds—a curl of white flesh with a reddish tip.

"*Phew,*" he yelled out, holding his nose, "*here it is!*"

As his group hurried over to get a look at it, a female officer named Sindi Leo arrived at the intersection in her patrol car. She was a ten-year veteran of the police department, a short, robust, and round-faced brunette in her thirties, known for her efficiency and self-assurance on the job, and also for her forthrightness in chiding her male colleagues whenever she believed they were behaving in a chauvinistic manner. While she respected Sergeant Hurley's refined and right-minded disposition, Sindi Leo often felt when in his presence that she was being privately judged, and now, as she headed in his direction, she noticed that he was frowning at her. He really doesn't want me here, she told herself (and later repeated to me in an interview); she also overheard him complaining in a low voice to his men: "This is why I don't like women police officers. . . ." She was not entirely sure what he meant, but as she joined him and the others in the field—they were circled around the spot where the penis lay, saying nothing to one another as they gazed down upon this helpless little piece of masculine pride that had proven to be so vulnerable to a woman's vengence—she could well understand it if her fellow officers regarded her arrival to be ill-timed. She had intruded upon a male moment.

But she also had orders to take pictures of the penis as soon as it had been found, and so, without objection from the blushing Sergeant Hurley, she held up her 35-mm Nikon camera and snapped a few pictures of him pointing a finger toward the place where it had landed. After she had finished, Hurley asked that she go to the Bobbitts' apartment and photograph the bloodstained interior, and then deliver the pictures, along with the key to the apartment, to Detective Weintz at the hospital. When she did so, she saw the detective talking to Lorena Bobbitt in the presence of Janna Biscutti. Weintz then directed Sindi Leo to retrieve the knife that Lorena had thrown into the refuse container in front of Janna Biscutti's nail salon in Centreville.

"You'd better hurry," Janna called out to Sindi Leo as the latter walked toward her patrol car. "It's Wednesday. It's trash-collection day."

The penis had by this time been lifted out of the grass by one of the rescue workers, Mike Perry (an off-duty cop who had served in the Marine Corps during the mid-1980s); Perry, accompanied by two other rescue volunteers, hopped into their ambulance and, with sirens wailing and lights whirling, drove swiftly through the early Washington-bound commuter traffic toward the hospital. Shortly before 7:00 a.m., the trio burst through the swinging doors of the rear entrance and one of the men, pointing to the penis contained in a clear plastic bag that was held high by a partner, asked the ER doctor on duty, Dr. David M. Corcoran, who had relieved Dr. Sharpe, "Is *this* it?"

"I guess so," said Dr. Corcoran. Two nurses came forward through the corridor toward Dr. Corcoran, wanting to get a glimpse of the penis, but the rescue men pushed past them into the room where John Bobbitt lay waiting, flanked by his two surgeons. One of them, Dr. James Sehn, had been there for more than a half hour, while Dr. David E. Berman had just arrived. He had gotten there as quickly as he could, but, since his wife was then vacationing with their child at Rehoboth Beach, Delaware, it had been Dr. Berman's duty to feed and walk the two family dogs before departing for the hospital. At approximately 7:30 a.m., Dr. Berman and Dr. Sehn concentrated their attentions on John Bobbitt, beginning what would be a nine-and-a-half-hour-long operation.

Sergeant Hurley was now back in his office, where someone had placed near his desk an ersatz plaque made of silver foil, bearing the inscription "Awarded to Sgt. Hurley—1st Place Winner of the PRT (Penis Recognition Technician) Award." Ignoring it, Hurley sat down and wrote out his report for the daily police files. He had thought about referring to John Bobbitt's injured body part as an "appendage" but then changed his mind, and so in his report of Wednesday, June 23, 1993, he wrote:

Shortly after 5 a.m., a male subject arrived at the hospital with his penis cut off. The subject stated that his wife cut this off as he slept. Shortly after he got to the hospital his wife called to report that she had been raped by her husband and that she cut his penis off after the rape. The wife came to the hospital. As she was in route to the hospital the husband gave permission to search his apartment for his lost part.

We searched the apt. with Rescue to no avail. After she arrived she told us she carried the penis to the intersection of Maplewood and Old Centreville and threw it out the window. After a short search it was located and transported to the hospital by Rescue. As I write (7:32 a.m.), Detective Weintz is at the hospital trying to sort this whole thing out. The success of the operation that is now being performed is very questionable. . . .

Just when you think you've seen it all.

—Sgt. William Hurley.

26

Many may wonder why I didn't leave my husband sooner. Although I thought about it many times the reason is commitment—commitment I learned as I grew up in a very loving family in Venezuela. My mother and father have been married for 25 years and are still very much in love. They taught me to be committed to your spouse for life and that divorce wasn't an option. A large part of my "American Dream" was to be married to one man for the rest of my life. I wasn't perfect, but I was dedicated to our success as a young couple and to make our marriage work regardless of the cost. Through it all, I maintained a strong belief in God and continually held out hope that somehow through counseling and forgiveness, our marriage would eventually be saved. . . .

In the middle of June, 1993, I was desperate. . . . On June 23, shortly after 3 a.m., John returned home intoxicated and I was once again brutally attacked and forcibly raped against my will. . . . Everyone has a limit, and this was beyond mine.

Copyright, 1993, Lorena L. Bobbitt. All rights reserved.
Contact: Paradise Entertainment Corp., Culver City, Calif., 90230.
Alan Hauge, 818/773-1317

THE ABOVE STATEMENT WAS COMPOSED FOR LORENA BOBBITT BY a relatively obscure California-based screenwriter and director who was temporarily serving as her media consultant—Alan Hauge, a stocky, blue-eyed, sandy-haired individual who looked much younger than his fifty years and who flew into Virginia to attend meetings and press conferences with Lorena, dressed in the fashion adopted by many who dwell along the fringe of fame in the entertainment industry: cowboy boots, jeans, a baseball cap, and a leather jacket, in a pocket of which was a regularly ringing cellular phone that Hauge invariably answered in an upbeat voice and with a smile on his face. No matter what he heard on the other end, Hauge's facial expression suggested that he was receiving good news.

He had been introduced to Lorena through an ex-colleague in film production who had become a friend of Janna Biscutti's in Virginia, and in the course of planning Lorena's dealings with the press, Hauge persuaded Lorena to cooperate with him in the writing of a screenplay about her life. Although he had never before written or directed a successful feature, Hauge owned the movie rights to the story of James Dean, the Hollywood star who died at twenty-four in an auto accident in 1955 after being in three notable films—*East of Eden, Giant,* and *Rebel Without a Cause.* It was in 1988 that James Dean's heirs sold the film rights to Hauge because the latter's script presented a more positive image than that of other prospective writers, who tended to focus upon the late actor's alleged drug problems, his rumored intimacies with men, and his natural kinship with the rebellious and lonely characters that he portrayed on screen. But when I first met Hauge in Manassas during the summer of 1993, shortly after Lorena Bobbitt's appearance at her preliminary hearing—and *five years* after Hauge had first won approval from Dean's relatives—he conceded to me that the Dean project was not yet ready for production, although he insisted that it would one day become a major motion picture, and he felt similarly about his future film based on the life and times of Lorena. He further explained that both of these would be shot within a commodious building that he owned just west of Los Angeles, in Culver City. He called his building "GMT Studios," adding that the letters stood for "Great and Mighty Things" and had been drawn from his reading of the Prophet Jeremiah ("Call unto me, and I will answer thee, and show thee great and mighty things, which thou knowest not").

Alan Hauge was a devout Bible-quoting Christian, a man whose statements and comments often aroused my skepticism, although my opinion of him was probably influenced by the fact that he consistently refused to support my designs on Lorena. He did not mind talking to me about his own career, but he had insisted that Lorena stay away from me while she adhered to his plan that she grant early interviews only to *20/20* and *Vanity Fair,* both of which would go public with her comments shortly before her first court appearance in the fall. Displeased with this arrangement, I did everything I could to make contact with her behind Hauge's back, timing my initiatives to those days when I knew he was not in Virginia. I appealed in person to Lorena's main attorney, James Lowe, seeing him on three occasions after showing up at his office unannounced. I tried to pursuade Janna Biscutti to allow me to speak with Lorena in Janna's home, where Lorena had been staying since the incident. I sent letters directly to Lorena and mailed her inscribed copies of my books. But these and similar efforts on my part were unavailing, and moreover, whether Alan Hauge was in Los Angeles or elsewhere, he quickly learned about what I was up to, and when he returned to Manassas, I would hear about it. "I understand you're adding to Lorena's reading list," he said to me one afternoon as we crossed paths near the courthouse. He was smiling, as usual.

I was not sure what to make of him, nor how to deal with him effectively. Quite apart from his wrangler style of dress, he was smoothly cosmopolitan and also indiscriminately congenial, in the manner that many ministers exhibit when greeting their parishioners after Sunday services. And yet with all his tactfulness and bonhomie, Hauge remained stubbornly unpersuadable as far as I was concerned, and his attitude contrasted greatly with the cooperation I was receiving from the gentleman who was handling John Bobbitt's publicity. With John Bobbitt, I had as much access as I desired—a privilege that I appreciated, though it was very time-consuming due to Bobbitt's tendency to repeat himself.

John Bobbitt's media consultant, Paul Erickson, was a lean and loquacious bachelor of thirty-two, who dressed conservatively and had earned a degree in economics from Yale University in 1984. Erickson stood six feet four inches and had curly dark hair receding at the crown and deep-set brown eyes that seemed to reflect intensity whether he was devoting himself to his professional responsibilities or to such favorite pastimes as skydiving, downhill skiing, swimming, and playing jazz on his saxophone. Among his businesses was a real estate development firm that he operated out of his office in Washington, D.C., and, on a short-term basis, he participated in a variety of other endeavors, sometimes assisting political candidates who shared his views as a Republican. During the first five months of 1992, Erickson served as the campaign manager for Pat Buchanan as the latter sought the party's presidential nomination. In the summer of 1993, much to Erickson's surprise but soon with the realization that this was another kind of politically driven event, Erickson was working to enhance the public image of John Bobbitt.

Erickson first became involved with John through a business associate who was friendly with one of Bobbitt's surgeons and had asked Erickson to recommend a law firm that might defend the recuperating ex-marine against the charge of sexual abuse being instituted by Lorena. Erickson knew many attorneys in and around Washington (he himself, though he had never practiced law, had received a law degree from the University of Virginia in 1988), but he did not begin to solicit counsel for Bobbitt until he had gone to Manassas and queried Bobbitt extensively about what would most likely be debated in court. Erickson had not been predisposed toward John Bobbitt prior to their meeting; on the contrary, the pretrial media coverage had inclined Erickson toward Lorena's perspective. Her life with John Bobbitt must have been intolerable, Erickson had thought; she was married to a dangerous man and had little choice but to defend herself.

But after Erickson had listened to John Bobbitt's side of the story—and had spent time as well with other people who were familiar with the couple during their four-year marriage—Erickson concluded that Lorena's version was self-serving and far from the whole truth. Erickson then got in touch with a female attorney in Alexandria who had been among his classmates in law school; she, in turn, introduced him to a partner in her firm, a soft-spoken slender and tweedy man of forty-six named Gregory Murphy, who had also earned his law degree at the University of Virginia. Murphy was a litigator with broad experience in both criminal and civil matters—international drug trafficking, defense contractor frauds, patent infringements, bankruptcies, divorces, and real estate closings, and he had once successfully defended a bull-breeding farm engaged in a legal dispute over the sperm rights to a dead animal that had been touted as a potentially valuable progenitor. After the judicial ruling, Gregory Murphy's clients presented him with a memento of his victory—a brown walking stick formed from the lacquered skin of a bull's penis. Murphy kept it in his office and, when Erickson came to see him, Murphy amusingly explained what it was; both men agreed that it might represent a favorable omen *if* Murphy decided to take on John Bobbitt as a client.

Murphy was initially hesitant. In the past he had compiled a fine record in court defending women against husbands described as abusive; but now Murphy wondered if he could be equally effective in seeking justice for a husband so described, especially one depicted in the media as a barhopping ex-marine. However, after Murphy had accepted Erickson's suggestion and had gone to meet with Bobbitt in person, he came to believe, as had Erickson before him, that Bobbitt's version had legal merit and might well lead to an acquittal. John Bobbitt had insisted convincingly that he had not raped his wife prior to the maiming, and the doctor who had examined Lorena's body at the hospital after the incident had reported finding no sign of physical trauma or recent intercourse. Lorena had also remained calm during the examination, the doctor stated in his report, demonstrating none of the hysteria that he usually observed when in the presence of women complaining of rape. Lorena's grievances at that time seemed to have focused more on what she described as John Bobbitt's deficiencies as a lover—". . . he doesn't wait for me to have an orgasm," she had said in that tape-recorded interview with Detective Peter Weintz after surrendering to the police. "He's selfish. . . . I don't think it's fair. So I pulled back [the] sheets. Then I did it."

Gregory Murphy and others on his legal staff worked throughout the summer and fall of 1993 to prepare for John Bobbitt's defense. They verified the facts that would be offered in court. They deposed several people who might be summoned to testify. They also coached Bobbitt as much as possible, in the hope of improving his communication skills before he was required to speak in the presence of a jury. Paul Erickson, meanwhile, continued to serve as Bobbitt's media consultant, although neither Erickson nor Murphy believed they could do much before the trial to offset what they judged to be Lorena's public-relations advantage. They saw the press as overly receptive to publishing articles containing feminists' statements linking Lorena's case to the national campaign on behalf of battered wives, and Lorena had additional backing from well-organized groups of Latin Americans in Virginia, Maryland, and Washington, D.C.—many of whom had been encouraged to rally behind her by the region's Spanish-language radio station WILC, whose manager had been petitioned by Alan Hauge at the suggestion of Lorena. (Lorena also had an idea on who might play her in the movies if Hauge could get their film project produced: Marisa Tomei, the dark-haired actress whom Lorena saw as closely resembling herself, and whose lively performance in the recently released *My Cousin Vinny* Lorena had seen and admired.)

The fact that Hauge had arranged for Lorena's forthcoming appearance on *20/20* and in the pages of *Vanity Fair* did not preclude Paul Erickson from seeking similar outlets for his client. The television show and the magazine writer would have welcomed giving John Bobbitt a chance to present his viewpoint; but Erickson had ruled against it. After I had called his office and had left a message questioning his decision, Erickson faxed me with his explanation: "John lacks the verbal or mental skills to become either an articulate champion or a martyr. And if he attempted either role and failed, he would almost certainly doom his criminal defense in the process. We as outsiders have no right to require of John that he spend ten to twenty years of his life in a futile attempt to write 'Letters from a Manassas Jail' about a struggle that is beyond his comprehension, though symbolically connected to his anatomy." Erickson went on to say that while Alan Hauge might aspire to transforming Lorena Bobbitt's image into that of Rebecca of Sunnybrook Farm, Erickson himself believed that she was motivated by a "psychopathic personality." "Psychopathic behavior is extremely rare among women," Erickson conceded.

> While fully 5% of the adult male population of the U.S. is psychopathic, considerably less than 1% of the adult female population can be so diagnosed. The severity and uniqueness of this attack, however, certainly makes Lorena a prime candidate for review. You will have noticed that I have ignored any explanation of Lorena's behavior attributable to the "battered wife syndrome." This is because in my opinion the facts of the case do not support such a conclusion. Lorena was not in imminent and continuing danger of extreme physical harm; there was no triggering event the morning of the attack sufficient to have caused a sudden and unusually violent response. . . . Lorena was almost certainly a jealous wife, but was not in any extreme sense a battered one.

Erickson theorized further that Lorena's South American temperament combined with her cultural folklore suggested to her that penis severing is an appropriate response to male abandonment or infidelity.

Although I had never visited Lorena's native country of Ecuador and was certainly unqualified to comment on the "penis-severing" tendencies of its women, I believed that Erickson's last statement was absurd—and yet months later, from the Ecuadorean capital of Quito, the Associated Press reported:

> A feminist organization Friday threatened to castrate 100 Americans if Ecuadorean-born Lorena is given a sentence for cutting off her husband John's penis in June, in an apparent bid to halt his alleged sexual abuses. . . . The National Feminist Association of Ecuador made the threat in telephone calls to several local news media. The association also organized a protest demonstration at midday Friday outside the U.S. Consulate in the port city of Guayaquil, 170 miles southeast of Quito. About 100 people bearing signs branding the case as racist shouted slogans in support of Lorena Bobbitt and collected signatures in solidarity. Mrs. Bobbitt was born in the small southern town of Bucay, where her relatives have held religious services to pray for a favorable verdict.

Unrelated to the Bobbitt episode—but how could I be sure?—would be a later remark made by Nobel Prize–winning author Gabriel García Márquez, who, while in Mexico attending an international congress on the Spanish language, pointed out that in Ecuador there were no fewer than 105 words for the male sexual organ, many of which were unknown in Spain. His statement, reported in the *New York Times*, offered no explanation as to why.

27

Wᴴᴇɴ I ꜰɪʀꜱᴛ ᴡᴇɴᴛ ᴛᴏ Mᴀɴᴀꜱꜱᴀꜱ ꜰᴏʀ *Tʜᴇ Nᴇᴡ Yᴏʀᴋᴇʀ* ɪɴ July 1993, it was understood that the "marital sexual abuse" case against John Bobbitt would go before a jury in September and the "malicious wounding" case against Lorena Bobbitt would be heard in November. Although nearly two hundred members of the media hoped to attend these two events in a building where the largest courtroom could accommodate only forty-two spectators, I had been promised a good seat by an important county official whom I had cultivated shortly after my arrival in Virginia—an individual who claimed to have read and admired my book about the Mafia (*Honor Thy Father*) and who soon became my frequent dinner guest at the most expensive restaurant in Manassas.

But a few days before the first trial was supposed to begin, the judge announced a delay, doing so at the request of the prosecutor's office. It seemed that a key witness for the prosecution, a forensic scientist who had been asked to analyze microscopically some of the evidence that the police had collected earlier in the Bobbitt couple's bedroom, would be unable to testify during the period set aside for the first trial; and so the judge postponed this trial until November, and moved Lorena's trial to January 1994.

I was not happy with this, for it changed my approach to the article that was due in September. I had thought of beginning my piece with a description of the crowded courtroom on the opening day of the first trial, and I had foreseen my lead concentrating on Lorena Bobbitt as she took the witness stand and began testifying against her husband, who would be seated at the defense table just ten feet away. Among the spectators in court would be members of his family from Niagara Falls who had stalwartly assisted him since the incident: his foster parents, his brothers and sisters-in-law, his uncles, his aunts, and his twenty-six-year-old cousin, Todd Biro, who had been in the recovery room in June on the day after the cutting, and had asked aloud, "What do you want us to do, John?" Todd Biro had already let some family members know what *he* had in mind. He had favored personal retaliation. He had seen himself stalking Lorena through the streets of Manassas and, as quickly and privately as possible, doing away with her. But John Bobbitt, lying on his back in the hospital bed, had turned toward his cousin and said, "Todd, don't do anything."

I had learned of this exchange during one of my midsummer interviews with John Bobbitt, and I had been surprised that he had favored restraint rather than revenge against his wife after what she had done to him on the previous day. But a week before his scheduled trial in September, his comments to me about Lorena were decidedly hostile, and I guessed that he was aggravated as well by the possibility that the jury might decide the case in her favor. If found guilty, John Bobbitt could be sentenced to prison for as many as twenty years.

But no matter what the jury might conclude, nor how the trial itself might proceed, I was looking forward to writing about it, centering my entire story within the courtroom, the one place that would draw to it all the individuals who were involved in the trial tangentially or directly—the feuding couple, their attorneys, their consultants, their supporters, their debunkers, their deliberators, the judge, and the media. I was particularly eager to hear in person the testimony of Lorena, whom Alan Hauge had prevented me from interviewing, but whose appearance in court would provide me with my first view of her in the same room with her husband. I would be able to observe and report upon whatever discomfort they brought to each other, and they would both undoubtedly be pressured by each other's attorneys during cross-examination. If all went according to plan, I would get my article in print days before Lorena's appearance on *20/20* (to be aired on Friday night, September 24) and the soon-to-follow interview with Lorena in *Vanity Fair*.

However, the judge's postponement of the first trial meant that I could not use the courtroom as my locale *if* I was to meet my deadline and deliver the piece to Tina Brown's office in time to be included within the issue that would be on the newsstands on Monday, September 20. And so I worked long hours in my motel room organizing my notes and then began writing what would be a ten-thousand-word article entitled: "Incident in Virginia." It began with an excerpt from a French novel that I had read years ago (the aforementioned *Germinal* by Emile Zola), and this was followed by a quotation from the statement that Lorena Bobbitt had made to Detective Peter Weintz on the day of the cutting.

Incident in Virginia
by Gay Talese

Mouquette was already unfastening and drawing off the trousers, while the Levaque woman raised the legs. And mother Brulé, with her dry old hands, separated the naked thighs and seized this dead virility. She took hold of everything, tearing with an effort which bent her lean spine and made her long arms crack. The soft skin resisted; and she had to try again, and at last carried away the fragment, a lump of hairy and bleeding flesh, which she brandished with a laugh of triumph.

"I've got it! I've got it!"

Shrill voices saluted with curses the abominable trophy.

"Ah! swine! you won't fill our daughters any more!"

Zola, "Germinal" (1884)

"He didn't care about my feelings. . . . He always has orgasm, and he doesn't wait for me to have an orgasm. He's selfish. I don't think it's fair. So I pulled back [the] sheets. Then I did it."

From Lorena Bobbitt's taped statement to Det. Weintz, Manassas, Va., June 23, 1993.

This week, the nation that officially abhors sex and violence but can never get enough of it, may be further indulged by the televised tale-bearing of the miserably-married Mrs. Lorena Bobbitt, who, after claiming to have been sexually abused in her marital bed by her ex-Marine husband, extracted her revenge in the form of a red-handled twelve-inch kitchen knife (bought at the Ikea home products center in Woodbridge, Virginia) with which she severed two-thirds of her dormant spouse's penis, whereupon she fled with it in her car for a quarter of a mile before tossing it along the roadside and driving on to the home of a woman who employs her as a manicurist.

That the husband would not only survive the experience but would have his penis retrieved and reattached less than ten hours later by two surgeons in a nearby hospital, are events perhaps no more remarkable than the fact that Mr. and Mrs. Bobbitt would soon each sign separate agreements with media consultants eager to sell their conflicting versions to the entertainment industry. . . . This century that came of age with Dr. Freud and his notions of penis envy, might end with an unenvied ex-Marine and his malfunctioning member serving a twenty-year prison term for abusing his knife-wielding wife.

. . . As women in times past have been accused of being witches and seductresses, traits that many pious men believed were cultivated in the Garden of Eden, it has since become common to blame men for whatever woes women complain about, and to see (if not actually to seize upon) the penis as the problem. Why else would the women in Zola's novel feel compelled to pluck it from the body of the late and avaricious Monsieur Maigrat, a shopkeeper who had been withholding bread during the post-Revolutionary class struggle? Did he not deserve to have that evil extension of his personality sundered and stuck on a stick by Mother Brulé, to be paraded amid the gleeful cries of women denouncing it as an "evil beast"? Was not Mrs. Bobbitt a similarly enraged and oppressed person when she removed, if only temporarily, that male weapon that Lawrence in *Lady Chatterley's Lover* acknowledged to be "the terror of the body," making men incapable of having "a proper reverence for sex"?

If these ruminations seem irrelevant to the upcoming cases concerning the Bobbitt couple, it should be noted that the Virginia prosecutor, Paul Ebert, who will be directing the cases against both the husband and wife, remarked on August 4 to the many reporters covering Mrs. Bobbitt's preliminary hearing: "I've never seen a case draw as much attention . . . if she'd cut something else off, or had she killed him, I doubt you'd all be here today. . . ."

My article went on to describe the family background of John and Lorena Bobbitt: how they met, why they married, the marital incompatibility that prompted a series of 911 calls to the police, and finally to the morning of the mutilation. I was not displeased with the article that I faxed into Tina Brown's office on Thursday morning, September 9, but I was then so tired after writing all night that my satisfaction was probably derived from having met my deadline. It reminded me of my youthful days as a daily journalist, writing under pressure, doing my best, while realizing that I was capable of doing better had there been more time. After I had sent in my final page, I called the telephone operator at my motel, requesting that calls to my room be withheld. I wanted and believed that I had earned the right to sleep undisturbed for the remainder of the morning and into the afternoon.

When I woke up, it was nearly 4:00 p.m. I noticed an envelope tucked under the door. It contained a faxed letter from Tina Brown.

Dear Gay:

I just tried calling you on the phone but the receptionist said you were not taking calls, and since I have to go out for a couple of hours I wanted to get my thoughts down clearly, since I know the time and energy that has gone into this piece.

Alas, I think it might have been an impossible assignment after all. . . . Perhaps because you did not have access to the wife, or perhaps because the Marine is simply a dull, dim-witted guy. . . . I do not feel I know any more about this couple than I did after reading the newspapers. . . . My instinct is that this might wind up as your own initial layout of the material for something you would then go on to develop and explore in a book. . . .

I was disappointed in the extreme. I had not only blown an opportunity to be published in *The New Yorker* but I had let down the editor who had in the past often professed admiration for my work, and on this occasion it had been me who had failed to fulfill a story idea that had been of my own choosing. Yet I believed that there was *still* time for me to redeem myself, so I immediately faxed her back:

Dear Tina:

Would you let me try a revised version, with the hope of getting it into the September 20 edition? . . . Even if it's just ten pages long, a pre-trial piece on the themes we've talked about and what this couple represents about the U.S.A. today, and that we don't read about much. You say that you've learned little that you hadn't heard before—well, you heard most of it from me! And nobody but me has gotten access to the emasculated male, a contemporary symbol . . . a part of the White Ghetto we don't read about—the tattooed white trash from inner cities who escape to places like the U.S. Marines (where they get discipline/macho status/financial security; but then, after they're discharged, often end up like him, working at Burger King, 7-Eleven, etc.).

What's the angle on her? She's a Mall Girl, a Material Girl, an ambitious Latina who saw him as a Marriage to America, to the Green Card, etc. . . .

The following morning, this came from Tina Brown:

Dear Gay:

I brooded on what you said all the way to the office and I think it will be absolute madness for you now to try to do a short and skimpy column from this piece. You will expend more pain and no gain. . . .

Best, Tina

A fortnight later, still thinking that I could salvage the situation, I accompanied John Bobbitt to his foster parents' home in Niagara Falls and joined several family members on Friday night, September 24, to watch *20/20*. Before the program began, John Bobbitt had predicted that his wife would have tears in her eyes as she complained to the ABC correspondent about her marriage, and this turned out to be true. But I thought that she had probably gained considerable sympathy from the TV audience, and I myself responded favorably to a shot showing her seated on an upholstered chair in Janna Biscutti's living room, presumably reading a hardcover book that she held open in front of her. A close-up camera view of the book's title was clearly shown on the screen. It was *Unto the Sons*, one of my books that I had sent her.

Dear Tina:

I spent the weekend in Niagara Falls, New York, in the home of John Bobbitt and his family watching the ABC-TV *20/20* show in which Lorena Bobbitt told the nation what an awful man and husband he was; and by the reaction of John Bobbitt and his kin in their living room as the ABC-TV show was going on, I think I have a good scene . . . many scenes to be included in this forthcoming piece I have in mind. . . .

With the John Bobbitt trial (for "abuse") coming up on November 8, it might not be a bad idea to get into print just before that trial. This will allow me to make full use of my research, dealing with what the reading public does not know, even from the Lorena Bobbitt cooperation with ABC and the piece in *Vanity Fair*. . . .

Finally, on October 5, Tina Brown ended our correspondence about the Bobbitts.

> Dear, dear Gay,
> . . . I have come to feel that we should really kiss off this penile saga and have you do something more rewarding. In a strange way the exposure has told me all I need to know and the success of the piece now depends on so many undefinables that may not be gettable—the luck that one of these dreary and incoherent people will be worthy of dramatic rendition or that somehow you will turn up some psychological rosebud that will justify our voyeuristic involvement or that we can somehow strain to make this a metaphor for a war between the sexes, etc., etc. . . . . Hell, Gay, it's just too hard. . . . Let's try and dream up something else more worthy of your energies.
>
> Best, Tina

In a gesture of generosity that sweetened to a degree Tina Brown's decision, she did permit me to attend the trials as a correspondent for *The New Yorker*. Although I did not tell my journalistic colleagues in Manassas that my assignment had been terminated, I now felt differently about myself as I sat in the courtroom each day among members of the working press. I sensed that I was now more an observer, less a reporter. I listened carefully to the proceedings, but I rarely took notes. I knew that if I someday wanted to describe the trials in a book of my own, as Tina Brown had suggested, it would be relatively easy for me to obtain all the transcripts and to go back and read old newspaper clippings that had dealt with the trials.

The "marital sexual abuse" case against John Bobbitt began on the early afternoon of Monday, November 8, after a morning in which many prospective candidates for jury selection had been interrogated and had finally been reduced to the required number. Nine jurors were women; three were men. This did not augur well for John Bobbitt, it seemed to me, but I would be proved wrong. After a three-day trial, during which much of Lorena's testimony was perceived by the jury to be contradictory and unconvincing—the female jurors were especially doubtful about the trustworthiness of her recollections—John Bobbitt was acquitted.

His foster mother, seated in the front row, suddenly leaped to her feet after the foreman's announcement and cried out, "Oh, *yes!*" John Bobbitt stood up, pumped his fist in the air, then turned to embrace his attorney, Gregory Murphy. The prosecutor, Paul Ebert, expressed disappointment. "I believed her," he said at a news conference. He had little doubt that

Lorena had been raped, he reiterated, but he also believed "that what she did in response was not justified." Lorena, who had gone home during the jury's four-hour deliberation, received the news via a cell-phone call made from outside the courtroom by Janna Biscutti. Lorena had listened quietly, and then began to cry. Her media consultant, Alan Hauge, had no comment for the press, although the ruling had all but negated his chances of obtaining enough money to finance a film built around Lorena's personal story. Such a project had been predicated on the assumption that Lorena's character would be presented heroically— a woman who had justifiably defended herself against a rapist husband, and such a characterization of John Bobbitt could now be refuted by his lawyer in light of the acquittal.

The acquittal had come about, according to one juror whom I interviewed after the trial, because the jury had placed a lot of faith in the physician who had testified that he had found no sign of forced sex when he had examined Lorena at the hospital. Another juror had further explained, "If someone had heard her scream, or if there had been some sort of bruising, that would have been more substantive evidence." A third juror told me that in addition to Lorena's unconvincing recounting of what had occurred, she projected an uncertain presence on the witness stand—she had not looked directly at the jury, nor at her husband, as she testified; she had sat almost sideways on the stand, using her long and dangling dark hair as a kind of veil within which she cloaked her countenance. She seemed to be hiding from who she was.

Lorena, to be sure, would change all this when she next appeared before a jury at the "malicious wounding" trial, which would begin on Monday, January 10, 1994. She requested that her attorney, James Lowe, bolster the legal staff—he would add Blair Howard and Lisa B. Kemler. Kemler offered valuable advice on how Lorena should appear in court: her posture, what she should wear, her hairstyle.

"Lorena's a changed person," one reporter remarked as Lorena walked into the courtroom with her attorneys on the opening day. "She's completely made over." Lorena's long hair was pulled back in a clip from her face, making her complexion seem lighter, since it was no longer shadowed by low-hanging curls. With a crucifix hanging around her neck, she sat next to her attorneys at the defense table, and, when it came her turn to testify, she made eye contact with the jury and spoke with more clarity and less timidity than she had done at the first trial. Even before she had taken the stand, the opening statement delivered by Lisa Kemler described her as a woman of changeable character and impressionability, a frantic and fearful wife who had been provoked by a horrible husband into behaving horribly. Lorena had been guided by an "irresistible impulse" when she had taken a knife to her husband, said Kemler, a slender brunette who wore a dark suit and directed her comments to the jury in a self-assured manner. "Ladies and gentlemen," she said in conclusion, "what we have is Lorena Bobbitt's life juxtaposed against John Bobbitt's penis. The evidence will show that in her mind it was his penis from which she could not escape, that caused her the most pain, the most fear and the most humiliation. And I submit to you, that at the end of this case, you will come to one conclusion—and that is that a life is more valuable than a penis."

Disagreeing with all this, of course, was the fifty-six-year-old prosecutor, Paul Ebert. He had lost the first case to John Bobbitt, and, making every effort not to lose again, he made good use of a blond and articulate thirty-five-year-old female attorney who worked in his office, Mary Grace O'Brien, who responded to Lisa Kemler's statement with one of her own. "This is not about self-defense," said O'Brien. "It is not about insanity and most certainly it is not about a choice between a life and a penis. This is a case about anger. It is a case about revenge. And it is a case about retribution." Taking a step toward the defense table and casting her blue eyes down upon Lorena, Ms. O'Brien said sharply, "What *she* did cannot be excused, it cannot be condoned, and it cannot be justified!"

During the eight-day trial, forty-two witnesses were summoned to testify before a jury that was made up of seven women and five men. One of the witnesses for the defense was a Continental Airlines flight attendant in his late twenties named Michael Dibblee, who, with his girlfriend, a United Airlines flight attendant, had been renting an apartment next door to John and Lorena Bobbitt at the time of the incident. Dibblee had returned home after an international flight on the evening of June 22. After sleeping for a few hours, he had been awakened before dawn by what he thought were the sounds of sexual activity coming from the Bobbitts' bedroom on the other side of the wall.

Dibblee was accustomed to hearing people having sex, often being registered in hotel rooms next to them when on extended trips away from home—and, thanks to Nytol, he usually managed to get his rest even amid the resounding rhythm of a headboard hitting against the wall within an adjacent room, set in motion by a copulating couple. But the sounds coming from the Bobbitts' bedroom in the early-morning hours of June 23 were "different from anything I'd heard before," he said in a pretrial deposition and in interviews with the press. He explained that Lorena had been "screaming" in a manner that told him she was experiencing little pleasure and much misery. It was possible that she was being molested.

Michael Dibblee was, therefore, a potentially valuable witness in Lorena's defense. He could lend credibility to her claim that her husband had raped and brutalized her on the morning of June 23. In the first trial, the jury had disbelieved her, in part because there had been no reports of screaming or sounds of a struggle coming from the Bobbitts' apartment before the cutting. Dibblee's failure to make his information known in time for use in the first trial had not helped the cause of the prosecutor, Paul Ebert. When Ebert later asked Dibblee why he had not told the police about the screaming when they had interrogated him shortly after the incident, Dibblee replied that he was not asked if he had heard anything; they had mainly seemed interested in his impressions of the Bobbitt couple, and, since he traveled so much, Dibblee could only say that he knew little about his next-door neighbors. He would greet Lorena from time to time on the staircase they shared, or in the parking lot, and he would sometimes see John Bobbitt at the pool, swimming, sunbathing, or trying to flirt with some of the young female bathers, including on one occasion Dibblee's own girlfriend, who responded to Bobbitt with immediate indifference.

Taking the witness stand at Lorena's trial, Dibblee explained to one of the defense attorneys, James Lowe, that he had flown in from Paris on the evening of June 22 and was fatigued as he arrived at his apartment and had soon gone to bed. His girlfriend, Lorna, was already asleep.

"Now, on the morning of 23d June, did you hear anything?" asked James Lowe.

"Yes, sir, I did," said Dibblee, mentioning that the Bobbitt couple seemed to be "having sex," except that, every few seconds or so, Lorena "would blurt out a scream." Dibblee said his girlfriend slept through the noise the entire time, while he continued to drift in and out of sleep as he tried to reassure himself that what he was hearing through the wall were "just two folks having sex."

"Did you think it was *normal* sex?" Lowe asked, the implication being that it might have been *forced* sex.

Before Dibblee could reply, the prosecutor, Paul Ebert, got to his feet, frowned in Lowe's direction, and called aloud to Judge Herman A. Whisenant: "Your Honor, I would object to *that*. . . ."

"Sustained," the judge said without hesitation.

Ebert sat down, contented, but he still seemed to be rankled by the defense attorney's line of questioning. Paul Ebert rarely repressed his feel-

ings in a courtroom, or anywhere else in this part of Virginia, where he
had been born and reared and where, since becoming the county prosecutor twenty-six years before, he had been recognized as a formidable force
for probity, if not always justice with compassion. A large man with graying blond hair, blue eyes, and the ruddy complexion of the outdoorsman
that he was—his office was decorated with carved ducks and wildlife photos and was strewn with hunting magazines—Ebert had so far sent seven
convicts to death (a record for a Virginia prosecutor), and, together with
his thirteen assistants, he had prosecuted 2,416 new cases during the previous year, which was a 55 percent increase from a decade earlier. An outside attorney named Daniel Morissette, having competed unsuccessfully
against Ebert in a capital murder case, said that Ebert usually "destroys
defendants" during cross-examination.

When it came time for the cross-examination of Michael Dibblee, Ebert
got up from his chair slowly, smoothed out the wrinkles from the back of
his dark suit with his big hands, and ambled over to the witness stand.

"Mr. Dibblee," he began, speaking in a leisurely manner and with a
slight southern drawl, "you said you heard people having sex, and you had
heard similar noises, except this was not rhythmic?"

"As I heard before in hotel rooms, sir," Dibblee said.

"Now, is it fair to say that the other instances you heard were people
having sex, at least they were making noises, loud noises?"

"Yes, sir."

"Both parties?"

"More so the woman than the man," Dibblee said.

"And the woman would be screaming?" Ebert asked.

"Yes, sir."

". . . And would it be fair to say that, from your experience, when
people have sex, they scream?"

"No, sir, I guess it wouldn't be. I'm sure people have had sex in a hotel
room next to me when I haven't heard them."

"But there are people that have sex and they scream, you've heard
that?"

"Yes, sir, I have."

"Now," Ebert continued, "you *speculate* they're having sex, I take it."

"Okay," Dibblee conceded.

"You didn't see them having sex?"

"No, sir."

"You heard screams."

"Yes, sir."

"It was your opinion that these persons were engaged in sexual inter-course where these screams were being uttered."

"Correct," said Dibblee with a casual nod.

"When *you* have sex," Ebert quickly asked, "does *your* partner scream?"

Dibblee's face reddened. Up until this point he had been courteous and cooperative, responding in the amiable manner that he practiced on air-planes; now, however, Dibblee had lost his composure, and, turning toward Judge Whisenant, he asked in a high-toned voice almost trem-bling with indignation, "Sir, do I have to answer *that*?"

"If it please the Court," Ebert interrupted, "*he's* the one who brought this up."

The judge agreed with Ebert, and ordered Dibblee to respond.

". . . On occasion," Dibblee said sheepishly.

"*What's that?*" asked Ebert, as if unable to hear.

"On occasion, I would say."

"Every time?"

"No, sir," Dibblee said, shifting on the stand, "not *every* time."

"And do you *force* your girlfriend to have sex?"

"No, sir, I do *not*!" Dibblee declared.

"But she screams whether you force her or not?"

"Is this *arousing* to you that you're asking me these kind of questions?" Dibblee asked, glaring at the prosecutor.

"What's *that*?" shouted Ebert, unaccustomed to being challenged.

"Is this *arousing* to you that you're asking me these kind of questions?"

"*You* answer my question, sir!" Ebert insisted, and at the same time he gestured toward the judge, who then turned toward Michael Dibblee.

"Mr. Dibblee," Judge Whisenant said softly but formally, "just answer the question."

"Can I hear the question again?"

"The question is," said Ebert, "does your girlfriend scream whether you force her to have sex or not?"

"Your *Honor*," said Lorena's attorney Blair Howard rising to his feet, "I've got to object to this . . . this is totally irrelevant."

"If it please the Court," Ebert said, ". . . it's not *his* witness, and, for that matter, I ask the Court to admonish Mr. Howard and have him sit down."

As Blair Howard sat down, his colleague James Lowe got up to say, "Your Honor, I think we *are* reaching a point where going into his sex life is a little *much* on cross-examination—"

"If it please the Court," Ebert cut in, "the very purpose for this man's testimony is to establish that he heard somebody having sex, although he didn't *see* it. He assumed from the noises that he heard that these people were having sex. And I think I'm entitled to inquire as to how he reached his opinion or conclusion. And *they* brought it out, I didn't."

"All right, sir," said Judge Whisenant, "I'm going to allow that question because that was the purpose on direct examination. He was called and he so testified as to what was going on. There was no objection to that question. Go ahead, sir." The judge nodded toward Dibblee, instructing him to answer Ebert.

". . . Yes," said the crestfallen Dibblee, "on occasion my girlfriend would scream while having sex."

"More often than not?" Ebert asked.

"It varies, sir."

"It *varies?*" asked Ebert. "And would it be fair to say that when you have sex she screamed more often than not?"

"Yes," Dibblee went on, "I guess that would be fair to say."

"Would she scream loud enough for other people as far as you're concerned to hear it in the apartment project?"

"I wouldn't know."

Dibblee seemed to be almost listless at this time. He had entered the courtroom in the morning touted as a strong witness for the defense, but while on the stand he had been embarrassed and humiliated, and, when Ebert finally finished, Dibblee sighed with relief. After the judge had thanked him for his testimony, Dibblee left the courtroom and headed for the lobby. Along the way a reporter for the *Washington Post* caught up with him, and in the next day's story Dibblee was described as "distressed." Dibblee had told the reporter that he was en route to see his girlfriend, who was at home watching the trial on television. The Court TV Network was providing gavel-to-gavel coverage of the daily proceedings. The network had a national audience of approximately 14 million viewers.

The procession of defense witnesses who followed Dibblee to the stand were more successful than he had been in voicing their support for Lorena and emphasizing to the jury that her marriage to John Bobbitt had depressed her, had dehumanized her, and had brought her much physical suffering. Lynn Acquiviva, a customer at the nail salon that employed Lorena, recalled seeing her at work "with extensive bruising" on the top and sides of her head. Another customer, Roma Anastasi, described Lorena as characteristically "tense, nervous, and very sad." A onetime neighbor of Lorena's, Mary Jo Willoughby, had remembered her at times as ". . . hysterical . . . crying, just shaking." The assistant manager at the Bobbitt couple's apartment building, Beth Ann Wilson, told the jury that

"Lorena seemed to be intimidated by John, had a hard time looking towards him." One of Erma Castro's daughters not only denounced John Bobbitt to the jury but presented them with some of the Polaroid pictures that she had taken of Lorena's bruised body in 1991 after Lorena had quarreled with her husband and had sought refuge in the Castro household. These photos were offered in evidence by Lorena's attorneys.

More than a dozen witnesses would testify on behalf of Lorena before she herself took the witness stand on the afternoon of the third day of the trial—Wednesday, January 12. For two and a half hours on this day, and well into the following day, Lorena sat answering the cordially posed questions of her attorney James Lowe, who was hoping to present her to the jury as a virtuous young woman who had been raised in a Latin American family that subscribed to the moral teachings of the Catholic Church.

"What is the family view concerning premarital sex?" Lowe asked.

"My family wouldn't allow it," said Lorena.

"What is the family view concerning unchaperoned dating?"

"My family wouldn't allow it."

"Did you have any unchaperoned dates before you came to America?"

"No, I didn't."

"What is the family view on abortion?"

"My family would not allow it."

"On divorce?"

"My family would not allow it."

"Was there any background of violence in your family as you grew up?"

"No, no."

"How do you believe that differences should be resolved within the family?"

"My parents will close the door or just talk about the matter. Just resolve the problems talking. No yelling, no screaming, no violence."

Her first experience with screaming and violence came via her husband, she said, adding that he was easily infuriated. She recalled a time when she was preparing Thanksgiving dinner in their new home in Manassas during her second year of marriage. Her mother was then visiting from Venezuela, and her husband, John, was sitting in the living room watching a football game on television. Lorena decided on her own to switch the channel to the Macy's Thanksgiving Day parade, explaining to her husband as she did so that her mother would find this program more enjoyable than football. He reacted by jumping up from his chair, shoving her across the room, and then—after he had run out of the house and had climbed up on the roof—tearing down the antenna.

Lorena remembered that John had also behaved wildly and had man-handled her after they had gotten into an argument over what kind of Christmas tree they should purchase and display in their home during the holiday season. He had wanted a pine tree. She had preferred a plastic tree.

"To me, a plastic tree is a tradition," she explained to James Lowe. "In South America, you can't have pines. It's not cold weather. So, I guess it meant a lot to me, because I grew up with a plastic tree."

And how was this issue settled?

"He squeezed my face really tight, and he said, 'Don't tell me what to do,' and he pushed me around," said Lorena. "And he told me again, 'Don't tell me what to do.' And he slapped me and then he pulled my skirt up."

"Did that put you in a mood to have sex?" asked James Lowe.

"No," she said. "I escape. I ran away from him."

James Lowe later asked Lorena to describe the morning of June 23, 1993, when, after her husband had allegedly raped her and had then fallen asleep, she had gotten out of bed and walked into the kitchen.

"I just tried to calm myself down," she said, "and I pour some water from the refrigerator, and . . . the only light that was on was the refrigerator light, and I saw the knife. . . ."

"Do you remember cutting him?" Lowe asked.

"No, I don't remember that. No, sir, I don't remember that. . . ."

During the cross-examination, conducted by the assistant prosecutor Mary Grace O'Brien, Lorena was questioned further about what she remembered from the morning of June 23.

"You don't remember cutting your husband's penis off?" O'Brien asked.

"No, ma'am, I don't."

"It's your testimony that the last thing that you remember was being in the kitchen, holding a knife?"

"Yes, ma'am. I was in the kitchen holding the knife. . . ."

"After time passed, you calmed down some, didn't you, over the months that have passed since then?"

"Ma'am, it's really hard to, even now, go through the situation. I really wish that I could forget about it."

"I'll *bet* you do," O'Brien said sarcastically.

"Yes, ma'am," Lorena said, tearfully. "I wish I could just forget about it. . . ."

O'Brien's cross-examination continued for more than an hour, touching upon many phases of Lorena's life—her girlhood in Latin America; her settling in Virginia under the guardianship of Castro; her working for

Janna Biscutti as a nanny and nail sculptress; her involvement with John Bobbitt and her willingness, while claiming to be a practicing Catholic, to marry him outside the Church ("It was *his* idea," Lorena told the jury). But O'Brien kept returning to the main question in this case: What was Lorena's state of mind when she severed her husband's penis on the morning of June 23? Had she been so traumatized and depressed as to be governed by what her attorneys called an "irresistible impulse"? Or did she attack her husband in a spirit of maliciousness? If the jury found her guilty of "malicious wounding," she could be fined and could serve twenty years in prison. There was no doubt in the minds of Mary Grace O'Brien and Paul Ebert that Lorena had known what she was doing at the time, and had approached John Bobbitt calculatedly and maliciously. "This is a man who was asleep in his own bed," O'Brien told the jury; "he was defenseless." Instead of using a knife, O'Brien went on to say, Lorena should have left the apartment after the alleged rape and gone directly to the police station to file a report.

But the defense attorney Blair Howard differed with O'Brien when it came his turn to speak. Lorena had been unable to think clearly at the time of the cutting, Howard explained as he delivered his closing argument on Thursday, January 20, the seventh day of the trial. "This lady is ill," he said, nodding toward Lorena, who was seated at the defense table, maintaining a posture of serenity as the eyes of the entire jury were now focused upon her. "This lady has been stripped of all dignity, of all self-confidence," Howard continued in a soft voice that invited commiseration. "She's been done in by the man she loved, the man that she tried to be a good wife to, the man she was faithful to. And as a result of all this battering, she needs a lot of help. She needs *your* help. And I would say to you that by your verdict, ladies and gentlemen, you can restore a little bit of self-respect so she can walk out of this courtroom not heaving and crying, but with her head up. It has been a tremendous ordeal. I know in my heart you're going to do the right thing. And that's because justice, ladies and gentlemen, is for all. For the weak as well as the strong. Thank you."

By the time Blair Howard had sat down, it was midafternoon, and although Judge Whisenant had promptly dispatched the jurors into the deliberation room, the day ended without their reaching a verdict. Lorena left the court building shortly before 6:00 p.m., accompanied by her attorneys and her close friends Janna Biscutti, Erma Castro, and the latter's two daughters. Lorena walked out into the cold wind and through the snowy sidewalks toward the parking lot, being greeted along the way by hundreds of Latin American supporters who held up signs reading NO ESTÁS SOLA ("You Are Not Alone"), and they were cheering repeatedly,

"Lo-Re-Na . . . Lo-Re-Na . . . Lo-Re-Na!" She was hatless and wore a dark wool coat, and in her arms she held a teddy bear and a bouquet of flowers that someone had given her. Though she smiled and blew a kiss toward a camera crew, she refused to speak to the press as she slowly moved ahead through the crowd, closely guarded by two police officers and her friends.

"Sometimes women have to take the law in their own hands," I was told by an Ecuadorean journalist who was standing next to me. Her name was Maria Gomez and she was covering the trial for a television station in Quito. "What Lorena did was very brave," Gomez said as we watched Lorena climbing into Janna Biscutti's car and being driven away. Parked along the curbs of the streets around the court building were nearly twenty satellite trucks, and among the masses of pedestrians were vendors selling penis-shaped pieces of chocolate candy and T-shirts bearing the messages LOVE HURTS, and MANASSAS, VA.—A CUT ABOVE THE REST. There had been a press release distributed earlier in the week by the town's information bureau, reminding readers that the Bobbitt cutting had *not* occurred within the city of Manassas but, rather, within the territory of Prince William County.

On the following day, Friday, January 21, the court building's lobby and corridors were once more filled with spectators and journalists who were eagerly anticipating the jury's verdict. Throughout the morning and most of the afternoon the jurors had remained in the deliberation room, reviewing and debating the relevance of the evidence. At one point their discussions became so raucous that the bailiff knocked on the door and requested that they control themselves.

At 4:00 p.m., the jury sent a message to Judge Whisenant, asking him to clarify the meaning of "irresistible impulse." After he had done so, the jury spent another hour in discussion. At approximately 5:00 p.m., they had come to a decision. This information was conveyed by the guards to the reporters and other people gathered in the corridor, and soon they were lining up and making their way into the courtroom, which within seconds was packed to full capacity. With the appearance of Judge Whisenant, followed by the arrival of the seven women and the five men who constituted the jury, the courtroom clerk called out in a stentorian voice, "Members of the jury, have you reached a verdict in the case?"

"Yes," they answered collectively.

"Is this your unanimous verdict?"

"Yes."

"Would the defendant please stand," said the clerk. Lorena rose from her chair at the defense table. She was wearing a black skirt, a white silk

blouse with a crucifix hanging around her neck, and her posture was perfect. Her three attorneys stood close by as the clerk proceeded to read
aloud from a piece of paper that had been prepared by the jury foreman:

". . . We the jury find the defendant, Lorena Lenore Bobbitt, not guilty
of malicious wounding, as charged in the indictment, by reason of
insanity."

Gasps were heard throughout the courtroom. Lorena stood motionless,
not indicating how she felt about the verdict. Finally she turned toward
her attorney Lisa Kemler, who was positioned to her right, and asked, "Is
that *good?*"

"Yes," said Kemler with a slight smile. "You're free."

John Bobbitt had not been in the courtroom on this final day, but his
foster parents, appearing that evening on Larry King's television show,
reported that John was "dumbfounded" by the jury's decision. However,
the executive vice president of the National Organization for Women,
Kim Gandy, applauded the verdict. "We're glad the jury rejected the
twisted argument that a battered woman should be locked up in a prison
cell," she said.

In the next day's *New York Times*, an editorial writer posed the
question:

What are Americans to make of the Bobbitt verdict? Some will pronounce it fair, a justification for revenge against abuse, and perhaps
the verdict will indeed make some abusive men think twice before
they strike again. But violence cannot be the standard answer to
violence.

The Bobbitt case is the story of a violent, sick marriage that went
over the edge. Maybe Lorena Bobbitt was temporarily insane, as the
jury voted. Maybe driven by anger, weariness and suffering, she
knew what she was doing but no longer cared. . . .

I returned home to New York thinking that I no longer cared, either,
although I could not easily discount the fact that I had invested six
months on this story and had little to show for it except for two thick
folders filled with my notes and my ten-thousand-word magazine article,
which Tina Brown had refused to publish in *The New Yorker*. After I had
filed away this material near my desk—labeling it: "The Bobbitts—a work
in progress (1993–1994)"—I thought that I would reread it someday
soon, reminding myself that Tina Brown had said it might be worthy of
a short book.

Years passed, however, and I never got around to doing it.

28

DURING THE ALMOST FIFTY YEARS THAT I HAVE LIVED AMONG millions of New Yorkers whose origins and spiritual beliefs are representative of most of the world's nationalities, races, religions, languages, and eccentricities, I have become closely acquainted with very few of the city's 400,000 residents of Chinese birth or ancestry—a circumstance that I attribute as much to their traditional reticence and insularity as to whatever Oriental wisdom and discriminating taste they may possess in keeping their distance from me.

I have, in fact, become friendly with only two Chinese New Yorkers. One is Dr. Allan Jong, a slender, bespectacled, and soft-spoken psychiatrist close to my age, who practices on Park Avenue and is one of nearly thirty children sired by an itinerant Cantonese merchant who had three wives and a dozen concubines. The other is Jackline Ho, a petite, strikingly attractive, and adventuresome woman I mentioned earlier, who resides near me in a penthouse apartment and also maintains hillside homes in Hong Kong and in the Kona district of Hawaii, and who is often accompanied to dinner parties and restaurants by two men from whom she is divorced—her first ex-husband, a homosexual, and her second, a heterosexual.

Jackline Ho and Dr. Jong had never met, nor had I ever tried to arrange it, believing that what these two assimilated Asians needed least in New York was an introduction to each other. It was not only that I assumed that they lacked compatibility—Dr. Jong was reticent, refined, and sagacious; Ms. Ho was assertive, streetwise, and capricious—but it seemed to me that in their social and professional lives they preferred to associate almost exclusively with non-Chinese New Yorkers, and this was apparently consistent in their choices of partnerships in marriage. Jackline Ho's two husbands, though differing in their sexual orientation, were both American-born, white, Anglo-Saxon Protestants, while Dr. Jong's two wives were both American-born and Jewish.

"He was hung up on Jewish girls," wrote his first wife, the author Erica (née Mann) Jong, in her 1973 best-selling novel, *Fear of Flying*. The main male character in the book (the heroine's husband) is Dr. Bennett Wing, a Chinese-American psychoanalyst who "practically never sweats" and has "long, thin fingers" and "hairless balls" and a "lovely swivel to his hips when he screwed." While I am of course aware that works of fiction are offered as products of a writer's imagination, it nevertheless seemed to me, knowing Dr. Allan Jong as I did, including when he was naked—we often showered together after playing tennis at the Seventh Regiment Armory's indoor club on Park Avenue—that the fictional figure of Dr. Bennett Wing in *Fear of Flying* bore a close physical resemblance to my tennis partner Dr. Allan Jong, whom I knew to have hairless testicles, fingers that were long and thin, a markedly swivel-hipped motion as he ran around the tennis court, and, while he doggedly pursued every shot, he practically never sweat.

I had befriended Jackline Ho about twenty years after I had met Dr. Jong. I had been given her private New York telephone number by her second husband, the heterosexual one, in 1995, three years after their divorce. This husband was J. Z. Morris, the tall and blondish forty-five-year-old land developer based in Sarasota who had acquired 206 East 63rd Street in 1973. He believed she might be helpful to me in what I was trying to write after I had put aside the Bobbitt material in the latter part of 1994, when I had revived my interest in writing a nonfiction novel set within the five-story brick structure at 206 East 63rd Street, which I had privately identified as the "Willy Loman of buildings in New York." J. Z. Morris had gradually converted it into a modern commercial property in which the upper three floors were rented out to tenants using the space for offices, studios, or showrooms, while the lower two floors and the basement were, of course, designed to accommodate a two-tiered dining establishment, several of which had by now come and gone.

During Jackie Ho's thirteen years of marriage to J. Z. Morris, beginning in 1979, she occasionally helped her husband in overseeing the property, not infrequently taking it upon herself (since her penthouse apartment was a few doors away and she was untimidly mercenary in matters of business) to pursue and admonish those tenants who were habitually late in paying the rent. Following her amicable divorce from Morris in 1992—so amicable that he continued to stay with her when visiting New York and was welcomed as well as her houseguest in Hawaii and Hong Kong—she continued to assist him in looking after the old building at 206 East 63rd. What I hoped to get from her for use in my book, which was tentatively entitled *The Building*, was some interesting information about the tenants she had come to know during her years as the rent collector and manager of the property—insights and anecdotes that might add to the research I had already done, and might further enliven my narrative as I sought to describe this place as if it were a multiplex movie house, a five-story structure layered with real-life dramas, comedies, romances, and mysteries. If I dug deeply enough and interviewed enough people, I often reminded myself as I fantasized, I might be able to find here, at this single address, along this shadowed side street in the middle of Manhattan, a story line that would span the entire twentieth century.

I saw my story as beginning during the horse and buggy era of Frederick J. Schillinger, and then advancing into the motorized age of Frank Catalano (who, as you remember, purchased the storage business from Schillinger's heirs and replaced Schillinger's horse-drawn moving vans with trucks), and finally progressing into the period of reconstruction and modernization as personified by J. Z. Morris and Jackie Ho and their diverse and changing cast of tenants, which included a travel agent, a freelance photographer, an engraver, an Italian designer of women's shoes, a Gypsy fortune-telling family, a two-partner law firm, and a procession of restaurant proprietors who never seemed to survive economically at this address for very long. No fewer than nine restaurants had opened and closed at 206 East 63rd since J. Z. Morris had renovated the building. I had patronized every one of them, starting with Le Premier in 1977, and, being sentimental about restaurants and easily pleased as a customer, I was both saddened and bewildered by the frequency of foreclosures.

As I said earlier, my old friend Nicola Spagnolo, the third restaurateur to try his luck at 206 East 63rd Street, had closed Gnolo in the spring of 1985, following an eight-month history that almost led him into personal bankruptcy. The two-floor restaurant space went unrented for the next fifteen months. In the winter of 1986, however, it was taken over by an optimistic and audacious gourmand named Marvin Safir, a cousin of an acquaintance of mine at the *Times*, the columnist William Safire, the latter having added an *e* to his surname because he thought it would encourage the pronunciation he preferred: *sah-fire*, rather than *say-fur*. His cousin Marvin was nearly sixty when he opened the fourth restaurant at the Sixty-third Street address, calling it Moon's because his boyhood nickname had been "Moon." He had previously owned two small praiseworthy restaurants, one on the West Side, the other further uptown on the East Side, but at this point in his life Marvin Safir wanted a more spacious dining interior so that he might rival the triumphant and trileveled "21" Club on West Fifty-second Street, where, as a onetime patron, he

believed he had never received from the proprietors and waiters the deferential treatment known to the man by whom he measured himself: his
late father, Leo Safir, a flamboyant ladies' man and bon vivant who had
manufactured men's robes and been referred to in the garment industry as
"the Bathrobe Baron." Although the decor at Marvin Safir's Moon's imi-
tated the "21" Club (dark wood paneling, gleaming brass appointments),
and although he had hired a distinguished chef who had cooked in the
White House for President Gerald Ford, Moon's restaurant never managed to draw sufficient numbers of customers to support its high overhead
and compete with "21"; it closed after two years, in 1988, having lost
more than $2 million. "The restaurant business," said one of Marvin
Safir's partners, "is an oxymoron."

The fifth restaurant to open at 206 East 63rd did so during the holiday
season of 1988. It was called John Clancy's East, and was an uptown affiliate of the critically acclaimed and financially solvent two-story John
Clancy's seafood specialty eatery that had opened downtown in 1981 on
West Tenth Street in Greenwich Village. The restaurant's founder and
namesake was an introverted ex–U.S. Marine Corps' cook during the
Korean War named John Clancy, who preferred to work in the kitchen
while his extroverted partner, Sam Rubin, stood near the front door,
greeting customers and escorting them to tables. Since the two partners
looked alike—both were tall, bearded, and balding—and since Clancy
continued to distance himself from his clientele while preparing the
meals, most customers assumed that the sole owner and namesake of John
Clancy's was Sam Rubin. After John Clancy had gone into semiretire-
ment in 1984, Rubin did become the sole owner, and, having purchased
the legal use of the trade name, Rubin used it in 1988 when he expanded
uptown with John Clancy's East at 206 East 63rd Street. Rubin had been
persuaded to take over this moribund space that had been Moon's by a
friend and fellow restaurateur named Michael Schwartz, an articulate and
personable New Yorker in his fifties, who had been so sanguine about the
Sixty-third Street venture that he volunteered to underwrite it and to
assist Rubin personally in its operation.

Michael Schwartz had grown up in a family that had long owned and
operated restaurants in the Wall Street area, and he took pride in being a
shrewd investor in dining properties and an experienced administrator in
all aspects of the business. Michael Schwartz's enterprising grandfather
from Austria-Hungary, Sigmund Schwartz, had arrived in New York in
the 1880s, and, as a part-time waiter at a restaurant downtown on Chambers Street, Sigmund Schwartz was known to tell his customers compli-
mentary things about *another* restaurant nearby in which he also worked

as a part-time waiter *and* had a small investment. By 1902, having
enlarged upon his investment, Sigmund Schwartz was sufficiently affluent
to launch his wholly owned Schwartz restaurant on Church Street. In
1927, his son Henry opened a second Schwartz not far away on Broad
Street. In 1967, the grandson Michael Schwartz introduced Michael One
on Trinity Street, and in later years had Michael's on Broadway and
Michael's on John Street.

But after Michael Schwartz had signed a contract with J. Z. Morris for
the sublease of the dining space for John Clancy's East, Schwartz would
prove to be no more adept than Marvin Safir had been in overseeing a
profitable enterprise at 206 East 63rd Street. Schwartz and his partner
Sam Rubin were equally perplexed by this situation, and so was the *New
York Times* food critic at the time, Bryan Miller, whose 1989 review of the
restaurant began: "John Clancy's, one of the best seafood restaurants in
Greenwich Village, recently opened a handsome new branch at 206 East
63rd Street called John Clancy's East. A recent visit found that the fish
have not fared well on their migration upstream. This is puzzling because
the chef, Lynn Aronson, used to run the downtown kitchen. . . ." Defending the chef's cooking at John Clancy's East, however, was the veteran
critic Mimi Sheraton, who in her popular newsletter referred to the
restaurant as "practically what the doctor ordered," and Sheraton added,
"Nowhere will you find a thicker, more delicately woodsy fillet of smoked
trout with a fluff of horseradish-flecked whipped cream or larger, firmer
shrimp served with horseradish and a puree of sweet red peppers. Dill-
scented gravlax, the raw salmon marinated to near translucence . . .
equally good are the little necks, steamed in a good-to-the-last-drop
tomato fennel broth." Still, John Clancy's East was unable to lure enough
customers to sustain itself beyond 1991. In dissolving the partnership
with Sam Rubin, Michael Schwartz recalled a remark made to him long
ago by his late father: "There are no answers in the restaurant business."

The sixth restaurant at 206 East 63rd opened in 1992 under the aus-
pices of a vivacious thirty-nine-year-old black woman named Yvonne
Bell, who was popularly known as "Lola" Bell, and who specialized in
Caribbean cooking. Born in New York City of immigrant parents from
Jamaica, and aspiring to a career as a singer and dancer, Lola Bell worked
during her teenage years as a waitress in order to support herself between
auditions; but since none of her auditions led to professional fulfillment,
she continued to work in restaurants, becoming in time a hostess and
manager of a place near lower Broadway and the Flatiron Building. Here
she cheerfully greeted and seated her customers in a way that made them

feel very welcome and wanted, and she also gained distinction by dressing sumptuously, favoring colorful gowns shimmering with sequins, and light-catching rhinestone earrings and bracelets, and she often covered the close-cropped hair on her small head with one of a multiplicity of stagy wigs. She soon attracted crowds of regular customers, one being the celebrated Broadway dancer and director-choreographer Geoffrey Holder, in front of whom she had once auditioned unsuccessfully. "You don't have to be onstage," he said, referring to her restaurant job. "This is your stage."

In 1985, she attained marquee status in the dining world after acquiring the financial backing to open Lola's at 30 West 22nd Street. It not only featured her specialties—spicy Caribbean fried chicken, shrimp and chicken curry, honey-glazed ham steak with black-eyed peas and collard greens—but on Sundays she added what she called a "gospel brunch." Between noon and 3:00 p.m., while her customers were being served, they were serenaded by a standing group of black men and women who were among her churchgoing choir friends. The fact that the singers received favorable notices in newspaper columns brought in additional customers. But along with the commercial success of Lola's restaurant arose managerial disagreements between Lola Bell and her partners that would remain unresolved, and would lead in 1992 to her departure from Lola's and her acceptance of financial help from Michael Schwartz (who had been among her Sunday brunch customers) to take over the space vacated by John Clancy's East at 206 East 63rd Street. She would rename the place Lolabelle.

She changed the old decor but otherwise infused the dining area with her customary charm and exuberance, her Caribbean culinary specialties, and, on Sundays, her gospel brunch. She also decided to entertain her dinner guests on two or three nights a week with the accompanying sounds of reggae musicians, jazz combos, and vocal soloists. She believed that the possibility of success on Sixty-third Street would be fostered by the presence of live music, and so she alternatively used the second floor and sometimes the first floor as well in featuring Lolabelle as a combination restaurant and supper club. Since she would not be opening the place for lunch on weekdays—none of the five previous restaurants at this address had drawn a large-enough luncheon crowd to offset their midday operating costs—she would be counting on an increased volume of business at night to make a profit after meeting her expenses, which included J. Z. Morris's monthly rent of $14,000, nearly $3,000 a month for the electricity, $2,000 for the linen, $1,500 for the water, $850 for private cartage, perhaps $30,000 to purchase the food and liquor, plus a weekly total cost of about $10,000 in salaries for the kitchen crew and dining room staff. Still, she started out convinced that Lolabelle would soon triumph as an establishment.

It would not happen. Her business began promisingly, but then, slowly but steadily, it went into decline through 1993 and into 1994. The crowds that had patronized her at Lola's downtown did not flock to Lolabelle uptown. The quality of the food uptown was the same as it had been downtown, the prices were the same, the voices of her Sunday gospel singers were the same, but the revenues generated were hardly the same. After a bit more than two years at 206 East 63rd Street, Lolabelle ceased to exist.

Five months after it closed—Lola Bell had meanwhile signed a television contract to anchor a food show—a *seventh* restaurant prepared to make its debut at 206 East 63rd. It was the Napa Valley Grill. It was being financed by a young New York investment banker and food fancier named Michael Toporek, who, having become enamored of northern California during his sojourns in the wine country, sought to transfer some of its ambience and flavor to Sixty-third Street.

Prior to the restaurant's opening, Toporek spent extravagantly on interior alterations and renovations. He sent his workmen inside to knock a square hole through one side of the second floor so that the lengthy tropical plants he planned to hang upstairs would dangle below and be visible to the customers seated in the main dining room on the first floor. He furnished both floors with comfortable silk-covered green banquettes and tables covered with fine linen, as well as china decorated with floral engravings. In the rear of the first floor, next to the door leading into the kitchen, he spent $35,000 on the construction of a seven-foot-high circular brick wood-burning oven. On the sidewalk overlooking the entranceway he replaced the beige canvas marquee labeled LOLABELLE with a sprightly tricolored one that was a blend of yellow, pink, and violet and that spelled out in scripted lettering NAPA VALLEY GRILL.

In a printed statement that was included with the opening-night menus, Michael Toporek explained, "While traveling through the Napa Valley last year and enjoying the fine food and wine the region has to offer, my wife and I heard an interesting story that helped inspire the concept behind this restaurant. We heard that a well-known movie producer has a vineyard in his backyard where he also has a wood-burning brick oven and an open grill. One of his favorite ways to spend an afternoon is to have his friends over, enjoy great wine from his own vineyard, great pizza from his wood-burning oven and fine food from his grill. What we hoped to create here is a place where people could relax, feel comfortable, and have fine food and wine with friends, as if they were sitting in our backyard."

A large crowd gathered at the Napa Valley Grill to attend the opening-night party on March 21, 1995. During the summer and fall of 1995, however, there were far fewer customers being served. And then on a cold day in late November while I was passing the Napa Valley Grill during a midafternoon stroll—only two days after I had last dined there—I saw the front door padlocked, the dining room vacated, and a FOR RENT sign posted behind the plate-glass window. I was startled to learn about the sudden demise of the Napa Valley Grill, for despite its brief tenure of only eight months, it had largely fulfilled my expectations of what a desirable neighborhood restaurant should be. Its service had been friendly and efficient, its food attractively presented, and its maître d' used to wink at me knowingly whenever I walked in during uncommonly busy evenings without a reservation, indicating that he would seat me ahead of whoever else was waiting but lacked my status as a recognized regular.

I immediately tried to contact Michael Toporek at his apartment uptown on York Avenue, hoping to gain his insight into what had gone wrong at the Napa Valley Grill. But he neither returned my calls nor replied to my letters, and I never again caught a glimpse of him walking around in the vicinity of East Sixty-third Street. He was dodging his creditors, I was later told by one of his friends, who went on to say, "As a restaurant owner, Michael made a cardinal mistake—he fell in love with his restaurant. He took five months to fix it up, and spent a fortune fussing over it. Whatever he bought was the best quality, the best workmanship, but when he *finally* opened up his restaurant, he was too deeply in debt to continue to run it. His creditors were swarming into his place all the time, demanding to be paid for their construction work, their food and beverage deliveries, the delinquent utility bills and other charges." I also learned, after calling J. Z. Morris in Sarasota, that Michael Toporek was usually in arrears with the monthly rent, and when Toporek would see Jackie Ho coming in to collect it, he would try to elude her by retreating into the kitchen and then descending via the rear staircase into the basement's wine cellar.

In January 1996, a new group of restaurant investors had arrived at 206 East 63rd Street, and, after they had spent some weeks redecorating the place and otherwise preparing for the opening of the *eighth* restaurant on this site, they removed from above the front door the Napa Valley Grill's tricolored awning and replaced it with a green one bearing the name Tucci. The name honored the northern Italian hometown of the fiancée of the new chef, a New York–born Portuguese-American named

Cliff Pereira, who had met his Piedmontese lady friend, Marguerita, two years before when they were both working in the kitchen of Le Madri on West Eighteenth Street. But the chef's subsequent conflicts with the financial backers of Tucci (a five-man consortium consisting of two lawyers, a retired raincoat manufacturer, and two admen known for their work on the Miller Lite commercial—"Tastes Great, Less Filling") provoked his dismissal in June 1996, a little more than four months after Tucci had opened.

I had met Cliff Pereira a number of times before his departure and had been impressed with his engaging personality. I saw him as one of many media-conscious New York chefs who were consumed with Food Network aspirations. He liked to step out of the kitchen after the final serving and, while wearing his white toque and a broad smile, he would stroll around the dining room of Tucci, greeting the guests and seeking their opinions of the dinners that he had prepared for them. It was my feeling that the restaurant's owners—one or two of whom posted themselves at night near the front door, greeting the arriving guests—would have preferred that their chef remain in the kitchen, where they thought he belonged, rather than making public appearances in the dining room and occasionally taking bows. But there was no stopping him. He was a product of this period in which the media were heralding the restaurant business as a glamorous growth industry and chefs were being extolled as culinary artists with drawing power and the potential to extend their influence beyond the swinging doors of the kitchen. An article entitled "The Chef as Mogul" was published in the *New York Times Magazine*, and it told the story of an ambitious ex–kitchen worker named David Bouley, who at the age of fifteen had washed dishes after school in a Connecticut restaurant, and who at the age of forty-four was a millionaire posing for the *Times* cover photo in the manner of a Hollywood studio magnate, wearing dark glasses and a blue denim shirt and speaking into a cellular phone while reclining in the sun. As the chef and co-owner of Restaurant Bouley, which opened on Duane Street in downtown Manhattan in 1987, David Bouley's exceptional cooking and presentation quickly drew crowds of customers and show business celebrities, the *Times Magazine* article pointed out, and within a few years his place would have a four-star rating and be grossing about $9 million annually.

Food fortunes were being made throughout the 1980s and 1990s not only in New York but around the nation under the personalized leadership of several other "mogul chefs," among them Wolfgang Puck of Los Angeles, Paul Prudhomme of New Orleans, and Charlie Trotter of Chicago. The average American citizen was now eating out about four times a week, and such magnetic New York chefs as Charlie Palmer and Jean-Georges Vongerichten were individually attracting so many customers that each man was prompted to create four separate menus and advise the cooking in four different restaurants under their aegis— contributing to the numerical growth of full-service restaurants in New York from thirteen thousand in the 1980s to seventeen thousand in the 1990s, with a comparable increase nationwide. But as I continued to gather information about the restaurant industry, I kept wondering why, amid so much prosperity and growth and the public's ever-expanding embrace of restaurants as a nightly necessity, there was only continuing disappointment and instability in the restaurants that I was patronizing at 206 East 63rd Street.

What was wrong here? Was this site jinxed, as I had been told by Nicola Spagnolo? Was the ouster by Tucci's ownership of its chef, Cliff Pereira, merely the latest example of the flawed managerial judgment peculiar to this locale that might be called a restaurateurs' graveyard and the catacombs for short-term cooks? I was aware that most of the proprietors and managers of these ephemeral restaurants at 206 East 63rd Street had functioned successfully for long periods of time in other locations, and there was nothing in the outward appearance of this street that would suggest it was unwise to invest here. The building 206 was on the south side of East Sixty-third, just a few doors east of the heavy pedestrian traffic that flowed along Third Avenue, and down the street from Tucci, closer to Second Avenue, was the Bravo Gianni restaurant, which had so far prospered at 230 East 63rd for more than a dozen years, having opened in 1983. Moreover, these two restaurants were the only public dining establishments open for business on Sixty-third Street between Second and Third avenues, which was, in turn, a densely populated residential area lined with high-rises occupied by thousands of potential customers who, it seemed to me, could by themselves sustain the existence of at least half a dozen restaurants on this street alone.

But insofar as 206 East 63rd was concerned, the site was seemingly haunted. Yet I knew from my research that the particular location of a restaurant was irrelevant to the issue of its survival—witness the success of Elaine's. Even more inconvenient than Elaine's, as I mentioned earlier, is Rao's restaurant on 114th Street near the East River, but masses of people nevertheless spend large sums on taxis and limos in order to dine at this small Italian spot that has existed in East Harlem for more than one hundred years and eschews credit cards and even discourages its diners from choosing what they might prefer to order from the menu. The owner's aggressive son, who serves as the maître d', announces the evening's specials in such a persuasive manner that people are reluctant to overrule him. I have seen Mafia bosses being bossed around at Rao's by the owner's son. The restaurant is filled with boisterous people, the juke-box music is too loud, the customers are forced to sit on uncomfortable wooden benches and chairs. And yet getting a reservation at Rao's is diffi-cult even if one telephones weeks in advance. Long-tenured customers have laid claim to all of Rao's tables for every night of the week, no doubt in the spirit of those early-nineteenth-century San Carlo opera box hold-ers in Naples who carried keys that enabled them to lock their seats in an uplifted position whenever they were not occupying them.

Trendiness also has nothing to do with a restaurant's long-term success. There is a staunchly reactionary place called Gino on Lexington Avenue south of Sixty-first Street that has been operating profitably for more than fifty years while dwelling in a time capsule created in the postwar 1940s. The daily menu at Gino features most of the same choices offered by its opening-night chef in 1945, and the restaurant clings to an unchanging policy of no reservations, no credit cards, and no waiters wearing earrings (Gino's waiters, incidentally, are probably the straightest middle-class family men in New York; whenever one of them dies or retires, he is replaced by a waiter who closely resembles him in manner and appear-ance). Unchanging as well is Gino's decor, its preference for artificial flowers, and its tomato red wallpaper pattern, which exhibits several rows of jumping zebras dodging hundreds of flying arrows. Half of the zebras on the wall are shown lacking a single stripe near the tail. Since the neigh-borhood artist who designed the original wallpaper in 1945 forgot to add a stripe across the rump of one of the two zebras that he drew leaping together in the same direction (a sketch that would serve as the prototype for every pair of zebras shown vaulting the length of the wallpaper), *half* of the zebras on the walls at Gino are short-striped due to the artist's negli-gence. Still, whenever Gino is compelled to change its wallpaper, it does so with an exact replica—one that flawlessly renders every other zebra with a missing stripe.

Shortly after the Tucci partnership had replaced Cliff Pereira with a very complaisant chef named Matthew Hereford—Pereira had mean-while been hired to oversee Giorgio Armani's full-service café on the lower level of the designer's shop on Madison Avenue near Fifty-seventh Street—I feared that I had been wallowing for too long in the woes of the restaurants at 206 East 63rd Street. I felt that I was losing perspective as a writer because I had been spending too much time gathering information without pausing to evaluate it. What did I intend to do with all this mate-rial? What was my story?

Since writers often do not know what they are writing until *after* they have written it, I decided in the summer of 1996 to halt my research for a while and attempt to write a magazine article about the problem-prone restaurants of 206 East 63rd that had regrettably become part of *my* problem. Getting something into print might quickly boost my morale, I thought, and also help me to eventually determine what material was worthy of inclusion in a book, *if* any of it was. And so I sat at my desk for several days reviewing my notes and outlining what I anticipated would be an article of about three thousand words. After tossing into the wastebasket several pages filled with sentences and paragraphs that I wanted no one to read, I wrote:

For nearly twenty years in New York I have dined regularly at a neighborhood restaurant that regularly abandons my neighborhood, discharging its employees and bolting its front door in the brick building at 206 East 63d Street, between Second and Third avenues, for various periods of time while dust covers its bar and its owners digest their losses.

Then after a few months, or sometimes more than a year, another restaurant with a new name and new owners opens for business at the same address, using the same kitchen and some of the same old pots but otherwise eager to separate itself from whatever bad tastes or unfavorable impressions may be lingering in the palates or memories of those individuals who have eaten there before. There is a new menu and service staff. There are newly-purchased tables, chairs, and lighting fixtures. The interior brick walls are scraped clean or perhaps repainted in different colors and adorned with new tiles, sconces, pictures, and mirrors intending to deflect any reflections of the past. There are also predictions by the new owners that they will succeed on this spot where their predecessors have failed. And there are veteran diners like myself who, drawn as much by curiosity as hunger, return again and again to savor the varied specialities concocted by the rotation of chefs who since 1977 have found temporary employment within the two floors and basement of this five-story tan brick building that so far has been the locale of eight different restaurants and dozens of partners. . . .

Before I had finished the article, however, I received a phone call from a friend of Cliff Pereira's, telling me that Tucci—which had been in business for barely five months—would soon be sold. I found this difficult to believe, for the restaurant had appeared to be operating at full capacity during the many evenings I had been there, and I now dreaded the idea of putting aside what I was writing and doing additional research. I telephoned Gerald Padian, a thirty-four-year-old attorney who was one of Tucci's five investors. He was unavailable when I called, but he soon got back to me and confirmed that a deal to dispose of the restaurant might be in the offing. He proposed that we get together later in the week, suggesting that he would have more to say at that time.

Among the quintet of Tucci's backers, Gerald Padian was the one I liked the most, and, not incidentally, he was the one who most eagerly cooperated with me in my work, and he also seemed to be genuinely interested in hearing my recounting of the unhappy histories of the restaurants that had preceded Tucci at 206 East 63rd Street. Ever since I had met him at the opening of Tucci, he had been friendly and forthcoming, and, since we were both avid sports fans, we subsequently spent lots of time talking together after dinner while watching Yankee baseball games and other events on the television he had installed above Tucci's bar.

Gerald Padian was born Catholic in the Bronx. He was a solidly built six-footer with jet black hair, green eyes, and a roundish pale-skinned face with a heavy jaw that had often been bruised in the boxing ring during his schoolboy years as a pugilist and in the bar fights he had occasionally gotten into while working as a concrete mixer and manual laborer in order to help pay his way through Fordham Law School. His paternal grandfather, Michael Padian, had briefly been a professional prizefighter in his native Ireland, and, after coming to America and settling down as a workingman with a family, Michael had given boxing instructions both to Gerald's father and later to Gerald himself. Gerald's maternal grandfather, of Spanish-French ancestry, had owned and operated a tavern on West 116th Street, which, Gerald liked to recall, had been filmed in scenes of *The Pawnbroker*, a movie starring Rod Steiger.

Gerald Padian's law office was on East Fifty-sixth Street, seven blocks south of Tucci. On evenings when it was his turn to oversee the dining operation, Padian usually arrived at the restaurant attired in lawyerly fashion—dark suits, white shirts, buffed shoes, and silk neckties that were never flashy but were sometimes loosely knotted. It seemed to me that Padian was at heart a blue-collar man who was resigned to wearing white shirts and neckties as part of his uniform as an officer of the court. And while he minimized the fact that he was fast with his fists, he impressed me as an individual who regularly foresaw unpleasant situations heading his way that he had to confront.

Before dawn one day during his third year at law school, while walking near Lincoln Center toward the Fordham library, where he planned to study for an exam, he was followed on the sidewalk by a young black man who called to him, "Hey, can I have a moment of your time?" Padian did not respond, and kept walking. Then the man caught up with him and, face-to-face, repeated the question more urgently: "Can I have a moment of your time?" This guy's weird, Padian thought, and he's about to mug me, so Padian quickly grabbed him by the throat and shoulders and, with a vigorous shove, sent him staggering backward off the curb into the street.

Padian continued on toward West Sixtieth Street and Amsterdam Avenue at a quickened pace. Suddenly he was squinting into the glare of klieg lights and stepping on a cord of electrical wiring that lay across the sidewalk, and he saw in front of him a group of men busily engaged with their movie cameras and sound equipment. "Cut!" yelled one of the men angrily, and then Padian recognized the director Woody Allen, who was frowning at him and cursing loudly. Padian had interrupted a scene that Allen was shooting for *New York Stories*. The young black man, a production assistant who was supposed to prevent pedestrians from disturbing the filmmakers, now arrived at Padian's side and said sarcastically, "Thanks a lot! I was only asking for a moment of your time, trying to keep you from walking on the set when the cameras were rolling!" Padian was too embarrassed to say anything to the man or to Woody Allen, although the latter continued to curse him. Padian then slowly retreated from the set and continued on his way toward the library.

After graduating from Fordham Law School in 1988, he was hired as an associate in the litigation department of Weil, Gotshal & Manges, a large firm known primarily for its bankruptcy and corporate work. Among his young colleagues there was a fellow Fordham graduate of Armenian ancestry named Richard Tashjian. After working together for four years at Weil, the two of them left to establish their own firm, Tashjian & Padian, specializing in commercial litigation. One of their first clients was the owner of the Café Society nightclub on Twenty-first Street and Broadway, who was filing for bankruptcy in 1992. Padian and Tashjian tried to recruit outside investors who might open another nightclub there, but instead they met a wealthy individual who was willing to spend $1.5 million to convert the club site into a restaurant. Padian and Tashjian assisted him with the legal matters and also contributed funds of their own to participate in the partnership. The restaurant would be called Metronome, and the chef hired to run the kitchen was Cliff Pereira. Three years later, after Padian and Tashjian had severed their ties to Metronome and had negotiated with J. Z. Morris to take over the Napa

Valley Grill's vacated space at 206 East 63rd Street, Pereira was invited by Padian to work with the five-man partnership that would launch Tucci.

Even before its opening in February 1996, Padian revealed himself to be the most decisive of the Tucci partners, having a clear vision of how to operate the business profitably and avoid the practices of the Napa Valley Grill's owner, Michael Toporek, who had "fallen in love with his restaurant" and had ended up owing creditors about $500,000. Padian's place would be a trattoria, quite informal, and with a quick turnover. He would hire fewer waiters and kitchen workers than Toporek had for the Napa Valley Grill, decreasing the weekly payroll from twelve thousand dollars to below nine thousand. Padian's menu would reduce the food and beverage prices, making it possible for a Tucci customer to spend on average between twenty-five and thirty dollars per dinner with an appetizer and a glass of wine, which was roughly ten to fifteen dollars less than the average check at the Napa Valley Grill. Padian increased the seating capacity in the main dining room by moving in very small tables, each with a top measuring twenty-four inches square, and as a result seventy-five customers would be accommodated in a space that had formerly served a maximum of sixty. And since the tops were made of an attractive composite marble, Padian chose not to cover them with linen tablecloths. The laundry charged ninety-eight cents to wash a single tablecloth, and by avoiding this expenditure, he estimated a monthly saving of a few thousand dollars. He profitably disposed of Toporek's sleek and expensively designed cherry-wood bar, putting in its place a castoff antique bar purchased for less than two thousand dollars from a warehouse in Harlem, which had obtained it from a bankrupt resort hotel in the Pocono Mountains of Pennsylvania. Padian auctioned off Toporek's silk-cushioned chairs and replaced them with unpadded wooden chairs, which he believed would reduce the comfort level of Tucci's customers and encourage a faster rate of turnover.

(Months later, after Tucci had opened and the Napa Valley Grill's assets had been liquidated, Michael Toporek was dining with friends at a restaurant in Sag Harbor, Long Island, and found himself sitting in a silk-cushioned chair that was comfortable and somehow familiar. When he looked down to examine it, he realized he was sitting in one of the chairs that he had bought for his Napa Valley Grill.)

In late June 1996, a few days after hearing that Tucci might soon be sold, I met with Gerald Padian at the Tashjian & Padian law firm on East Fifty-sixth Street. The receptionist greeted me by name, having seen me on earlier occasions, and waved me in the direction of Padian's office. He was seated behind his desk, completing a phone call, when I walked in.

Displayed on the wall behind him was a large framed photograph showing Muhammad Ali brandishing his gloved fists over the fallen body of Sonny Liston. After hanging up the phone, Padian stood to shake hands and offered me a chair. We chatted for a while about the Yankees, and then he quickly changed the subject and asked me a question in an offhanded way that caught me by surprise: "How'd you like to buy Tucci?"

Thinking he was kidding, I remained silent.

"No, I mean it," he said. "You *like* the restaurant business, as you've told me lots of times, and I think you'd really be good at it."

I did admit that during my boyhood I had often dreamed of owning a restaurant.

"Well, now's the time," he said, adding that Tucci was on the verge of becoming quite successful. Lowering the food and beverage prices had been a good idea, he believed, drawing more and more customers every night, and he described the new chef as a first-rate employee who was eager to continue doing his fine job in the kitchen. Padian went on to explain that the only reason he was now tempted to relinquish the restaurant was the sudden growth of his law practice, making it increasingly difficult for him to function effectively all day as an attorney and at night as a restaurant owner. His controlling personality, he admitted, had perhaps led him to devote himself excessively to the management of Tucci, while his partners seemed to be too willing to let him do their share of the work. But this situation had to change, he said. He wanted to spend more time with his fiancée (whom he planned to marry within the coming months) and it was also now necessary for him to take more business trips out of town, most recently flying to J. Z. Morris's home state of Indiana to attend to matters involving Morris's multimillionaire father.

As Padian was telling me this, leaning back in his chair with his feet propped up on the desk, his phone was ringing constantly, and while he apologized for each interruption, he readily reached out to accept every call. I sat across from him, thinking about the possibility of my becoming a proprietor in the restaurant world. I wondered what price Padian had in mind, and whether it was *his* share that he was proffering or if the entire five-man partnership intended to unload Tucci. I was intrigued by the notion of fulfilling my boyhood fantasy and also writing about the restaurant business from the *inside*, as George Orwell had done so effectively in *Down and Out in Paris and London*. But it also occurred to me that if I became an investor, familiar as I was with the restaurants at this location, I might become so preoccupied with the economic survival of Tucci that I would never find the time or energy to write anything. Writers are renowned for discovering things to distract them from their work.

I recalled a story about a fellow *Times* man named Meyer Berger, who, after complaining endlessly to his wife about his inability to finish a magazine article, heard her declare one morning that she was leaving him alone in their apartment for the rest of the day and would be locking the door behind her, taking his key with her. She told him that when she returned, later in the afternoon or by early evening, she fully expected that he would have finished his article, adding that he had nothing else to think about, since she had *already* attended to all the household chores: She had washed the breakfast dishes, had prepared his lunch, had cleaned the apartment—even the windows were washed, having been done a day earlier by a service company. Eight hours later, she returned, to find her husband smiling and apparently pleased to see her at home. She discovered, however, that while he had not written a single page, every piece of silver that they owned was on display on the sideboard or in the cupboard, shining, buffed, and freshly polished.

If I invested in Tucci, I was concerned that I would not only be diverted from my writing but would be deprived of the pleasure I had always derived as a restaurantgoer, one who liked going to many different places on a regular basis. I would be confined to one place, night after night. I would be restricted in ways familiar to my friend Sidney Zion when he operated Broadway Joe's, and thus was no longer able to be, as he preferred to be, a man about town venturing in and out of various New York bars and eating places. Another resident of New York named Warner LeRoy, a portly gentleman who favored wearing expensively tailored embroidered jackets and damask waistcoats and was far more experienced and skilled in running restaurants than Sidney Zion had been—LeRoy had founded such splendiferous dining establishments as Maxwell's Plum and Tavern on the Green—told me in an interview that there were two rules a restaurant owner should follow in order to succeed. The first rule, said LeRoy, was to avoid drinking alcohol. (As he mentioned this, I thought about the heavy-drinking Marvin Safir, who had owned Moon's at 206 E. 63rd and had lost $2 million, prompting one of Moon's partners to remark, "The main problem at Moon's was that Marvin Safir was its best customer.") The second rule, according to LeRoy, was that a restaurant owner should never appear to be bored when in the presence of his customers. This was easier said than done, LeRoy conceded, for sometimes a restaurant's best customers are self-important people who talk too much and are accustomed to being listened to even when they are boring. They are not aware that they are boring, LeRoy went on, and yet it is never the job of a restaurateur to inform them of this; indeed, being as diplomatically inclined as he was, LeRoy said that whenever he was conversing with boring people, he often nodded his head encouragingly and sometimes raised an eyebrow in a feigned indication of heightened interest. Warner LeRoy's acting abilities were probably linked to his family background. His grandfather had started Warner Bros. and his father had produced and directed *The Wizard of Oz*.

But as a potential proprietor of Tucci, what could I find helpful from my talk with Warner LeRoy? Not much, I thought. I did not want to abstain from my usual predinner dry martini, nor would I want to surround myself almost every night with a social circle of customers, especially those who were presumptuous and tedious. And so when Gerald Padian hung up the phone and resumed our conversation with the question "Have you come to a decision about Tucci?" I replied, "I'm sorry, but I think I'd be better off staying out of it. I'm having enough trouble writing about restaurants, and—"

"Oh, but you'd be *good* at this business," he interrupted. When I said nothing, he continued in a softer voice: "Won't you at least give it a little thought?"

"Okay," I said, "I'll think about it, but I'd also like to know a little more about the business, and maybe spend some time hanging around the kitchen."

"Fine," Padian said quickly. "I'll arrange it. When would you like to come in?"

"Whenever," I said.

Padian reached for his phone and spoke for a while to the Tucci chef, Matt Hereford. After hanging up, Padian leaned back in his chair and smiled. "You're hired," he said. "You can come in tomorrow morning at ten sharp. You'll be working with the chef and the cooks throughout the day. You'll be helping out on the salad station, the pasta station, and the grill. They'll have a uniform waiting for you. And, I promise, you won't have to wash any dishes."

29

W HEN I ARRIVED IN FRONT OF TUCCI THE FOLLOWING MORN-
ing, I saw a panel truck parked at the curb and heard the driver
cursing to himself as he unloaded boxes of fruit and vegetables
along the sidewalk while swatting away the mosquitoes and gnats that
were buzzing around his balding head and his rosy-cheeked round face,
which was dripping with sweat, even though the shimmering midsummer
sun was hidden behind the high-rises and the expected heat wave was
hours away from penetrating the streets of the city.

Stacked high along the curb near the truck were several black plastic
bags filled with the previous day's garbage from Tucci, which the cartage
company was supposed to have collected at dawn and which the insects
had been hovering around until being attracted to the newly arrived fresh
fruit and vegetables. I paused to count the number of bags. There were
twelve. I knew from talking to Padian that cartage companies could tell
how well a restaurant was doing by how much garbage it piled up, and so I
assumed that the accumulation of a dozen bags supported Padian's notion
that Tucci was doing quite well.

The front door was unlocked, but before I entered I heard the driver
calling to me in a voice bearing a Slavic or German accent: "Mister, you
vill hold open, yah?" He headed toward me, pushing a two-wheeled steel
dolly stacked with boxes, and I held open the restaurant's green wood-
framed front door as wide as the hinges would allow, and then I stood
aside as he brushed past me, nodding his head once and displaying on his
face a quirky expression that I accepted as a smile. I followed a few paces
behind him as he moved past the rows of empty tables in the dining room
and then slowly forced open the swinging doors of the kitchen with the
front edge of the dolly.

"Hello, Hans," said Matt Hereford, sitting on a stool behind the salad
table, looking up from the slips of paper spread out in front of him.
"They're waiting for you downstairs." Hans lowered the dolly to the floor

and, after lifting up the top two boxes with his hands and holding them in front of his chest, turned around and walked a few steps to the rear before heading down a narrow wooden staircase to the basement, where the preparatory kitchen was located and where a radio was now tuned loudly to Latin dance music.

"Welcome," Hereford said, seeing me approaching and getting up to shake my hand. "I'm glad you're here, and hope you'll find it interesting." He was a slender, soft-spoken, fair-haired individual in his early thirties, whose pale forehead was only a shade darker than the white linen cap that rested upon it, and, as if wishing to lend distinction to his otherwise plain-featured face, he'd endowed it with a Vandyke beard and mustache. His white linen jacket was spotless and hardly wrinkled, and the flat-topped cap that he wore was more like a fez than the high-crowned floppy toques donned by most of the chefs I knew. After handing me a freshly laundered white jacket and cap similiar to what he was wearing, he said, "I hope these will fit." I removed my Panama hat and tried on the cap, which fit perfectly. Though the jacket was quite large, it was what I preferred because it slipped easily over my beige jacket and it had a collar flap that I could button across the throat and protect my tie and shirt from kitchen splatter.

Hereford gave me a tour of the kitchen, showing me where the grilling was done and where the salads and desserts were prepared. Lined along the white-tiled walls were sinks, stoves, refrigerators, and a dishwasher, and in the middle of the room were counters, a chopping block, and a freestanding rack, on the shelves of which were pots, pans, plates, cooking utensils, and also a white plastic printer that within a few hours would begin relaying the customers' luncheon requests after they had been coded into the dining room's computer by the service staff. Although I did not mention it to Hereford, I had visited this kitchen on earlier occasions, having been shown it initially in 1977 by the French-born proprietor of Le Premier, Robert Pascal, the first restaurateur in this building. It seemed to me that Pascal had been the original owner of nearly everything I now saw in Tucci's kitchen, save for the printer, and the place was in need of restoration and repair. There were dents in the metal cabinets and shelves, cracks in the tiles, and the stove was encrusted.

I followed Hereford down the wobbly steps into the preparatory kitchen, which, like the kitchen above, had white-tiled walls and counters that were obviously not new, but the place abounded with a youthful energy and jolliness that seemed to be in rhythm with the radio music being transmitted by one of the Spanish-language stations. I heard coming from the back of the room the voices of three or four white-capped workers who were singing along with the recorded sounds of Roberto Carlo as they leaned over sinks and counters while scrubbing potatoes, washing heads of lettuce, and slicing carrots, onions, celery, and cucumbers. I saw Hans kneeling in the center of the room, surrounded by half a dozen boxes that he had opened, and, in his accented way of speaking, but with no lack of self-assurance, he was describing what was packed in the boxes to a tall, broad-shouldered, dark-complected man who stood over him, wearing a white apron and cap. He was the head cook, I was told by Hereford. His name was Miguel Peguero and he was from the Dominican Republic. I had seen Peguero's name on the list of Tucci employees that Gerald Padian had faxed me earlier, and I remembered it because Peguero had been described as a onetime prospect with the Minnesota Twins baseball organization, an infielder who had suffered a career-ending injury during spring training a few years earlier. Now he was on the roster of Tucci, and yet he did not appear to be discontented with where he was; I heard him laughing loudly at something that a fellow worker had called out in Spanish from across the room, and he maintained a bemused expression as Hans knelt in front of him and zestfully directed Peguero's attention to the panoply of fruit and vegetables that was contained in the boxes.

"Beautiful zucchini I have brought you, yah?" Hans said, quickly adding, "And I have also brought you beautiful romaine lettuce . . . and beautiful eggplant, and potatoes, and arugula, and shiitake mushrooms, and potatoes, yah?" Hans then paused, waiting for a word or nod of approval from Peguero; but the latter withheld it until he had bent down and closely examined the contents, sometimes picking up a piece of fruit or a vegetable and raising it to eye level, then staring at it, smelling it, squeezing it lightly, testing for overripeness, I assumed, or perhaps checking for the possibility that a worm was lurking within. Only after Peguero was satisfied with what he saw did he take his ballpoint pen and mark "OK" on the order sheet that was tucked in the pocket of his apron. He had phoned in the order the night before, and before dawn this morning it had been collected at the Bronx wholesale market by Hans, who had himself done the selecting at the various fruit and vegetable stalls before making his deliveries to Tucci and the other restaurants that relied upon his judgment and accepted, no doubt with a grain of salt, his tendency to describe as "beautiful" almost everything he brought.

"But these potatoes are not so good," Peguero said finally, lifting a few of them and then dropping them back into the box. He had momentarily held on to one of them and twirled it between his fingers a few times, as if feeling for the seam on a baseball.

"So we take the potatoes back," said Hans unhesitatingly, shoving the box aside—a box that, for all I knew, he might later be delivering to another restaurant and describing the contents as "beautiful."

After Hans had left, having waved good-bye to Peguero and to another kitchen employee whom he knew by name, Hereford escorted me over to meet Peguero, explaining that he would serve as my mentor and companion for the rest of the morning. This pleased me, for instead of my having to begin the day discussing food preparation, about which I had learned little from my mother and about which I cared no more than she did, I could talk baseball with Miguel Peguero if he was willing—and, fortunately for me, he was. He was also quite fluent in English, more so than most of the South American baseball players whom I have interviewed, and during our morning together—while I stood watching him slicing meat, deboning fish, and making enough lasagna to feed more than a dozen customers—I learned how he had gone from being a disabled and unemployable athlete to becoming a contented team player in the kitchen of Tucci.

He told me that he had broken an ankle while running to first base four years before on a soggy field in Fort Myers, Florida, and despite his medical treatment and his rehabilitation exercises, he had been unable to recover his earlier speed on the base paths or his range as an infielder; and so his longtime dream of becoming a big leaguer had ended before his twenty-third birthday. When I asked him if, prior to his injury, he thought he had been talented enough to compete on baseball's highest level, he replied affirmatively but modestly, alluding to the fact that in the minor leagues he had played with a number of people who would be elevated to the majors, including his ex-roommate and fellow infielder, Enrique Wilson.

But speculating on what might have been was a waste of time, Peguero suggested, emphasizing that as soon as he had physically been able to move around without crutches, he traveled to New York with his Dominican bride, and, while sharing a Bronx apartment with a few of their relatives, he sought whatever opportunities were available to newcomers like himself, young men with limited options and without green cards. One of the places where he worked was in the kitchen of a Manhattan restaurant in the East Forties, starting out as a dishwasher. But as he appeared every night to scrub dishes, he was also surveying the room and closely observing the other workers as they functioned at various positions, noting in particular the skills and ingredients they used in producing the appetizers, the sauces, the main courses, the desserts, and the specialties of the day. It did not take long before Peguero believed he was capable of performing each task on a highly professional level, and as he recounted this to me, I had visions of him as a ballplayer standing on first base after hitting a single and, while he thought about stealing second, studying the pitcher's every gesture and movement on the mound.

Since the place where Peguero had been hired as a dishwasher had a rapid rate of employee turnover, he was soon promoted to more interesting and challenging assignments at the salad station and the grill. Three years later, in 1996, after he had worked for a while as a cook in a second restaurant, he accepted a higher salary to serve directly under Matt Hereford in Tucci's kitchen. Hereford prepared the menus, made decisions regarding the workers' schedules, and was nominally in charge of everything that occurred in the rear of the restaurant. But it seemed to me, after I had spent a few days there, that the workers saw Peguero as their leader, even though he never asserted himself, nor did he set himself apart from the others. Still, he was obviously a presence, one to whom the others came for advice and consultation, and they usually nodded in agreement with what he said to them. He was inches taller than his co-workers, being a six-footer, and had big shoulders, narrow hips, a long dark-skinned face, and brown eyes that were large and alert, and he moved around the floor and up and down the staircase with agility and grace, showing no signs of his old injury.

He and Matt Hereford both arrived for work at approximately the same time, shortly after 9:00 a.m., but it was my impression that Peguero worked harder and certainly put in longer hours. Hereford would sometimes leave the building prior to the serving of dinner. Hereford was then dating a sister of Gerald Padian's fiancée. Peguero would spend much of the morning and afternoon in the preparatory kitchen, wielding a knife delicately and precisely in separating fat from meat, and removing myriad fish bones with his tweezers, and then at approximately 6:00 p.m., he was upstairs in the main kitchen, beginning to cook dinner; he was there until nearly midnight.

Flanking him at the grill almost every night was the assistant cook, Ray Perez, who had been born in Brooklyn of Mexican parents, and Lindomar De Mouvra, a Brazilian who performed many tasks but specialized in none of them. Working at an adjacent counter, which was closer to the kitchen's swinging doors, was the pasta cook, José Rosendo, who was a native of Mexico, and the pizza maker, Andres Artigas, who had been born in Uruguay. There were one or two kitchen workers who shied away from conversing with me; perhaps they feared that I would expose them as illegal aliens, or maybe they were unable to communicate in English. There was a dishwasher, however, who spoke English quite well, and he took the initiative in introducing himself to me shortly after I had met Miguel Peguero.

"Hello," he said, extending his right hand after drying it off with a towel. "My name is Manuel Bonete, and I am from Ecuador."

"Ecuador," I repeated, "*that's* where Lorena Bobbitt is from. You know who she is, don't you?"

"Oh yes," he said enthusiastically. "She is very famous in my country." After I had mentioned seeing her many times in person at the trial, he told me that she had visited Ecuador during the past week and had been at the palace in Quito to attend a luncheon hosted by Ecuador's president, Abdalá Bucaram.

A few months later, I read in the *New York Times* that the Ecuadorean congress had voted to remove President Bucaram from office because of what it called his "mental incapacity."

Inasmuch as Gerald Padian had not established a limit to the frequency of my visits to Tucci, I came and went with regularity throughout the summer of 1996 and into the winter of 1997, usually appearing when there were no customers and when the employees, who had become quite accustomed to my presence, were so preoccupied with their tasks that they more or less ignored me, allowing me to wander around at will. As I explored the vastness of the basement, which was nearly one hundred feet long and twenty-five feet wide—and which housed a wine cellar, a pantry, a glass-enclosed office, two bathrooms, a cloakroom, and the preparatory kitchen, which took up most of the space—I reminded myself that this area had once been the domain of a dozen dray horses. They had slept and been fed here when Frederick J. Schillinger operated this building as a warehouse, beginning in 1907. A freight elevator had transported the horses up to their wagons, which had been parked within what was now the main dining room of Tucci. The dining room had been renovated and repainted so many times during the last two decades as a result of the rotating restaurateurs that there were few remaining signs of the fine work done here by the celebrated Sam Lopata, who had designed this building's first restaurant, Le Premier, in 1977. Although the critic Mimi Sheraton had condemned Le Premier's cuisine and high prices, she had raved about its design, calling it an "absolute stunner . . . a dazzlement of Art Deco splendor at its most sensual and flattering . . . as romantic as a valentine."

Sam Lopata, who was thirty-four at the time, had been born in Paris during the Nazi occupation. His father, a milliner, had been arrested during a roundup of Jews and would not survive Auschwitz. In 1971, after studying architecture at the École Nationale des Beaux-Arts in Paris,

Lopata moved to New York, where he eventually befriended his fellow Frenchman, the restaurateur Robert Pascal, who had commissioned him to create the ambience at Le Premier. Lopata then moved on to design several other restaurants in New York and elsewhere. In 1986, he was named "Restaurant Designer of the Year" by *Time* magazine. Ten years later, he died of cancer in New York at the age of fifty-four. In the *Times* obituary, the onetime owner of the restaurant Lutèce, André Soltner—who had once hired Lopata to provide Lutèce with a face-lift—described Lopata as "an indefatigable perfectionist who approaches walls and floors, tables and chairs, as an artist approaches a canvas." But the only reminder of Lopata's decorative style within 206 East 63rd Street in 1997 was the five-tiered coffered ceiling of the auxiliary dining room on the second floor of Tucci.

The dining room staff at Tucci consisted of five waiters, three waitresses, a bartender, and two "runners," the latter being young men who carried trays laden with food from the kitchen to the seated customers. The dining room crew were entirely fluent in English, although only two of them were native-born Americans. One was the bartender, an attractive and vivacious red-haired woman named Elizabeth Edwards, whose possessive boyfriend had been a nightly visitor to the bar until the management had ordered him to stay away. The other was a dark-haired, stocky waiter in his late thirties named Andy Globus, whose grandfather had been a neurosurgeon and his father an advertising executive. After Andy had dropped out of the Borough of Manhattan Community College in the early 1970s, he had drifted into restaurant service and had worked in several places before coming to Tucci in 1996. Andy Globus's associates at Tucci were at least ten years his junior, and they included a waiter from Romania named Givan Stevans, a waiter from Sardinia named Vittorio Scarpa, a runner from Bangladesh named Mohammed Matin, and a waitress from Poland, Monica Kosciolowiez, who had come to the United States on a student visa and divided her time between waiting tables at night and attending classes during the day at nearby Hunter College.

Andy Globus shared his nearby flat on First Avenue with a Tucci waiter from Russia, Konstantin Avramov, a tall and prematurely balding man of twenty-seven with an oval face, brown eyes, a courteous manner (his father and grandfather had both been Soviet diplomats, serving, respectively, in Czechoslovakia and Austria), and a well-defined muscular body that he maintained by working out in a gym for two hours every afternoon. Konstantin Avramov had been born in Moscow in 1970, and at seventeen was called into the army, serving for two years and considering himself lucky not to have been sent to Afghanistan, which he viewed as comparable to America's involvement in Vietnam. After being discharged as a sergeant in 1990, following the completion of Russia's withdrawal from Afghanistan a year earlier, Konstantin returned to Moscow filled with a sense of malaise and estrangement. He had no idea what he wanted to do. As a teenager, he had grown up feeling quite comfortable with the political system, and, while it did not encourage individual ambition unless it served the system's interests, he believed that the government's intent was to satisfy the basic needs of the people, offering job security and pensions and at least a modicum of identity with the awesome power and status of the state.

He had been raised in relatively privileged circumstances, he told me one afternoon at Tucci, recalling his comfortable and happy family and the fact that his parents and grandparents had often hosted dinner parties for their many friends and acquaintances employed within the government. His family and their guests took turns entertaining one another in their homes, never in restaurants, and he described his mother as a superb cook who planned the menu several days in advance of a party. He had always been impressed with her social energy and culinary creativity, her way of preparing traditional Russian food heavily flavored with Asian and European spices, which he thought had prompted within him a curiosity about people living in faraway places.

Konstantin's first job after leaving the army was as a trainee in a Moscow hotel owned by a Canadian corporation, and it was then that he began to sense that his country was beginning to decline as a superpower. Many of his fellow veterans and ex-schoolmates, lacking his family's connections, were unable to find jobs. "Nobody is offering us anything" was the phrase that he often heard, and there were also complaints about the high cost of things that had formerly been affordable and available. The grocery store patronized by his mother now had many empty shelves, and the dinner parties were quickly discontinued. A friend of Konstantin's began traveling regularly to Belgium to obtain luxury cars to drive back and sell to members of the newly emerging enterpreneureal class that was prospering in the wake of the national crisis. After the demise of the Soviet Union in 1991, Konstantin quit his job at the hotel and left for Belgium to join his friend in the car-selling enterprise.

A year later, more affluent than he imagined he would ever be, he flew with his friend to the United States, arriving at JFK. After sleeping for three nights on airport benches without being queried by security personnel, Konstantin and his companion rode the subway into Queens and rented an apartment in a neighborhood that had many Russian-speaking residents. Later in the year, on his own, Konstantin moved into an East

Village apartment and found a job in a floral shop in the West Twenties that was managed by a Polish man who spoke Russian no better than Konstantin spoke Polish, but they communicated well enough to work together. Konstantin remained on the job for nearly three years, meanwhile gaining fluency in English, and, after taking six hundred dollars from his savings, he registered for classes at a training school for waiters and bartenders on Seventh Avenue near Thirty-seventh Street. His first restaurant job was in a French bistro on First Avenue at Fifty-seventh Street, near the Queensboro Bridge. A year later, in 1995, he was waiting tables in the Museum of Modern Art's restaurant on West Fifty-third Street, and in 1996 he found work at the newly opened Tucci, where he met Andy Globus and moved uptown to share Globus's apartment.

Even before I had begun talking at length to Konstantin, I felt as if I had met one of his spiritual kinsmen in the character of the exiled Russian waiter named Boris, whom George Orwell had written about a half-century earlier in *Down and Out in Paris and London*. Like Konstantin, Boris had spent part of his youth in the Russian army. Boris had served during World War I as a captain, until his rank and income had been eliminated by the Communists during the Revolution, whereupon Boris fled to Paris and, being impecunious and reduced at times to sleeping under the bridges of the Seine, he struggled to support himself as a waiter.

" 'Ah, but I have known what it is to live like a gentleman,' " Boris was quoted in Orwell's book as telling his fellow waiters, most of whom were Italian or German. "There is hardly such a thing as a French waiter in Paris," Orwell wrote, although he conceded that when a man becomes a waiter, he tends to forget his origins and dwells in a world of illusions. "He lives perpetually in sight of rich people, stands at their tables, listens to their conversation, sucks up to them with smiles and discreet little jokes," Orwell wrote. "He has the pleasure of spending money by proxy. . . . He will take pains to serve a meal in style, because he feels that he is participating in the meal himself." Orwell went on to write about Boris: "Though he had never saved more than a few thousand francs, he took it for granted that in the end he would be able to set up his own restaurant and grow rich."

Konstantin had similar aspirations in New York, which he often expressed to me as we sat together at midday in Tucci's dining room, both of us folding napkins and stuffing newly printed menus into plastic covers. "I will one day own a great restaurant," he assured me, adding confidentially that he had already met some wealthy New Yorkers who were eager to finance him whenever he was ready to venture out on his own. His personable manner helped him make friends easily at the health club and wherever he associated socially, and it seemed to me that he was the most optimistic of the Tucci employees. It also struck me as ironic that this ex-soldier from the Red Army who had witnessed the crumbling of communism in his homeland would be envisioning his capitalistic ascendancy in the food business while working in this restaurant site, which had known so many failures and foreclosures.

Still, he arrived for work every day in high spirits and was dressed for success in Armani-style suits that he had purchased on sale. In the evenings, his face flushed and his muscles pumped up as a result of his late-afternoon workout, he moved swiftly around the dining room in his waiter's attire, catering to his customers efficiently and obligingly. "I really like working at Tucci," Konstantin told me one day.

It was not long after my conversation with Konstantin that I learned from Gerald Padian by telephone that he and his partners would be selling the restaurant within a few days. I should not have been surprised, but I was. I was also devastated. I had finally gotten my foot in the door, thanks to my relationship with Padian, and now he was leaving, and if I wanted to continue my research, I would have to try to ingratiate myself with a new group of restaurant owners—headed, according to Padian, by a wealthy man of Greek ancestry from Fort Lee, New Jersey. There was a good chance that Mr. Fort Lee would not want me hanging around his place all day, and then I'd be back to where I was before—a customer, this time at the *ninth* restaurant to open for business at 206 East 63rd Street.

"Is there any chance your deal will fall through?" I asked Padian hopefully.

"No, everything's set and we're signing the papers in my office on Monday," he said, meaning March 10, 1997.

He had opened Tucci thirteen months before, in February 1996.

"Do you think that Konstantin and Andy Globus and the rest of them know about this?" I asked Padian.

"No," he said, "and I'd appreciate it if you'd keep it to yourself until I tell them after dinner on Sunday night."

"I thought your business was doing pretty well," I said.

"It was," Padian agreed, but he repeated what he had often told me before: It was very difficult and time-consuming to be simultaneously responsible for running a law firm *and* a restaurant. He also reminded me again that his days as a late-night bachelor were soon coming to a close—he was getting married in less than two months and, since he was approaching the age of thirty-five, he believed that he was ready for a home life; and he went on to explain that, inasmuch as none of the other Tucci backers were willing or able to assume the leadership role of the restaurant, he was receptive to the idea of selling the sublease to the 206 East 63rd Street space to the gentleman from Fort Lee. Padian meanwhile promised that he would remain in touch with me, and, before hanging up, he wished me the best of luck with my book.

Later that day, I received a note from my editor at Knopf, my publisher, asking that I bring him up-to-date on how my work was progressing. My editor had proven himself to be a man of infinite patience, but I knew that he would be feeling some anxiety when a writer was as tardy as I had been in giving him something to read. So I faxed him back with the promise that he would be receiving a written report from me in a day or so, and then I immediately began to review my voluminous notes entitled "Restaurants—a work in progress," hoping to draw from this material a summarized account of what I was trying to accomplish and then describing it in an outline that I would send to my editor. I had not read through my research material in quite a while, and as I began to peruse it that evening and on the following morning, picking my way through hundreds of pages of typed notes that were spread out along the two tables that flanked my desk, I realized that I had gathered lots of information that I had forgotten I had collected. Some of it was in the form of extraneous data and detail about Elaine's or the "21" Club or other restaurants that were not central to my main interest, and there were also many references to what other writers had published in the past about the restaurant business and dining in general. I had excerpted paragraphs from Joseph Wechsberg's biography of Le Pavillon's owner, Henri Soulé, including the latter's remark that a restaurant's success was very much influenced by the presence of beautiful women. I had paraphrased an observation made in a novel by Philip Roth to the effect that Jewish people liked dining in Chinese restaurants because Chinese waiters could never tell whether or not the customers were Jewish. From a book by Truman Capote I had reprinted a comment made by one of his characters, Lady Ina Coolbirth, who, while having lunch with a friend at La Côte Basque, remarked, "There is at least one respect in which the rich, the really very rich, *are* different. . . . They understand vegetables. Other people—well, anyone can manage roast beef, a great steak, lobsters. But have you ever noticed how, in the homes of the very rich, at the Wrightsmans' or Dillons', at Bunny's and Babe's, they always serve only the most beautiful vegetables, and the greatest variety? The greenest petits pois, infinitesimal carrots, corn so baby-kerneled and tender it seems almost unborn, lima beans tinier than mice eyes, and the young asparagus! the limestone lettuce! the raw red mushrooms! zucchini. . . ." I also included in my notes from Capote's book his demurral, "Champagne does have one serious drawback: swilled as a regular thing, a certain sourness settles in the tummy, and the result is permanent bad breath. Really incurable. . . ."

Some of what I found within my stacks of research had *not* been placed there with the intention of including it in my book. It was, instead, a private account of my state of mind during the days and months that I had been gathering information, a kind of diary that revealed my personal thoughts and impressions about the people I was interviewing and the places I had been and my ongoing doubts, vacillations, and rationalizations about the work I was trying to do.

"Why in the hell do I remain involved in matters of such dubious interest as the Willy Loman Building and all these retro restaurants on Sixty-third Street?" I asked myself in a memo, and I questioned myself further:

"Has the waywardness of my own life made me compatible with the floundering forces that apparently guide this place? . . .

"When I started delving into the origins of the building's ownership was I exploring the possibility, illogically but inexorably, that hidden in the history of Schillinger's warehouse was evidence of an unfortunate incident or misadventure that might help to explain the legacy of lost causes inherited later by the restaurateurs? And, furthermore, might these revelations point to a theme that underlies my new book?

"Possible title for the book: 'We Shall Now Praise Unfamous Men.'

". . . Get serious."

In another memo I asked myself some difficult questions and then replied in a way that made me feel better:

"Why am I not writing this book faster? Do I have 'Writer's Block'? No, you're not suffering from 'Writer's Block,' you're just showing good judgment in not publishing anything at this time. You're demonstrating concern for readers in not burdening them with bad writing. More writers should be doing what you're doing—NOT writing. There's so much bad writing out there, why add to it? The bookshelves of America are lined with the second-rate work of first-rate writers. Many of these writers have a built-in audience and so the editors will publish their stuff. They'll publish whatever sells. But the writers should be blocked. It would be a good thing for the writers' reputations, for the publishers' production costs, and for the reading standards of the general public. There should be a National Book Award given annually to certain writers for NOT WRITING."

Another memo to myself contained a paragraph that I believed belonged in my restaurant book, if, of course, I ever wrote the book:

"Every day in the dining world there is somewhere a diaspora, a casting out of cooks, and of waiters wearing clip-on bow ties, and of bartenders who will go to their graves knowing the favorite drinks of hundreds of customers—customers who never knew their bartenders' last names. . . ."

And:

"The midday kisses exchanged between the maître d's and the ladies who lunch are quintessential manifestations of unfelt affection. . . ."

And there was another memo with questions that were repetitive of those asked elsewhere in my research files:

"Where is the center point of your story? Is it 'The Building' that you're writing about, or the Rise & Fall of the Retro Restaurants situated within the building?

"What is the connection between the building and its occupants other than the fact that Schillinger's workhorses and Tucci's kitchen workers occupied a common ground at opposite ends of the twentieth century?

"Why are you, who are supposed to be writing a personal book, devoting your attentions to this faithless piece of real estate at 206 E. 63rd?

"What's your response to these questions?

"Answer: I think that I cannot directly respond to these questions because the issue has less to do with the building and its occupants than with me and my natural, though at times misguided, affinity for people and places that exist in the shadows and side streets of the city and other overlooked places in which there are untold stories awaiting my discovery and development. Oh, I know this sounds grandiloquent, but considering where I come from, the distant dunes of South Jersey, where instead of reading childhood literature I scanned menus, and where my homelife was happiest when dining with my stylish mother and my relaxed and contented father in mediocre restaurants, is it any wonder that after moving to New York I would find comfort with, and compassion for, some of the city's unheralded and struggling restaurateurs and would moreover be inclined to become their chronicler? In addition, I must acknowledge something of a personal identity with the building at 206 E. 63rd—it has held its ground, as I have, during decades of urban renewal and changing trends in my neighborhood and, like me, it has so far survived the wrecking ball. The venerable building is unmentioned in the guidebooks of Old New York but at various times throughout the century it has provided shelter and sustenance for hundreds of people from all over the world. It was built by the German-born Frederick Schillinger and later passed into the hands of the Italianate teamster Frank Catalano, whose heirs subsequently leased it to the Anglo-American entrepreneur in Florida, J. Z. Morris, whose ex-wife from Hong Kong, Jackie Ho, presently assists him in the not-always-easy task of collecting the monthly rent from the alternating restaurateurs whose employees have included a bus boy from Bangladesh, a cook from the Dominican Republic, and a waiter from Russia who fled his homeland to make his mark in this building that regularly reinvents itself and in which I must quickly find a worthy story to present to my editor."

30

Hoping to simplify for my editor what I had not yet figured out for myself, I began the first draft of my outline with the suggestion that my forthcoming book would be in the genre of a famous novel written a half-century ago and entitled *Grand Hotel*. I had not read the book, which had been written by a Vienna-born author named Vicki Baum, but I had seen a film version of it recently on television and it seemed to me that there was a similarity between what I was trying to do—recounting the tales of many people who at various times had occupied the old building at 206 E. 63rd—and what the filmmakers had presented on the screen: They had dramatized several stories involving a number of employees and guests who regularly crossed paths within the corridors and suites of the Grand Hotel, which in the novel was situated in Berlin in the years between World War I and World War II.

As I gave more thought to my outline, however, I began to doubt that my editor would be impressed with my seeming lack of originality in mentioning *Grand Hotel* as a point of comparison. But why, I asked myself, should I even acknowledge *Grand Hotel* in my outline? It had *not* been a source of inspiration to me. The idea of recounting a variety of stories from the vantage point of a single place had been on my mind long before I had been made aware of Vicki Baum's novel, and indeed this approach had probably been used by storytellers in centuries past. Did not Boccaccio in *The Decameron* relate the stories of a group of people who were gathered together in a country manor near Florence? And, in a different location, wasn't this narrative structure employed by Chaucer in *The Canterbury Tales*? On the other hand, wasn't I definitely stretching the point here and deviating from what I was supposed to be doing in my outline—selling my editor on the idea of what I was doing?

I decided perhaps in the interest of expediency to restrict the scope of my outline to the story about the restaurant business rather than the building, because I knew that my editor cared somewhat about food preparation. (He had recently published a cookbook by David Burke, then the chef of the popular Park Avenue Café, though his primary interests lay elsewhere—five of the books he had published had won Pulitzer Prizes.) My editor had also dined with me once at Tucci and had seemed to share my fascination with the fact that so many of the employees were foreign-born. And so in the outline to Jonathan Segal, my editor at Knopf, I wrote:

Dear Jon:
   During our recent dinner at Tucci you'll recall that I introduced you to a waiter from Moscow, a waitress from Warsaw, a cook from the Dominican Republic, etc., . . . and now I'd like to write about these and other restaurant workers in a book about new-wave immigrants, successors to the types of people I portrayed in *Unto the Sons*. . . . You've read all my past work, both in long and short versions—i.e., short works like *The Bridge,* and long efforts like *The Kingdom and the Power*—and you know how I develop characters as a way of reflecting a history of a time and place that historians tend to ignore. . . . And I think that if my next book was set within the milieu of a restaurant, the result would be compelling. . . .

A few days later I received a letter from Jonathan Segal:

Dear Gay,
   I've thought long and hard about the restaurant book. I'm sure it would be an interesting book. But I don't see it selling very many copies. I don't know what else to say. At your level, we need a book with very large sales potential. I don't think this is it.
   I know you've put a lot of time and effort into this, so you won't be pleased. I'm sorry for that.
   Where do we go from here?
   Let's talk. . . .

Let's talk about what? I asked myself, distressed with his response. Should I send him a revised proposal, shifting the emphasis away from the restaurant and back to the building? One of my problems in writing about the building was the absence of a lively contemporary figure who could singularly personify the place, who could represent it with enough panache and distinction and individual appeal to satisfy even my minimum needs as a nonfiction writer with a soft heart for secondary characters. As it was, I had been picking my way through the atavistic plaster dust and cobwebs of this building for many years in a vain attempt to discover something more useful than what I already had, which was a stack of photographs of Schillinger with his horses, and Catalano with his trucks, and the tenants' rental records loaned to me by the building's largely absentee leaseholder, J. Z. Morris.

I had followed up on Morris's suggestion that I interview his former wife, Jackie Ho, and even before I had arranged a meeting with her—it took me months to do this, as she regularly professed to being engaged with matters that were more important than whatever I had in mind—I began to ponder the possibility (while striving to uplift my sagging spirits) that she might represent the missing link in my quest for a figure to embody my chosen building. She had been associated with it for nearly twenty years, beginning in 1979, when she began helping J. Z. with the building's management and the rent-collecting chores. She undoubtedly knew lots of stories about the tenants who presently or in the past had occupied space on the fifth, fourth, and third floors, like the Gypsy fortune-tellers who had been evicted for forgetting to turn off their bathtub's water, drenching the diners in the restaurant below. Her personal background was also said to be uncommonly eventful, which I learned not only from conversing with J. Z. but with her first husband as well, a cordial fifty-five-year-old gentleman of youthful appearance named Winter Evans, an executive in the knitwear business on Seventh Avenue, with whom I dined a few times at Elaine's along with his German boyfriend, an international banker.

Evans told me that he had married Jackie Ho during the winter of 1970, after being paid a few thousand dollars to do so by a tycoon in the electronics industry. Evans had initially met the man through a mutual acquaintance in New York, and had Evans not been told in advance that the man was a rich and resourceful mensch who commanded a global enterprise, Evans would never have guessed it. The man was a shy, unprepossessing, slope-shouldered individual in his middle fifties who, when meeting Evans for the first time, limply shook hands and introduced himself quietly as "Mel." Evans would never know Mel's last name, nor would he know much about Mel's private life beyond the fact that he was married, supported a wife and children in the suburbs, and did not wish to alter his family situation even though, as Evans later described it to me, Mel was "gaga" over Jackie Ho.

Evans believed that Mel had met her in 1969 when he was traveling on business in Tokyo. Jackie was then living there as a nineteen-year-old student who had come from Hong Kong to continue her education; but she had become so enamored of her newfound freedom in Tokyo that she never got around to registering for classes. Mel was eager to bring her to New York and set her up in an apartment convenient to his midtown office, and it occurred to him that the simplest way to arrange this, as well as to establish her legal residency, which was what she wanted, was to have her marry an American citizen who was a homosexual—and the individual who came to mind, since he was aware of no other candidate, was Winter Evans.

Evans was then twenty-seven, and, though well educated (he had earned a degree in biology from the University of Wisconsin in 1965, and had later taken postgraduate classes in hotel management at Cornell), he had not yet found a satisfactory career when he came to know Mel in 1970. Evans then held a junior position in a New York public-relations firm owned by an older man who had been his lover for a few months but was becoming difficult to deal with. During the previous year, Evans had served as a bartender at a club in Miami and had also taken a turn modeling bathing suits in Palm Beach. But while financial considerations were certainly a factor in enticing Evans to marry Jackie Ho in 1970—in addition to the bonus from Mel, Evans would live with Jackie in a rent-free apartment—he also discovered after their introduction that she was physically stunning, and he suddenly fancied the notion that she might influence him in ways that would be considered normal by most of his friends and relatives back home in Green Bay, Wisconsin.

During the first year of their marriage, however, he would make love to her on only two or three occasions, he told me. He actually thought that he was beginning to enjoy being in bed with a woman, but Jackie thought differently. "Oh, this isn't what you want," she told him one night, convincing him that their marital arrangement would be best served if the two of them restricted their sexual intimacies to other men. And so during the remaining eight years of their marriage, Winter Evans had his boyfriends, and Jackie Ho had hers, going off with whomever she pleased when Mel was not around. Evans had never imagined, until knowing Jackie, that a woman could be so self-directed and determined to do as she pleased. Mel's money had earned him neither her fidelity nor gratitude, Evans told me; and one day in the apartment after Mel had handed her ten thousand dollars to cover the costs of her forthcoming visit to Hong Kong, she became very upset after she had removed the cash from an envelope and had counted it.

"*This* is chicken money," she declared to him, and she quickly proceeded to tear up dozens of hundred-dollar bills and hurl them at Mel, who was seated across from her on a sofa. Mel said nothing at first, but Evans, who was standing nearby, noticed that he was beginning to blush and then the corners of his mouth began to turn upward, forming a tricky, frozen smile. "I think he was actually enjoying this," Evans told me. "He had this big cigar, and Jackie was throwing money in his face, and he had never seen anything like this before—it was a *first* for him, seeing all that money torn up. It was like a guy with a lot of money going to Las Vegas and losing ten grand at roulette in an hour, and thinking it was a terrific deal. . . .

"And yet, not every man gets turned on by the same thing," Evans conceded, citing as an example Edward VIII's decision to give up the power and glory of the British throne in 1936 in order to marry a twice-divorced American woman from Baltimore, Wallis Simpson. "He'd been sheltered all his life in that domineering Victorian family, and then he falls for this woman," Evans remarked, "who maybe had a trick pelvis, but in any case she was an eye-opener for him, and he says to himself, This is real life!, and he suddenly no longer wants to be a king, and he says to his mother, 'Get my brother to do this, because I'm walking off' . . . and he walks off to become the Duke of Windsor. . . ." History is replete with women who turn the heads of rich and powerful men, Evans went on to say, mentioning Pamela Harriman and Jacqueline Onassis, and what he suggested was their Chinese equivalent—Jackie Ho.

"It's not necessarily a sexual thing that these women have going for them—it's more of a head thing," Evans speculated. "These women get into certain men's heads and make these men crave being around them. In Jackie's case, it's the strength of her spirit—she brings to men a kind of backbone; she's basically a stern woman. She's no dominatrix. She's no tomboy. But there's something vaguely masculine about her—never mind her beautiful body, her clothes, her hair, all her beautiful jewelry—*she* is in control, and she gives certain men what they want, which is denial. She never calls men; they're always calling her—'Can I see you?' 'No, I'm busy,' 'What are you doing Saturday?' 'I'm out of town.' 'Where will you be next Thursday?' 'I don't know yet.' It goes on and on, a cat-and-mouse game, and certain guys love it. She doesn't get close to many women. The only woman who played any important role in Jackie's life was her paternal grandmother in China. . . ."

I had been told the same thing by Jackie's second husband, J. Z. Morris: It had been this grandmother who had influenced Jackie's character and style, her solipsistic nature and tendency to be more pragmatic than romantic. The grandmother was a worldly and well-to-do woman from a distinguished Cantonese family, and after her opium-addicted husband had died prematurely, she moved the family from Canton to Hong Kong in advance of the Communist takeover of the mainland. Jackie's father grew up in Hong Kong as an underachiever who resisted hard work and hardly ever expressed himself, deferring most often to his mother's judgment. After he had gotten married and saw his first child, however, he admitted to his wife his irrepressible disappointment. He had wanted a son instead of the daughter who would be born to them in 1950 as Ho Ching Sheung, and would be called "Jackie." His daughter would resent him throughout her girlhood, and, shortly after her eighteenth birthday, with her grandmother's financial support and encouragement, she left China for Japan.

Her guardians in Tokyo were members of a Japanese family that had met her grandmother during previous visits to China. One member of the Japanese family was a socially active woman in her mid-thirties named Mia Kobayashi, who regularly held receptions in her Tokyo apartment, where the guest list often included Americans—employees from the U.S. embassy, American military officers on leave from Vietnam, and American civilians on business trips. Mia sometimes invited Jackie to attend these events not only because Jackie was a lovely young adornment and was mature beyond her years but also because Jackie was eager to practice her English. Jackie learned English quickly and well, and, after a year and a half in Tokyo—meeting Mel during this time—she had a better understanding of English than did Mia Kobayashi herself. Mia had in the interim become involved with a middle-aged American whom she thought was a mogul in the movie business. But after Mia had visited the man's home in Las Vegas and had noticed that his residence was surrounded by trucks, she wondered aloud, "Aren't you in the *movie* business?" "No," he said, "I told you I was in the *moving* business." Mia's visit to Las Vegas was quite brief.

Whatever misunderstandings Jackie Ho would later have in New York with Mel were easily resolved, Winter Evans told me, as long as Jackie had her way. Evans recalled that after Jackie had torn up Mel's money and had thrown it into his face, Mel had soon returned to the apartment with another envelope, this filled with enough cash to satisfy Jackie's expectations that her visit to Hong Kong should be budgeted at no less than twenty thousand dollars. Evans would sometimes accompany Jackie overseas, especially when the purpose of the trip was to ski, which they both enjoyed and at which Jackie excelled, even though she had never seen snow until she had turned eighteen and had taken her first skiing lesson during a weekend in Sapporo, Japan.

Evans would continue to be Jackie's skiing partner, confidant, and consort long after she had eased Mel out of her life, which she did by 1973. "He'd become a waste of makeup" was how she had put it to Evans, using a phrase that she often used when explaining her change of heart toward certain men who had formerly seemed to matter to her. Jackie was meticulous in making herself up before going out at night, Evans explained to me. She scrutinized herself in front of her bedroom mirror as she carefully applied her cosmetics, and adjusted her hair, and tried on her jewelry (much of it designed by Bulgari, although some had come from her grandmother). Jackie's body, too, was a reflection of her dedication to physical health, her working out daily in a gym, Evans went on to say, emphasizing that her well-toned and slender figure had changed little during the nearly thirty years he had known her. Many men had since come and gone, but Evans had remained a constant factor in her life, her oldest American friend; after she had divorced him in order to marry J. Z. Morris in 1979, he had served as the couple's best man. When J.Z. moved his things into Jackie's penthouse, taking over Evans's closet space, Evans moved *his* things into what had been J.Z.'s pied-à-terre on the fifth floor of the building at 206 East 63rd Street.

But even though I had been recommended to Jackie by Winter Evans and J. Z. Morris, she resisted my interview requests throughout 1997 and into 1998, saying always that she was too busy to see me, while at the same time saying it was okay to call her. She was friendly on the telephone but otherwise elusive. I wondered if she saw me for what I was, a man whose interest in her she could put to no practical purpose, and I was therefore a waste of makeup. Or maybe, as I recalled what Evans had said about her, she saw me as a potential player in her "cat-and-mouse game." However, I remained interested in her as an audacious woman of no doubt beguiling charm who might loom large in my projected book about the Willy Loman Building; and I was surprised and encouraged one afternoon when she returned a message of mine and agreed to meet with me. "I'm leaving for Hawaii tomorrow," she said, "but I'll be back in a month or so. Call me back then and we'll make a date."

I had meanwhile followed my editor's advice and put aside the restaurant saga, conceding to myself that it was probably wise to do so. I had been unable to get a handle on the material after years of research. I could never understand *why* 206 East 63rd was the worst address in the *Zagat* guide and why it symbolized failure within the restaurant industry. I knew only that whoever opened a restaurant at 206 East 63rd was likely to have a dyspeptic experience. Still, I occasionally stopped in to have dinner.

The investors from Fort Lee, New Jersey, who had bought Tucci from Gerald Padian and his associates in March 1997, decided to keep the restaurant's name, while repainting it in brighter colors. The exterior walls, which had been green, were redone in a salmon tone similar to that of the much-praised Sign of the Dove restaurant located a few blocks uptown, and they replaced Padian's green canvas marquee with a red one. In the dining room they installed an elaborate new backbar, and also a new rug for the staircase, and white linen cloths now covered the black marble-topped tables that Padian had left uncovered. Extra personnel were added to the service staff, and the food prices were increased. The chef that Padian had hired, Matt Hereford, was retained, although the chief cook, Miguel Peguero, quit to accept a higher-paying job at a New York social club where Padian was a member.

The general manager brought in by the New Jersey backers was a high-spirited though prickly individual named Larry Rosenberg. In his mid-forties and a native of Brooklyn, Rosenberg was slight of build, dark-haired, and mustachioed, and he was quite distinct in his manner of dressing, possessing a wardrobe that consisted of several Nehru-style jackets of varying shades, which he hung on a pipe in the basement at Tucci and alternatively wore while greeting customers upstairs for lunch and dinner. Though trained as a pastry chef, Rosenberg had risen to management positions in a number of restaurants before coming to Tucci, and he took pride in the fact that there was no task in the trade that he could not satisfactorily perform—he could cook, tend bar, wait tables, and supervise a staff. "In a pinch, I can do anybody's job," he told me one night after my second meal there, "and so I don't have to take any funny stuff from these people who work for me."

Disliking what he interpreted to be a cavalier attitude on the part of Andy Globus, one of the holdover waiters from Padian's time, Rosenberg fired him within three weeks. During his first six months as Tucci's manager, Rosenberg dismissed half a dozen other employees as well, including the waiter from Russia, Konstantin Avramov. Rosenberg had learned from a busboy that Konstantin had been overheard talking in the kitchen about the likelihood that he would soon open a place of his own, whereupon he would offer superior positions to several of his friends among the Tucci staff. Konstantin denied these allegations as soon as Rosenberg had brought them up, but Rosenberg fired him anyway. Konstantin was eventually hired as a waiter at the Coco Marina restaurant in the World Financial Center. Five months after Rosenberg had fired him, Rosenberg himself was looking for a job.

The New Jersey backers, unimpressed with the return they were receiving on their investment, decided to close Tucci in the spring of 1998, a little more than a year after they had bought it from Padian's group. The final dinner would be served on Sunday night, April 5. I was among the closing-night crowd.

As I sat at a corner table behind the bar, sipping a predinner drink in the company of my wife and two of our friends, I could not help (despite being privy to the many unfavorable comments made about Larry Rosenberg by Konstantin Avramov et al.) feeling sorry for Rosenberg as I watched him standing stiffly at the door, dressed in his navy blue Nehru jacket, evoking the image of a dutiful and dour sea captain posed on the deck of a sinking ship. His dark eyes were downcast and he spoke softly and succinctly as he acknowledged the arriving customers, seeming to be more disappointed than pleased by their abundant number—no fewer than 170 diners, which was unusually high for a Sunday night, and it would produce at the end of the evening revenue of $6,430. And *yet*, as Rosenberg later complained to me, not one of the restaurant's backers from New Jersey had made an appearance during the restaurant's last night to say farewell to him or to the workers, who, in most instances, had shown up to fulfill their obligations on the eve of their unemployment.

"Oh, part of me is relieved that we're getting out of here," Rosenberg told me, pausing briefly after delivering the menus, "and yet there's another part of me that really wished we'd made it." But one of the mistakes that he acknowledged making a week earlier was in forewarning two of his favorite waiters that Sunday would be Tucci's last night. "And how did you think they thanked me?" Rosenberg asked, and then quickly answered: "They thanked me by abandoning me. They disappeared. And so I've been shorthanded since then, and tonight we have all this business, and I have to help the waiters and busboys and also be at the door." While I nodded with understanding, it was obvious that many customers were intolerant of the slow service they were receiving, and they complained often to Rosenberg, calling to him from across the room:

"Where's the waiter?"

"What's the problem here?"

"Where's our food?"

"What's taking so long?"

"Everything's coming along," said Rosenberg, trying to reassure them as he moved up and down the aisles, helping his waiters and busboys; "everything's on the way."

"Well, if you don't get it here in a minute," said one customer with three companions, "we're out of here."

Rosenberg's conciliatory manner suddenly changed. His dark eyes narrowed, and he walked toward the man.

"Well, why don't you leave *now*?" he asked, with his upraised right hand pointing toward the door.

"We *will*," the man said immediately, getting up and heading toward the exit, with his companions following.

As Rosenberg watched them leave, I removed a pen from my pocket and noted on a piece of paper what I had just seen. Rosenberg turned toward me.

"You looking for a quote?" he asked.

Before I could reply, he struck a theatrical pose. He placed his hands on his hips, tossed his head back, and, dancing in the aisle, began to mimic the song that Al Jolson had made famous in the 1920s film *The Jazz Singer*—"Toot Toot Tootsie Goodbye." He serenaded the restaurant crowd with:

> Toot, Toot, Tucci goodbye
> Toot, Toot, Tucci don't cry
> The choo-choo train that takes me away from you,
> No words can say how sad it makes me.
> . . . Toot, toot, Tucci . . .
> Goodbye. . . .

31

IN THE LATE SUMMER OF 1998, FOUR MONTHS AFTER LARRY ROSEN-
berg had closed Tucci, Donald Trump's estranged wife, Marla Maples,
in partnership with Bobby Ochs, a restaurateur who was a friend of
hers, announced that they would soon open a restaurant at 206 East 63rd
Street called Peaches. This would be the tenth partnership seeking success at this address. The new restaurant was named Peaches because
Marla Maples had been born in the Peach State of Georgia. When I first
heard the news, having received a fax from J. Z. Morris's office in Sarasota, I tried to pay no attention. I was finished with the restaurant story. I
had eaten my last meal at that losers' location.

In holding Morris's message, however, I was drawn to the surname of
Ms. Maples's partner—*Ochs*. Was Bobby Ochs related to the Ochs family
that owned the *New York Times*? If so, should this not command my interest? How extraordinary it would be, I thought, if Bobby Ochs was a blood
relative of the newspaper's late patriarch, Adolph Ochs, who had left his
assets to his offspring, hoping that they would emulate him at the helm of
the *Times*—and yet there was perhaps a black sheep among them who,
after discrediting himself, had been ostracized by his kinsmen and was
destined to grovel for his livelihood in the pits of the dining profession at
206 East 63rd Street.

But what if Bobby Ochs and his forthcoming Peaches would emerge as
a critical and commercial success? Would this not earn Bobby Ochs a
prodigal son's return to the bosom of the *Times*-owning family?

Aware that it is easier to track down restaurateurs *before* they become
important or self-important, I hastened over to 206 East 63rd Street. I
had no idea what Ochs might look like, but Marla Maples would be easily
recognizable because her photograph had often appeared in the press in
connection with her career as an actress and model and, of course, her
marriage to the real estate king, Donald Trump, which was currently in its
third and final year. However, when I arrived at the restaurant site early

in the afternoon, a few days before the scheduled opening of Peaches, I saw no sign of the blond-haired southern belle; I saw only two painters retouching the lower ledge of the building's facade in a honey-colored shade and a workman standing on a ladder under the marquee, tightening a peach-striped canvas awning. The security man posted behind the front door told me that Ms. Maples was out of town and Ochs was out to lunch, but after I had shown him the fax from J. Z. Morris and had further identified myself, he permitted me to enter the restaurant and look around.

I was immediately impressed by the many changes and improvements that had occurred since the closing of Tucci, and it was obvious that lots of money had been spent on the new decor—a sum that I would later learn was in excess of $750,000. Indeed, the place was now so altered in appearance that it was difficult for me to associate it with its troubled past, and not since the opening of Le Premier in 1977 did I feel as optimistic about the future prospects of the proprietors at this address. Everything here was of the highest quality and design, luxuriously appointed and carefully painted—none of the slapdash brushstrokes and plaster cracks that had marked the walls and wainscoting of Tucci. The second-hand bar that Gerald Padian had bought from a warehouse in Harlem had been scrapped. On the second floor was a glistening new mahogany bar that was twice as long as Padian's bar. A grand piano stood next to it. This would be part of the locale of the one-hundred-seat supper club and cabaret at Peaches. The seven-foot-high brick pizza oven that had been erected in the rear of the dining room below by the Napa Valley Grill owner, Michael Toporek, had been discarded for a U-shaped banquette uphostered in a beige print fabric. The dining room's walls were cream-colored; there were potted palms standing on pedestals along the edges of the room; and hanging from the ceiling were round honey-colored glass fixtures with copper rims. The tables were larger and more widely spaced than they had been at Tucci, although the seating capacity of ninety at Peaches would exceed Tucci's by fifteen.

"Hello, I'm Bobby Ochs," said the man who approached me from behind, and as I turned, I saw a slender six-footer in his mid-fifties with horn-rimmed glasses, dark eyes, graying curly hair, and a neatly trimmed salt-and-pepper beard. Personable to a fault, and with little prompting from me, he proceeded to describe in detail what I had observed in passing, and while he credited Marla Maples with making most of the key decisions with regard to the ambience of Peaches, he also mentioned that she had been assisted by two women who were feng shui consultants.

There had recently been an article in the *Times* describing feng shui as a melding of certain principles in the Chinese Taoist and Tibetan Buddhist tradition that presumably offered guidance to people wishing to experience more "energy" and "harmony" in their places of work and their residences; it was further suggested that such goals might be achieved merely by the rearrangement of furniture, the relocation of kitchens, and the removal of structural columns, overhead beams, and other objects that might limit the flow of energy. Inasmuch as Marla Maples had previously hired feng shui proponents to work with the designers and decorators of some of Donald Trump's properties, and had been pleased with the results, she invited two of them to examine the space at 206 East 63rd Street shortly after she and Bobby Ochs had acquired the sublease. Ochs told me that he had initially been skeptical about seeking advice from the feng shui women, but after showing them around and hearing their comments, and later reading their report, he realized that he was in total agreement with their recommendations. The restaurant's entranceway should be rebuilt and made "more welcoming"; the bar area should be on the second floor, not the first, thus adding space and energy to the dining room; and the pizza oven was best eliminated, being described in the report as a "money burner." The adoption of these and other proposals would make Peaches similar in design to one of Bobby Ochs's favorite New York restaurants—Le Colonial, a two-floored Vietnamese restaurant at 149 East 57th Street, between Third and Lexington avenues. "That place has a lively bar upstairs and a wide-open dining room below that's doing a terrific business," he told me, becoming so enthusiastic about the possibility that Peaches might exceed Le Colonial in popularity that I was reluctant to interrupt him with the question that had drawn me here.

"Are you by any chance related to the Ochs family of the *New York Times?*" I finally asked.

"Oh, I'm often asked that," he replied, recalling that during his boyhood in the Bronx the teachers would usually commence the school year by asking each of the students to rise in their classrooms, introduce themselves by name, and also say a few words about their parents. "Whenever I mentioned that my father was Adolph Ochs, the teacher would cut in and ask, 'The Adolph Ochs?' and I'd say, 'Of course, the Adolph Ochs.' 'Oh,' the teacher would say, 'I didn't know your father owned the *New York Times,*' and I'd say, 'No, my father, Adolph Ochs, is a dental mechanic on One Hundred and Sixty-seventh Street and River Avenue.'"

The two Adolphs were *not* related, Bobby Ochs told me, although he believed that his late father might be deserving of a footnote in the annals of the dental profession. His father had made the false teeth worn by the exiled Russian leader Leon Trotsky, not long before the latter had

been murdered in Mexico in 1940 by agents of Trotsky's rival, Joseph
Stalin. Trotsky had passed through the United States while en route to
Mexico, Ochs explained, and it was during Trotsky's brief stay in the
Bronx that he had somehow become a dental patient of Bobby Ochs's
father, Adolph.

I thanked Bobby Ochs for this information. Privately, however, since
hearing that he was unrelated to the *Times's* ownership, I was no longer so
interested in his personal story nor the fate of Peaches restaurant. I did
attend the opening-night party in late September 1998, and I dined there
occasionally after that, but on those occasions I never once saw Marla
Maples on the premises. There *was* a large portrait of her by LeRoy
Neiman hanging on the wall near the entrance, but she herself was either
out of town—a *New York Post* columnist wrote that she was working on a
television pilot in Los Angeles—or she was, as I also read in the papers,
preoccupied in New York with matters regarding her marital breakup
with Donald Trump or her litigation involving a man who had formerly
served as her publicist and had allegedly stolen seventy pairs of her shoes
and also some of her lingerie and panty hose.

In her absence, Bobby Ochs ran Peaches cheerfully and without apparent effort each night, and, from what I was able to observe as an occasional customer (once dining there with J. Z. Morris), the restaurant was
doing well enough, although my judgment was, as usual, untrustworthy.
In early May 1999, as I was passing 206 East 63rd during my usual midday
stroll, I saw Bobby Ochs alone in the dining room and decided to pay him
a visit.

"Sorry," he said as I entered, "but we're closed."

"Closed for the afternoon?" I asked.

"No, closed for good," he said.

"I can't believe it," I said; "you seemed to be doing fine."

"No we weren't," he said, "but I still don't know what I could have
done differently around here. The food was good; the prices were
right. . . ."

He invited me to join him at one of the empty tables, and for the next
hour or so he tried to analyze what had caused the downfall of Peaches.
As he delivered what was essentially a monologue, his voice sometimes
almost inaudible and markedly morose, I sat across from him taking notes;
and, after returning home, I sent the following message by fax to J. Z.
Morris in Sarasota:

Friday, May 7, 1999

Dear J.Z.—

I was just with Bobby Ochs in his now-defunct Peaches restaurant listening to him discussing the reasons—the how many reasons?—that led to his having to close the place after barely seven months of operation. I think that in a mental sense he is almost shell-shocked at this time. I felt so sorry for him as he unburdened himself in this abandoned dining room that was buzzing with flies—a forlorn atmosphere interrupted occasionally by a ringing telephone dialed by people wanting a dinner reservation, or by the door knockings of a mailman who wanted to know how much longer he should be delivering mail to Peaches at this address? There was also a visit from a young woman who had been a customer and she inquired as to the whereabouts of a man she'd often met in the bar in the upstairs lounge weeks before (she'd been smitten by him, but lost his phone number); and there also arrived at the door a now out-of-work waitress asking Bobby Ochs when she'd be receiving her promised pay? He promised that she'd receive her money on Friday evening.

Once or twice during my stay with him he received visits from rental agents wanting to see the place. So far as I could tell, Ochs has no takers; but he has not lost hope. As depressed as I think he is, he tries hard not to show it . . . although the clouds did seem to be very heavy and dark in this vacant restaurant today. The plants situated above the banquettes had not been watered in days, and their leaves were turning brown, and in the kitchen the garbage cans were filled with refuse. I watered the plants, and warned Bobby that rats would be visiting soon if he did not get the kitchen cleaned up. He agreed to do it. He is very agreeable and likeable. But he still wonders why he failed to make a success of this business. All he could do was list his possible shortcomings and errors in judgment; and he is not reluctant to take all the blame. Maybe, he suggests, it was wrong to have moved the bar upstairs. Maybe if the downstairs dining room had been furnished with a bar and had people gathered around it waiting for tables, the potential customers looking in from the sidewalk would have found the place more inviting and desirable. There were several other things that were mentioned—but what did it matter now? Approximately $750,000 was invested in improving this place beyond what the Tucci owners had done; and the results were nil. . . .

A few months later, J. Z. Morris told me that yet another restaurant, a kosher Italian dining establishment named Il Patrizio, would open at 206 East 63rd Street. This would be the eleventh partnership to take a risk at this address. This time, however, I was determined to stay away. What was the point of returning? What could I find there that I had not already found, and that my editor had not already told me he did not want me writing about? Still, I *had* to write something. I had signed a book contract in 1992, and now seven years had elapsed, and how could I justify this expenditure in time?

I spent the spring and early summer of 1999 going through my research files, rereading my notes, and rewriting some of the sections of various works that I had labored over but had never come close to finishing. There was the fifty-four-and-a-half-page section dealing with Frederick J. Schillinger and the origins of the "Willy Loman Building." There was a forty-page introduction to my memoir, beginning with my arrival in 1949 at the University of Alabama. There were sixty pages of a travel book that described my first visit to Calabria in 1955. There was a book outline and ninety typed pages of notes concerning the financial struggles of the Chrysler automobile company, a subject that I had first pursued in 1982, conducting many interviews with Chrysler officials in Detroit and their Mitsubishi partners in Tokyo.

I had put aside this material in 1983, and had more or less forgotten about it while concentrating on the research and writing of *Unto the Sons*. Reviewing the Chrysler material now, in 1999, I considered the possibility of using some of it in an updated story about Chrysler's onetime leader, Lee Iacocca, an interesting man, whom I had remained in touch with since his retirement from the auto company and his relocation to Los Angeles, where he was now hoping to launch a company that manufactured electric bicycles. On reflection, however, I decided that an updated story about Iacocca probably belonged in a magazine, perhaps as a profile in *The New Yorker*.

There was also in my filing cabinet a few folders labeled "The Bobbitts—a work in progress (1993–1994)." I would have probably discarded this long before had it not been for the advice of *The New Yorker*'s editor, Tina Brown, who suggested that it might someday be worthy of a short book. In the years since then, as tidbits of new information about the Bobbitt couple appeared occasionally in the press, I would collect it and insert it into my folders. There was a paragraph in 1995 announcing that the couple had finalized their divorce. It was also reported that Lorena Bobbitt, after having been forgiven by the jury for removing her husband's penis, had resumed her career as a nail sculptress at a shopping mall in northern Virginia. There were many tabloid references to John Bobbitt at various times between 1995 and 1997 as he resided in Las Vegas and elsewhere in Nevada and also in Southern California, working sporadically as a tow-truck operator, a lumper, a bartender, a pizza deliverer, and a performer in pornographic films (although his penis was unable to achieve the full tumescence it had known prior to its last encounter with Lorena). In addition, John Bobbitt made a few nightclub appearances as a stand-up comic, and in one routine he made reference to his ex-wife: "The last thing I told her was that I wanted a separation, and she took it literally."

Included in the Bobbitt folders were a few paragraphs that I myself had written:

> While John Bobbitt received no credit from the nation's lexicographers, his mishap is singularly responsible for the P-word entering the English language as it is now commonly spoken by men and women in the everyday world and is being published unhesitatingly in the headlines of family newspapers. Had John Bobbitt received a penny every time "penis" had appeared in newsprint and been articulated on television and radio broadcasts since he unwittingly removed the fig leaf from the word, he would now be extremely rich. He did earn about $400,000 for his guest appearances as a curiosity on talk shows and for his half-erect debut as a porno stud, but most of this money was retained by his media adviser and his attorneys as compensation for his legal bills and other operating expenses during and after the trials.
>
> The Hollywood agent for Lorena Bobbitt, Alan Hauge, has failed so far to sell her story to a movie studio but he said that he had earned her considerable sums of money from her appearances on foreign and domestic television shows and the interviews she gave to magazines overseas. These funds, Hauge said, enabled her to put a down payment on a new home in Virginia, and to arrange for her parents and her younger sister and brother in Venezuela to emigrate to the U.S.A. and stay with her. . . .

In early December 1997, after I had returned to New York from a sojourn in Alabama—where I spent time with Selma's sixty-seven-year-old mayor Joseph T. Smitherman, who had served nine terms in office but would lose the next election to a youthful black candidate named James Perkins—I was more than surprised to find on my answering machine a message from Lorena Bobbitt. Her recorded voice was soft, timid, but urgent. "Please call me back as soon as you can," she said; "I'm in trouble." On the tape she explained that she had been arrested by the Virginia police in the aftermath of a noisy domestic dispute with her mother, and now Lorena had a favor to ask: Would I be willing to testify in her behalf as a "character witness"?

Absurd, ridiculous, laughable—these were the words that came to my mind as I replayed the tape. I was to be a character witness for a woman who, after cutting off her husband's penis, had been arrested following an altercation with her mother?

And, I reminded myself, Lorena had been no help to me whatsoever when I had needed her during my assignment for *The New Yorker.* If I had then gotten Lorena's cooperation in the form of an interview, Tina Brown would have surely published my article, or so I preferred to believe. Why didn't Lorena rely upon the magazine writer from *Vanity Fair* and the correspondent from *20/20,* both of whom she had favored with interviews, to be her character witnesses?

Still, I returned her call. And when she heard my voice, she began to cry. She pleaded with me to attend her trial. She was being charged with assault and battery. The case would be heard in early April 1998. It would take place in the same courthouse where, four years earlier, she had given her ingenue performance as the abused wife of John Bobbitt. I was actually too curious to miss her forthcoming appearance in court, and so on the phone I promised that I would be there. The occasion would also provide me with my first opportunity to see her mother as well as her father and her younger sister and brother, and this might help me to decide whether or not I wished to continue with my research on the Bobbitt saga as part of my vaguely defined book, which might be called *Down and Out in America.*

On the eve of the court date, I flew from New York to Washington's Dulles Airport and was met near the baggage-claim section by Lorena, who hastened toward me with her arms extended, smiled, and kissed me on the cheeks. At twenty-nine, she was as slender, pretty, and carefully groomed and attired as she had been on the day the jury had exonerated her in the penis case. After thanking me for coming, she turned to introduce me to her new boyfriend, who followed a few paces behind her. He was a gangling, heavyset, casually dressed, dark-haired individual in his thirties named David Bellinger. He bent down slightly as we shook hands—he was six-four (Lorena was five-two). The couple seemed to be very comfortable in each other's presence and Bellinger was at once cordial and accommodating toward me, taking the initiative to carry my luggage out of the airport to the parking lot, where his red sports car awaited us. Bellinger ran an auto accessories business in Woodbridge, Virginia, and his car was replete with such paraphernalia.

As we drove toward my motel—Lorena insisted on sitting in the back—he told me that he and Lorena had started dating during the past year, having first met after they had begun taking night courses at Northern Virginia Community College. He said that even before meeting her in person he had been attracted to her from seeing her on television and in news photos during the media blitz of 1993–1994, and he would sometimes drive past the courthouse while the trials were in progress. He imagined her sitting in the crowded courtroom facing the jury, and at such times he was always sympathetic to her cause and very optimistic that she would win her freedom.

There were questions I wanted to ask David Bellinger, but I resisted. This was neither the time nor the place to pose such questions, certainly not with Lorena in the car. Still I wondered, Did he and Lorena, whom I assumed to be lovers, ever get into arguments? Did he ever think that he was in a precarious position as Lorena's bedmate? Did he sleep on his stomach? I recalled the advice given in 1993 by the maimed John Bobbitt to an investigating police officer in the hospital: "Be careful who you date."

After registering at my motel, I had a drink in the lobby with David and Lorena and learned a bit more about her quarrel with her mother. Lorena, who following her divorce from John Bobbitt had resumed using her maiden name, Gallo, told me that she and her mother had often argued about money and other matters since the elder Gallos had moved from Venezuela into her home in 1994. Lorena had hoped that her parents would adjust to a new way of life, but instead they held to their old Latin American traditions and measured her by their expectations. They made little effort to understand English, tuned in almost exclusively to Spanish-language radio stations, and tended to treat her as if she were a naïve and dependent daughter, whereas it was *they* who were dependent on *her*. They lived rent-free, relied upon her to drive them around, and, when shopping or otherwise engaged with people unable to communicate in Spanish, expected her to serve as their interpreter. Eventually she helped them to find work outside the home, menial tasks that did not demand fluency in English, and at the same time she saw to it that her teenage brother, Fabrizio, was enrolled in school and that her sister, Vanessa, four years her junior, was hired as a trainee at her nail salon.

Lorena's difficulties with her parents worsened after she had met David

Bellinger and the latter began offering her advice on how she might more effectively manage her finances. It was he who encouraged her to take into strict account the monthly expenses incurred by her and her family and to expect the others to contribute to the payments. There was not much expressed disagreement about this from Lorena's family, but when Bellinger, who was quick with numbers and adept with his computer, printed out the bills with suggestions of appropriate apportionment, Lorena's parents *did* feel resentment. He was an outsider, they reminded her when he was not around, and he was now meddling in their personal affairs. But Lorena, who had experienced bankruptcy during her years as Mrs. Bobbitt, welcomed having David as a buffer, as a responsible and reliable friend who was not only interested in her solvency but in reaffirming her independence within the complicated closeness of her not yet fully assimilated Latin American family. Even though she and David were not living together, he was an imposing presence in her household. She also had a key to his apartment, and it was to him she had fled following the confrontation with her mother and the arrival of the police.

Lorena told me she was confident that the judge would rule in her favor. It was her mother, forty-nine-year-old Elvia Gallo, who had provoked the argument and had struck first, although in the ensuing scuffle Elvia had gotten the worst of it. She had scratches on her neck, facial bruises, and a speck of blood in the corner of her left eye; it was while in this condition that Elvia ran outside the house to complain to a neighbor, a Puerto Rican woman, who in turn telephoned the police and repeated Elvia's assertion that she had been beaten up by her daughter.

When meeting with the police, however, Elvia changed her story, insisting that it was *she* who was at fault. It had perhaps belatedly occurred to her that the interests of the Gallo family would not be well served if Lorena went to jail. The police listened noncommittally as Elvia made her statement through an interpreter, and they also took several photographs of her scratched neck and bruised face. A warrant was immediately issued for Lorena's arrest. Soon the county prosecutor's office released a statement advocating that the case against Lorena be brought before a judge.

On the morning of the court date—April 2, 1998—I sat in the courtroom a few rows behind Lorena and her attorney, listening as her mother took the stand and repeated what she had told the police—*she* had been the attacker, not her daughter. Elvia Gallo's testimony was refuted, however, when her neighbor was on the stand and recalled that on the day of the incident Elvia had come tearfully to her door, beaten and battered, and had described how Lorena had just attacked her with her fists. At the conclusion of the neighbor's testimony, Judge James B. Robeson said that he, too, believed that Elvia had been brutalized by Lorena.

"If you ask me if I think she is guilty, I'd say yes," the judge admitted. But still, he went on to say, "I have reasonable doubt . . . so I'll find her not guilty."

Lorena showed no reaction to Judge Robeson's verdict; she simply reached over and shook hands with her defense attorney, William Boyce, and whispered, "Thank you." Then she turned around and thanked me, although I had not been called to testify. Later in the corridor, she embraced her mother and father and then introduced me to them. Elvia and Carlos Gallo were both lean and short, and after forcing a smile and shaking hands with me, they quickly backed away, seeming to be intimidated by the advancing presence of members of the media.

"My mother and I love each other very much," Lorena declared, stepping forward to face three newspaper reporters, two photographers, and a television camera crew—a tiny fraction of the press coverage she had drawn years earlier. "We live together; we work together," Lorena said, and, nodding toward her mother, she continued: ". . . Blood is thicker than water." Boyce told the press that Lorena was "very happy to have this episode behind her, and she'd like to resume a normal life free of publicity." He added, "Hope springs eternal."

Among the small crowd of onlookers stood Lorena's nineteen-year-old brother, Fabrizio, whom I tried, without success, to engage in conversation, and Lorena's twenty-five-year-old sister, Vanessa, who was actually quite friendly and communicative. A bit more petite than Lorena but equally attractive in her physical appearance and attire, Vanessa told me what I had already learned from speaking with Lorena the previous evening: Vanessa had recently gotten married and was no longer residing at the Gallo household—a decision that Lorena said had riled her parents (and particularly her mother) not only because Vanessa seemed to hardly know the young man but because he was Chinese. His immigrant family currently operated a Chinese restaurant in a nearby northern Virginia community. Neither he nor any of his kinsmen had come to the courthouse on this day, but, after mentioning that I would like to meet them, both Lorena and Vanessa agreed that they would try to arrange it when I next came to Virginia.

32

A s I FLEW BACK TO NEW YORK THAT AFTERNOON THINKING
about the Gallo family, and the fact that Lorena now had a Chinese brother-in-law, I was still not exactly sure what I was writing
about, but I nevertheless felt that I was part of it. I was both an observer
and an exemplar of the ongoing process of American assimilation and
conflict, of newcomers influenced by old traditions and fears and often a
misconstrued sense of what was relevant and important. How *American* it
was of the Spanish-speaking Gallo parents (recently settled on the outskirts of the nation's capital) to object to their daughter's decision to
marry a young neighbor of Chinese origin, and how *American* it was of
their daughter to marry him anyway.

I remembered how my convent-educated wife, Nan, had similarly
upset *her* parents decades earlier when she had traveled alone to meet me
in Rome, and, after having assured them that we would get married
within the chapel of the Trinità dei Monti, overlooking the Piazza di
Spagna—a site that had been consecrated by a sixteenth-century Pope
and that Nan had extolled as the spiritual center of her Sacred Heart education—we got married instead in a civil ceremony overseen by an Italian
Communist magistrate within the city's principal municipal hall, in the
Piazza del Campidoglio.

It had not been my idea to seek a change of venue for the wedding, nor
had I even wanted to be married. Prior to the arrival of my bride-to-be in
June 1959, I had been dwelling in solitary bliss in a hotel suite near the
Borghese Gardens, luxuriating in the fact that my expenses were being
paid by the *New York Times Magazine* after I had persuaded its editor to
allow me to write a piece about the city's famous boulevard, the Via
Veneto, where the director Federico Fellini was then filming scenes to be
included in his forthcoming movie, *La Dolce Vita*. I had briefly interviewed him through an interpreter while visiting the set, and I had spoken as well with one of the stars, Marcello Mastroianni, whose suavity

and nonchalance on the screen projected a romantic style that I someday hoped to emulate in real life.

After working at the desk in my hotel room every day for two weeks, I finally organized and outlined my material and began to type out the opening pages of the article on my Olivetti portable:

It is said that the most sophisticated street in the world is Rome's Via Veneto, a tree-lined promenade that is flanked by expensive hotels, sidewalk cafés, and *boulevardiers* whose eyes miss nothing.

This is the street that has seen everything. Back in the horse-and-chariot age it was part of the lovely gardens in which Messalina, the naughty wife of the Emperor Claudius, held her orgies. The Emperor Aurelian, in 271 A.D., built his famous wall along here— then the barbarians broke through it and plundered the villas, and then came the Saracen, Bourbon, and World War II invaders to sack it some more.

Under this street is a chapel adorned with the skulls of more than 4,000 Capuchins, and nearby is the spot where Raphael used to relax after a hard day at the Vatican. It was here that Pauline Bonaparte's perfumed carriage passed on its way to her villa; where Benito Mussolini went horseback riding. . . .

Today sleek Fiats and Alfa-Romeos whiz through the holes in the Aurelian Wall and later this summer travelers from around the globe will come here to sit in the sidewalk cafés, drink, stare—and be stared at. They will slump in chairs under the umbrellas, their legs crossed, their eyes roving, the heads moving from side to side like spectators at a tennis match. Before them will pass some of the world's richest men and loveliest women. Italian armchair connoisseurs will whistle softly at the women and often compliment them with a *"bona"* or *"bellissima."* . . .

I finished the three-thousand-word piece on June 1, and two days later, after the editor had accepted it for publication in an early-summer issue, I taxied to the airport to meet Nan and begin what I thought would be a ten-day vacation together in Rome—and *not* a matrimonial occasion at the altar of the Trinità dei Monti. I later listened with disbelief and anguish as Nan shared her intentions with me, doing so after her luggage had been carried into my suite and while the two of us were having what had begun as a pleasant lunch at Rosati's sidewalk café.

"You *can't* be serious," I said, or something to that effect—I cannot recall exactly what I said, or what Nan said, other than the fact that, in the most tactful way possible, it was made clear to me that if I wished to continue my two-year-old relationship with this green-eyed beauty who had the temerity to tell her parents that she was marrying me before telling *me*, my bachelorhood would soon be ending. It also must have occurred to me, though I was then only twenty-seven and relatively inexperienced in *les affaires du coeur*, that in matters most *personally* and *directly* affecting the lives of involved couples—be it the decision to marry, or to have children, or to buy or sell a house, or to sue for divorce—the woman's will invariably prevails.

Still, I believe that Nan was unhappy with my lack of enthusiasm for the potential joys of wedlock (feelings that I traced back to my claustrophobic upbringing in a home where my parents thought that an ideal marriage was one in which one's spouse was never out of sight), and so after Nan had visited the Trinità dei Monti and learned that weddings were no longer held there—the only place that represented special meaning to her as a marital site—she suggested that we might as well be married outside the Church. I got the impression, though she never articulated it, that she was now experiencing doubts about my worthiness as a husband (doubts perhaps previously conveyed to her by her mother), and while Nan did not want to leave Rome unmarried, since marrying me had been the expressed purpose of her trip, I think that she was anticipating, at least subconsciously, a happy day in the not-too-distant future when, after she had met the right man, she would marry him properly in front of a priest and in the presence of her family and friends.

The two of us coexisted with recurring feelings of resignation for the rest of the week in the Eternal City, waiting to be contacted by the office of the registrar, where we had applied for a marriage license and had given the chief clerk a fifty-dollar gratuity in the interest of expediency. The clerk himself delivered the license to us at our hotel on June 8, five days after Nan's arrival, and he also gave us directions to the municipal hall, where we were to appear two days later for the official ceremony.

On the eve of our wedding, Nan and I went to dinner at the Hostaria dell'Orso and ordered a bottle of champagne. Before we had received it, I excused myself from our table to greet one of my favorite authors, Irwin Shaw, who was standing at the bar chatting with a few other men. Shaw, a broad-shouldered, ruddy-faced, gregarious individual in his mid-forties, had played football for Brooklyn College but had achieved fame and fortune as a writer of short stories (I had practically memorized the opening paragraphs of "The Girls in Their Summer Dresses" and "The Eighty-Yard Run") and such best-selling novels as *The Young Lions*, which later became a movie starring Marlon Brando. I had recently read in a news column that Shaw's latest novel, which was set in Rome and was called *Two Weeks in Another Town*, had just been optioned by Hollywood.

After I had approached him and had congratulated him on his latest accomplishment, I was pleased to hear that he remembered meeting me years before in Paris, where he kept an apartment and was friendly with a *Times* colleague of mine, who had introduced us.

"What brings you to Rome?" he asked.

"I came to write about the Via Veneto for the Sunday *Times Magazine*," I said, "but a few days ago my girlfriend arrived from New York *with my birth certificate!* We've been dating for two years, and she thinks it's time we made it official."

"Who *is* this woman?" he asked.

"Her name is Nan Ahearn, and she works at Random House," I said.

"Random House! They're the best. They're *my* publishers. . . ."

We walked over to my table, and I introduced Nan to Irwin Shaw. Her large green eyes widened, and with a smile and gracious handshake, she complimented him on his work.

"This woman's got good taste," he whispered into my ear. "You're lucky to be marrying her. Who's the best man?"

"I don't have one," I replied.

"Yes, you do," he said. "You have me."

The next morning, in front of an ornate building overlooking the Piazza del Campidoglio, which had been designed by Michelangelo, Nan and I were met by Irwin Shaw and two of his closest friends in Italy—a courtly and personable gentleman named Pilade Levi, who was the Rome representative of a Hollywood studio, and Levi's attractive and equally engaging companion, Carol Guadagni, who headed the Rome office of the William Morris Agency. Shaw had undoubtedly sensed that Nan and I were uneasy about what we were about to do, and so he brought along his friends to lend their support and encouragement—which they did. But in actual fact, once the ceremony had begun, I ceased to think about what had concerned me earlier (that is, the good life would soon be over) and concentrated instead on how amazing it was that Nan would travel so far to be with me, and that the two of us would now be standing together in a huge and magnificent hall, hearing our marital vows being intoned in Italian by a handsome magistrate whose chest was crossed with a tricolored sash and who stood before a high-backed damask chair behind a table draped with a velvet cloth that displayed an emblazoned seal in gold lettering: *S.P.Q.R.* (the Senate and People of Rome).

After the ceremony, Shaw gave Nan and me a wedding party in a ballroom across the street from the American embassy on the Via Veneto. It was a festive occasion, attended by many people who were then active in the filming of *La Dolce Vita*, including Federico Fellini and Marcello Mastroianni—which brightened my spirits for about twenty-four hours, or until the following day, when our bridal suite was sizzling with an angry phone call from my bride's mother in New York.

"But *Mummy* . . ." I heard Nan trying to explain, "but *Mummy* . . ."

From the drift of their conversation and from what I found out later, my wife's mother became furious when she learned from the wedding story in that morning's *Times* that we had been married by a civil official rather than a priest. It had been a tiny story buried near the bottom of the social page, and I was surprised that Nan's mother had even noticed it.

Gay Talese Marries Miss Nan I. Ahearn

Miss Nan Irene Ahearn, daughter of Mr. and Mrs. Thomas J. Ahearn, Jr., of Rye, N.Y., was married Wednesday in Rome to Gay Talese. He is the son of Mr. and Mrs. Joseph F. Talese of Ocean City, N.J. The ceremony was performed in City Hall on Capitol Hill by City Councilor Renato Ambrosi de Magistris.

Mrs. Talese, a former student at the Rye Country Day School, was graduated from the Convent of the Sacred Heart, Greenwich, Conn., and in 1955 from Manhattanville College. She was presented in 1951 at the Westchester Cotillion. She is with Random House publishers in New York. The bridegroom, a member of the staff of the New York Times, was graduated from the University of Alabama in 1953.

In the interest of reportorial fairness and perhaps the continuation of my marriage, I do not think it is prudent of me to reveal any more information about my private relationship with Nan and her family. And yet since it was I who introduced the subject of my marriage and the irritation that it caused my mother-in-law in particular, I believe that readers are entitled to more of an explanation than I am comfortable about disclosing—accepting as I do my wife's prerogative to edit and amend whatever I might wish to publish about our marriage, the circumstances that preceded it, and the reactions that it provoked.

My own parents, to be sure, did not reveal what they thought about the marriage. Whatever misgivings they might have had about Nan as their daughter-in-law or about not being invited to the wedding, they kept to themselves. Italian-American couples of their generation were customarily reticent about discussing personal matters that caused them pain or discomfort, no doubt being influenced to some degree by the traditional southern Italian code of silence, known as *omertà*. Nan's family, however, being more securely ensconced in the American mainstream—Nan's banker father was three generations removed from Irish soil, and her mother's forebears first arrived from England in 1631—were more forthright in expressing their views on just about everything that interested them; and yet this does not provide *me* with much leeway when it comes to writing about *them* or my marriage to their daughter. Such topics are tacitly "off the record." After all, what I know about my in-laws and my wife came to me through circumstances quite different from how I operate as a fact-gathering writer, pursuing people for interviews with the understanding that the information is for public consumption.

If I were a practitioner of fiction, a creator of novels, plays, or short stories, I would have the option of doing what these writers can do whenever they feel compelled to write intimately about themselves and/or individuals whom they are close to—they can change everybody's names and otherwise falsify the facts in ways that they hope will protect their works from lawsuits or other forms of redress arising from so-called injured parties. And thus what is most truthfully and tellingly conveyed about private life in public literature and other means of communication is categorized and conveyed as "fiction." But as I have already tried to explain, since I am a fastidious exponent of *non*fiction—a reportorial writer who does not want to change names, who avoids using composite characters in narratives, and who makes every effort to adhere to factual accuracy—I am in a quandary here because I suspect that there exists a conflict of interest between my role as a writer and myself as a subject in this section of my story. Therefore I must recuse myself and defer to another writer, Arthur Lubow, who separately interviewed Nan and me on several occasions in 1991 for a *Vanity Fair* magazine piece that he was researching and that was pegged to the publication in early 1992 of my book *Unto the Sons*.

In Mr. Lubow's article, which appeared in the February 1992 issue of *Vanity Fair*, he wrote:

> Talese had never wanted to get married. In 1957, when he was a *Times* sportswriter, he was introduced to Nan Ahearn, a recent graduate of Manhattanville College of the Sacred Heart. Like many well-bred girls in the fifties, she was working at respectable jobs until she found a husband.

In Gay she saw a handsome young man with a passion for books and a single-minded ambition to be a writer. He had little in common with the boys who had escorted her to Princeton games and to the Stork Club and to the Westchester Cotillion, at which she made her debut. Those boys would be lawyers and bankers like her father, a handsome man who wore three-piece suits and consoled himself with alcohol. Her father paid attention only when she talked to him of philosophy or literature. She had majored in those subjects at Manhattanville.

For Gay, this dark-haired young woman with enormous green eyes might have been Judy Jones in F. Scott Fitzgerald's "Winter Dreams," a short story he loved so much that he had typed it out to see how it was constructed. Fitzgerald's protagonist was, like Gay, a tradesman's son in a summer resort, for whom the cultured, classy, glamorous Judy Jones was the incarnation of every youthful dream. So for Gay was Nan Ahearn. After an initial date at Toots Shor, during which Nan concluded he was more full of himself than anyone she had ever met, they hit it off. . . .

In May 1959, the *New York Times Magazine* dispatched Talese to Rome to write about the Via Veneto. Back in New York, Nan wrote him moony letters until he cabled her to come join him. With great animation, Nan, at fifty-eight still a beautiful, wide-eyed postdeb, tells me what happened next.

"On the way to lunch I went to Alitalia and booked the ticket for the next day," she remembers. "I called Mummy and Daddy and said, 'Can I have dinner with you tonight?' Which was a strange thing to ask. Of course, they said yes. I was just doing it one step at a time. I told them that I had received a cable from Gay asking me to marry him. It was totally untrue, a bald-faced lie. Mummy said, 'No, you have to be married here with the family.' I think I wept and carried on. I know I did. My mother said, 'You don't know what it's like to live with a writer. You weren't brought up for it.' But my father said, 'Go cable Gay.'

"The next morning I called Gay's parents very early and asked would they please send Gay's baptismal certificate. . . . That afternoon my mother came in and during lunch we went shopping for my trousseau. There was so much logistics involved that there wasn't time for reflection. On the plane that night, the man next to me, just making conversation, said, 'Where are you going?' I said to Rome. He said, 'Why?' I said, 'To get married.' And for the first time, I thought, Holy good night—what have I done?'"

When she got off the plane, she saw Gay in the lounge, his dark head buried in his sleeve, the image of dejection. He sensed what was about to happen. . . .

A civil wedding was arranged by one of Talese's heroes, Irwin Shaw. . . .

For a young writer who traced his lineage from Fitzgerald through Shaw, the auguries seemed right. A telephone call from Nan's mother in Rye to their Rome hotel was the initial upset. Suzanne Ahearn had learned from a *Times* wedding notice about the civil ceremony. Outraged, she told Nan that a wedding outside the church was invalid. Nan began to cry. Gay grabbed the phone and told his mother-in-law not to interfere. . . .

The newlyweds did have the Ahearns over to dinner in their shabby apartment (a third-floor room in the house that Gay and Nan would acquire in 1974 for $175,000). But that was the last time Gay would see them. "I think I felt challenged in a serious way," he says. . . . When their daughters were born, Nan visited Rye with them by herself. . . .

Nan and I celebrated our fortieth wedding anniversary on June 10, 1999. We dined alone at our summer place in Ocean City, and, after opening a special bottle of wine, exchanged gifts. I gave Nan a long strand of pearls and she presented me with two pairs of hand-crafted shoes she had ordered from a bootmaker on Lexington Avenue. During the evening, we received congratulatory calls from our daughters in New York—Pamela, thirty-five, a painter, and Catherine, thirty-two, the photo editor of *Quest* magazine. They both lived with boyfriends in apartments not far from our Manhattan residence, and, as we usually did every week, we made plans to meet for dinner.

Throughout our marriage, Nan continued to work full-time in the book business. After thirteen years as an editor at Random House, she moved to Simon & Schuster for seven years, and then in 1981 joined the Boston-based Houghton Mifflin company as the editorial director of the New York office. Eventually she became Houghton Mifflin's editor in chief and publisher, spending a few days each week in Boston. But in 1988, after explaining to her colleagues that she was "resigning from the Boston shuttle," she left Houghton Mifflin to become a senior vice president in New York with Doubleday & Co., and in 1990 began issuing her writers' works under her own imprint: Nan A. Talese/Doubleday.

In April 1999, together with the actress Meryl Streep and NBC's Katie Couric, Nan received the Matrix Award, given annually to women for their contributions toward the enhancement of communication. A month later, at a banquet sponsored by the United Jewish Appeal Federation of New York, Nan was again an honoree.

In July 1999, while Nan was a guest lecturer in California at the Stanford publishing course held every summer for a week or so on the Palo Alto campus, I was at home in New York, trying to write and extricate myself from the literary logjam that had stagnated my professional life. When I was not parrying with words and paragraphs at my desk, I was indulging in nerve-calming diversions—rearranging things in my office, removing and rewashing the filter in my air-conditioner, tuning in to baseball games and other sporting events on my small television screen. For me it was a channel-surfing summer. It was when I first felt the urge to fly halfway around the world to interview Liu Ying, the young Chinese woman who had missed that important kick in the China–United States women's World Cup finale, costing her team the match.

The Chinese players, as you will recall, had undoubtedly entered the Rose Bowl knowing that special importance was being attached to this contest by high-level Party leaders in their homeland, where there existed unfriendly feelings toward the United States in the aftermath of the accidental bombing of the Chinese embassy in Belgrade by an American plane. The United States government's explanation that the targeting had been unintentional was greeted skeptically by Chinese officials, reflecting the latter's mistrust of American foreign policy, as was reported in the press throughout the summer and into the autumn of 1999. I had also read several newspaper and magazine articles indicating that heightened security arrangements would be imposed in October as the Chinese Communist Party marked its fiftieth year in power. There would be public displays of tanks, missiles, and millions of troops marching past rows of Politburo members assembled on reviewing stands. There would be multitudes of security guards checking everyone's credentials, especially those of foreigners. It was admittedly not an ideal time for me, an unaccredited American writer, to be wandering around the country seeking to interview a young woman possessing deficient skills as a soccer player. Who would believe that I would travel so far for such a purpose? And, moreover, I had reasons of my own not to be in China during the late summer and fall of 1999.

I had promised to go with Nan on a European sojourn, a kind of postanniversary wedding gift that we were giving to each other. After a few days in Paris, we would join other couples on a bicycle tour of the Bordeaux wine country, and then in mid-September we would fly to Barcelona and embark on a two-week cruise of the Mediterranean.

According to the sailing schedule of our Cunard liner, the *Royal Viking Sun*, we would be in Florence on September 28, and in Rome on October 1 (where we planned to revisit our marital site); and on October 3, after moving along the southern Italian coastline and past the mountain ranges of Calabria that had long loomed over my ancestry, Nan and I would arrive on the morning of October 8 in Athens. We would remain there for four days, and then fly together to Germany on October 12, and part company at the Frankfurt airport. Nan was expected at the Frankfurt Book Fair, a weeklong event that she had often attended in the past, whereas I was to return to New York on a flight to JFK.

This was our plan, and we followed it precisely until the final day of our excursion. After I had accompanied Nan to the Frankfurt airport's baggage carousel, and then escorted her out to where a German driver was waiting to take her to her hotel, I returned to the terminal to await the announcement of my flight, which was five hours later. As I was hauling my belongings on a trolley and idly surveying the merchandise on display in duty-free shops and other stores, I passed the entrance of the airport's Sheraton Hotel and noticed a sign announcing that the hotel had a health club. I thought it would be a good idea to register for a room and have a workout and perhaps a massage prior to my flight. I was in no particular hurry to get back to New York.

Two hours later, having been to the gym and enjoyed the massage, I was wearing a robe and relaxing in my hotel room, reading through some of the notes that I had brought with me on the cruise. Among the material was a slim folder labeled "Wrong-footed Chinese soccer maiden—a work in progress." It contained several pieces about the World Cup soccer match and my letter to Norman Pearlstine, the magazine boss at Time, Inc., suggesting that an article might be done on Liu Ying.

As I was getting dressed and rearranging my luggage prior to checking out, I reached into my jacket for a slip of paper on which Nan had written the phone number of the Frankfurterhof, which was where she was staying while attending the book fair. I dialed the number but was unable to reach her. My call was soon transferred to a man at the front desk, who asked, "May I take a message for Mrs. Talese?"

"Yes, thank you," I said. "Please tell her that her husband called to say that he is canceling his flight to New York and is going to China, and he'll get back to her when he knows where he'll be staying."

Later that night, I was on a jet heading east.

Five months would pass before I would return home to New York.

33

ON ARRIVING IN BEIJING, I REGISTERED AT THE CHINA WORLD Hotel and was assigned to an attractive suite on the fourteenth floor, which had large windows and looked out upon several gleaming multistoried buildings rising in the polluted sky of this capital city that had a population of 12 million people, not one of whom I knew.

My plan, such as I had one, was to meet somebody who could facilitate my introduction to Liu Ying—but who? I decided that it would be unwise to approach the officials at the Chinese Sports Ministry directly, imagining that they would just entangle me with red tape, and I also did not think that it would be productive if I went to the American embassy, given the present state of U.S.-China relations. I did believe, however, that there was an individual in Beaverton, Oregon, who could help me.

He was Philip H. Knight, the founder and chairman of Nike, Inc., based in Beaverton. I had met him a year earlier through my wife. During one of his business trips to New York, he had gone to Nan's office to discuss the publication of a book he was writing in his spare time, a work of fiction having nothing to do with Nike. His wife, Penny, was with him in New York, and, after the four of us had dined one night at Elaine's, he handed me his business card and suggested that I contact him whenever I was in the vicinity of Oregon.

I had no idea how his novel was progressing when I arrived in China, but I knew that Nike was flourishing throughout the country—manufacturing tons of sneakers, employing thousands of Chinese factory workers; and it occurred to me that there was probably no one of my acquaintance who had more influence in China than Philip Knight. He surely possessed in abundance what the Chinese call *guanxi*—"connections." The word *guanxi* had often been referred to in *The Beijing Guide Book* that I had bought at the Frankfurt airport and had kept with me during my eleven-hour flight into Asia. In a chapter headed "Doing Business," the book's author noted:

China's Confucian society has been for millennia based upon personal relationships and the obligations pertaining to them. Familial relationships are paramount, followed by those among old friends. Known as "guanxi," personal relationships or connections permeate the business and bureaucratic arenas, forming an invisible network which often provides the most expedient way of getting anything done. . . . Beijing is a veritable "guanxi" bazaar, filled with "guanxi" peddlers, brokers and speculators. Whatever your scope of business, it is important to keep in mind these key elements of "guanxi."

I dialed Philip Knight's office from my hotel room, having, fortunately, kept his business card in my address book. Although he was unavailable when I called, his secretary promised that she would deliver to him the fax message that I said I would send within the hour.

In my fax to Philip Knight, after recalling our dinner together at Elaine's, I explained why I was in China and offered him a synopsis of my soccer idea, emphasizing that it was not my intention to portray Liu Ying unfavorably but, rather, to suggest that, like most competitive performers who have encountered setbacks, she is guided by a "comeback spirit"—a spirit compellingly expressed by Michael Jordan in one of his famous commercials for Nike.

"In that commercial," I reminded Philip Knight, "Michael Jordan is telling us about the numerous times when he has missed important shots, and the countless contests that were consequently lost, and yet following each defeat he expresses determination to keep going, to give it another shot. . . ." At the conclusion of my fax, I sought Knight's advice on how I should properly proceed in China, hoping that he would put me in contact with someone who might eventually make it possible for me to have a face-to-face meeting with Liu Ying.

Later that day, I received a reply from Knight's office saying that my fax had been received and that he would get back to me as soon as possible. Two days later came a message from Philip Knight himself—one of four from him that I would receive during my early days in China, all of them encouraging in tone but also cautioning me to maintain my patience. "As you might imagine," he wrote in one fax, "Chinese Officials are not always enamored with the idea of talking to the U.S. press." In another message: "Dear Gay: China is a big country compiled of many different dialects, attitudes and regional barriers, all presided over by a government in conflict with itself," and he added, "I don't know where all this leads, but I do believe you will not be sorry you have gone on this search/adventure. Best regards, Phil."

The most important thing that he did for me was to refer me to Nike's chief representative in Beijing, an amiable round-faced gentleman in his mid-thirties named Patrick Wang, who had been born in Shanghai but had attended colleges in Oregon and New York and spoke English fluently and heartily. He was Nike's ambassador to the Chinese sports regime and therefore not lacking in *guanxi*. Shortly after I had spoken to him and had enjoyed the first of our many dinners together, he called to inform me that the soccer authorities would be sending a car and driver to pick me up at my hotel within a few days, or a week at most, and would take me to a location in the western hills of Beijing, where I would witness a practice session by the team and receive an introduction to Liu Ying.

While awaiting this occasion, and keeping Nan informed of my activities via faxed messages to the Frankfurterhof and later to our home in New York, I read through my guidebook and selected sites that I planned to visit, and I familiarized myself as well with the public spaces existing within the China World Hotel, a massive brownish-toned curved glass emporium that offered an aerial view of the city from its Horizon Club lounge on the twenty-first floor, and there was also a double-leveled shopping mall below its main lobby. According to the China World's brochure, the hotel consisted of nearly eight hundred guest rooms, all with color television sets, bedside controls, and minibars; and the recreational facilities included three indoor tennis courts, a skating rink, a twelve-lane bowling alley, and a large gymnasium and swimming pool. Beyond the revolving glass doors of its entranceway was a marble-floored reception area flanked by two decorative stone elephants, and behind the elephants was a fountain and a two-hundred-foot-long room lined with vermilion columns. On the right side of the room, atop a three-stepped platform and surrounded by a brass and glass banister, was a café with a few dozen tables served by young Asian waitresses who wore high-necked red silk gowns with a gold circled pattern, and whose tight-fitting skirts were slit open on both sides up to the middle of their thighs.

I spent an hour or more here almost every day, having breakfast or lunch while writing postcards and letters and reading the official English-language *China Daily*, which the concierge provided free of charge, and the *International Herald Tribune*, which was on sale in the lobby for the equivalent of about three dollars in Chinese yuan. The front page of the *China Daily* regularly showed pictures of high-level Party officials posing with visiting foreign dignitaries and executives of global enterprises, and there were editorials and articles stressing the importance of China's impending acceptance into the World Trade Organization

(WTO). There were also many references to China's seventy-three-year-old President Jiang Zemin's fifteen-day visit to France, England, Portugal, Morocco, Algeria, and Saudi Arabia, a goodwill tour that the paper celebrated as "China's major diplomatic campaign at the threshold of the new century"—a campaign promising to promote China's "great potential and vast prospects" for economic expansion and prosperity.

Having never before been a daily reader of a Communist newspaper, I found it diverting to see how its evaluation and coverage of foreign and domestic affairs was at variance with how the news about China was prioritized and offered in the *International Herald Tribune*.

In the *Tribune:* "China's state-owned enterprises are dying, noncompetitive even in its restrictive system. . . ."

In the *China Daily:* "China's socialist democracy and legal system is the only guarantee for the country's rapid economic development. . . ."

In the *Tribune:* "Mr. Jiang's security police forcibly detained more than a dozen members of the Falun Gong, the banned spiritual group, who had dared to unfurl a yellow banner and meditate in Tiananmen Square. . . ."

In the *China Daily:* "Seattle's streets were transformed from a battle zone to a near-police state on Wednesday, one day after broken glass and booming tear gas volleys shattered the peace [as] the city struggled to scrub itself clean for WTO delegates meeting here. . . ."

As I sat in the café reading newspapers, which often included *USA Today* and the dailies from Hong Kong, I was eavesdropping on the English-speaking people gathered at the surrounding tables. Staying at my hotel were dozens of Americans who were here on business (I had exchanged amenities with some of them in the elevator, receiving, in turn, their business cards—Motorola, Whirlpool Corp., Delphi Automotive Systems, RR Donnelley & Sons, Caterpillar, Inc.); and while it was not always possible to hear clearly above the crowd noise in the café and the piped-in music (Broadway hits, golden oldies, 1970s rock 'n' roll), it did seem to me that the loudest voices in the room belonged to American engineers and contractors who, while dining and usually drinking bottles of Tsingtao beer, expressed their displeasure at having to deal with the Party bureaucrats who regulated the city's building industry. "We don't even have clearances yet, and they're sending their inspectors over to check out our cement mixers and cranes," declared a burly red-haired man in his mid-thirties who wore a tight-fitting tan jacket and a loosely knotted necktie. As his companions nodded in agreement, he went on: "*And* they're sticking us with the same miserable foreman and crew we had last time."

Across from me, seated alone and eating a shrimp salad while talking on a cell phone, was a slender, carefully coiffed blonde in her forties who was wearing a pink linen suit and was becoming increasingly upset by what she was hearing. "Look, Max," she shouted at one point, "you don't seem to realize I'm sticking my neck out here. We're already in for three million, and we need another million. . . . What do you *mean*, "that's difficult"? . . . You told me last week you could swing it. . . . Yes you *did*, Max. You said we had our friend in Seattle with us. . . . Now you're saying we *don't*? . . . Well, so we have a real emergency here," she said, and, before clicking off, added, "Bottom line, Max, you *lied* to me."

In the latter part of the afternoon, after the local schools had closed for the day, I would often see groups of Chinese teenagers, wearing baggy jeans and T-shirts and with their spiky brightly tinged hair glossed with gel, making their way through the lobby and heading downstairs in the direction of Starbucks and an Internet center; and on weekends many young Chinese married couples would come to the café for lunch, accompanied by their young children. More often than not, these children were unruly. They crawled under tables, ran through the lobby, and screamed mightily when pursued and reclaimed by their parents. I supposed that they represented what I had been reading about—the "spoiled" and emerging masses of youngsters currently being reared without siblings in the homes of relatively affluent mothers and fathers who were part of China's burgeoning middle class.

The one-child policy, initiated in 1979, had been presented as a protective measure against famine. Although more than 22 percent of the world's population resided in China, it accounted for only 7 percent of the world's arable land. And so in the hope of preventing an oversized and underfed society, the government decided that couples should restrict themselves to only one offspring (except for parents who were employed in farming, or who had previously produced a disabled child, or were members of ethnic minorities dwelling in rural areas). But while the government would estimate that 330 million births had been avoided between the years 1979 and 1999, it nevertheless believed that the current population of 1.3 billion was about 100 million more than desirable, and the most negative by-product of the one-child policy was the countless number of females being aborted, or otherwise disposed of, by parents guided by the traditional belief that they would be assisted more substantially during their elderly years by a son than a daughter.

There were now 120 boys born for every 100 girls in China, according to data released by the Chinese Academy of Social Sciences. All the children I had observed running wildly around my hotel were male—the youngest majority within a pampered generation coming of age within the People's Republic. "These are the 'little emperors,'" a Beijing-based reporter wrote in *USA Today*, adding that they were "the most visible result of China's sometimes brutal effort to brake runaway population growth." The article quoted a Chinese professor of psychology as saying, "They are the VIP in the family . . . they just consider themselves and don't think about others."

In a memo to myself, I noted: "If the U.S. government thinks that it's having a tough time dealing with the Chinese policy makers now, just *wait* until these 'Little Emperors' take over."

A few hundred feet beyond the China World Hotel's circular driveway was Chang'an Boulevard, the principal thoroughfare in Beijing. There were eight lanes for motor vehicles, flanking roads for bicyclists, and a wide tree-lined promenade on which I regularly strolled during the middle of the afternoons and early evenings, mingling with multitudes of Asians who in most cases seemed to look right through me—the Cantonese word for white people is *gweilo* ("ghosts")—but occasionally my path was blocked by street hustlers wanting to sell me compact discs, newly released American films, software, and other items that I assumed were in the category of pirated merchandise.

One afternoon, I felt my jacket being gently tugged from behind, and, after pausing and turning around, I faced a smiling boy of about ten who proceeded to point his fingers insistently down toward where I was standing. As I waited in confusion, he quickly removed a rag and a plastic tube from his pocket and squirted cream upon my shoes before kneeling to give me a shine. After he had finished, and I could not decide what to offer him in Chinese currency, I dangled a dollar in front of him, which he snapped out of my hand, then bowed his head slightly and disappeared into the crowd.

"This kid knows how to create his own market," I wrote on a hotel memo pad I carried. "The 'Little Emperors' might learn a thing or two from him."

Although much of Chang'an Boulevard was characterized by office towers and residential high rises, there still existed many smaller buildings with storefronts occupied by grocers, clothiers, jewelers, cobblers, appliance salesmen, travel agents, and the proprietors of tablecloth restaurants as well as fast-food enterprises. McDonald's was about to launch its fifty-eighth site in the city. There was outdoor cooking, too, done by sidewalk chefs whose sizzling pans and steaming cauldrons rested upon metal stands or were spread out within plastic-windowed boxcars that measured approximately five-by-five feet and were clamped atop the rear wheels of tricycles.

I had, of course, read many stories about China's ever-increasing number of automobile owners, and there was ample evidence of a motorized society in the backed-up traffic that marked Chang'an Boulevard during rush hours; but the city's bicyclists and tricyclists continued to embody a large and unrelenting presence—millions of people pedaling to work every morning, and each evening returning home along the magnolia-lined roadway. There were no reflectors on any of the bikes, and so the nighttime riders were mainly noticeable as red specks of light flickering from the burning ends of the cigarettes they held between their teeth. Why did the cyclists lack reflectors? I could as easily have asked, Why did most of the Mercede-Benz vehicles that I saw in Beijing have missing hood ornaments? If I were to hazard a guess, I would respond in both instances with a single word: *pilferage*. But in any case, millions of people moved ahead every night and day by means new and old along parallel lines leading toward the twenty-first century. It had just been announced that Beijing's newest commercial complex, the Oriental Plaza—which would open within a year and consist of eight chrome blue glass office towers, a luxury hotel, and a convention center—would also have an indoor parking facility to accommodate eighteen hundred automobiles and twelve thousand bicycles.

A few blocks west of the Oriental Plaza on Chang'an Boulevard was the moated and Mao-muraled gateway leading into the ancient imperial palace and its walled environs, an area frequently referred to as the Forbidden City. It is so called because during most of the five hundred years that dynastic figures had enthroned themselves at this unnumbered address, starting with the Ming in 1406 and ending with the Qing in 1911, the preserve was off-limits to people not of the imperial court, except those being summoned for execution, or those who were employed as the emperor's concubines and eunuchs—the latter being, according to my guidebook, "not just castrated but also dismembered."

To the south of the Forbidden City, on the other side of Chang'an Boulevard, was Tiananmen Square, a vast stone plaza of about one hundred acres, which was said to be capable of accommodating 1 million standees. It seemed to me that at least fifty hard-surfaced soccer fields could be marked off here. I made my estimate as I paused along the grainy gray sidewalk that rimmed the northern edge of the square's white stone sward. The square had been repaved recently to smooth the parade route for the troops that had participated in the Communist Party's fiftieth-anniversary ceremony on October 1. With the aid of my illustrated guidebook and the data it provided, I was able to familiarize myself with the monuments erected within the square, and the two buildings that bordered its east and west sides.

To the west was the Great Hall of the People, a starkly grand structure that was listed as being one thousand feet long and having a main auditorium with a seating capacity of ten thousand. The building had been designed and constructed during the 1950s in architectural tribute to Stalinistic Russia, a style that influenced most of China's state buildings until there arose Sino-Soviet disagreements in the 1960s over the future course of international communism—quarrels that prompted the Russian leader Nikita Khrushchev to remove his engineers and consultants from large Soviet-assisted projects in China and to terminate foreign aid.

On the eastern side of the square, almost as large as the Great Hall and basically its architectural twin, was the Museum of Chinese History. Within its display cases and along its walls were relics, artifacts, scrolls, enamelware, metalwork, ivory, embroidery, and paintings that were said to represent the evolution of the revolution—the rise of Chinese people from a primitive society to a slave society, to a feudal society, to a colonial society, and finally to a society that, in the quoted words of Chairman Mao, "stood up."

On the southern side of Tiananmen Square, behind a granite obelisk, was Mao's mausoleum. It was completed in 1977, a year after his death, and contained his body in a crystal sarcophagus. "Join the enormous queue of Chinese sightseers," said my guidebook, "but don't expect more than a quick glimpse of the body as you file past the sarcophagus. At certain times of the year the body requires maintenance and is not on view." From my distant vantage point of the mausoleum's staircase, I could see no sign of anyone entering or leaving, although elsewhere in the square there were hundreds of people, or maybe thousands, walking around—couples holding hands, toddlers with balloons, gray-haired men and women, some using canes and wearing Mao jackets—and also dozens of other elderly people, all of them men, busily engaged in flying colorful kites, often assisted by boys young enough to be grandchildren. It was a sunny, windy autumn day. The gold-starred red flag of China was waving briskly atop a steel pole set in a granite foundation. "If you get up early you can watch the flag-raising ceremony at sunrise, performed by a troop of PLA [People's Liberation Army] soldiers drilled to march at precisely 108 paces per minute. . . . The same ceremony in reverse gets performed at sunset, but you can hardly see the soldiers for the throngs gathered to watch."

I saw no such gatherings now because it was midafternoon, and although I could imagine few sights more welcoming to a newly arrived stranger in a foreign city than the sight of soaring and swooping kites, I was nevertheless hesitant about entering Tiananmen Square and becoming part of the crowd. Mixed in with everyone, no matter where I looked, were the blue-uniformed police officers. Some patrolled in pairs; others gathered in small groups near the flagpole and obelisk, talking among themselves while surveying their surroundings. At any moment I half-expected to see them spring into action, pursuing and arresting individuals affiliated with the outlawed Falun Gong, a Chinese group that during the past summer had begun to express its unhappiness with the regime by staging surprise vigils in various parts of the capital, including in its most public space, the square.

I had never heard of the Falun Gong until I started reading about it in China. The *International Herald Tribune* had published several articles about it, some appearing on page one, describing it as a spiritual movement comprising "hordes of ordinary people seeking health and happiness" through meditation and ritualistic exercises evoking "elements of Buddhism, Taoism and traditional *qigong* exercises that are said to harness cosmic forces in the body" and even "supernatural powers." It was estimated that the Falun Gong had 10 million members in China and a growing number in foreign countries. Its founder and leader, Li Hongzhi, currently lived in the borough of Queens, New York, having left China in 1998. He and his aides maintained contact with their followers via E-mail and cellular telephone.

Unlike the student-led protests of ten years ago, in 1989, the Falun Gong was made up mostly of middle-aged or elderly Chinese citizens—retired schoolteachers, phased-out factory workers, clerks, hairdressers, civil servants, bureaucrats, and others who were not benefitting from China's economic reforms and who expected, at the very least, to be allowed to seek their own sense of spiritual contentment and salubrity through meditating and practicing their exercises in public places in accord with the prescriptions of the Falun Gong. On April 25, 1999, without a word of warning to government authorities, ten thousand adherents of the Falun Gong assembled in various parts of central Beijing in an appeal for official recognition. Not only was their request denied but the government would label them an "evil" and "disastrous cult"; and, between the spring and autumn of 1999, approximately three thousand of the Falun Gong were arrested.

The swiftness and resoluteness of the crackdown contrasted with the government's slow response ten years earlier to the launching of the students' pro-democracy campaign in Tiananmen Square. At that time—

April 1989—students in Beijing began to congregate in Tiananmen Square to criticize the government's unwillingness to negotiate with them on the issue of additional freedom. As days passed and as the protest movement increased in size and intensity (being joined by students from the provinces and applauded by many ordinary citizens and workers), the police and military surveyed the situation closely from the sidelines but otherwise did not actively interfere.

Among the marchers who must have surely drawn their attention was a six-foot blond man of about two hunded pounds—an American named Philip Cunningham, who, after attending Cornell University and the University of Michigan, moved to Asia in the 1980s to begin his career as a freelance writer and television producer specializing in Far Eastern politics and culture. Being sympathetic to the grievances of the students, many of whom he had met while taking courses at the Beijing Teachers University, he not only accompanied them to the square but often served as their interpreter when they began giving interviews to the foreign press. During this time, he also kept a daily journal describing the protesters' six-week-long confrontation with the government, which extended from the latter part of April into early June 1989; the journal would serve as the foundation for a memoir he would eventually complete a decade later while spending a year in the United States as a Nieman Fellow at Harvard University. Philip J. Cunningham's memoir, entitled *Reaching for the Sky*, would be published in the spring of 1999 as a tenth-anniversary commemorative of the mass demonstrations in Tiananmen Square. In the book, he would recall:

> In April, Tiananmen Square had only briefly been traversed by student protesters; by mid-May they owned it. The government's indecision and inability to react firmly to the early demonstrations encouraged the student vanguard to keep on pushing. The initial official tolerance of the student protests lent credence to the idea that at least some of China's top leaders tacitly supported the cause.

At times the demonstrators numbered as many as one million people. Their organizers and most active supporters installed loudspeakers in the square, held rock concerts, slept at night in pup tents, and during the day blocked traffic along Chang'an Boulevard while strolling around with banners advocating democracy. Their takeover of Tiananmen coincided with the arrival in China of Mikhail Gorbachev, the first Soviet leader to visit the country in decades. Gorbachev kept his distance from the crowd, while his host, China's leader, Deng Xiaoping, "made no secret of his humiliation at not being able to welcome him with the traditional Tiananmen ceremony," according to the author and Pulitzer Prize–winning *New York Times* writer Harrison Salisbury, who was then in Beijing.

The dissent continued with a prolonged hunger strike. When martial law was declared on May 19, the government condemned the protesters as criminals and warned bystanders not to fraternize with them in the square or anywhere else, but the demonstrators would not disappear. Three protesters threw paint at Mao's portrait overlooking the main gate of the Forbidden City. A thirty-seven-foot-high Styrofoam statue called the "Goddess of Democracy" was erected on a six-foot-high platform in the forefront of the square on May 29. It overlooked Chang'an Boulevard and faced the portrait of Mao. When armored personnel carriers were sent to clear the crowd from the square on the night of June 3, they were initially halted by a defiant crowd.

"The crowd cried for revenge on the metal monster that had bullied its way through with reckless impunity," Philip Cunningham wrote in his memoir. "Despite my pacifist inclinations, it was thrilling to watch the crowd pound the tank with bare hands. The APC wheels had gotten enmeshed in the makeshift road barrier . . . someone with a Molotov cocktail had set the APC on fire. . . . I watched from 20–30 feet away as the students tried to extract from the burning vehicle the man who had nearly killed them. Some people in the crowd felt less mercy. . . . The back door of the ambulance swung open and the injured soldier was about to be yanked out when the vehicle lurched forward, and raced off in the direction of the Beijing Hotel."

The best-known leader of the 1989 protest movement was a twenty-three-year-old woman named Chai Ling. Prior to the uprising she had been involved with her studies as a graduate student in educational psychology at Beijing Normal University. She was married to a fellow student. It was her husband rather than herself who was passionately engaged in political affairs, she later explained to interviewers. She had merely been a follower. But once the student marchers started to make headlines around the world, it was she who emerged as the movement's main mobilizer and spokesperson. I remembered reading about her regularly in the press throughout the spring of 1989, and my memory of her had been refreshed prior to my impulsive trip to China by Ian Buruma's piece entitled "Tiananmen, Inc." that appeared in *The New Yorker* in late May 1999.

The story of Chai Ling could be read as an American success or as a Chinese failure. . . . She was seen on television all over the world almost every day for nearly a month: a small, frail girl in a grubby white T-shirt and jeans, admonishing, cajoling, entertaining, and hectoring the crowds through a megaphone that often seemed to hide her entire face. . . . Chai's speech on May 12 moved hundreds of people to go on a hunger strike when the government ignored the students' demands for "dialogue," and she galvanized the support of many thousands of others. "We the children," she said, her reedy voice breaking, "are ready to die. We, the children, are ready to use our lives to pursue the truth. We, the children, are willing to sacrifice ourselves. . . ."

But she is also remembered for another speech, recorded two weeks later in a Beijing hotel room by an American reporter named Philip Cunningham. This speech became the centerpiece of a 1995 documentary film about Tiananmen, *The Gate of Heavenly Peace*. The film is harshly critical of the student leaders, and particularly of Chai. In the scene in the hotel room, she is semihysterical. Government troops have moved into Beijing. Factions within the student movement are quarrelling about tactics, aims, pecking orders, and money.

Chai is overwrought: "My students keep asking me, 'What should we do next? What can we accomplish?' I feel so sad, because how can I tell them that what we actually are hoping for is bloodshed, the moment when the government is ready to butcher the people brazenly? Only when the square is awash with blood will the people of China open their eyes. Only then will they really be united. But how can I explain any of this to my fellow-students?"

Columns of Chinese infantry and many tanks invaded the center of Beijing on Sunday, June 4, 1989, having been ordered to do so by a government no longer willing to be reticent. As Harrison Salisbury would report in his book published in 1992, *The New Emperors: China in the Era of Mao and Deng*, the government had become convinced that "evil elements" had penetrated the ranks of the students, and thus an assault was essential. "Neither then nor later were the evil elements identified," Salisbury wrote, adding, "There were vague references to foreign agents— presumably the CIA, Taiwan, and Hong Kong. In fact, such agents were spotted in the square, but no evidence indicated they played any role except possibly as a conduit for funds from Hong Kong." Prior to the PLA offensive, the troops had received instructions to keep signs of "violence and bloodshed away from the view of witnesses and cameras," Salisbury wrote, but the PLA's aggressions were nevertheless recorded by the media even though "two CBS men lost their cameras and were beaten and held overnight in the Forbidden City," and reporters from Taiwan and Hong Kong were also arrested and detained for several hours. "The government claimed no one had been killed in the square," Salisbury continued, but "the volume of gunfire in and around the square made this ridiculous. . . . Best guess: between 1,000 and 2,000 killed in Beijing, perhaps 300 in and around the square."

From then, Tiananmen Square would be best known in the Western press, and in the minds of most Americans, as the place where the reactionary forces of China had initiated mass murders of unarmed students. Tiananmen thus became a single word signifying oppression—a catchword, a *cause* word that critics of China would thereafter use to smear and pockmark the square that Mao had earlier designed to memorialize his Long March. "Tiananmen entered our vocabulary as shorthand for the grotesque crushing of dissent," said an editorial in the *Far Eastern Economic Review,* based in Hong Kong.

Some journalists and commentators, however, would in time amend their findings, maintaining that the square itself had *not* been part of the killing field. "As far as can be determined from the available evidence, no one died that night in Tiananmen Square," wrote Jay Mathews, a *Washington Post* reporter who was in Beijing on June 4 and who in 1998 would publish in the *Columbia Journalism Review* a critical essay about the Tiananmen coverage. "A few people may have been killed by random shooting on streets near the square," Mathews continued in his critique, entitled "The Myth of Tiananmen," "but all verified eyewitness accounts say that the students who remained in the square when troops arrived were allowed to leave peacefully. Hundreds of people, most of them workers and passersby, did die that night, but in a different place and under different circumstances," Mathews wrote, adding that "the resilient tale of an early morning Tiananmen massacre stems from several false eyewitness accounts in the confused hours and days after the crackdown." Among the unreliable sources cited by Mathews was a student leader named Wu'er Kaixi, "who said he had seen 200 students cut down by gunfire, but it was later proven that [Wu'er Kaixi had] left the square hours before the events he described allegedly occurred."

Wu'er Kaixi, Chai Ling, her husband, and several other student leaders not only eluded incarceration but managed to get out of the country.

"The circumstances of Chai's escape from China are mysterious," Ian Buruma's 1999 piece in *The New Yorker* reported.

She has never talked about what happened, perhaps to protect those who helped her, but there are stories about how she got out concealed in a wooden crate. All most people know is that she suddenly emerged in Hong Kong in April of 1990. From there she went to Paris, and then to the United States. While she was on the run in China, supporters of the democracy movement had her nominated for the Nobel Peace Prize. Earlier this year [1999] I met Chai at an outdoor café in Cambridge, Massachusetts, where she has been living since 1996, when she enrolled at the Harvard Business School.

Buruma's article mentioned that Chai Ling had divorced her Chinese husband and was planning to marry a senior partner in a global strategy consultancy firm based in Boston. Buruma also wrote that Chai Ling was employed as the CEO of an Internet company backed by executives from Reebok and Microsoft.

As I lingered along the edge of Tiananmen Square observing the crowds on this peaceful autumn afternoon in 1999, I wondered if the so-called Tiananmen Massacre (this is how most of the Western press would persistently refer to what had happened in Beijing on Sunday, June 4) was comparable to the Bloody Sunday that I had witnessed along the highway in Selma, Alabama, back on March 7, 1965. Footage shot that day would add Selma's name to the world's gazetteer of places with horrible images, footage linking it in my mind with the square in Beijing that I was now seeing for the first time but *seeing* through the reflected memory of having seen it repeatedly in recent years on American news broadcasts and documentaries. My sense of contemporary history had been influenced by the airing of what television programmers had chosen to show because it had visual appeal—that is, the image of the diminutive Chai Ling shouting and sobbing in front of thousands of her followers in an attempt to inspire them, the image of an unidentified young man stepping in front of a moving tank on Chang'an Boulevard and causing it to stop, the image of young people wearing headbands being chased through the streets by helmeted PLA soldiers firing tracer bullets in the sky while other soldiers demolished the "Goddess of Democracy" statue in Tiananmen Square.

"Reporters created a kind of epic story that showed good pitted against evil, young against old, freedom against totalitarianism," said Richard Gordon, codirector of the 1995 documentary called *The Gate of Heavenly Peace*. He could have been talking about Selma's Bloody Sunday. No one died in Selma on that day, but the scenes captured by the television cameras were evocative, showing as they did the onrushing lawmen wearing gas masks and brandishing their weapons within clouds of smoke above the heads of black demonstrators lying on the ground. In covering the Beijing protest movement of 1989, the press "found a simplified narrative irresistible," wrote Carolyn Wakeman, a journalism professor and author, in her essay entitled "Beyond the Square," published in 1999 in the *Media Studies Journal*. Wakeman wrote that the "compelling footage" of the turmoil in Beijing "appealed to broad media audiences never before interested in China," and at the same time it prompted in other Americans deep-seated conflicts about the Chinese people. "For more than a century Americans have oscillated between seeing the Chinese as noble peasants and Oriental demons," Wakeman wrote. "Missionaries, businessmen, the military, and journalists have each contributed different elements to the picture of China that has emerged in the United States."

Among the misleading impressions conveyed by the news coverage of the Beijing story, said Jay Mathews in the *Columbia Journalism Review*, was the perception that the PLA soldiers had singled out the students for punishment, when in fact their main targets were the rebellious masses of workers who had allied themselves with the students. Unhappy with their uncertain status in an increasingly changing China, the workers fused their frustrations with those of the students, and, prior to the crackdown, the number of protesting workers had far exceeded the student representation. The government saw its stability threatened more by the workers than by the relatively privileged student element. And as Jay Mathews pointed out in his critique, it was predominantly the names of workers and innocent bystanders that filled the death lists, while it was also true that "a few soldiers were beaten or burned to death by angry workers."

Still, it was the alleged victimization of the students that had caught the fancy of the media, Mathews emphasized, and "over the last decade, many American reporters and editors have accepted a mythical version of that warm, bloody night." He mentioned that when President Bill Clinton visited China during the summer of 1998 and was welcomed in Tiananmen Square, the press coverage of Clinton's trip continued to remind readers that the square was once "the site of the student slaughter" (*New York Post*); was "where the pro-democracy demonstrators were gunned down" (*USA Today*); and was "where Chinese students died" (*Baltimore Sun*). The *Wall Street Journal*, in recalling the "Tiananmen Square Massacre," described it as the place where "hundreds or more" demonstrators had been killed by the invading troops.

"Given enough time, such rumors can grow ever larger and more distorted," Mathews wrote. "When a journalist as careful and well-informed as Tim Russert, NBC's Washington bureau chief, can fall prey to the most feverish versions of the fable, the sad consequences of reportorial laziness become clear. On May 31 [1998] on *Meet the Press*, Russert referred to 'tens of thousands' of deaths in Tiananmen Square."

I stood for about twenty minutes along the northern edge of Tiananmen Square, seeing it as a vast photo op, a backdrop for opportunism, a space open to exploitation by those with a vested interest in doing so. It was where people came to make news. In a way, it was what the Golden Gate Bridge represented to suicidal publicity seekers. It was where they went to make a big splash, and, if they survived, they made headlines. Chai Ling had challenged the Communist regime in Tiananmen Square, had survived, and had ended up going to Harvard and becoming a CEO.

I felt sure that members of the outlawed Falun Gong would soon be making an appearance here, following in the footsteps of the long-departed students. Without casting doubts on the spiritual sincerity of the Falun Gong's leaders, I gathered that they were quite adept in reaching out to the media. During the first week after my arrival the leaders had held clandestine press conferences with Western journalists and had managed to get lots of favorable publicity—stories that portrayed the Falun Gong as an oppressed group whose civil liberties were being violated merely because its members wished to meditate and perform ritualistic exercises in Tiananmen and other public places. Although the government had begun arresting Falun Gong members months before I arrived in China, the organization remained boldly confrontational and newsworthy, being the subject of such headlines and stories as appeared in the *International Herald Tribune:*

Falun Gong
Steps Up Resistance Campaign;
New Arrests in Tiananmen Square Fail to
Break Sect's Determination

... over the past few weeks, thousands of adherents of a popular Buddhist-like sect have poured into Beijing to undertake a quiet and surreal challenge to the government's three-month-long crackdown on their group, called Falun Gong. In five consecutive days of silent protests on Tiananmen Square ... Falun Gong followers have expressed their opposition—peacefully but stubbornly—to the Communist Party's decision to ban their group on July 22. ...

I waited for another ten minutes, idly watching as people continued to wander around the square or sit on the stone steps of the Great Hall, or fly kites while standing in front of Mao's mausoleum—but *still* no sign of the Falun Gong. As a reporter, I had hoped to see in person what I had been reading about. But now I decided that it was probably better that I return to my hotel. I was in town on a tourist visa. My story was the soccer lady. So I turned away from the square and retraced my route along Chang'an Boulevard, passing once more the little boy with the shoe-shine rag, and the hustlers of black-market films and CDs, and the women whispering "massagey-massagey," and the yellow-helmeted workers at the construction site of the Oriental Plaza's chrome blue glass office buildings and convention center.

When I was within a few blocks of my hotel, I turned to the left and entered "Silk Alley," a crowded and noisy market street that was lined with hundreds of booths selling a great variety of famous-brand merchandise at low prices that could be negotiated downward—Gucci shoes listed at thirty dollars a pair, a Louis Vuitton handbag for twenty-five dollars, a Cartier watch for twenty dollars, a pair of Nike sneakers for fifteen dollars, North Face parkas for ten dollars, a Ralph Lauren sweatshirt for five dollars. There were also antiques, used household goods, curios, copies of Mao's *Little Red Book*, baseball caps representing every team in the major leagues, and thousands of T-shirts emblazoned with the names of recognizable people and places, and even T-shirts depicting Tiananmen Square, with its name printed in English. I bought two of them for a dollar, returned to the hotel, and mailed them to my daughters in New York.

34

AFTER I HAD BEEN IN BEIJING FOR A LITTLE MORE THAN A WEEK, I received word from Patrick Wang's office at Nike that on the following day, if I would be standing in front of my hotel at 2:00 p.m., I would be met by representatives of the soccer association; and so I was.

Two Asian men, one a slender and sharp-featured individual in his mid-thirties wearing a black turtleneck polo shirt and a navy blazer, the other a stockily built younger fellow wearing a colorfully striped sports shirt and an identical blazer, walked directly toward me as if they knew who I was. After a quick nod and a handshake, they presented me with their business cards, extending them in an almost ceremonial manner with both hands. As they introduced themselves—the older one was Liu Dian Qiu, the younger Li Duan—I regretted that I did not have a card to give them. I had never had business cards. How should I describe my business?

I followed the men to a black sedan that was parked at the curb, its doors held open by one of the hotel's red-uniformed doormen. At the direction of Liu Dian Qiu, I sat in the back next to Li Duan while Liu slipped into the driver's seat. In the passenger seat was an attractive almond-eyed woman wearing a beige silk blouse and a gray jacket. She turned to smile while handing me her card. Her name was Chen Jun. She was with the soccer association's advertising department. Like the other business cards, hers was printed in English on one side and had Chinese characters on the other, and in the left-hand corner was a tiny image of the Forbidden City resting on a soccer ball.

As we drove along Chang'an Boulevard, approaching the real Forbidden City, I sat trying to communicate with Li Duan in English. He spoke haltingly, but I was grateful for his efforts. Up front, Chen Jun and Liu Dian Qiu—his card identified him as the soccer association's "vice general manager"—were speaking to each other in what I assumed was Mandarin. They never once tried to explain anything to me, and this would be true throughout our time together for the rest of the day. Either they could not speak English or chose not to in my presence. In either case, I decided I should not have been surprised; except for those Chinese who had gone to school or resided in places where English was the primary language, such as Nike's Patrick Wang, or who were specially trained as translators and interpreters within the upper echelons of international political and business affairs, it was unreasonable of me to expect to meet English-speaking Chinese while traveling here under these circumstances. Even at the China World Hotel, where many Americans were registered, there were relatively few employees who were fluent in English, except for the concierge and his colleagues.

When our vehicle paused for a red light at the Forbidden City intersection, I briefly turned away from my backseat companion to steal a glance through the side window at Tiananmen Square. I could see a few kites flying high over the parade grounds, and hundreds of pedestrians moving around unhurriedly, and only two police officers on guard. I guessed that the Falun Gong demonstrators were taking the day off.

Our motor ride continued for more than an hour without us arriving at our destination. After we had reached the end of Chang'an Boulevard, we had turned right and circled around a ramp onto a modern highway that took us past warehouses and coal yards and soot-smeared apartment buildings, most of which were painted pink or tan and had laundry hanging within their glass-enclosed balconies.

As we proceeded, I learned what I could from Li Duan about the women's soccer team. I could not figure out from his business card what exactly he did for the soccer association—his vaguely defined job title was "Player Transfer"—but he did say that he was an ex-athlete, one who had played soccer for a few seasons within the men's municipal league, and that he currently served as an administrative assistant with varied chores to perform, including that of being my interpreter, although he apologized for not being fully up to the task. As for the Chinese women's national team, Li Duan suggested that it was probably superior to the men's national team, the latter being lazy and lax. I told him that I had recently read a similar opinion expressed in the sports section of the *China Daily*; in fact, I had seen a cartoon there showing a male soccer player driving a sports car with his nose in the air and with one of his arms around the shoulders of a frizzy-haired woman (she was smoking a cigarette and clasping a bundle of cash), and in his other hand he gripped an XO-labeled bottle of cognac. Standing nearby, primly posed on a pedestal while embracing a large trophy, was a woman in a soccer uniform. Above the cartoon was the headline CONGRATULATIONS TO OUR MEN'S SOCCER ALSO-RANS. The men's team of 1999 had done poorly in international competition and had failed to qualify for the 2000 Olympics. The women's team, however, even before it had walked onto the field in California to play the Americans, had received a phone call from the Beijing office of President Jiang Zemin saying that the players would be welcomed home as heroines no matter what happened in the World Cup finale.

Earlier at my hotel, I had written out a list of questions in preparation for my interview with Liu Ying, and now in the car I handed the list to Li Duan, hoping that he would be able to understand my English well enough to translate it accurately into Chinese and communicate it to the soccer lady. I also gave him a photocopy of a *New York Times* article by George Vecsey that I thought would be appreciated by Liu Ying and her teammates. Vecsey's piece, published some weeks after Liu Ying's failed kick had resulted in the American team's triumph, questioned the ethics and tactics used by the American goalkeeper Briana Scurry when she had blocked Liu Ying's shot in the final minutes at the Rose Bowl.

WHEN IS IT GAMESMANSHIP, AND WHEN IS IT CHEATING? asked the *Times* headline, and in the article's opening paragraphs, George Vecsey explained:

The world championship was in the balance when Briana Scurry strode to the goal line on July 10 in the Rose Bowl. The American goalkeeper had picked out her victim, the third Chinese player to take a penalty kick in the shootout that would decide the Women's World Cup.

"That one girl—her body language didn't look very positive," Scurry said later. "It doesn't look like she wanted to take it. She'd been running on the flank and she was tired. I looked up at her and said, 'This one is mine.'"

It was one thing to choose which opponent was most likely to be weak. It was another thing for Scurry to choose her tactics. By her own admission, Scurry decided to improve her chances by ignoring the rules of the penalty kick.

In a quick and practiced move, Scurry bolted two steps forward—in violation of the rule—and cut off the angle for Liu Ying, her opponent. With superb reflexes, Scurry then dived to her left and tipped Liu's shot wide of the goal. That one stop would shortly give the United States the championship, and newfound fans of soccer would admit they were teary-eyed watching Scurry's celebration.

Since then, the poised goalkeeper has become one of the most popular of the Yanks, but there has been a minor swell of criticism that the Americans had to break a rule in order to win. . . .

Li Duan examined Vecsey's piece for a few minutes without comment and then turned his attention to my list of questions for Liu Ying:

1. What's your reaction to the *New York Times* report that quotes Briana Scurry as saying that she singled you out as her victim—"this one is mine"—and that your "body language didn't look very positive" and it didn't look like you wanted to take the penalty kick, and that you were "tired" from running on the flank?

2. After blocking your kick, Briana Scurry was described by some people as being "in violation of the rules." Do *you* believe that she violated the rules?

3. After the game was lost, and you left the field, what did you hear from your teammates and the coach? What was in your mind then, and later during your long flight back home to China?

4. Three months have now passed since you missed that kick—do you replay it in your mind? If so, how will you prepare yourself for the next penalty kick you might have to take, perhaps in the upcoming Olympics in Australia when you might again be facing Briana Scurry?

As Li Duan paused over my list of questions, and then looked at them again two or three times without turning toward me, I wondered if what I had written had struck him as being too invasive of Liu Ying's privacy or too insensitive to the anguish that Liu Ying might still be experiencing. I had no idea how the local press wrote about Chinese women athletes after the latter had fallen short of expectations. Perhaps such matters were approached more delicately by the media, and I thought it possible that Liu Ying had never before faced a foreign interviewer, an American no less. But I reasoned that since Li Duan worked within the soccer association, he could advise me on whether some of my questions should be withdrawn or rephrased. I did *not* want my first meeting with Liu Ying to go badly. I hoped to see her not just once but on later occasions. If I could win her confidence, and that of her teammates, I might be in a position to hang out with them as they prepared to compete in the 2000 Olympics to be held during the following autumn in Sydney, Australia. *That* is where this story might be leading me, I thought as I imagined a crowded Olympic stadium and the sight of Liu Ying kicking the ball into the net past the outstretched body of Briana Scurry, and thus vindicating herself by earning a Gold Medal. In the meantime, I hoped that Liu Ying, who had been largely ignored by the American press except for George Vecsey's article, would accept my presence as her opportunity to tell her side of the story.

"Well, what do you think?" I asked Li Duan after he had handed me back my list and I had put it in my pocket.

"No problem," he said.

"You mean all my questions are okay to ask?"

"No problem," he repeated.

I could only hope that Li Duan read English well enough to pass judgment on what I had written. In my brief time in China, I had noticed, particularly at my hotel, that the two English words used most often by Chinese employees who otherwise spoke no English were *no problem*. The hotel's chambermaids, porters, waitresses, lobby clerks, and other employees responded to any request I made with a smile and a "No problem." Perhaps they had picked up the words after hearing them said repeatedly by American businessmen reassuring their would-be Asian partners. The employees came to believe that this was simply a courteous response; they could continue to do what they were doing and politely ignore what was being asked of them by responding, "No problem."

Finally we arrived at the soccer site. It was in the hills west of Beijing in a remote and bosky place called Xishan and was actually part of a military installation. It was surrounded by brick walls affixed with barbed wire and its entrance was guarded by two rifle-bearing soldiers. As our car stopped at the checkpoint, one of the soldiers strolled forward to scrutinize us; as soon as he recognized our driver, Liu Dian Qiu, he waved us through and saluted as we passed. Without acknowledging the salute or even turning away from the steering wheel, Liu Dian Qiu shifted the vehicle abruptly into gear and sped ahead on a gravel road, kicking dust up along the sides of our vehicle. Liu Dian Qui obviously enjoys a certain status around here, I thought; no doubt he is emboldened by an abundance of *guanxi*.

We soon stopped next to a two-story brick building, one of the barracks currently serving the women players as their dormitory. After stepping out of the car, Liu Dian Qiu headed directly into the building, followed by his female colleague Chen Jun. My interpreter, Li Duan, took my arm and together we walked in the opposite direction in silence, following a tree-lined path until we came to a green pasture in which a soccer field was marked off. In the middle of the field were rows of young women wearing red shorts and shirts, jumping up and down while bouncing soccer balls on their heads. They were being watched by middle-aged men who wore peaked caps and warm-up suits and who, I assumed, were coaches and trainers. I tried to locate Liu Ying. I vaguely knew what she looked like from having seen her on television during the World Cup match, and there had also been a blurry photo with Vecsey's *Times* article, one showing her leaning backward as she watched the lunging figure of Briana Scurry blocking her kick. But now that I was standing behind the white chalk of the sidelines, forty or fifty yards away from the rows of jumping, dark-haired, ball-bouncing young women, I could not tell which one of them had lured me here from the other side of the world.

I stood watching while Li Duan wandered off to exchange a few words with two young Asian men who had just arrived on the sidelines carrying a tripod and a camera bearing the letters *CCTV*. They were from the Central Chinese Television Network and I assumed they were here to get film clips of the practice session for inclusion on a sports show. I remained alone for the next ten minutes, continuing to observe the women. They were now standing on one leg while extending the other leg in a bent-kneed position and balancing a ball on their toes. They then kicked the ball a few inches in the air and retrieved it securely on the tops of their soccer shoes. After doing this several times successfully, they spread themselves around the field, rearranging themselves into four circles of six players, and, with a single ball assigned to each circle, they practiced short-distance passing, swiftly and accurately. As their pace picked up, they varied their manner of kicking: They kicked the ball not only with their toes but with their insteps and the outer edges of their feet.

At the sound of a coach's whistle, they began to jog around the field, encircling it three times, and as they came closer to where I stood, I could plainly read the white numerals printed on their red jerseys—and finally I was able to see Liu Ying, number 13. She was small and boyish, and her black hair was cut shorter than that of most of her teammates, many of whom had long hair pulled back in ponytails or braided. She quickly moved past me with the others and ran along a path leading toward their two-storied quarters, a flat-roofed rectangular brick building that had a double row of windows trimmed with white stone and was architecturally similar in design to an old-style Holiday Inn.

My interpreter came over to say that we should follow them; ten minutes later, after he had briefly left me in the foyer and had gone off to find her—I heard women's laughter coming through the halls and smelled the aroma of cooking coming from a dining area nearby—he returned with Liu Ying, although she had positioned herself so closely behind him that it was not until he had stepped aside that I realized it was she.

She was now wearing a full-length red warm-up suit that had the Chinese flag with its gold stars stitched upon the upper left side of the jacket. Piercing her left ear was a gold ring. She had wide-set eyes, a round face, stood around five-four, and she was trying to smile, although she appeared to be quite shy, or ill at ease. We shook hands. She said something in Chinese that I assumed were welcoming words. Then she led us down the hall to her bedroom, a small space of about ten feet by twelve feet. There were two cots placed along the sides of the walls, both covered with army-style olive drab blankets. If she had a roommate, and I guessed that she did, since there were two cots, the roommate was staying away. There were no chairs. Liu Ying gestured for me to sit next to her on the cot, while the interpreter sat on the cot across from us. I tried to introduce myself and explain why I had come to China to see her, but it was a slow and awkward process. I would say something to her in English and pause while the interpreter communicated with her in Chinese, but this led to lots of back-and-forth conversation between them in Chinese; either she did not understand his interpretation of what I was trying to say, or *he* had not understood me well enough to convert my English into words that she could understand well enough to respond to.

I then removed from my pocket the article by George Vecsey, held it in front of her, and then waited to see how she might respond to the photograph showing her watching helplessly as Briana Scurry blocked her kick. I pointed to the headline over the article—WHEN IS IT GAMESMANSHIP, AND WHEN IS IT CHEATING?—and asked the interpreter if he would translate the question it posed. I also pulled out the list of questions I had shown him earlier in the car, but this time I read the questions aloud and slowly, and after he had assured me that he understood, I asked him to take all the time he needed to get her reaction to the key issues raised in Vecsey's article:

What did she have to say about the possibility that Briana Scurry had violated the rules?

What about Scurry's observation that Liu Ying had been too "tired" to kick straight, which led Scurry to conclude confidently "This one is mine"?

And now that three months had passed, was Liu Ying still haunted by that moment in the Rose Bowl?

As the interpreter concentrated his attentions upon Liu Ying, and as I sat listening as they conversed back and forth in Chinese, I saw various expressions coming into her face—her eyes narrowing, furrows in her forehead, her lips tightening. She seemed at times to be sad or angry, although I could not tell which. But the interpreter had definitely gotten her attention, and then he recounted her replies to me:

She did not appreciate what was said about her in the *Times*. She did not like Briana Scurry. "Yes, I was tired," she acknowledged, "but all the girls on the field were tired. We had played in two overtime periods." She disrespected Scurry for violating the rules. "How can a person like that be called a winner?" she asked. As to how she felt after missing the kick, she said that she had cried afterward. Commenting on the flight back to Beijing, she admitted to thinking, "I hope we never get there. I do not want this plane to arrive in Beijing. Better it should stay in the sky forever."

I was particularly struck by her last response—"Better it should stay in the sky forever." I was writing it in my notes, when, suddenly, into the room came the man who had driven us here, Liu Dian Qiu. He stood near the doorway, speaking firmly to the interpreter, and shook his head disapprovingly at the *Times* article he saw spread out on the cot. Then he waved us out of the room. I could not tell if he was infuriated or merely officious, but, following the lead of my interpreter, I got up and left. Liu Ying remained behind.

We waited in the foyer until we were again joined by Liu Dian Qiu, who was followed by Chen Jun, whom I had not seen since our arrival. Liu Dian Qiu then began a lengthy conversation with my interpreter, who, in turn, told me that my interview with Liu Ying was over and that we would soon be headed back to my hotel, but that we would first dine here with the soccer team.

Five minutes later, I was having dinner. I was not with the team. They were at a long table across the room, and I saw Liu Ying looking away, talking to one of her mates. I was at a smaller table, seated between my interpreter and Chen Jun, along with their boss, Liu Dian Qiu. It was a buffet-style dinner. I had helped myself and greatly enjoyed what I was eating. I had often gone to Chinese restaurants in downtown Manhattan and elsewhere, and I was pleased with the fact that I could adroitly use chopsticks. As I sure-handedly picked my way through the food, I hoped that the people around me were aware of this and approved.

35

W HAT I THOUGHT I NOW NEEDED WAS AN INTERPRETER FOR my interpreter. It had been naïve, if not arrogant, of me to assume that the women's soccer team should have facilitated my meeting with Liu Ying by providing me with someone who was completely bilingual, someone on the order of the English-speaking, dark-suited young Asian gentleman whom I had seen the day before in the hotel lobby standing next to the slim blond-haired president of the Hewlett-Packard company, Carly S. Fiorina, assisting her as she was queried by a dozen members of the Chinese press. As they peppered her with questions, her interpreter swiftly communciated them to her in English and just as quickly relayed her remarks in English back to the Chinese journalists. He was a double-tongued wizard playing Ping-Pong with words, unhesitatingly shifting back and forth from English to Chinese, Chinese to English, English to Chinese. I was indeed impressed as I stood watching near the concierge's desk, and the entire press conference was over in ten minutes, after which Carly Fiorina was met by a delegation of older Chinese and American men who escorted her to a luncheon elsewhere in the hotel, followed by her interpreter.

He must be highly paid, I thought, and interpreters of such competence were no doubt greatly in demand in this country because so many important people from other parts of the world were now in China on business, or diplomatic assignments, or making speeches at luncheons and dinners attended by joint venturists and policy makers. I had read in the *China Daily* that the U.S. treasury secretary, Lawrence H. Summers, was soon scheduled to address the American Chamber of Commerce of Beijing, and that the German chancellor, Gerhard Schröder, would be arriving the following week to meet Party officials in the Great Hall. Within a fortnight, the Chinese leaders would greet United Nations Secretary-General Kofi Annan.

The former U.S. secretary of state, Dr. Henry Kissinger, who had helped to arrange President Richard Nixon's historic trip to China in 1972, was regularly in the country these days in his role as an international business consultant, and, indeed, on the afternoon after I had returned from my meeting with Liu Ying, I read a news item saying that Kissinger was currently in Beijing, and my knowing concierge told me that Kissinger was staying, as usual, at the International Club, a few blocks west of us on Chang'an Boulevard. I had occasionally chatted with Kissinger in recent years at New York dinner parties hosted by such friends as the former executive editor of the *Times*, A. M. Rosenthal, and, recalling that Kissinger was an avid soccer fan, it occurred to me that I should approach him and ask him if he might open a few doors for me at the highest levels of the Chinese sports ministry. At the very least, I might meet one of his assistants and learn where to hire a first-rate interpreter.

After I had faxed a note to Kissinger's suite seeking an appointment, I immediately sent a second fax to the Nike office of Patrick Wang, telling him about my experiences earlier in the day at the soccer camp.

Dear Patrick:

I'm grateful for all you've done in arranging for me to see Liu Ying today. I found her to be interesting, sincere, and forthright, and, as I told you when we first met for dinner, I think she has a good story to tell about the challenges facing women athletes in contemporary China.

Unfortunately, I was not able to communicate with her today as I had hoped because of language problems. With all due respect—and I would appreciate it if you would regard this as confidential—the interpreter I was given, Li Duan, does not speak English with facility. If you spoke with him for two minutes, you'd know what I mean. But my dilemma is this: I cannot say to the soccer authorities that the interpeter they chose for me is inadequate. They might take offense. They might not even know that he doesn't speak English well, since they apparently speak no English themselves. Still, if I try to bring in my own interpreter, they might object. They wouldn't want me to be showing up with someone they hadn't cleared. And finally, if they find out that their designated interpreter, Li Duan, is not good at the job, they might fire him. He seems to be a nice fellow. I think he's married and has a seven-year-old son. I don't want to cause trouble.

But my interview today, as I say, dragged on too long—and was then abruptly ended by the boss, Liu Dian Qiu. How do you think I can improve upon this situation when, and if, I get a second meeting with the soccer player?

After I had sent this fax to the Nike office, I wished that I had given more thought to what I had written. It was possible that I was behaving impetuously and impatiently, confirming some of the worst notions that Asians had about Americans. Here I was in China, expressing disappointment over the fact that the young man, Li Duan, did not speak English well enough, when I myself, like most Americans, made little effort to understand foreign languages. Whatever French and Spanish I had learned in school, I had long forgotten, and I had not even learned to speak Italian, the native language of my father. Instead of complaining about my Chinese interpreter, I should have been praising him, remembering that Li Duan was an ex-athlete and lower-level bureaucrat who had somehow picked up enough English to perform a real service for me earlier that day; he had managed to get me some usable quotations from the soccer player, who was facing me for the first time and yet exposed her emotions in the aftermath of her missed kick, and who had said of the plane carrying her back to China, "Better it should stay in the sky forever."

Days passed without my receiving a reply to the fax I had sent to Kissinger, nor did he or his assistants return my follow-up phone calls to his hotel. But I did hear promptly from Patrick Wang's secretary at Nike, and she told me that Patrick had arranged for my presence the next day at a luncheon to be attended by Liu Ying and four other Beijing-born women who played for the national team; since the following day was a Saturday and Patrick was taking the day off, he himself would accompany me and help with the interpreting.

I met him in the lobby the next day at noon. He was smiling, as usual, and graciously dismissive of my expressed concern that I was burdening him with my problems. "Oh, don't worry," he assured me, "I'm happy to help. I only wish it wasn't so difficult to find good interpreters. This situation will change. But now there are simply not enough good ones to go around." We walked out toward his car. He was more casually dressed than I had seen him before, now wearing a sports jacket, a polo shirt, and a peaked blue cap, on the front of which was the white swooshed symbol of Nike.

After a twenty-minute drive across town, we turned into a street that led us in the direction of Workers Stadium in central Beijing. It was a hulking oval-shaped structure supported by gray steel rafters and soot-covered concrete walls, and the outer edges of its grandstand roof were lined with red flags. It could seat about sixty thousand spectators, Patrick said, making it the second-largest stadium in China. The *largest* stadium, he added with as much modesty as his pride would allow, was the eighty-thousand-seat arena in his home city of Shanghai.

Near the north gate of Workers Stadium, which was where he parked the car, was a restaurant called Havana Café. In its front window was a sign in English reading FOODS & MUSIC, FULLY EXPRESS LATIN FLAVOUR! I thought this was where we were having lunch, but Patrick led me across the parking lot and into one of the side doors of the stadium. Only men's soccer was played here, he said. The women used a smaller stadium on the south side of the city that can accommodate about thirty-five thousand spectators. The success of the 1999 women's team, however, especially as it contrasted with the poor performance of the men, had led many male followers of the game to lend their support to the women; today's luncheon—held in a private men's club within Workers Stadium—was evidence of this.

After passing through the lobby, where the walls were decorated with framed photographs of male soccer players and coaches as well as the administrators and sponsors of professional soccer in Beijing, we entered a large dining hall where about two hundred people, almost all of them men, cheerfully chatted and laughed with one another as they sat drinking wine and beer. All the tables were covered with green-and-white-checkered cloths, and there were bowls filled with flowers in the center. In the front of the room, too far away from me to get her attention, I saw Liu Ying wearing her red warm-up suit and seated on the dais next to four of her teammates and the head coach.

As we found places to sit at a long table in the corner, I noticed that Li Duan, my appointed interpreter, was waving at me from across the room and was headed in my direction. I was momentarily embarrassed. I vaguely recalled his saying something about a luncheon after he had escorted me back to my hotel following soccer practice; I now wondered if I had neglected to call him, as I should have, to confirm my interest in coming here. If I *had* been neglectful, it was yet another reminder of our difficulties in communicating. Still, he approached me with a smile and a handshake, and after I had introduced him to Patrick Wang, he sat down next to us just as a group of fleet-footed waiters began moving up and down the aisles balancing trays bearing bowls of steaming food and gallon-sized glass pitchers filled with beer, which they plunked down on the tables. Whenever the waiters noticed that a guest's beer glass was half-empty, they would grab the pitcher and pour forth more beer in a manner of such effusion and unmeasured nonchalance that the rising foam would cascade over the lip of the glass, dousing the tablecloth and sometimes trickling to the floor. This seemed to be a popular way of pouring beer in Beijing. In my short time in the city, I had seen servers doing the same thing at my hotel and other places I had visited; no matter if they were pouring beer from pitchers, bottles, or cans, they would pour so much of it into a glass that it would overflow—a symbolic sign of abundance and generosity, I guessed, although I never inquired further.

The program began after lunch as the master of ceremonies, a television sports commentator, stepped up to the microphone on the speaker's platform and encouraged the applause of the crowd by gesturing in the direction of the six honored guests seated at the dais. He explained that the coach and five local women would be departing on the following Monday with the rest of the team to travel to distant locations in China and to foreign countries to compete in dozens of exhibition matches as a tune-up for the 2000 Olympics. This luncheon, he said, represented a kind of pep rally for the team, a way of wishing the women well in their forthcoming ventures. Then he called to the microphone four female soccer fans who had been invited to the luncheon to read aloud the statements that each had prepared in homage to the team.

As the women took turns reading, I sat between Patrick Wang and Li Duan, listening as they interpreted for me, although I was not paying much attention to the praise being bestowed upon the players; I was thinking instead about what the master of ceremonies had mentioned earlier to the audience—that the soccer team was leaving town within two days for an extended journey into the interior of China and elsewhere in Asia to practice for the Olympics, and *this* meant that my self-appointed assignment with Liu Ying would be indefinitely delayed unless I could somehow get permission to leave on Monday with the team, *and* could get clearance for a worthy interpreter to accompany me.

Immediately after the luncheon ended, I excused myself from Patrick Wang. Taking Li Duan aside, I asked, "Who has the authority to get me on that plane?"

"No press allowed," he said. "Only the team is going. They are having closed practice sessions, very private. . . ."

"Are you going?" I asked Li Duan.

"No, I must stay in the office," he said.

"Look," I went on, "I came a long way to meet this girl, and I got only that one interview, and now what?"

"We thought you got what you wanted," he said, "and that now you return home. Maybe you come back some other time."

"*Listen to me,*" I said, holding on to Li Duan's right arm and raising my voice for the first time, hoping I was not pushing my luck (reminding myself that I was here on a tourist visa), "I came to China with good intentions. I came to do an understanding story about Liu Ying. I came a *long* way. I'm now sixty-seven years old. How much longer do you think I can wait? If I leave now, I might not live long enough to come back to China. Do you *understand?*"

Li Duan said nothing for a few seconds, but his expression softened. I sensed that I had touched something within him. Maybe one of his parents or a close relative was dying. Whatever it was, his eyes moistened.

"Yes, I understand," he said, "but I do not know what I can do. The team is training in private. It is the rule. . . ."

"Well," I said, coming up with the idea for the first time, "what about me interviewing her parents? Are they in Beijing?"

"Her father is dead," he said, "but, yes, her mother lives in Beijing."

"In America we have what we call 'soccer moms,'" I said. "Maybe I can write about her as a Chinese 'soccer mom.'"

He thought about it and then nodded.

"Yes," he said, "no problem."

"You can arrange for me to see her?"

He again nodded, repeating, "No problem."

During the next two or three days, while I waited to hear from Li Duan, I visited the offices of several Beijing-based Western journalists in the hope that they might know of an excellent interpreter I might hire on a part-time basis. I went first to the *New York Times* bureau, which was located close to my hotel, in a compound behind Chang'an Boulevard. The government agency that issues press licenses expected foreign journalists to maintain their offices and residential quarters within one of the bulky brick buildings within the compound, which was surrounded by a wall and had guards posted at the entrance. The guards checked the identities of everyone entering the compound—the correspondents, their families, their household employees, the staff workers, *and* whoever wanted to visit for social or professional reasons. This meant that if a foreign correspondent conducted an office interview with an outsider, the latter's identity would be known to the guards. Thus interviews dealing with political or other potentially sensitive subjects were usually conducted by the correspondents well beyond the gates of the compound.

After I had shown my passport to one of the guards, I was met by a *Times* employee who came down to greet me. As I followed him along a path toward the building in which the *Times* office was located, I wondered if reporters in China could operate more freely if they were *not* accredited. Perhaps I enjoyed more liberty as a hotel guest on a tourist visa than if I were working here for the *Times*. I was not living in the compound and playing cat-and-mouse games with the authorities whenever I wanted to slip away to interview a member of the Falun Gong or some other controversial figure. In my case, however, I was pursuing a relatively inconsequential subject, such as women's soccer. But even in *this* area, I reminded myself, the authorities had shown themselves to be controlling. I recalled the military checkpoint at the soccer camp, and my aborted interview with Liu Ying, and the fact that Li Duan had told me I could not follow the team to its next destination. Perhaps Li Duan has been assigned to keep tabs on me, I thought; maybe he is my portable gatekeeper. Still, I now needed him to deliver Liu Ying's mother. And *if* he delivered, as promised, I could probably learn more about Liu Ying from her mother than I could from Liu Ying herself. In any case, I needed Li Duan as well as someone who could bridge the linguistic gap between us.

As I arrived in the *Times* office, I met the bureau chief, Erik Eckholm, who greeted me cordially and introduced me to his wife, Elisabeth Rosenthal, who also covered China for the newspaper. In the office were English-speaking Asians working at their desks, and it was my hope that one of these might be receptive to earning extra money as my interpreter during his off-hours from the *Times*. I approached the subject obliquely to Eckholm, sensitive to the possibility that he might think that *I* thought his staff was so poorly paid that it was susceptible to moonlighting. And so I digressed for a while, and we talked at length about our mutual friends in the New York newsroom, and I described in detail my story idea about the soccer player, which he professed to find interesting. When I finally hinted that my efforts would be enhanced by the presence of a good linguist, he nodded in agreement, but without offering a suggestion; however, he did invite me to a dinner party that he and his wife were giving the following evening at their apartment within the compound, and I accepted immediately.

As it turned out, I had a fortuitous meeting with one of the guests, a slender, sandy-haired man in his thirties named Chris Billing, the Beijing bureau chief of NBC News. During and after dinner, he questioned me about my work, and, even before I had sought his help, he seemed to understand what I needed and volunteered to assist me. Unlike most foreign correspondents who were married and had children, Chris Billing was a bachelor and he liked going out at night. He had a car, a driver, and spoke fluent Mandarin. He also played tennis two or three times a week, and, at his suggestion, I met him for mixed doubles the following afternoon at my hotel's tennis facility, where he introduced me to our partners, two English-speaking Chinese women in their early thirties, who turned out to be excellent players.

Our games were often disturbed, however, by the ringing sounds coming from the cell phones that the women had left in their handbags near the net posts. Putting aside their rackets, they would hasten toward their phones, apologizing to Chris and me for interrupting our game, but it was clear they believed their calls were important, *too* important to ignore. I think both women held executive positions within private firms; both were married to successful husbands (too busy to play tennis), and one of the women (or maybe both) had a youngster at home being cared for by a nanny or a grandmother. In any case, Chris and I played *singles* while our doubles partners stood on the sidelines holding tiny gleaming phones to their ears and jabbering in Mandarin perhaps to a colleague in the office or, indeed, to a "little emperor" at home. But despite these interruptions, I enjoyed being back on a tennis court and was pleased to have in Chris Billing a new American friend who knew his way around Beijing and was including me in his social plans.

The two of us dined that night in a back-street restaurant in a congested residential area with cobblestoned alleyways lined with single-level courtyard houses. During the evening, I alluded to my recent visit to Tiananmen Square, which led Billing to invite me to the NBC office the following day to view several hours of tape taken during the six-week confrontation of 1989. It was an offer I accepted. I was also grateful to him a week later: He was expected briefly in New York, and while there he saw my wife, Nan, and volunteered to carry back to China a suitcase containing some of my suits and other clothing made of a heavier fabric than what I had brought with me to Beijing a month earlier following our fortieth-anniversary cruise in the Mediterranean. But before he left Beijing, he gave me the phone number of a woman whom he hoped was what I was seeking in an interpreter. She was a refined and highly educated woman, he said, who both spoke and wrote English, and, since she had recently retired from a full-time position, she had flexible hours and was looking forward to hearing from me. Her name was Fu Cuihua.

I promptly telephoned Madam Fu, and she said she would come to my hotel as soon as she could, maybe within the hour. This pleased me because I had just received a fax written in Chinese—sent by Chen Jun of the soccer association's advertising department—and I was eager to have it translated. In less than an hour, the concierge notified me that Madam Fu had arrived in the lobby and was on her way up. I left my suite on the fourteenth floor and walked down the hall to meet her at the elevator. When the door opened, I saw a tiny woman coming out unsteadily but with determined resolve. She seemed not to notice me as she hurried past, taking several mincing steps in the wrong direction while holding on to the wall with one hand for support.

"Madam Fu?" I called out, pursuing her from behind. "Madam Fu?"

"Oh, yes," she said, stopping and turning around. She regarded me with a tentative smile. Refocusing her eyes from behind her steel-framed spectacles, she said, "I'm afraid I am a little dizzy. These elevators go so fast, they make me dizzy."

"Would you like to hold on to my arm?" I asked as she removed her hand from the wall.

"Oh, no," she said, "I will be fine once I sit down. It just takes a while for me to get used to how fast the elevators are in these tall buildings." I guessed that Madam Fu was in her sixties, if not older. She was not much taller than five feet and weighed maybe one hundred pounds. She was demurely dressed, wearing what might have been in vogue during the days when Chinese women first ceased to emulate the fashion of Chairman Mao.

She followed me through the corridor, then into my suite. Seeing a cushioned chair, she headed toward it and sank into it. "Water," she said, "I could use a bit of water." I removed a bottle from the refrigerator and poured the contents into a wineglass and handed it to her. As she slowly sipped from the glass, she glanced around the room at the polished paneling, the mirrored backbar, the pale blue damask pillows on the sofa, and the coffee table, on which was a vase containing the fresh flowers that were brought in daily by the chambermaid. In the far corner of the room was a banquet table that served as my desk, and, in its center, surrounded by stacks of folders and yellow lined pads, was an electric typewriter I had borrowed from the concierge. He had retrieved it from the storage room, where it had been discarded by the secretary of the banquet manager after she had switched to a computer. "Nobody uses typewriters in China anymore," the concierge explained after dispatching a porter to bring it to me. It was an IBM Wheelwriter 3 model, exactly like the ones I had purchased twenty-five years ago and continued to use in New York and New Jersey.

After Madam Fu had drunk less than half of the water, and had politely waved off my attempt to refill her glass, she asked: "You are a writer?"

"I try to be," I said.

"Well, then, " she said with a snap in her voice, "how is it that I can be of service to you?"

I was pleased that she spoke English in such a clear and formal manner, preferring to associate it with my younger years, when people seemed to communicate with more care and when an IBM electric typewriter was less anachronistic.

"I just received this fax written in Chinese," I said. "It comes from a woman named Chen Jun, who is employed by the soccer assocation. Are you well enough now to translate it for me?"

"I shall try," she said, taking the page in her tiny hands, which were as small as a child's. She studied the writing for several seconds, her eyebrows arched over the rim of her glasses, her facial expression absorbed with intensity. "This message was not written by Chen Jun," she said. "It was forwarded to you from the office of Chen Jun, but it is composed by someone named Liu Ying."

"She's the soccer player I'm interested in," I explained.

"Well, in this message she is actually telling you about her mother," Madam Fu went on. Liu Ying must have been told about my forthcoming meeting with her mother, I thought; then I listened as Madam Fu began to translate aloud:

"'It was very difficult for my mother to bring up her three children because she had to overcome a lot of difficulties. Even when I was very young I loved sports and I needed to be strong to do the exercises, so my mother often cooked special food just for me. My mother doesn't understand soccer and she does not go to watch the games. I began to live in the school's dormitory at the age of twelve, and would only go back home on holidays. But my mother gives me a mother's love. She has been my spiritual pillar. . . .'"

Madam Fu's voice began to weaken, and then she paused.

"I am sorry," she said finally, "but I feel like I am about to fall on the floor."

"Let me call the hotel doctor," I quickly said, and she nodded and asked if she could lie down. I showed her into the bedroom and she stretched out on top of the covers and waited until the doctor arrived. He went in to see her, and when he came out, he told me she would be all right, but urged that we put her in a taxi and let her go home, where she could rest.

Together, we walked Madam Fu down the hall toward the elevator, and she was very apologetic. I arranged for a hotel car, and gave her the fee for her time, although she accepted it with reluctance. After she had gone, I thanked the doctor and returned to the lobby, thinking that I must not let Chris Billing know about this incident, nor should I further depend upon Patrick Wang of Nike. These men had done too much for me already; from now on, I decided, I must be more on my own.

I noticed a stack of *China Daily* newspapers on the side of the concierge's counter and it then occurred to me to contact one of the editors there; surely, since it was an English-language periodical, it was a likely place for me to seek advice and perhaps even be introduced to a candidate. After the concierge had arranged for me to see one of the editors there whom he knew and had accompanied me to the taxi stand and given the directions to the driver, I was on my way to the *China Daily* building, which I reached in less than twenty minutes. It was an L-shaped white modern structure lined by large rectangular-shaped sealed windows, and behind its wide glass entranceway was a marble-floored lobby. The receptionist was expecting me, and, after a guard had escorted me up the elevator into a conference room, I was greeted by a smiling Asian gentleman in his mid-fifties who wore a bow tie and a dark suit and spoke English in the same exacting manner as Madam Fu.

"So, I understand you are an authority on the game of soccer as played by youthful Chinese women," he began.

"Not exactly," I said, "but I am interested in one of the players." I had already described my story idea so often to so many people that I could relate it by rote, and so I barely listened to myself as I now succinctly recounted to the editor the circumstances that had drawn me into the orbit of Liu Ying, my following in the trajectory of an errant kick through a dozen time zones into the Orient in search of what I was yet eager to discover. The editor appeared to be puzzled by what I was saying, and so he abruptly changed the subject and asked, "May I show you our newsroom?"

As I followed him through the corridor, he explained that the *China Daily*, which was founded in 1981, had a circulation of about 300,000 and was the only English-language newspaper in the nation. It was read mainly by Chinese natives who were learning English and by Westerners who were touring or residing here. Among the paper's dozens of staff members were four or five Americans who held annual contracts as grammarians—"polishers" was how he referred to them, and they were expected to review all the words and phrases written in English by the Chinese headline writers and reporters and to make sure that everything was properly parsed and nothing was printed that might represent "Chinglish." He did not offer examples of "Chinglish," and I thought it imprudent of me to request any; but I guessed that what he had in mind were such sentences as I had recently seen printed on a sign displayed in a flea market frequented by tourists: TAKE MORE CARE OF YOUR BELON GINGS.

The newsroom of the *China Daily* consisted of rows and rows of cubicles, within which men and women sat silently facing computer screens. There are modern newsrooms similar to this one in thousands of cities throughout the world, I thought, from Beijing to Copenhagen to Denver, vast and muted spaces in which people of many colors and languages practice journalism in an ambience so different from what I knew as a young man working on the third floor at the *Times*, where three hundred reporters could be seen at a single glance, making clattering sounds with their fingertips on the metal keyboards of bell-ringing typewriters, their facial expressions alternating between frustration and satisfaction, all within view of everyone else, and all calling aloud to copyboys whenever they wanted their completed stories to be rushed to an editor. Journalism was then performed with resonance and impartible vivacity, whereas it was now the work of walled-in scriveners delivering stories to their editors with the click of a mouse. It was so quiet within the *China Daily*'s crowded newsroom that I could distinctly hear, rising from a cubicle, the sound of a soft-spoken man conversing on a telephone in an accented American voice that I took to be Texan.

"Who's that talking on the phone?" I asked the editor.

"His name is Mr. Charles Dukes. He is one of our polishers."

"Would you allow me to have a word with him?"

"No problem," said the editor, "as soon as he completes his call."

Within minutes I was being introduced to Charles J. Dukes, a stocky, square-jawed middle-aged man who had a full head of chestnut brown hair and a carefully clipped goatee that was almost entirely gray.

"I'd be glad to talk to you," Charles Dukes said after we had shaken hands, "but I have to get out of here for a while and get something to eat. I'm due back in an hour."

"May I join you?" I asked. Dukes looked at the editor, exchanged some words in Chinese, and then said, "Sure."

After I had thanked the editor, I followed Dukes out of the building and across the street into one of the typical neighborhood restaurants that the Chinese referred to as a *huoguo*, and that Americans called a "hot pot," because in the center of each table was a cauldron filled with bubbling broth surrounded by trays of raw meat, vegetables, and hot peppers. The customers seated at the tables would drop their selected food into the cauldrons with their chopsticks, and seconds later would dip their chopsticks back into the cauldrons and retrieve the now steaming and cooked morsels of food ready to be eaten. Dukes started out with an appetizer of something I did not recognize, while I ordered only a bottle of Tsingtao beer, which the waiter poured so freely that the foam flowed onto the tablecloth.

Dukes told me that he had come to Beijing during the previous year, having applied to the *China Daily* after he had seen a help-wanted ad placed by the paper on the Internet during the spring of 1998. At that time he had been editing his hometown weekly in Malakoff, Texas, a position that he liked well enough but did not mind leaving, being a divorcé with grown children and thus at liberty to accept whatever he thought might reawaken what was left of his sense of adventure. Although he had majored in journalism at the University of Texas in Arlington, and had been a staff writer for ten years on the *Athens Daily Review* in Athens, Texas, he had intermittently left Texas journalism to accept consulting jobs with oil companies and other multinational corporations that sponsored his travels in the Middle East, Europe, Peru, the North Sea, and the Arctic Slope. He had earlier learned Mandarin while earning a master's degree in Asian studies at the University of Hawaii, and he said that this had probably weighed in his favor when he had submitted his application to the *China Daily*. But his interest in Asia actually dated back to 1967, he said. He was then twenty years old, embarking on a tour as a U.S. paratrooper in Vietnam.

He had not only experienced hand-to-hand combat there, he said, but had fatally shot two Vietnamese soldiers, a fact of which he was neither proud nor prone to discuss at length with his Chinese coworkers and acquaintances—and especially not with the father of his Chinese girlfriend in Beijing. During the war, her father had been a bomber pilot serving with the Vietcong. Although Dukes's girlfriend, Nanfei, was thirty years younger than himself—she had just turned twenty-one—he had proposed marriage to her, and she had accepted after discussing it with her family. Nanfei was a very talented artist, Dukes said, and he was spending all of his nonworking hours helping her to find exhibitors and buyers of her paintings—which was his way of explaining, after I had raised the question, that he lacked the time to assist me as an interpreter.

"But I might have *the* perfect person for you," he said. "She's a Chinese-American. She works with us as a polisher. She's young and smart. I think she's done some reporting on papers back in the States. She's not dating anybody, as far as I know, so she's probably free at night. After we get back to the office, I'll introduce you. Her name is Sharline Chiang."

While I am mindful of the fact that sometimes things sound or appear to be too good to be true, after meeting Sharline Chiang and speaking with her briefly, I was convinced, as Dukes had suggested, that she was perfect for my purposes. To begin with, she was immediately available for interpreting during her off-hours from the *China Daily*, and, as well as being bilingual, she was well mannered and personable. She wore her dark hair back in a braid, and her square-framed modish glasses set off her dark-eyed look of intelligence. She was twenty-nine, had a bachelor's degree from Rutgers University in New Jersey, and in 1995 had earned her master's from the Columbia University Graduate School of Journalism in New York.

Her workday had finished when I met her, and after I suggested that we continue our conversation over dinner at my hotel, she agreed. In the taxi she explained that she was the only child of Chinese immigrants who had gone to the United States in the late 1960s, adding that many of their kinsmen had lost contact with one another during the turmoil of the Japanese invasion of the 1930s and the Chinese civil war of the mid-forties. Although Sharline's paternal grandparents had escaped to Taiwan prior to the Communist takeover in 1949, taking six of their eight children, two others had been unavoidably left behind—a younger brother of her father's and an older sister. Nearly forty years would elapse before her father, then fifty-nine and residing in New Jersey, would be reunited with them at a family gathering in Taiwan in September 1996. Sharline, who was then employed as a reporter for the *Press-Enterprise* in Riverside, California, flew to Taiwan to join them, and now, three years later, working in Beijing on a one-year contract as a polisher, she was on a kind of sabbatical, reclaiming a sense of her heritage in mainland China.

When we arrived in the lobby of my hotel, the concierge waved and called out to me, "You have visitors waiting for you in the café."

As we entered it, I saw my intrepid interpreter, Li Duan, heading toward me with his right hand extended and a smile on his face.

"I am very happy that you are here," he said. "I have telephoned your room many times, but no answer." He then went on to say, as he nodded in the direction of a woman seated at one of the tables, "I have brought to you the lady who is the mother of Liu Ying."

36

AFTER I HAD INTRODUCED SHARLINE CHIANG TO LI DUAN, leaving for later whatever difficulty I might have in explaining to him that I had just hired her for additional assistance as an interpreter, he led us through the crowded café toward a table at which sat the mother of Liu Ying, a slender and refined-looking woman of fifty-four who wore a black-and-white houndstooth checked coat and had short, wavy brown hair, a smooth-skinned, angular face, and dark eyes that reflected warmth as she stood to greet us. Her name was Sun Zhixian—or, as I referred to her from then on, Madam Sun.

As she spoke to my two interpreters, I departed to get an extra chair and summon a waiter to bring menus. When I returned, the three of them were conversing animatedly, and so I joined them as a spectator and took pleasure in the fact that my two interpreters seemed to be getting along, with Sharline Chiang helping herself to the pack of Red Pagoda cigarettes that Li Duan had laid on the table. Madam Sun politely refused Li Duan's offer of a cigarette, but she did not back away from the table as trails of smoke floated past her, and I guessed that she shared with most of the residents of Beijing—a city polluted by coal burners, construction dust, gas fumes, and gusts of westerly sand blown in from the direction of the Gobi Desert—a tolerance toward the puffers of Red Pagodas and other brands. Smoking was permitted in all the restaurants and other public places I had visited since my arrival in China (including in the elevators of my hotel), and I assumed that whatever health threats arose from the inhalation of cigarettes, those threats were minimized in the murk of 8 million tons of coal burned each year in Beijing alone.

As we three enjoyed our cocktails and canapés, and Madam Sun sipped from a glass of coconut juice, I asked Li Duan to tell her that I had received a fax from her daughter saying what a wonderful mother she was; I also asked him to get her to explain why her daughter had chosen to become a full-time soccer player. As Li Duan spoke to Madam Sun, I noticed that Sharline Chiang had removed a pen and pad from her handbag and had jotted down what I assumed was my question, and she was now poised with a pen for Madam Sun's reply. I was concerned, for I thought that perhaps we should have extended to Madam Sun the courtesy of knowing in advance that there would be a written account of our interview; but on the contrary, after she had glanced at Sharline's notebook and seen that the words were in Chinese characters, she smiled. She could read in her own language what she was telling us. From then on, it seemed to me, she was very cooperative and candid.

"I am not exactly sure why my daughter became a soccer player," she said, "but I think she inherited her interest in the game from her father, my late husband, who played soccer in school and was very athletic all his life. He was a physical education teacher at our neighborhood school. Unfortunately, he did not live past the age of thirty-three. He was knocked off his bicycle by a truck one night in 1978, and died instantly. Liu Ying was only four. She hardly knew him. But I still think she connects with him through the game. She grew up watching soccer matches on television, and watching the boys playing soccer in school, and she would often stand on the sidelines criticizing them—"You are not doing this right; you are not doing that right"—and a teacher said to her one day, 'Well, if you can do better, why don't you play?' Girls did not play soccer in school, but the principal allowed her to play with the boys, and she did very well. When she was eight or nine, and did not have a soccer ball to kick, she was out in the streets kicking pebbles and small rocks. The other little girls had nice shoes, but my daughter's shoes were always scratched and tattered from kicking stones. When she was fifteen, in 1989, she was transferred from the middle school to a special school that emphasized soccer. When she was eighteen, she was promoted to the national women's team as a substitute player. She accompanied them to the Olympics in Atlanta in 1996, and, when one of the starters was injured, she was sent in for twenty minutes. The team did not win, but she passed accurately and played aggressively. Soon she became a starter, and since then has traveled all over the world. And so I now have a daughter who makes her name with her feet."

As we progressed through dinner, with Li Duan continuing to do the interpreting while Sharline Chiang kept jotting down the questions and answers, Madam Sun wanted us not to ignore the fact that she was the mother of two other children—a thirty-year-old son, Liu Tong, currently employed as a sales representative in Beijing for a door-manufacturing company, and a twenty-five-year-old daughter, Liu Yun, who was a cashier and bookkeeper at a leading department store on the western end of

Chang'an Boulevard, not far from their home. Liu Yun was actually the fraternal twin of Liu Ying, Madam Sun explained. Neither of Liu Ying's siblings were athletically inclined, and they watched soccer matches only when Liu Ying was participating. Madam Sun also mentioned that her seventy-eight-year-old mother was an active part of her household, and that the latter helped to raise the children when she, Madam Sun, had been sent to work on a dairy farm during the decade-long Cultural Revolution, which continued through 1977.

"I cried when I had to leave home," she recalled, "but it was a time of a national crisis. There had been a great famine a few years before, and millions of people were moved from the cities to the countryside to work and live with the farmers. I spent more than eight years on a farm. I actually first went in 1967, a year before I got married and began to have children. I had been living with my parents and other relatives in the old-style courtyard house that we still live in today, on a narrow lane a few blocks west of the Forbidden City. My grandfather, an attorney, bought the place in 1911 after the fall of the last emperor. The house was later inherited by my father, a chemical engineer who attended a Jesuit-tutored college in Beijing before the Party takeover. The farm where I worked was many miles from the city, a five-hour bus ride one way, and my visits home were infrequent. On the farm I stacked hay, fed the animals, and worked in the fields. At night I slept in communal quarters with other young women."

During one of her visits home, she was introduced to the man who would become her husband. She met him through her mother, a teacher in the elementary school where he was the physical education instructor. The wedding was an unceremonious and unphotographed occasion, at which the marital couple both wore blue Mao suits. Following the birth of their son in 1969, her husband began earning extra money as a construction worker after school, while she remained employed on the farm, returning home two or three times a month. This routine continued until 1974, when, following the birth of the twin daughters, she managed a transfer from her farming job to a lamp-making factory in the outskirts of the city, making it possible for her to live at home but nevertheless requiring a two-hour bus ride to and from work.

Her home was overcrowded, being occupied by her immediate family, her extended family, and by a dozen of what she described as "neighbors," the latter being nonrelatives assigned to live on her parents' property by the state housing authority. Since there was insufficient shelter in Beijing to accommodate the city's burgeoning population, home owners were expected to share their living space with tenants designated by the state. Landlords such as her parents were in no position to resist, nor did they dare to complain. If they had complained, they would have risked being branded as bourgeois elitists at a time when Chairman Mao was extolling the virtues of proletarianism and promoting a class-leveling campaign, one offering equal opportunities for the privileged and better-educated elements to learn firsthand from the peasants what it was like to exist on the lower level of the social order. Revolutionary committee leaders and other zealots set all the standards when it came to public and private behavior and expressionism, and they heckled, harassed, and otherwise silenced manifestations of dissent and nonconformity. As the firstborn child of parents with an advanced education and diminishing influence, Madam Sun served as her family's representative and hostage during the Cultural Revolution.

As she recounted her story, I did not perceive in her manner, nor in her words as translated by Sharline Chiang, any indication of disapproval toward the authorities who had exercised such vast and arbitrary control during the Cultural Revolution. I found her lack of expressed resentment surprising even as I recalled reading that Chinese people hardly ever revealed their inner feelings to outsiders, and I also reminded myself that my wonderment about her seeming stoicism might be based on the fact that, residing in New York, I regularly lived among crowds of chronic complainers. More lawyers and psychiatrists probably thrived in New York than anywhere else in the world. I also thought that her apparent absence of self-pity or contentiousness might represent her confidence and fortitude, her determination not to be humbled by an ill-tempered and punitive period in Chinese history, during which she and millions of her countrymen were subjected to deprivation, social humiliation, and no doubt betrayal from many others whom they had trusted.

What little I knew about the Cultural Revolution had come from history books and novels written by Americans or Chinese exiles, and such accounts were more or less in accord with how the Cultural Revolution would later be summarized in the *Times* by its correspondent Howard W. French—a "decade-long descent into madness." Yet out of this madness, and perhaps because she recognized it for what it was, Madam Sun had adjusted and endured; and now I imagined her, together with millions of other middle-aged and elderly Chinese survivors of Mao's demented decade, as being part of the backbone of a transforming China, and I recalled Friedrich Nietzsche's comment: "What does not kill you will make you stronger."

Immediately after we had finished dinner, Li Duan apologized for having to leave, explaining that he wished to return home and spend time with his young son. It was shortly after 7:00 p.m. He asked if Sharline and I would accompany Madam Sun to her door, and I was happy to oblige. It afforded me an opportunity to see her neighborhood and perhaps receive an invitation into her home.

As our taxi proceeded slowly through the traffic of Chang'an Boulevard in the direction of the Oriental Plaza and the Forbidden City, Madam Sun pointed to a large white modern building on the north side of the boulevard; it was the Jianguo Garden Hotel and she said that this was where she had come to watch the televised broadcast of the World Cup match in California. "I would have preferred to watch the match at home," she said, "but the sports association had invited all the players' mothers to be guests of the hotel and attend the Mother's Hope Dinner on the evening before the game. The dinner was held in a private room in the hotel and everybody was very enthusiastic and friendly. The mothers were from different parts of China, and had been brought to Beijing on planes, buses, and trains. The coach's wife was there and also some Chinese reporters. Most of us were meeting for the first time, but we suddenly felt very close because of our daughters being bonded to one another and to all of us, as well. A child leaves home and the mother's heart must follow.

"After dinner we went to our rooms, but I don't think anybody slept much that night. At three a.m. we were awakened and met for breakfast in a hall where a large television screen was set up, and soon we saw our daughters wearing their red uniforms, representing China, playing soccer, and running up and down the field. There was no score; they started taking penalty kicks. The tension was terrible, and when Liu Ying's kick was blocked, I began to feel tears in my eyes. Everybody was now crying, each for our own reasons. I cried for my daughter's pain and my pain. Everyone tried to console me, but I just wanted to go to my hotel room. I did not want the others to see more of how I felt."

Our taxi had turned off the boulevard and we were now passing through an alleyway that was crowded with pedestrians and bicyclists and was lined on both sides by gray stone walls that were about seven feet high and were cracked and crumbling in many places. Within a matter of moments we had moved from a city of modern hotels and office towers to what my guidebook described as a classically antiquated Chinese neighborhood in which millions of walled-in residents occupied centuries-old single-story homes with lattice-arched entranceways opening out to an ancient alleyway called a *hutong*.

Although relatively few people during the dynastic period had ever ventured into the Forbidden City, there were many *hutongs* leading

toward it, traveled no doubt by traders and servants and various kowtow-
ing opportunists who wished to congregate in the proximity of power and
who eventually established communities along the fringes of the imperial
preserve. Into one such community came a certain attorney from southern China in 1911 to conduct his practice and acquire a house on favorable terms in the wake of the abdication of the emperor. After the
attorney had taken title to the house, he welcomed into it his bound-
footed wife, who was conveyed through the *hutong* in a bridal sedan, an
enclosed chair with poles in the front and back hoisted by two carriers.
The address of the house—74 Wuding Hutong—was where Madam Sun,
the late attorney's granddaughter, directed our taxi driver to stop.

She asked if we wished to come in, and after I had paid the driver,
Sharline and I followed her toward the unpainted swinging exterior doors
of the entranceway. The overhanging latticework was falling apart and
the double doors lacked the decorative clasps and intricate carving that I
had seen in picture books memorializing *hutong*s and their quadrangle
houses with slanted tiled roofs and inner open courtyards. In the days
prior to the Cultural Revolution, when Mao saw these houses as reflecting bourgeois values and his Red Guards often vandalized them, the
courtyards were typically graceful areas of serenity in which flowers and
trees were grown, caged birds sang, goldfish swam in aquariums, and
family members communicated with one another while their children
played. To whatever degree this is an idyllic image of the past chosen for
publication in a picture book by a nostalgic editor opposed to Beijing's
present-day urban renewal campaign and the land developers' eager-
ness to replace the *hutong*s with wider thoroughfares and demolish the
old-style houses in favor of high-rises, I must say that I was unprepared
for the wretched scene that greeted me as Madam Sun led us into what
had once been a courtyard, into what I imagined had once been an arbor
of congeniality. Now the area was overrun with weeds and dilapidated brick shacks that housed what Madam Sun had earlier referred to as
her "neighbors." Some of the occupants stood outside their doors watching us quietly, while others were busily engaged in chores—removing
laundry from the clotheslines, tinkering with rust-covered bicycles, stacking circular chunks of coal with holes in the middle resembling oversize
bagels. In one corner of the yard was an outhouse with corrugated tin
walls and a leaky tiled roof covered with a tarpaulin secured in place by
an overlay of heavy wooden planks and several bricks.

After Madam Sun had acknowledged her neighbors with a nod, she
turned left and headed toward a rectangular building on the eastern side
of the original compound, which was where she now lived in two adjoin-

ing rooms. In one room was a table, a couple of carved wooden chairs, and an armoire, on top of which was an old suitcase that she identified as belonging to her late grandmother. As a young girl, Madam Sun used to wash her grandmother's gnarled feet and help her hobble around; whenever Madam Sun saw the distinctive waddling walk of Charlie Chaplin in silent-era films, she was reminded of her.

In the other room was a mahogany-framed bed, a bureau with a mirror, and a potbellied stove, from which a metal pipe rose to an aperture near the ceiling, funneling coal fumes to the outdoors. Although Liu Ying no longer lived at home—she shared an apartment with another soccer player near the women's stadium in southern Beijing when not traveling with the team—she regularly returned home for overnight visits, and whenever she did, she slept on the cot that Madam Sun pointed to in the far corner of the room. Next to the cot was a cedar chest, and near it was a plastic compartmentalized container holding loafers, sneakers, and cleated soccer shoes. Hanging on the wall above the cot was a four-by-three-foot poster featuring a broadly smiling Michael Jordan.

"My daughter is now in Guam, competing in the Asia Cup," Madam Sun told us. "She telephoned last night. She telephones a few times a week no matter where she is. All the team members have cell phones, given to them by one of their sponsors, the Ericsson company. Now that she has a cell phone, I talk to her more than when she used to live here. But she was barely a teenager when she went off to room and board at the soccer academy, returning home only on weekends." Madam Sun recalled that during the weekend of the Tiananmen Square trouble in 1989, as the bloodshed began on Saturday night, June 3, and continued through the following morning, Liu Ying was staying at the family home. She was then fifteen. "My son was out walking on Saturday night and saw a lady get hit with a stray bullet," Madam Sun recalled. "I myself could hear the gun noises and lots of people screaming and shouting. The noise carried throughout our neighborhood. It didn't disturb Liu Ying, however. She lay on that cot all night, sleeping peacefully through all that noise and commotion. She was not aware of anything until we told her about it the next morning, and then she said, 'Oh, Mom, why didn't you wake me?' Later on Sunday, the two of us took a walk around the neighborhood and we saw vehicles turned upside down, and lots of rubble everywhere. Most of the people were very fearful and confused. . . ."

As we sat listening to Madam Sun, we were joined by an elderly but agile gray-haired woman who came in carrying a pot of steaming tea and three cups on a tray. As she smiled, the many wrinkles on her broad face deepened. She was wearing a gray worsted Mao-style jacket and a long sweater vest knitted in a pattern of beige and gray concentric squares. After she had poured the tea and handed a cup to each of us, she sat down on the bed next to Madam Sun, who, with seeming pride, introduced her as her mother. Her name was Zhang Shou Yi. She had turned seventy-five a few years earlier and had worked until then.

With some prompting on my part and no interruptions from her daughter, Madam Zhang began to speak to us about her youthful days in Beijing in the aftermath of the emperor's abdication. She was born in 1921 in a well-maintained courtyard house along a *hutong* a few miles west of where we now were. Her father ran an antiques business and also held a minor position within the local administration. As a child, she heard stories describing how the young emperor, sequestered for more than a decade behind the vermilion walls of the city he no longer influenced, idled away many hours pedaling his bicycle around the stone pathways of the preserve. While her formal education was perhaps superior to that of most of her neighboring female contemporaries, she had no special ambition beyond being married to a man of her father's choosing. Shortly after she had turned twenty-three, deemed to be an advanced age for a young woman harboring marital expectations, her father told her that he was in contact with an attorney who had a twenty-three-year-old son who was a worthy candidate for a marital arrangement. The son was in college, studying to become an engineer. While it was not then customary for young women to be introduced to prospective spouses, Madam Zhang told us that in her case, which she thought illustrative of the early twentieth century's modernizing tendencies—which had already freed many millions of Chinese women from a thousand-year-old tradition of crescent-footed dependence—she was permitted to have a meeting with her future husband prior to the actual ceremony. Fortunately for her, she liked him immediately.

Married in 1943, and moving into the courtyard house of her husband's family at number 74 Wuding Hutong, she would have six children. Three of her children—four including Madam Sun—and *their* children were also residing within separate quarters on the compound at the time of my visit, although I did not meet them. Madam Zhang told me that, in addition to herself, there were now twenty-six people lodged within her property—eleven family members and fifteen neighbors. She had a two-room suite on the northern side of the courtyard, which was the side customarily reserved for elders. Her bedroom was slightly more spacious than any other, and, of the five television sets hooked up on the property—two within the quarters of her neighbors—her newly purchased twenty-five-inch-screen Peacock model was the most reliable and emitted the most clearly delineated images in color.

It was this set that she had been watching as Liu Ying competed in the China-U.S.A. World Cup final. Madam Zhang and four members of her family—two of her sons and their wives—had gathered around the set in the early-morning hours, joining together in calling out words of encouragement toward a tiny red-shirted figure of a girl who wore number 13 and was shown running up and down the field, amid her teammates and opponents, focusing her attentions upon a soccer ball on the other side of the world.

On that morning, Liu Ying's twin sister and her brother were watching the game in the latter's bedroom, while their nearby neighbors were doing so in their courtyard dwelling. On the other side of the wall, within the rows of homes that lined the *hutong*, there were hundreds and perhaps thousands of other television viewers. Lights could be seen glowing in countless windows during the predawn darkness as the game began, and throughout the four-hour telecast the quiescence that usually accommodated late sleepers on Sundays, at least along the back streets of the city, was now penetrated by the lively commentary of a play-by-play announcer in California and by the soaring and syncopated sounds of people in China venting their responses through the raised windows of their homes—cheering, jeering, clapping, sighing, and finally voicing their displeasure and disappointment when the game was over and the Chinese team had been defeated by the Americans. As I have mentioned, more than 100 million people in China reportedly viewed the telecast. Nowhere was the final score more silently and sadly accepted than within the household at number 74 Wuding Hutong.

After turning off her television set and veiling it with a black cotton dustcover, Madam Zhang tried to comfort and reassure her kinsmen, who sat around her, most of whom seemed to be stunned. "It is a part of life," she said. When a few of her neighbors came in from the courtyard, she repeated, "It is a part of life." Throughout the morning, everyone remained within the walls of the compound. And then the telephone in Madam Zhang's anteroom began to ring, and her younger brother got up to answer it.

"Please let me speak to my mother," said the sobbing voice of Liu Ying. She was calling from Los Angeles.

"I'm sorry, she is not here," her uncle said, explaining that her mother had gone off to watch the game with the coach's wife and other women at a hotel, but he did not know the name of the hotel.

"Then let me speak to my brother," she said. As soon as her brother picked up the receiver, she began to cry: "Oh, it's all my fault, it's all my fault. . . ."

A day later, after the team had gotten off the plane in Beijing, Liu Ying's mother, along with the mothers of the other players, stood waiting in the marble-floored lobby of a reception hall near the airport while the arriving group of young women wearing red warm-up suits ascended from ground level via an escalator. After tossing their carrier bags to the floor, the young women ran with their arms outstretched and tears in their eyes to be embraced by their mothers. As they greeted one another, a chorus of sibilant sounds was heard through the lobby—*Mei shi, mei shi, ni mei shi ba: Ni ye mei shi ba?*—words not easily translated, my interpreter explained to me, but words meant to comfort, to express concern and regret while at the same time stressing positiveness and reassurance.

Still, as Madam Sun told us during our interview, the players and their families were not sheltered from the fact that millions of people in China had been let down by the outcome of the World Cup match. When Liu Ying's twin sister, Liu Yun, returned to her job in the department store on the day after the telecast, she was approached by many customers and coworkers, who asked, "What happened to Liu Ying? How could she have messed up when it was so important?"

"Oh, I'm so sorry," the sister replied, saying repeatedly, "please accept my apologies."

But such criticism subsided on the following day after there were stories in Chinese newspapers and on television claiming that the United States team had won the game unfairly, blaming the American goalkeeper for moving improperly in front of the net *before* Liu Ying had begun her penalty kick. Some of these reports were accompanied by photographs purporting to show Briana Scurry in the act of committing an infraction. Liu Ying's brother, Liu Tong, saw the photos and stories while surfing on the Internet, and, after printing them out, he distributed them to members of his family and several people he knew in the neighborhood.

Later in the week, the Chinese soccer players and the coaching staff were invited to the Great Hall to be greeted by President Jiang Zemin and receive medallions identifying them as honored citizens of the People's Republic. The women were uniformly attired in gray skirts and jackets, white blouses, and black pumps. As President Jiang walked toward Liu Ying and placed a ribboned medallion on her shoulders, he smiled and told her, "Don't worry, there will be another day, and you will have another opportunity."

CODA

I FOLLOWED THE FORTUNES OF LIU YING FOR THE NEXT FEW months, and then the next few years, waiting for her to have a heroic moment.

With her mother's cooperation and goodwill, I met with Liu Ying on a number of occasions during the latter part of 1999 and the winter and spring of 2000. After learning where the team would be participating in tournaments and exhibition matches within China and overseas, I took it upon myself (without further consultation with the soccer authorities) to become a frequent flier on Dragonair, Mandarin Airlines, and several international carriers.

Whenever possible, I booked flights that would take me to the soccer sites prior to the arrival of the team, allowing me time to mingle with members of the welcoming committee (usually a congenial group of banner-waving, flower-bearing boosters) as well as the local camera crews and print media who stood waiting in the lounges of the airports. It was my hope, and it was a hope invariably fulfilled, that I would meet someone who spoke English well enough for me to recruit them on a freelance basis to accompany me to soccer fields and help whenever the need arose for me to understand something being said in Chinese. This was not a problem in Hong Kong, where English was widely spoken, but it was crucial in such places as Tainan on the island of Taiwan, and along the mainland's southeastern port city of Xiamen, a onetime fishing village that in recent decades had blossomed into what was commonly conceded to be the smuggler's capital of the People's Republic of China.

When I flew into Xiamen to watch an exhibition game between the Chinese team and the national women's team of Australia, the entire municipal leadership was being scrutinized by hundreds of investigators from the central government who believed it was being fleeced by customs agents who were illegally importing into China merchandise and commodities worth nearly $7 billion—oil, automobiles, telephone equipment, semiconductors, cigarettes. This inquiry would eventually lead to the conviction of not only customs agents but also the deputy mayor, the police chief, regional Party bosses, bankers, and corporate executives, many of the latter affiliated with a large firm devoted to sponsoring soccer matches in the area. It was likely that I sat among some of these executives in the box seats of the Xiamen stadium while six thousand spectators cheered on the Chinese team that defeated Australia, 4-2, led by Liu Ying, who scored two goals. Liu Ying was very contented with her performance and afterward invited me (and my new best friend, a young Chinese advertising man who had mastered English while attending college in Perth, Australia) to spend time with her at the resort hotel where the team was staying, on Gulangyu Island, which was reachable by ferryboat; the hotel's main restaurant was serviced by waiters on Rollerblades.

I next saw Liu Ying in the southern Portuguese town of Albufeira, where the team was registered at a beachfront hotel for ten days in mid-March 2000 while competing in the seventh annual Algarve Cup games against many of the national teams slated to play in the forthcoming Olympics. I watched Liu Ying score a goal in a victory over Finland, and she played well defensively in the following games against Canada and Norway, although the Chinese lost to Norway, which, in turn, lost to the Americans in the finals of the Algarve Cup. I expected to see Liu Ying three months later in the United States, during the early summer, when the Chinese team would be visiting three cities (Hershey, Pennsylvania; Louisville, Kentucky; and Foxboro, Massachusetts) while participating in continued competition against teams from other nations. But she was unable to make the trip. She was in a wheelchair, hospitalized after a rival player had collided with her in late May during an exhibition match. Although three of her ribs were broken and she had sustained other injuries, she insisted that she would recover in time to compete in the Olympics, which is why, in early September 2000, I flew from New York to Sydney, Australia.

During what seemed to be an endless flight, the high point being the descent into Hawaii for refueling, my mind was adrift with dreamy, cliché-ridden scenarios in which I foresaw a Gold Medal showdown between the women of China and the United States, *and* a last-second scene in which Liu Ying would stand poised in a penalty kick situation
 . . . in a crowded and clamorous stadium
  . . . while many millions of people watched on worldwide television
  . . . as she lowered her head and kicked the ball

. . . beyond the outstretched reach of Briana Scurry
. . . who had blocked Liu Ying's earlier kick the year before
. . . and had boasted to the American press
. . . "This one is mine."

None of my imaginings transpired during the 2000 Olympics in Sydney. It would prove to be an event in which Liu Ying would never command the spotlight. Unable to play at full strength as a result of her earlier injury, she sat watching on the bench as her team was surprisingly overwhelmed by Norway, 3-0, in an early-round match that quickly eliminated China from further competition.

A few days later, I flew from Sydney to Beijing, seeing Liu Ying on three or four occasions during the month I remained there. She was disappointed but not pessimistic, believing that the team would reclaim its stature by increasing its commitment, and that she herself, on regaining full strength, would contribute much as a member of the starting lineup. The Chinese press, however, was now saying that the team was getting old and was injury-prone, and what was needed were younger players and a new coach.

I revisited China for two weeks in 2001 in the aftermath of many celebratory demonstrations arising from the International Olympic Committee's announcement on July 14 that Beijing had been voted the host city of the summer games of 2008. Among millions of cheering Chinese gathered in Tiananmen Square and along Chang'an Boulevard were Liu Ying, her mother, and many members of her family, although the news hastened efforts by land developers to modernize the city and replace hundreds of *hutong* communities with high-rises and avenues wide enough to accommodate three million vehicles, which was double the current amount.

When I returned to Beijing for a fortnight in 2002, the courtyard house in which Liu Ying had been born and reared was leveled and lost among acres of rubble. For a while there had been stubborn resistance from some home owners, who had cemented large lagged pieces of broken glass to the tops of their walls in an attempt to discourage intruders from climbing over; it was not burglars they feared as much as the ruffians who had been hired by land developers to throw stones through windows and commit other acts of destruction against people ignoring eviction notices issued by civil authorities. What had been a household of twenty-seven residents at number 74 Wuding Hutong was inevitably dispersed to various places, with only Liu Ying's mother and grandmother remaining together. Her grandmother received only $25,000 in credit toward the purchase of a $75,000 four-room dwelling on the fifth floor of an eighteen-story pink apartment building on the southern edge of the city. Their apartment, which I visited, had two bedrooms, electric heating, and a modern bathroom and kitchen. Displayed over the archway in the living room was a red wooden sign: 74 WUDING HUTONG.

I had planned to return to China in September 2003 to attend the World Cup matches scheduled to be hosted by the city of Shanghai, but the event was quickly relocated to the United States due to China's springtime SARS (severe acute respiratory syndrome) epidemic. Neither Liu Ying nor her teammates were taken ill, because they were insulated from the public. But in a warm-up match months prior to the World Cup, Liu Ying was again seriously injured. This time she dislocated her left knee, requiring surgery. She did eventually accompany the team to the United States, but her playing time was limited because she lacked her usual speed and agility. After the team had been eliminated in early-round competition by Canada, the new Chinese coach (who had taken over the team the year before and would, in turn, be fired a year later) informed Liu Ying that she was no longer a member of the national team. A youth movement was in progress, he said, with only four players from the twenty-two-member 1999 roster representing China in the 2004 Olympics in Athens. The youthful team would not represent progress, however, being overwhelmed by Germany, 8-0, followed by a 1-1 tie with Mexico, leading to China's early-round elimination. The Gold Medal went to the United States team that defeated Brazil, 2-1, in overtime.

With the assistance of translators, I thereafter remained in touch with Liu Ying via E-mail or fax, or telephone calls placed from my home in New York, with an interpreter listening on an extension. During a recent conversation, she told me that she was planning to return to school, a college in Beijing. She said that her present ambition was to become, like her father before her, a physical education instructor.

I had meanwhile put aside, with finality, my notes on Liu Ying, and had already begun to write:

Chapter 1

I am not now, nor have I ever been, fond of the game of soccer. Part of the reason is probably attributable to my age and the fact that when I was growing up along the southern shore of New Jersey a half century ago, the sport was virtually unknown to Americans, except to those of foreign birth. And even though my father was foreign-born—he was a dandified but dour custom tailor from a Calabrian village in southern Italy who became a United States citizen in the mid-1920s—his references to me about soccer were associated with his boyhood conflicts over the game, and his desire to play it in the afternoons with his school friends in an Italian courtyard instead of merely watching it being played as he sat sewing at the rear window of the nearby shop to which he was apprenticed. . . .

ACKNOWLEDGMENTS

I am most thankful to many friends and colleagues who encouraged me during the research and writing of *A Writer's Life*, but most particularly to my publisher, Sonny Mehta, and my editor, Jonathan Segal. Their patience and guidance through my working years at Knopf (beginning with *Unto the Sons*, published in 1992, and continuing through 2005, when I completed this book) fill me with gratitude, respect, and pride in our enduring friendship.

Finally, I wish to add a note in remembrance of my mother, Catherine E. Talese, who hoped that she would live long enough to see me finish this book. She died in Ocean City, New Jersey, on August 11, 2005, days after I had completed the manuscript. She was ninety-eight.

ABOUT THE TYPE

THE TEXT of this book has been set in Goudy Old Style, one of the more than one hundred typefaces designed by Frederic William Goudy (1865–1947). Although Goudy began his career as a book-keeper, he was so inspired by the appearance of several newly published books from the Kelmscott Press that he devoted the remainder of his life to typography in an attempt to bring a better understanding of the movement led by William Morris to the printers of the United States. Produced in 1914, Goudy Old Style reflects the absorption of a generation of designers with things "ancient." Its smooth, even color combined with its generous curves and ample cut marks it as one of Goudy's finest achievements.